KU-307-357

2 vols.

THE WORKS OF WILLIAM SHAKESPEARE

VOLUME SEVEN

THE SHAKESPEARE MEMORIAL THEATRE

Stratford-on-Avon

THE WORKS OF WILLIAM SHAKESPEARE

VOLUME SEVEN

Romeo and Juliet
The Taming of the Shrew
The Tempest
Timon of Athens
Titus Andronicus

THE PEEBLES CLASSIC LIBRARY
SANDY LESBERG, *Editor*

All Rights Reserved

ISBN 0-85690-045-1

Published by Peebles Press International
U.S.A.: 10 Columbus Circle, New York, NY 10019
U.K.: 12 Thayer Street, London W1M 5LD

Distributed by WHS Distributors

PRINTED AND BOUND IN THE U.S.A.

CONTENTS

ROMEO AND JULIET

DRAMATIS PERSONÆ

ESCALUS, *prince of Verona*
PARIS, *young nobleman kinsman to the prince*
MONTAGUE ⎱ *heads of two houses at variance with each other*
CAPULET ⎰
Uncle to Capulet
ROMEO, *son to Montague*
MERCUTIO, *kinsman to the prince and friend to Romeo*
BENVOLIO, *nephew to Montague and friend to Romeo*
TYBALT, *nephew to Lady Capulet*
FRIAR LAURENCE, *a Franciscan*
FRIAR JOHN, *of the same Order*
BALTHASAR, *servant to Romeo*
SAMPSON ⎱ *servants to Capulet*
GREGORY ⎰
PETER, *another servant to Capulet*
ABRAHAM, *servant to Montague*
An Apothecary
Three Musicians
Page to Paris; another Page; an Officer

LADY MONTAGUE, *wife to Montague*
LADY CAPULET, *wife to Capulet*
JULIET, *daughter to Capulet*
Nurse to Juliet

Citizens of Verona; Kinsfolk of both Houses; Maskers, Guards,
    Watchmen, and Attendants.

Chorus

SCENE.—*During the greater part of the Play, in Verona; once,
        in the Fifth Act, at Mantua.*

12

ROMEO AND JULIET

PROLOGUE

Enter Chorus

Chor. Two households, both alike in dignity,
In fair Verona, where we lay our scene,
From ancient grudge break to new mutiny,
Where civil blood makes civil hands unclean.
From forth the fatal loins of these two foes
A pair of star-crossed lovers take their life;
Whose misadventured piteous overthrows
Do with their death bury their parents' strife.
The fearful passage of their death-marked love,
And the continuance of their parents' rage,
Which, but their children's end, nought could remove,
Is now the two hours' traffic of our stage;
The which if you with patient ears attend,
What here shall miss, our toil shall strive to mend.   [*Exit*

ACT ONE

Scene I.   Verona, a Public Place

Enter Sampson *and* Gregory, *of the house of Capulet,*
with swords and bucklers

Sam. Gregory, on my word, we'll not carry coals.
Gre. No, for then we should be colliers.
Sam. I mean, an we be in choler, we'll draw.
Gre. Ay, while you live, draw your neck out o' the collar.
Sam. I strike quickly, being moved.
Gre. But thou art not quickly moved to strike.
Sam. A dog of the house of Montague moves me.
Gre. To move is to stir, and to be valiant is to stand: therefore, if thou art moved, thou runn'st away.
Sam. A dog of that house shall move me to stand. I will take the wall of any man or maid of Montague's.
Gre. That shows thee a weak slave; for the weakest goes to the wall.
Sam. 'Tis true; and therefore women, being the weaker vessels, are ever thrust to the wall:—therefore I will push Montague's men from the wall and thrust his maids to the wall.

13

Gre. The quarrel is between our masters and us their men.

Sam. 'Tis all one, I will sho v myself a tyrant: when I have fought with the men, I will be civil with the maids; I will cut off their heads.

Gre. The heads of the maids?

Sam. Ay, the heads of the maids, or their maidenheads; take it in what sense thou wilt.

Gre. They must take it in sense that feel it.

Sam. Me they shall feel, while I am able to stand; and 'tis known I am a pretty piece of flesh.

Gre. 'Tis well thou art not fish; if thou hadst, thou hadst been poor John. Draw thy tool; here comes of the house of the Montagues.

Enter ABRAHAM *and* BALTHASAR

Sam. My naked weapon is out: quarrel; I will back thee.

Gre. How! turn thy back and run?

Sam. Fear me not.

Gre. No, marry: I fear thee!

Sam. Let us take the law of our sides; let them begin.

Gre. I will frown as I pass by, and let them take it as they list.

Sam. Nay, as they dare. I will bite my thumb at them; which is a disgrace to them, if they bear it.

Abr. Do you bite your thumb at us, sir?

Sam. I do bite my thumb, sir.

Abr. Do you bite your thumb at us, sir?

Sam. Is the law of our side, if I say ay?

Gre. No.

Sam. No, sir, I do not bite my thumb at you, sir; but I bite my thumb, sir.

Gre. Do you quarrel, sir?

Abr. Quarrel, sir! no, sir.

Sam. If you do, sir, I am for you: I serve as good a man as you.

Abr. No better.

Sam. Well, sir.

Gre. Say 'better': here comes one of my master's kinsmen.

Sam. Yes, better, sir.

Abr. You lie.

Enter BENVOLIO

Sam. Draw, if you be men. Gregory, remember thy swashing blow.   [*They fight*

Ben. Part, fools!   [*Beating down their weapons*

14

Put up your swords; you know not what you do.

Enter TYBALT

    Tyb. What, art thou drawn among these heartless hinds?
Turn thee, Benvolio, look upon thy death.
    Ben. I do but keep the peace: put up thy sword,
Or manage it to part these men with me.
    Tyb. What, drawn, and talk of peace? I hate the word
As I hate hell, all Montagues, and thee.
Have at thee, coward.   [*They fight*

*Enter several persons of both Houses, who join the fray;
then enter Citizens, with clubs*

    First Cit. Clubs, bills, and partisans! strike! beat them down!
Down with the Capulets! down with the Montagues!

Enter CAPULET, *in his gown; and* LADY CAPULET

    Cap. What noise is this? Give me my long sword, ho!
    La. Cap. A crutch, a crutch! Why call you for a sword?

Enter MONTAGUE *and* LADY MONTAGUE

    Cap. My sword, I say!—Old Montague is come,
And flourishes his blade in spite of me.
    Mon. Thou villain Capulet!—Hold me not; let me go.
    La. Mon. Thou shalt not stir a foot to seek a foe.

Enter PRINCE, *with Attendants*

    Prin. Rebellious subjects, enemies to peace,
Profaners of this neighbour-stainéd steel,—
Will they not hear? What, ho! you men, you beasts,
That quench the fire of your pernicious rage
With purple fountains issuing from your veins,—
On pain of torture, from those bloody hands
Throw your mistempered weapons to the ground,
And hear the sentence of your movéd prince.—
Three civil brawls, bred of an airy word,
By thee, old Capulet, and Montague,
Have thrice disturbed the quiet of our streets,
And made Verona's ancient citizens
Cast by their grave beseeming ornaments,
To wield old partisans, in hands as old,
Cankered with peace, to part your cankered hate.
If ever you disturb our streets again,
Your lives shall pay the forfeit of the peace.
For this time, all the rest depart away:

You, Capulet, shall go along with me;
And, Montague, come you this afternoon,
To know our further pleasure in this case,
To old Free-town, our common judgment-place.—
Once more, on pain of death, all men depart.

    [Exeunt Prince, and Attendants; Capulet, Lady
       Capulet, Tybalt, Citizens, and Servants

    Mon. Who set this ancient quarrel new abroach?—
Speak, nephew, were you by, when it began?
    Ben. Here were the servants of your adversary
And yours close fighting ere I did approach:
I drew to part them; in the instant came
The fiery Tybalt, with his sword prepared;
Which, as he breathed defiance to my ears,
He swung about his head, and cut the winds,
Who, nothing hurt withal, hissed him in scorn.
While we were interchanging thrusts and blows,
Came more and more, and fought on part and part,
Till the prince came, who parted either part.
    La. Mon. O, where is Romeo? saw you him to-day?
Right glad I am he was not at this fray.
    Ben. Madam, an hour before the worshipped sun
Peered forth the golden window of the east,
A troubled mind drave me to walk abroad;
Where, underneath the grove of sycamore
That westward rooteth from the city's side,
So early walking did I see your son.
Towards him I made; but he was ware of me,
And stole into the covert of the wood:
I, measuring his affections by my own,
Which then most sought where most might not be found.
Being one too many by my weary self,
Pursued my humour, not pursuing his,
And gladly shunned who gladly fled from me.
    Mon. Many a morning hath he there been seen,
With tears augmenting the fresh morning's dew,
Adding to clouds more clouds with his deep sighs:
But all so soon as the all-cheering sun
Should in the farthest east begin to draw
The shady curtains from Aurora's bed,
Away from light steals home my heavy son,
And private in his chamber pens himself;
Shuts up his windows, locks fair daylight out,
And makes himself an artificial night.
Black and portentous must this humour prove,
Unless good counsel may the cause remove.
    Ben. My noble uncle, do you know the cause?
    Mon. I neither know it nor can learn of him.

Ben. Have you importuned him by any means?
Mon. Both by myself and many other friends:
But he, his own affections' counsellor,
Is to himself—I will not say how true—
But to himself so secret and so close,
So far from sounding and discovery,
As is the bud bit with an envious worm
Ere he can spread his sweet leaves to the air
Or dedicate his beauty to the sun.
Could we but learn from whence his sorrows grow,
We would as willingly give cure as know.

Enter ROMEO, *at a distance*

Ben. See, where he comes: so please you, step aside;
I'll know his grievance, or be much denied.
Mon. I would thou wert so happy by thy stay,
To hear true shrift.—Come, madam, let's away.

                          [*Exeunt Montague, and Lady*
Ben. Good morrow, cousin
Rom.   Is the day so young?
Ben. But new struck nine.
Rom.   Ay me! sad hours seem long.
Was that my father that went hence so fast?
Ben. It was. What sadness lengthens Romeo's hours?
Rom. Not having that, which having makes them short.
Ben. In love?
Rom. Out—
Ben. Of love?
Rom. Out of her favour where I am in love.
Ben. Alas, that love, so gentle in his view,
Should be so tyrannous and rough in proof!
Rom. Alas, that love, whose view is muffled still,
Should without eyes see pathways to his will!
Where shall we dine? O me! What fray was here?
Yet tell me not, for I have heard it all.
Here's much to do with hate, but more with love:
Why, then, O brawling love! O loving hate!
O anything, of nothing first created!
O heavy lightness! serious vanity!
Misshapen chaos of well-seeming forms!
Feather of lead, bright smoke, cold fire, sick health!
Still-waking sleep, that is not what it is!
This love feel I, that feel no love in this.
Dost thou not laugh?
Ben.   No, coz, I rather weep.
Rom. Good heart, at what?
Ben.   At thy good heart's oppression.
Rom. Why, such is love's transgression.

Griefs of mine own lie heavy in my breast;
Which thou wilt propagate, to have it pressed
With more of thine: this love that thou hast shown
Doth add more grief to too-much of mine own.
Love is a smoke made with the fume of sighs;
Being purged, a fire sparkling in lovers' eyes;
Being vexed, a sea nourished with lovers' tears:
What is it else? a madness most discreet,
A choking gall, and a preserving sweet.
Farewell, my coz.   [*Going*
    Ben.   Soft, I will go along;
An if you leave me so, you do me wrong.
    Rom.   Tut, I have lost myself; I am not here;
This is not Romeo, he's some other where.
    Ben.   Tell me in sadness, who is that you love.
    Rom.   What, shall I groan, and tell thee?
    Ben.   Groan? why, no;
But sadly tell me who.
    Rom.   Bid a sick man in sadness make his will;
A word ill urged to one that is so ill.
In sadness, cousin, I do love a woman.
    Ben.   I aimed so near, when I supposed you loved.
    Rom.   A right good mark-man! And she's fair I love.
    Ben.   A right fair mark, fair coz, is soonest hit.
    Rom.   Well, in that hit you miss: she'll not be hit
With Cupid's arrow; she hath Dian's wit,
And, in strong proof of chastity well armed,
From love's weak childish bow she lives unharmed.
She will not stay the siege of loving terms,
Nor bide the encounter of assailing eyes,
Nor ope her lap to saint-seducing gold:
O, she is rich in beauty, only poor,
That, when she dies, with beauty dies her store.
    Ben.   Then she hath sworn that she will still live chaste?
    Rom.   She hath, and in that sparing makes huge waste;
For beauty, starved with her severity,
Cuts beauty off from all posterity.
She is too fair, too wise; wisely too fail
To merit bliss by making me despair:
She hath forsworn to love, and in that vow
Do I live dead, that live to tell it now.
    Ben.   Be ruled by me; forget to think of her.
    Rom.   O teach me how I should forget to think.
    Ben.   By giving liberty unto thine eyes:
Examine other beauties.
    Rom.   'Tis the way
To call hers, exquisite, in question more.
These happy masks that kiss fair ladies' brows,
Being black, put us in mind they hide the fair:

He that is strucken blind cannot forget
The precious treasure of his eyesight lost.
Show me a mistress that is passing fair,
What doth her beauty serve, but as a note
Where I may read who passed that passing fair?
Farewell: thou canst not teach me to forget.
    Ben. I'll pay that doctrine, or else die in debt.

                                [Exeunt

SCENE II.—A Street

Enter CAPULET, PARIS, *and Servant*

    Cap. But Montague is bound as well as I,
In penalty alike; and 'tis not hard, I think,
For men so old as we to keep the peace.
    Par. Of honourable reckoning are you both;
And pity 'tis, you lived at odds so long.
But now, my lord, what say you to my suit?
    Cap. But saying o'er what I have said before:
My child is yet a stranger in the world;
She hath not seen the change of fourteen years:
Let two more summers wither in their pride,
Ere we may think her ripe to be a bride.
    Par. Younger than she are happy mothers made.
    Cap. And too soon marred are those so early made.
The earth hath swallowed all my hopes but she,
She is the hopeful lady of my earth:
But woo her, gentle Paris, get her heart,
My will to her consent is but a part;
An she agree, within her scope of choice
Lies my consent and fair according voice.
This night I hold an old-accustomed feast,
Whereto I have invited many a guest,
Such as I love; and you among the store,
One more, most welcome, makes my number more.
At my poor house look to behold this night
Earth-treading stars that make dark heaven light;
Such comfort, as do lusty young men feel
When well-apparelled April on the heel
Of limping winter treads, even such delight
Among fresh female buds shall you this night
Inherit at my house; hear all, all see,
And like her most whose merit most shall be:
Which, on more view of many, mine, being one,
May stand in number though in reckoning none.
Come, go with me.—Go, sirrah, trudge about
Through fair Verona; find those persons out,

Whose names are written there [*giving a paper*], and to
    them say,
My house and welcome on their pleasure stay.

> [*Exeunt Capulet and Paris*

Serv. Find them out whose names are written here?
It is written, that the shoemaker should meddle with his
yard, and the tailor with his last, the fisher with his pencil,
and the painter with his nets; but I am sent to find those
persons whose names are here writ, and can never find
what names the writing person hath here writ. I must
to the learned.—In good time.

Enter BENVOLIO *and* ROMEO

Ben. Tut, man, one fire burns out another's burning,
    One pain is lessened by another's anguish;
Turn giddy, and be holp by backward turning,
    One desperate grief cures with another's languish
Take thou some new infection to thy eye,
And the rank poison of the old will die.
Rom. Your plantain-leaf is excellent for that.
Ben. For what, I pray thee?
Rom.   For your broken shin.
Ben. Why, Romeo, art thou mad?
Rom. Not mad, but bound more than a madman is,
Shut up in prison, kept without my food,
Whipped, and tormented, and—Good-den, good fellow.
Serv. God gi' good-den.—I pray, sir, can you read?
Rom. Ay, mine own fortune in my misery.
Serv. Perhaps you have learned it without book:
but, I pray, can you read anything you see?
Rom. Ay, if I know the letters, and the language.
Serv. Ye say honestly; rest you merry.
Rom. Stay, fellow; I can read.   [*Reads*

"Signior Martino and his wife and daughters: County
Anselme and his beauteous sisters; the lady widow of
Vitruvio; Signior Placentio and his lovely nieces; Mercutio and his brother Valentine; mine uncle Capulet, his
wife and daughters; my fair niece Rosaline; Livia;
Signior Valentio, and his cousin Tybalt; Lucio, and
the lively Helena."

A fair assembly: whither should they come?
Serv. Up.
Rom. Whither?
Serv. To supper; to our house.
Rom. Whose house?
Serv. My master's.
Rom. Indeed, I should have asked you that before.

Serv. Now I'll tell you without asking. My master
is the great rich Capulet; and if you be not of the house
of Montagues, I pray, come and crush a cup of wine. Rest
you merry!   [*Exit*
  Ben. At this same ancient feast of Capulet's
Sups the fair Rosaline whom thou so lov'st,
With all the admiréd beauties of Verona:
Go thither; and with unattainted eye
Compare her face with some that I shall show,
And I will make thee think thy swan a crow.
  Rom. When the devout religion of mine eye
       Maintains such falsehood, then turn tears to fires;
And these, who, often drowned, could never die,
       Transparent heretics, be burnt for liars.
One fairer than my love! the all-seeing sun
Ne'er saw her match, since first the world begun.
  Ben. Tut! you saw her fair, none else being by,
Herself poised with herself in either eye;
But in that crystal scales let there be weighed
Your lady's love against some other maid
That I will show you shining at this feast,
And she shall scant show well that now shows best.
  Rom. I'll go along, no such sight to be shown,
But to rejoice in splendour of mine own.

                                              [*Exeunt*

Scene III.—A Room in Capulet's House

Enter Lady Capulet *and Nurse*

  La. Cap. Nurse, where's my daughter? call her forth
to me.
  Nurse. Now, by my maidenhead at twelve year old,
I bade her come.—What, lamb! what, ladybird!—
God forbid!—where's this girl?—what, Juliet!

Enter Juliet

  Jul. How now! who calls?
  Nurse.   Your mother
  Jul.   Madam, I am here.
What is your will?
  La. Cap. This is the matter.—Nurse, give leave awhile,
We must talk in secret.—Nurse, come back again:
I have remembered me, thou's hear our counsel.
Thou know'st, my daughter's of a pretty age.
  Nurse. Faith, I can tell her age unto an hour.
  La. Cap. She's not fourteen.
  Nurse.   I'll lay fourteen of my teeth,—
And yet, to my teen be it spoken, I have but four,—

                        21

She is not fourteen.   How long is it now
To Lammas-tide?
   La. Cap.   A fortnight and odd days.
   Nurse. Even or odd, of all days in the year,
Come Lammas-eve at night shall she be fourteen.
Susan and she—God rest all Christian souls!—
Were of an age: Well, Susan is with God;
She was too good for me.   But, as I said,
On Lammas-eve at night shall she be fourteen;
That shall she, marry; I remember it well.
'Tis since the earthquake now eleven years;
And she was weaned,—I never shall forget it,—
Of all the days of the year, upon that day;
For I had then laid wormwood to my dug,
Sitting in the sun under the dove-house wall:
My lord and you were then at Mantua.—
Nay, I do bear a brain:—but, as I said,
When it did taste the wormwood on the nipple
Of my dug, and felt it bitter, pretty fool,
To see it tetchy, and fall out with the dug!
Shake, quoth the dove-house: 'twas no need, I trow,
To bid me trudge.
And since that time it is eleven years;
For then she could stand alone, nay, by the rood,
She could have run and waddled all about;
For even the day before, she broke her brow:
And then my husband—God be with his soul!
'A was a merry man—took up the child:
'Yea,' quoth he, 'dost thou fall upon thy face?
Thou wilt fall backward when thou hast more wit,
Wilt thou not, Jule?' and, by my holidame,
The pretty wretch left crying, and said 'Ay.'
To see now, how a jest shall come about!
I warrant, an I should live a thousand years,
I never should forget it: 'Wilt thou not, Jule?' quoth he;
And, pretty fool, it stinted, and said—'Ay.'
   La. Cap. Enough of this; I pray thee, hold thy peace.
   Nurse. Yes, madam.   Yet I cannot choose but laugh,
To think it should leave crying, and say—'Ay:'
And yet, I warrant, it had upon its brow
A bump as big as a young cockerel's stone;
A perilous knock; and it cried bitterly:
'Yea,' quoth my husband, 'fall'st upon thy face?
Thou wilt fall backward, when thou com'st to age;
Wilt thou not, Jule?' it stinted, and said—'Ay.'
   Jul. And stint thou too, I pray thee, nurse, say I.
   Nurse. Peace, I have done.   God mark thee to his
       grace!
Thou wast the prettiest babe that e'er I nursed:

An I might live to see thee married once,
I have my wish.

    La. Cap. Marry, that marry is the very theme
I come to talk of. Tell me, daughter Juliet,
How stands your disposition to be married?

    Jul. It is an honour that I dream not of.

    Nurse. An honour! were not I thine only nurse,
I'd say thou hadst sucked wisdom from thy teat.

    La. Cap. Well, think of marriage now; younger than
        you,
Here in Verona, ladies of esteem,
Are made already mothers: by my count,
I was your mother much upon these years
That you are now a maid. Thus, then, in brief,—
The valiant Paris seeks you for his love.

    Nurse. A man, young lady! lady, such a man,
As all the world—why, he's a man of wax.

    La. Cap. Verona's summer hath not such a flower.

    Nurse. Nay, he's a flower; in faith, a very flower.

    La. Cap. What say you? can you love the gentleman?
This night you shall behold him at our feast:
Read o'er the volume of young Paris' face,
And find delight writ there with beauty's pen;
Examine every several lineament,
And see how one another lends content;
And what obscured in this fair volume lies,
Find written in the margent of his eyes.
This precious book of love, this unbound lover,
To beautify him, only lacks a cover:
The fish lives in the sea; and 'tis much pride
For fair without the fair within to hide.
That book in many's eyes doth share the glory
That in gold clasps locks in the golden story:
So shall you share all that he doth possess,
By having him making yourself no less.

    Nurse. No less! nay, bigger: women grow by men.

    La. Cap. Speak briefly, can you like of Paris' love?

    Jul. I'll look to like, if looking liking move,
But no more deep will I endart mine eye
Than your consent gives strength to make it fly.

Enter a Servant

    Serv. Madam, the guests are come, supper served up,
you called, my young lady asked for, the nurse cursed in
the pantry, and everything in extremity. I must hence
to wait; I beseech you, follow straight.

    La. Cap. We follow thee. Juliet, the county stays.

    Nurse. Go, girl, seek happy nights to happy days.
                                  [Exeunt

SCENE IV.—A Street

Enter ROMEO, MERCUTIO, BENVOLIO, *with five or six*
Maskers, Torch-bearers, and others

Rom. What, shall this speech be spoke for our excuse,
Or shall we on without apology?
Ben. The date is out, of such prolixity.
We'll have no Cupid hoodwinked with a scarf,
Bearing a Tartar's painted bow of lath,
Scaring the ladies like a crow-keeper;
Nor no without-book prologue, faintly spoke
After the prompter, for our entrance:
But, let them measure us by what they will,
We'll measure them a measure, and be gone.
Rom. Give me a torch; I am not for this ambling;
Being but heavy, I will bear the light.
Mer. Nay, gentle Romeo, we must have you dance.
Rom. Not I, believe me. You have dancing shoes
With nimble soles; I have a soul of lead
So stakes me to the ground, I cannot move.
Mer. You are a lover; borrow Cupid's wings,
And soar with them above a common bound.
Rom. I am too sore enpiercéd with his shaft
To soar with his light feathers; and so bound,
I cannot bound a pitch above dull woe:
Under love's heavy burden do I sink.
Mer. And, to sink in it, should you burden love;
Too great oppression for a tender thing.
Rom. Is love a tender thing? it is too rough,
Too rude, too boisterous, and it pricks like thorn.
Mer. If love be rough with you, be rough with love:
Prick love for pricking, and you beat love down.—
Give me a case to put my visage in: [*Putting on a mask*
A visor for a visor!—what care I
What curious eye doth quote deformities?
Here are the beetle-brows shall blush for me.
Ben. Come, knock and enter; and no sooner in,
But every man betake him to his legs.
Rom. A torch for me: let wantons, light of heart,
Tickle the senseless rushes with their heels;
For I am proverbed with a grandsire phrase;
I'll be a candle-holder, and look on:
The game was ne'er so fair, and I am done.
Mer. Tut! dun's the mouse, the constable's own word.
If thou are dun, we'll draw thee from the mire,
Or, save your reverence, love, wherein thou stick'st
Up to the ears. Come, we burn daylight, ho.
Rom. Nay, that's not so.

24

Mer.   I mean, sir, in delay
We waste our lights in vain, like lamps by day.
Take our good meaning, for our judgment sits
Five times in that ere once in our five wits.
    Rom. And we mean well in going to this mask.
But 'tis no wit to go.
    Mer.   Why, may one ask?
    Rom. I dreamt a dream to-night.
    Mer.   And so did I
    Rom. Well, what was yours?
    Mer.   That dreamers often lie.
    Rom. In bed asleep, while they do dream things true.
    Mer. O, then, I see, Queen Mab hath been with you.
She is the Fairies' midwife; and she comes,
In shape no bigger than an agate-stone
On the forefinger of an alderman,
Drawn with a team of little atomies
Over men's noses as they lie asleep:
Her waggon-spokes made of long spinners' legs;
The cover, of the wings of grasshoppers;
The traces, of the smallest spider's web;
The collars, of the moonshine's watery beams;
Her whip, of cricket's bone; the lash, of film;
Her waggoner, a small grey-coated gnat,
Not half so big as a round little worm
Pricked from the lazy finger of a maid.
Her chariot is an empty hazel-nut,
Made by the joiner squirrel or old grub,
Time out of mind the Fairies' coach-makers.
And in this state she gallops night by night
Through lovers' brains, and then they dream of love;
O'er courtiers' knees, that dream on court'sies straight;
O'er lawyers' fingers, who straight dream on fees:
O'er ladies' lips, who straight on kisses dream,
Which oft the angry Mab with blisters plagues,
Because their breaths with sweetmeats tainted are.
Sometime she gallops o'er a courtier's nose,
And then dreams he of smelling out a suit:
And sometime comes she with a tithe-pig's tail
Tickling a parson's nose as 'a lies asleep,
Then dreams he of another benefice.
Sometime she driveth o'er a soldier's neck,
And then dreams he of cutting foreign throats,
Of breaches, ambuscadoes, Spanish blades,
Of healths five fathom deep; and then anon
Drums in his ear, at which he starts and wakes;
And, being thus frighted, swears a prayer or two,
And sleeps again. This is that very Mab
That plats the manes of horses in the night

And bakes the elf-locks in foul sluttish hairs,
Which once untangled much misfortune bodes.
This is the hag, when maids lie on their backs,
That presses them and learns them first to bear,
Making them women of good carriage.
This is she—
    Rom.   Peace, peace! Mercutio, peace!
Thou talk'st of nothing.
    Mer.   True, I talk of dreams;
Which are the children of an idle brain
Begot of nothing but vain fantasy,
Which is as thin of substance as the air
And more inconstant than the wind, who wooes
Even now the frozen bosom of the north,
And, being angered, puffs away from thence,
Turning his face to the dew-dropping south.
    Ben.   This wind you talk of blows us from ourselves;
Supper is done, and we shall come too late.
    Rom.   I fear, too early; for my mind misgives
Some consequence, yet hanging in the stars,
Shall bitterly begin his fearful date
With this night's revels, and expire the term
Of a despiséd life, closed in my breast,
By some vile forfeit of untimely death:
But He that hath the steerage of my course
Direct my sail.   On, lusty gentlemen.
    Ben.   Strike, drum.

                                [Exeunt

Scene V.—A Hall in Capulet's House

Musicians waiting.   Enter Servants

    First Serv.   Where's Potpan, that he helps not to take
away? he shift a trencher! he scrape a trencher!
    Sec. Serv.   When good manners shall lie all in one or
two men's hands, and they unwashed too, 't is a foul
thing.
    First Serv.   Away with the joint-stools, remove the
court-cupboard, look to the plate.—Good thou, save me
a piece of marchpane; and, as thou lovest me, let the
porter let in Susan Grindstone and Nell.—Antony! and
Potpan!
    Sec. Serv.   Ay, boy; ready.
    First Serv.   You are looked for, and called for, asked
for, and sought for, in the great chamber.   ᛀ
    Sec. Serv.   We cannot be here and there too.—Cheerily,
boys: be brisk awhile, and the longer liver take all.

                                [They retire behind

Enter CAPULET, *&c., with the Guests, and the Maskers*

Cap. Welcome, gentlemen! ladies, that have their toes
Unplagued with corns, will have a bout with you:—
Ah ha, my mistresses! which of you all
Will now deny to dance? she that makes dainty, she,
I'll swear, hath corns. Am I come near you now?
Welcome, gentlemen! I have seen the day
That I have worn a visor, and could tell
A whispering tale in a fair lady's ear,
Such as would please; 't is gone, 't is gone, 't is gone.
You are welcome, gentlemen!—Come, musicians, play.
A hall, a hall! give room; and foot it, girls.
                              [*Music plays, and they dance*
More light, ye knaves! and turn the tables up,
And quench the fire, the room is grown too hot.—
Ah, sirrah, this unlooked-for sport comes well.
Nay, sit, nay, sit, good cousin Capulet,
For you and I are past our dancing days:
How long is 't now, since last yourself and I
Were in a mask?
Sec. Cap.   By 'r lady, thirty years.
Cap. What, man! 't is not so much, 't is not so much.
'Tis since the nuptial of Lucentio,
Come Pentecost as quickly as it will,
Some five-and-twenty years; and then we masked.
Sec. Cap. 'T is more, 't is more: his son is elder, sir;
His son is thirty.
Cap.   Will you tell me that?
His son was but a ward two years ago.
Rom. What lady's that, which doth enrich the hand
Of yonder knight?
Serv. I know not, sir.
Rom. O, she doth teach the torches to burn bright!
It seems she hangs upon the cheek of night
Like a rich jewel in an Ethiop's ear;
Beauty too rich for use, for earth too dear!
So shows a snowy dove trooping with crows,
As yonder lady o'er her fellows shows.
The measure done, I'll watch her place of stand,
And, touching hers, make blessèd my rude hand.
Did my heart love till now? forswear it, sight!
For I ne'er saw true beauty till this night.
Tyb. This, by his voice, should be a Montague.—
Fetch me my rapier, boy.—What! dares the slave
Come hither, covered with an antick face,
To fleer and scorn at our solemnity?
Now, by the stock and honour of my kin,

To strike him dead I hold it not a sin.

 Cap.   Why, how now, kinsman? wherefore storm you
   so?

 Tyb.   Uncle, this is a Montague, our foe;
A villain that is hither come in spite
To scorn at our solemnity this night.

 Cap.   Young Romeo is 't?

 Tyb.   'Tis he, that villain Romeo.

 Cap.   Content thee, gentle coz, let him alone:
He bears him like a portly gentleman;
And, to say truth, Verona brags of him
To be a virtuous and well-governed youth.
I would not for the wealth of all this town
Here in my house do him disparagement;
Therefore be patient, take no note of him:
It is my will; the which if thou respect,
Show a fair presence and put off these frowns,
An ill-beseeming semblance for a feast.

 Tyb.   It fits, when such a villain is a guest:
I'll not endure him.

 Cap.   He shall be endured:
What! goodman boy!—I say, he shall:—go to.
Am I the master here, or you? go to.
You'll not endure him!—God shall mend my soul,—
You'll make a mutiny among my guests!
You will set cock-a-hoop! you'll be the man!

 Tyb.   Why, uncle, 't is a shame.

 Cap.   Go to, go to;
You are a saucy boy:—is 't so, indeed?—
This trick may chance to scathe you; I know what.
You must contrary me! marry, 't is time.—
Well said, my hearts!—You are a princox; go:
Be quiet, or—More light, more light!—For shame!
I'll make you quiet. What—cheerly, my hearts!

 Tyb.   Patience perforce with wilful choler meeting
Makes my flesh tremble in their different greeting.
I will withdraw: but this intrusion shall,
Now seeming sweet, convert to bitter gall.   [*Exit*

 Rom. [*To Juliet*] If I profane with my unworthiest
   hand
This holy shrine, the gentle sin is this,
My lips, two blushing pilgrims, ready stand
To smooth that rough touch with a tender kiss.

 Jul.   Good pilgrim, you do wrong your hand too much,
Which mannerly devotion shows in this;
For saints have hands that pilgrims' hands do touch,
And palm to palm is holy palmers' kiss.

 Rom.   Have not saints lips, and holy palmers too?

 Jul.   Ay, pilgrim, lips that they must use in prayer.

Rom. O, then, dear saint, let lips do what hands do;
They pray, grant thou, lest faith turn to despair.
Jul. Saints do not move, though grant for prayers'
        sake.
Rom. Then move not, while my prayer's effect I take.
Thus from my lips, by thine, my sin is purged.
                                    [*Kissing her*
Jul. Then have my lips the sin that they have took.
Rom. Sin from my lips? O trespass sweetly urged!
Give me my sin again.
Jul.   You kiss by the book.
Nurse. Madam, your mother craves a word with you.
Rom. What is her mother?
Nurse.   Marry, bachelor,
Her mother is the lady of the house,
And a good lady, and a wise, and virtuous.
I nursed her daughter, that you talked withal;
I tell you—he that can lay hold of her
Shall have the chinks.
Rom.   Is she a Capulet?
O dear account! my life is my foe's debt.
Ben. Away, be gone; the sport is at the best.
Rom. Ay, so I fear; the more is my unrest.
Cap. Nay, gentlemen, prepare not to be gone;
We have a trifling foolish banquet towards.—
Is it e'en so? Why, then, I thank you all;
I thank you, honest gentlemen; good night.—
More torches here!—Come on, then let's to bed.
Ah, sirrah, by my fay, it waxes late;
I'll to my rest.   [*Exeunt all but Juliet and Nurse*
Jul. Come hither, nurse. What is yond gentleman?
Nurse. The son and heir of old Tiberio.
Jul. What's he that now is going out of door?
Nurse. Marry, that, I think, be young Petruchio.
Jul. What's he that follows there, that would not
        dance?
Nurse. I know not.
Jul. Go, ask his name.—If he be married,
My grave is like to be my wedding bed.
Nurse. His name is Romeo, and a Montague;
The only son of your great enemy.
Jul. My only love sprung from my only hate!
Too early seen unknown, and known too late!
Prodigious birth of love it is to me,
That I must love a loathéd enemy.
Nurse. What's this? what's this?
Jul.   A rhyme I learned even now
Of one I danced withal.
                            [*One calls within,* "JULIET"
29

Nurse.   Anon, anon!—
Come, let's away; the strangers all are gone.
                                                        [*Exeunt*

Enter Chorus

Now old Desire doth in his death-bed lie,
    And young Affection gapes to be his heir:
That fair for which love groaned for and would die,
    With tender Juliet matched, is now not fair.

Now Romeo is beloved, and loves again,
    Alike bewitchéd by the charm of looks;
But to his foe supposed he must complain,
    And she steal love's sweet bait from fearful hooks:

Being held a foe, he may not have access
    To breathe such vows as lovers use to swear;
And she as much in love, her means much less
    To meet her new belovéd anywhere.

But passion lends them power, time means, to meet,
Tempering extremities with extreme sweet.   [*Exit*

ACT SECOND

Scene I.—By the Wall of Capulet's Orchard

Enter Romeo

Rom.   Can I go forward, when my heart is here?
Turn back, dull earth, and find thy centre out.
        [*He climbs the wall, and leaps down within it*

Enter Benvolio *and* Mercutio.

Ben.   Romeo! my cousin Romeo!   Romeo!
Mer.   He is wise;
And, on my life, hath stolen him home to bed.
Ben.   He ran this way, and leaped this orchard wall.
Call, good Mercutio.
Mer.   Nay, I'll conjure too.—
Romeo! humours! madman! passion! lover!
Appear thou in the likeness of a sigh!
Speak but one rhyme, and I am satisfied;
Cry but 'Ah me!' pronounce but 'love' and 'dove,'
Speak to my gossip Venus one fair word,
One nickname for her purblind son and heir,
Young Adam Cupid, he that shot so trim
When King Cophetua loved the beggar-maid!—
He heareth not, he stirreth not, he moveth not;

The ape is dead, and I must conjure him.—
I conjure thee by Rosaline's bright eyes,
By her high forehead and her scarlet lip,
By her fine foot, straight leg, and quivering thigh,
And the demesnes that there adjacent lie,
That in thy likeness thou appear to us!
    Ben.   An if he hear thee, thou wilt anger him.
    Mer.   This cannot anger him: 'twould anger him
To raise a spirit in his mistress' circle
Of some strange nature, letting it there stand
Till she had laid it, and conjured it down;
That were some spite: my invocation
Is fair and honest, and in his mistress' name
I conjure only but to raise up him.
    Ben.   Come, he hath hid himself among these trees,
To be consorted with the humorous night:
Blind is his love, and best befits the dark.
    Mer.   If love be blind, love cannot hit the mark.
Now will he sit under a medlar-tree,
And wish his mistress were that kind of fruit
As maids call medlars when they laugh alone,—
O, Romeo, that she were, O, that she were
An open *et cœtera*, thou a poperin pear!
Romeo, good-night:—I'll to my truckle-bed;
This field-bed is too cold for me to sleep.
Come, shall we go?
    Ben.   Go, then; for 'tis in vain
To seek him here that means not to be found.

                                    [*Exeunt*

Scene II.—Capulet's Orchard

Enter Romeo

    Rom.   He jests at scars that never felt a wound,—
           [Juliet *appears above, at a window*
But, soft! what light through yonder window breaks?
It is the east, and Juliet is the sun!—
Arise, fair sun, and kill the envious moon,
Who is already sick and pale with grief
That thou, her maid, art far more fair than she:
Be not her maid, since she is envious;
Her vestal livery is but sick and green,
And none but fools do wear it; cast it off.—
It is my lady; O, it is my love!
O, that she knew she were!—
She speaks, yet she says nothing; what of that?
Her eye discourses; I will answer it.—
I am too bold, 't is not to me she speaks.

Two of the fairest stars in all the heaven,
Having some business, do entreat her eyes
To twinkle in their spheres till they return.
What if her eyes were there, they in her head?
The brightness of her cheek would shame those stars,
As daylight doth a lamp: her eyes in heaven
Would through the airy region stream so bright,
That birds would sing and think it were not night.
See, how she leans her cheek upon her hand!
O! that I were a glove upon that hand,
That I might touch that cheek!
    Jul.   Ay me!
    Rom.   She speaks,—
O, speak again, bright angel! for thou art
As glorious to this night, being o'er my head,
As is a wingéd messenger of heaven
Unto the white-upturnéd wondering eyes
Of mortals, that fall back to gaze on him
When he bestrides the lazy-pacing clouds
And sails upon the bosom of the air.
    Jul.   O Romeo, Romeo! wherefore art thou, Romeo?
Deny thy father and refuse thy name:
Or, if thou wilt not, be but sworn my love,
And I'll no longer be a Capulet.
    Rom.   [*Aside*] Shall I hear more, or shall I speak at this?
    Jul.   'T is but thy name that is my enemy:
Thou art thyself, though not a Montague.
What's Montague? it is nor hand, nor foot,
Nor arm, nor face, nor any other part
Belonging to a man.   O, be some other name.
What's in a name? that which we call a rose
By any other word would smell as sweet;
So Romeo would, were he not Romeo called,
Retain that dear perfection which he owes,
Without that title—Romeo, doff thy name;
And for thy name, which is no part of thee,
Take all myself!
    Rom.   I take thee at thy word:
Call me but love, and I'll be new baptized;
Henceforth I never will be Romeo.
    Jul.   What man art thou, that, thus bescreened in night,
So stumblest on my counsel?
    Rom.   By a name
I know not how to tell thee who I am:
My name, dear saint, is hateful to myself,
Because it is an enemy to thee:
Had I it written, I would tear the word.
    Jul.   My ears have yet not drunk a hundred words
Of that tongue's utterance, yet I know the sound.

Art thou not Romeo, and a Montague?
    Rom. Neither, fair maid, if either thee dislike.
    Jul. How cam'st thou hither, tell me, and wherefore?
The orchard walls are high and hard to climb;
And the place death, considering who thou art,
If any of my kinsmen find thee here.
    Rom. With love's light wings did I o'erperch these walls,
For stony limits cannot hold love out:
And what love can do, that dares love attempt,
Therefore thy kinsmen are no stop to me.
    Jul. If they do see thee, they will murder thee.
    Rom. Alack, there lies more peril in thine eye
Than twenty of their swords: look thou but sweet,
And I am proof against their enmity.
    Jul. I would not for the world they saw thee here.
    Rom. I have night's cloak to hide me from their eyes;
And, but thou love me, let them find me here:
My life were better ended by their hate,
Than death proroguéd, wanting of thy love.
    Jul. By whose direction found'st thou out this place?
    Rom. By Love, that first did prompt me to inquire;
He lent me counsel, and I lent him eyes.
I am no pilot; yet, wert thou as far
As that vast shore washed with the farthest sea,
I would adventure for such merchandise.
    Jul. Thou know'st the mask of night is on my face,
Else would a maiden blush bepaint my cheek
For that which thou hast heard me speak to-night.
Fain would I dwell on form, fain, fain deny.
What I have spoke; but farewell compliment!
Dost thou love me? I know thou wilt say—'Ay,'
And I will take thy word; yet, if thou swear'st,
Thou may'st prove false: at lovers' perjuries,
They say, Jove laughs. O gentle Romeo!
If thou dost love, pronounce it faithfully:
Or if thou think'st I am too quickly won.
I'll frown, and be perverse, and say thee nay,
So thou wilt woo; but else, not for the world.
In truth, fair Montague, I am too fond;
And therefore thou may'st think my haviour light:
But trust me, gentleman, I'll prove more true
Than those that have more cunning to be strange.
I should have been more strange, I must confess,
But that thou overheard'st, ere I was ware,
My true love's passion; therefore pardon me;
And not impute this yielding to light love,
Which the dark night hath so discoveréd.
    Rom. Lady, by yonder blesséd moon I swear,
That tips with silver all these fruit-tree tops,—

Jul.   O, swear not by the moon, the inconstant moon,
That monthly changes in her circled orb,
Lest that thy love prove likewise variable.
Rom.   What shall I swear by?
Jul.   Do not swear at all;
Or, if thou wilt, swear by thy gracious self,
Which is the god of my idolatry,
And I'll believe thee.
Rom.   If my heart's dear love—
Jul.   Well, do not swear.   Although I joy in thee,
I have no joy of this contract to-night:
It is too rash, too unadvised, too sudden;
Too like the lightning, which doth cease to be
Ere one can say, 'It lightens.'   Sweet, good-night!
This bud of love, by summer's ripening breath,
May prove a beauteous flower when next we meet.
Good-night, good-night! as sweet repose and rest
Come to thy heart as that within my breast!
Rom.   O, wilt thou leave me so unsatisfied?'
Jul.   What satisfaction canst thou have to-night?
Rom.   The exchange of thy love's faithful vow for mine.
Jul.   I gave thee mine before thou didst request it;
And yet I would it were to give again.
Rom.   Wouldst thou withdraw it? for what purpose,
love?
Jul.   But to be frank, and give it thee again.
And yet I wish but for the thing I have;
My bounty is as boundless as the sea,
My love as deep; the more I give to thee,
The more I have, for both are infinite.
                                        [*Nurse calls within*
I hear some noise within; dear love, adieu!—
Anon, good nurse!—Sweet Montague, be true.
Stay but a little, I will come again.   [*Exit*
Rom.   O blessed, blessed night! I am afeard,
Being in night, all this is but a dream,
Too flattering-sweet to be substantial.

Re-enter JULIET, *above*

Jul.   Three words, dear Romeo, and good night, indeed,
If that thy bent of love be honourable,
Thy purpose marriage, send me word to-morrow,
By one that I'll procure to come to thee,
Where and what time thou wilt perform the rite,
And all my fortunes at thy foot I'll lay,
And follow thee my lord throughout the world.
Nurse.   [*Within*]   Madam!
Jul.   I come, anon.—But if thou mean'st not well,

I do beseech thee—
    Nurse. [*Within*] Madam!
    Jul.   By-and-by; I come.—
To cease thy suit, and leave me to my grief:
To-morrow will I send.
    Rom.   So thrive my soul,—
    Jul. A thousand times good-night!   [*Exit*
    Rom. A thousand times the worse, to want thy light.—
Love goes toward love, as school-boys from their books;
But love from love, toward school with heavy looks.
                            [*Retiring slowly*

Re-enter JULIET, *above*

    Jul. Hist! Romeo, hist!—O, for a falconer's voice,
To lure this tassel-gentle back again!
Bondage is hoarse, and may not speak aloud;
Else would I tear the cave where Echo lies
And make her airy tongue more hoarse than mine
With repetition of my Romeo's name.
    Rom. It is my soul that calls upon my name:
How silver-sweet sound lovers' tongues by night,
Like softest music to attending ears!
    Jul. Romeo!
    Rom.   My dear?
    Jul.   By what o'clock to-morrow
Shall I send to thee?
    Rom.   By the hour of nine.
    Jul. I will not fail: 't is twenty years till then.
I have forgot why I did call thee back.
    Rom. Let me stand here, till thou remember it.
    Jul. I shall forget, to have thee still stand there,
Remembering how I love thy company.
    Rom. And I'll still stay, to have thee still forget,
Forgetting any other home but this.
    Jul. 'Tis almost morning; I would have thee gone:
And yet no further than a wanton's bird,
Who lets it hop a little from her hand,
Like a poor prisoner in his twisted gyves,
And with a silk thread plucks it back again,
So loving-jealous of his liberty.
    Rom. I would, I were thy bird.
    Jul.   Sweet, so would I:
Yet I should kill thee with much cherishing.
Good-night, good-night: parting is such sweet sorrow
That I shall say good-night till it be morrow.
                               [*Exit*
    Rom. Sleep dwell upon thine eyes, peace in my breast!
'Would I were sleep and peace, so sweet to rest:

Hence will I to my ghostly father's cell,
His help to crave and my dear hap to tell.   [*Exit*

SCENE III.—Friar LAURENCE's Cell

Enter FRIAR LAURENCE, *with a basket*

   Fri. The grey-eyed morn smiles on the frowning night,
Chequering the eastern clouds with streaks of light;
And fleckéd darkness like a drunkard reels
From forth day's path and Titan's fiery wheels:
Now, ere the sun advance his burning eye
The day to cheer and night's dank dew to dry,
I must up-fill this osier cage of ours
With baleful weeds and precious-juicéd flowers,
The earth that's nature's mother is her tomb;
What is her burying grave, that is her womb:
And from her womb children of divers kind
We sucking on her natural bosom find,
Many for many virtues excellent,
None but for some, and yet all different.
O, mickle is the powerful grace that lies
In herbs, plants, stones, and their true qualities:
For nought so vile that on the earth doth live,
But to the earth some special good doth give;
Nor aught so good, but, strained from that fair use,
Revolts from true birth, stumbling on abuse:
Virtue itself turns vice, being misapplied,
And vice sometime's by action dignified.
Within the infant rind of this weak flower
Poison hath residence, and medicine power:
For this, being smelt, with that part cheers each part,
Being tasted, slays all senses with the heart.
Two such opposéd kings, encamp them still
In man as well as herbs,—Grace, and rude Will;
And where the worse is predominant,
Full soon the canker death eats up that plant.

Enter ROMEO

   Rom. Good-morrow, father.
   Fri.   Benedicite!
What early tongue so sweet saluteth me?—
Young son, it argues a distempered head,
So soon to bid good-morrow to thy bed:
Care keeps his watch in every old man's eye,
And where care lodges, sleep will never lie;
But where unbruiséd youth with unstuffed brain
Doth couch his limbs, there golden sleep doth reign

Therefore, thy earliness doth me assure
Thou art up-roused by some distemperature:
Or if not so, then here I hit it right,
Our Romeo hath not been in bed to-night.
    Rom. That last is true; the sweeter rest was mine.
    Fri. God pardon sin! wast thou with Rosaline?
    Rom. With Rosaline, my ghostly father? no;
I have forgot that name, and that name's woe.
    Fri. That's my good son: but where hast thou been,
        then?
    Rom. I'll tell thee ere thou ask it me again.
I have been feasting with mine enemy;
Where, on a sudden, one hath wounded me,
That's by me wounded; both our remedies
Within thy help and holy physic lies:
I bear no hatred, blessèd man, for, lo,
My intercession likewise steads my foe.
    Fri. Be plain, good son, and homely in thy drift;
Riddling confession finds but riddling shrift.
    Rom. Then plainly know, my heart's dear love is set
On the fair daughter of rich Capulet:
As mine on hers, so hers is set on mine;
And all combined, save what thou must combin
By holy marriage. When, and where, and how
We met, we wooed, and made exchange of vow,
I'll tell thee as we pass; but this I pray,
That thou consent to marry us to-day.
    Fri. Holy Saint Francis! what a change is here!
Is Rosaline, whom thou didst love so dear,
So soon forsaken? young men's love, then, lies
Not truly in their hearts, but in their eyes.
Jesu Maria! what a deal of brine
Hath washed thy sallow cheeks for Rosaline!
How much salt water thrown away in waste,
To season love, that of it doth not taste!
The sun not yet thy sighs from heaven clears,
Thy old groans ring yet in my ancient ears;
Lo, here upon thy cheek the stain doth sit
Of an old tear that is not washed off yet.
If e'er thou wast thyself and these woes thine,
Thou and these woes were all for Rosaline:
And art thou changed? pronounce this sentence, then:
Women may fall when there's no strength in men.
    Rom. Thou chidd'st me oft for loving Rosaline.
    Fri. For doting, not for loving, pupil mine.
    Rom. And bad'st me bury love.
    Fri.   Not in a grave,
To lay one in, another out to have.
    Rom. I pray thee, chide me not: her I love now

Doth grace for grace and love for love allow;
The other did not so.
    Fri.   O, she knew well,
Thy love did read by rote and could not spell.
But come, young waverer, come, go with me,
In one respect I'll thy assistant be;
For this alliance may so happy prove,
To turn your households' rancour to pure love.
    Rom. O, let us hence; I stand on sudden haste.
    Fri.   Wisely and slow: they stumble that run fast.
                                 [Exeunt

SCENE IV.—A Street

Enter BENVOLIO *and* MERCUTIO

    Mer. Where the devil should this Romeo be?
Came he not home to-night?
    Ben. Not to his father's; I spoke with his man.
    Mer. Why, that same pale hard-hearted wench, that
            Rosaline,
Torments him so that he will sure run mad.
    Ben. Tybalt, the kinsman to old Capulet,
Hath sent a letter to his father's house.
    Mer. A challenge, on my life.
    Ben. Romeo will answer it.
    Mer. Any man that can write may answer a letter.
    Ben. Nay, he will answer the master's letter, how he
            dares, being dared.
    Mer. Alas, poor Romeo, he is already dead! stabbed
with a white wench's black eye; run through the ear with
a love-song; the very pin of his heart cleft with the blind
bow-boy's butt-shaft; and is he a man to encounter
Tybalt?
    Ben. Why, what is Tybalt?
    Mer. More than prince of cats, I can tell you. O, he
is the courageous captain of compliments. He fights as
you sing prick-song, keeps time, distance, and proportion;
rests me his minim rest, one, two, and the third in your
bosom: the very butcher of a silk button, a duellist,
a duellist; a gentleman of the very first house, of the
first and second cause. Ah, the immortal passado! the
punto reverso! the hay!—
    Ben. The what?
    Mer. The pox of such antic, lisping, affecting fantas-
ticoes, these new tuners of accents!—'By Jesu, a very
good blade!—a very tall man!—a very good whore!'—
Why, is not this a lamentable thing, grandsire, that we
should be thus afflicted with these strange flies, these

fashion-mongers, these *pardonnez-mois*, who stand so much on the new form that they cannot sit at ease on the old bench? O, their *bons*, their *bons!*

Enter ROMEO

Ben. Here comes Romeo, here comes Romeo.

Mer. Without his roe, like a dried herring. O flesh, flesh, how art thou fishified! Now he is for the numbers that Petrarch flowed in: Laura, to his lady, was a kitchen wench; marry, she had a better love to be-rhyme her; Dido, a dowdy; Cleopatra, a gipsy; Helen and Hero, hidings and harlots; Thisbe, a grey eye or so, but not to the purpose.—Signior Romeo, *bon jour!* there's a French salutation to your French slop. You gave us the counterfeit fairly last night.

Rom. Good-morrow to you both. What counterfeit did I give you?

Mer. The slip, sir, the slip; can you not conceive?

Rom. Pardon, good Mercutio, my business was great; and in such a case as mine a man may strain courtesy.

Mer. That's as much as to say, such a case as yours constrains a man to bow in the hams.

Rom. Meaning to court'sy.

Mer. Thou hast most kindly hit it.

Rom. A most courteous exposition.

Mer. Nay, I am the very pink of courtesy.

Rom. Pink for flower.

Mer. Right.

Rom. Why, then is my pump well flowered.

Mer. Sure wit: follow me this jest now, till thou hast worn out thy pump, that, when the single sole of it is worn, the jest may remain, after the wearing, solely singular.

Rom. O single-soled jest, solely singular for the singleness.

Mer. Come between us, good Benvolio; my wit faints.

Rom. Switch and spurs, switch and spurs; or I'll cry a match.

Mer. Nay, if our wits run the wild-goose chase, I am done; for thou hast more of the wild-goose in one of thy wits than, I am sure, I have in my whole five. Was I with you there for the goose?

Rom. Thou wast never with me for anything, when thou wast not there for the goose.

Mer. I will bite thee by the ear for that jest.

Rom. Nay, good goose, bite not.

Mer. Thy wit is a very bitter sweeting; it is a most sharp sauce.

Rom. And is it not well served into a sweet goose?

Mer. O! here's a wit of cheveril, that stretches from an inch narrow to an ell broad.

Rom. I stretch it out for that word 'broad': which added to the goose, proves thee far and wide a broad goose.

Mer. Why, is not this better now than groaning for love? now art thou sociable, now art thou Romeo; now art thou what thou art, by art as well as by nature: for this drivelling love is like a great natural that runs lolling up and down to hide his bauble in a hole.

Ben. Stop there, stop there.

Mer. Thou desirest me to stop in my tale against the hair.

Ben. Thou wouldst else have made thy tale large.

Mer. O, thou art deceived; I would have made it short; for I was come to the whole depth of my tale, and meant, indeed, to occupy the argument no longer.

Rom. Here's goodly gear!

Enter Nurse and PETER

Mer. A sail a sail!

Ben. Two, two; a shirt, and a smock.

Nurse. Peter!

Peter. Anon?

Nurse. My fan, Peter.

Mer. Good Peter, to hide her face; for her fan's the fairer face.

Nurse. God ye good morrow, gentlemen.

Mer. God ye good den, fair gentlewoman.

Nurse. Is it good den?

Mer. 'T is no less, I tell you; for the bawdy hand of the dial is now upon the prick of noon.

Nurse. Out upon you! what a man are you?

Rom. One, gentlewoman, that God hath made himself to mar.

Nurse. By my troth, it is well said;—for himself to mar, quoth 'a?—Gentlemen, can any of you tell me where I may find the young Romeo?

Rom. I can tell you; but young Romeo will be older when you have found him than he was when you sought him. I am the youngest of that name, for fault of a worse.

Nurse. You say well.

Mer. Yea, is the worst well? very well took, i' faith; wisely, wisely.

Nurse. If you be he, sir, I desire some confidence with you.

Ben. She will indite him to some supper.

Mer. A bawd, a bawd, a bawd! So ho!

Rom. What hast thou found?

40

Mer. No hare, sir; unless a hare, sir, in a lenten pie, that is something stale and hoar ere it be spent.

> 'An old hare hoar,
> And an old hare hoar,
> Is very good meat in Lent:
> But a hare that is hoar,
> Is too much for a score,
> When it hoars ere it be spent.'

Romeo, will you come to your father's? we'll to dinner thither.

Rom. I will follow you.

Mer. Farewell, ancient lady; farewell, 'lady, lady, lady.'

[*Exeunt* BENVOLIO *and* MERCUTIO

Nurse. Marry, farewell!—I pray you, sir, what saucy merchant was this, that was so full of his ropery?

Rom. A gentleman, nurse, that loves to hear himself talk; and will speak more in a minute than he will stand to in a month.

Nurse. An 'a speak anything against me, I'll take him down, an 'a were lustier than he is, and twenty such Jacks; and if I cannot, I'll find those that shall. Scurvy knave! I am none of his flirt-gills; I am none of his skains-mates! —And thou must stand by too, and suffer every knave to use me at his pleasure?

Peter. I saw no man use you at his pleasure; if I had, my weapon should quickly have been out, I warrant you. I dare draw as soon as another man, if I see occasion in a good quarrel and the law on my side.

Nurse. Now, afore God, I am so vexed, that every part about me quivers.—Scurvy knave!—Pray you, sir, a word; and as I told you, my young lady bade me inquire you out: what she bid me say, I will keep to myself; but first let me tell ye, if ye should lead her in a fool's paradise, as they say, it were a very gross kind of behaviour, as they say: for the gentlewoman is young; and, therefore, if you should deal double with her, truly, it were an ill thing to be offered to any gentlewoman, and very weak dealing.

Rom. Nurse, commend me to thy lady and mistress. I protest unto thee.—

Nurse. Good heart! and, i' faith, I will tell her as much. Lord, Lord! she will be a joyful woman.

Rom. What wilt thou tell her, nurse? thou dost not mark me.

Nurse. I will tell her, sir,—that you do protest; which as I take it, is a gentlemanlike offer.

Rom. Bid her devise some means to come to shrift This afternoon;

And there she shall at Friar Laurence' cell
Be shrived and married.   Here is for thy pains.
   Nurse.   No, truly, sir; not a penny.
   Rom.   Go to; I say, you shall.
   Nurse.   This afternoon, sir? well, she shall be there.
   Rom.   And stay, good nurse; behind the abbey wall,
Within this hour my man shall be with thee,
And bring thee cords made like a tackled stair,
Which to the high top-gallant of my joy
Must be my convoy in the secret night.
Farewell; be trusty, and I'll quite thy pains.
Farewell; commend me to thy mistress.
   Nurse.   Now God in heaven bless thee!   Hark you, sir.
   Rom.   What say'st thou, my dear nurse?
   Nurse.   Is your man secret?   Did you ne'er hear say,
Two may keep counsel, putting one away?
   Rom.   I warrant thee, my man's as true as steel.
   Nurse.   Well, sir; my mistress is the sweetest lady—
Lord, Lord!—when 't was a little prating thing,—O,—
There's a nobleman in town, one Paris, that would fain
lay knife aboard; but she, good soul, had as lief see a
toad, a very toad, as see him.   I anger her sometimes, and
tell her that Paris is the properer man; but, I'll warrant
you, when I say so, she looks as pale as any clout in the
versal world.   Doth not rosemary and Romeo begin both
with a letter?
   Rom.   Ay, nurse; what of that? both with an R.
   Nurse.   Ah, mocker, that's the dog's name.   R is for
the—— No: I know it begins with some other letter:—
and she hath the prettiest sententious of it, of you and
rosemary, that it would do you good to hear it.
   Rom.   Commend me to thy lady.
   Nurse.   Ay, a thousand times.   [*Exit Romeo*
Peter!
   Peter.   Anon?
   Nurse.   Peter, take my fan and go before.

                                       [*Exeunt*

SCENE V.—CAPULET'S Garden

Enter JULIET

   Jul.   The clock struck nine, when I did send the nurse;
In half an hour she promised to return.
Perchance, she cannot meet him; that's not so.
O, she is lame! love's heralds should be thoughts,
Which ten times faster glide than the sun's beams,
Driving back shadows over louring hills:
Therefore do nimble-pinioned doves draw love,

And therefore hath the wind-swift Cupid wings.
Now is the sun upon the highmost hill
Of this day's journey; and from nine till twelve
Is three long hours,—yet she is not come.
Had she affections and warm youthful blood,
She'd be as swift in motion as a ball;
My words would bandy her to my sweet love,
And his to me:
But old folks, many feign as they were dead;
Unwieldy, slow, heavy and pale as lead.

Enter Nurse and PETER

O God, she comes!—O honey nurse, what news?
Hast thou met with him?   Send thy man away.
   Nurse.   Peter, stay at the gate.   [*Exit Peter*
   Jul.   Now, good sweet nurse,—O Lord, why look'st
       thou sad?
Though news be sad, yet tell them merrily;
If good, thou sham'st the music of sweet news
By playing it to me with so sour a face.
   Nurse.   I am aweary; give me leave awhile.
Fie, how my bones ache!   What a jaunt have I had!
   Jul.   I would thou hadst my bones and I thy news:
Nay, come, I pray thee, speak; good, good nurse, speak.
   Nurse.   Jesu, what haste? can you not stay awhile?
Do you not see that I am out of breath?
   Jul.   How art thou out of breath, when thou hast breath
To say to me that thou art out of breath?
The excuse that thou dost make in this delay
Is longer than the tale thou dost excuse.
Is thy news good or bad? answer to that;
Say either, and I'll stay the circumstance:
Let me be satisfied, is 't good or bad?
   Nurse.   Well, you have made a simple choice; you
know not how to choose a man. Romeo! no, not he;
though his face be better than any man's, yet his leg excels
all men's; and for a hand, and a foot, and a body, though
they be not to be talked on, yet they are past compare.
He is not the flower of courtesy, but I'll warrant him, as
gentle as a lamb. Go thy ways, wench; serve God.
What, have you dined at home?
   Jul.   No, no; but all this did I know before.
What says he of our marriage? what of that?
   Nurse.   Lord, how my head aches! what a head have I!
It beats as it would fall in twenty pieces.
My back—o' t'other side.—O, my back, my back!
Beshrew your heart, for sending me about
To catch my death with jaunting up and down!

43

Jul. I' faith, I am sorry that thou art not well.
Sweet, sweet, sweet nurse, tell me, what says my love?
Nurse. Your love says like an honest gentleman,
And a courteous, and a kind, and a handsome,
And, I warrant, a virtuous,—Where is your mother?
Jul. Where is my mother?—why, she is within;
Where should she be? How oddly thou repliest:
'Your love says like an honest gentleman,—
Where is your mother?'
Nurse.   O, God's lady dear!
Are you so hot? Marry, come up, I trow;
Is this the poultice for my aching bones?
Henceforward do your messages yourself.
Jul. Here's such a coil!—come, what says Romeo?
Nurse. Have you got leave to go to shrift to-day?
Jul. I have.
Nurse. Then hie you hence to Friar Laurence' cell;
There stays a husband to make you a wife.
Now comes the wanton blood up in your cheeks,
They'll be in scarlet straight at any news.
Hie you to church; I must another way,
To fetch a ladder, by the which your love
Must climb a bird's nest soon, when it is dark;
I am the drudge, and toil in your delight,
But you shall bear the burden soon at night.
Go; I'll to dinner; hie you to the cell.
Jul. Hie to high fortune!—Honest nurse, farewell.
                                              [*Exeunt*

SCENE VI.—Friar LAURENCE'S Cell

Enter FRIAR LAURENCE *and* ROMEO

Fri. So smile the heavens upon this holy act,
That after-hours with sorrows chide us not!
Rom. Amen, Amen! but come what sorrow can,
It cannot countervail the exchange of joy
That one short minute gives me in her sight.
Do thou but close our hands with holy words,
Then love-devouring death do what he dare,
It is enough I may but call her mine.
Fri. These violent delights have violent ends,
And in their triumph die, like fire and powder,
Which, as they kiss, consume. The sweetest honey
Is loathsome in his own deliciousness,
And in the taste confounds the appetite:
Therefore, love moderately; long love doth so;
Too swift arrives as tardy as too slow.

Enter JULIET

Here comes the lady.   O, so light a foot
Will ne'er wear out the everlasting flint:
A lover may bestride the gossamer
That idles in the wanton summer air,
And yet not fall; so light is vanity.
    Jul.   Good even to my ghostly confessor.
    Fri.   Romeo shall thank thee, daughter, for us both.
    Jul.   As much to him, else is his thanks too much.
    Rom.   Ah, Juliet, if the measure of thy joy
Be heaped like mine, and that thy skill be more
To blazon it, then sweeten with thy breath
This neighbour air, and let rich music's tongue
Unfold the imagined happiness that both
Receive in either by this dear encounter.
    Jul.   Conceit, more rich in matter than in words,
Brags of his substance, not of ornament:
They are but beggars that can count their worth;
But my true love is grown to such excess,
I cannot sum up half my sum of wealth.
    Fri.   Come, come with me, and we will make short work;
For, by your leaves, you shall not stay alone
Till the holy church incorporate two in one.

                          [Exeunt

ACT THREE

SCENE I.—A Public Place

Enter MERCUTIO, BENVOLIO, *Page, and Servants*

    Ben.   I pray thee, good Mercutio, let's retire:
The day is hot, the Capulets abroad,
And, if we meet, we shall not 'scape a brawl;
For now, these hot days, is the mad blood stirring.
    Mer.   Thou art like one of those fellows that when he
enters the confines of a tavern claps me his sword upon the
table and says, 'God send me no need of thee!' and, by
the operation of the second cup, draws it on the drawer,
when, indeed, there is no need.
    Ben.   Am I like such a fellow?
    Mer.   Come, come, thou art as hot a Jack in thy mood,
as any in Italy, and as soon moved to be moody, and as
soon moody to be moved.
    Ben.   And what to?
    Mer.   Nay, an there were two such, we should have

none shortly, for one would kill the other. Thou! why, thou wilt quarrel with a man that hath a hair more or a hair less in his beard than thou hast. Thou wilt quarrel with a man for cracking nuts, having no other reason but because thou hast hazel eyes. What eye but such an eye would spy out such a quarrel? Thy head is as full of quarrels as an egg is full of meat; and yet thy head hath been beaten as addle as an egg for quarrelling. Thou hast quarrelled with a man for coughing in the street, because he hath wakened thy dog that hath lain asleep in the sun. Didst thou not fall out with a tailor for wearing his new doublet before Easter? with another, for tying his new shoes with old riband? and yet thou wilt tutor me from quarrelling!

Ben. An I were so apt to quarrel as thou art, any man should buy the fee-simple of my life for an hour and a quarter.

Mer. The fee-simple? O simple.

Ben. By my head, here comes the Capulets.

Mer. By my heel, I care not.

Enter TYBALT and others

Tyb. Follow me close, for I will speak to them.—
Gentlemen, good den; a word with one of you.

Mer. And but one word with one of us? Couple it with something; make it a word and a blow.

Tyb. You shall find me apt enough to that, sir, an you will give me occasion.

Mer. Could you not take some occasion without giving?

Tyb. Mercutio, thou consort'st with Romeo,—

Mer. Consort! what, dost thou make us minstrels? an thou make minstrels of us, look to hear nothing but discords: here's my fiddlestick; here's that shall make you dance. 'Zounds, consort!

Ben. We talk here in the public haunt of men.
Either withdraw unto some private place,
And reason coldly of your grievances,
Or else depart; here all eyes gaze on us.

Mer. Men's eyes were made to look, and let them gaze:
I will not budge for no man's pleasure, I.

Enter ROMEO

Tyb. Well, peace be with you, sir. Here comes my man.

Mer. But I'll be hanged, sir, if he wear your livery:
Marry, go before to field, he'll be your follower;
Your worship, in that sense, may call him 'man.'

Tyb. Romeo, the love I bear thee can afford
No better term than this,—thou art a villain.

Rom. Tybalt, the reason that I have to love thee
Doth much excuse the appertaining rage
To such a greeting: villain am I none:
Therefore farewell; I see, thou know'st me not.
Tyb. Boy, this shall not excuse the injuries
That thou hast done me; therefore turn and draw.
Rom. I do protest, I never injured thee,
But love thee better than thou canst devise
Till thou shalt know the reason of my love:
And so, good Capulet,—which name I tender
As dearly as mine own,—be satisfied.
Mer. O calm, dishonourable, vile submission!
Alla stoccata carries it away.   [*Draws*
Tybalt, you rat-catcher, will you walk?
Tyb. What wouldst thou have with me?
Mer. Good king of cats, nothing but one of your nine
lives; that I mean to make bold withal, and, as you shall
use me hereafter, dry-beat the rest of the eight. Will
you pluck your sword out of his pilcher by the ears? make
haste, lest mine be about your ears ere it be out.
Tyb. I am for you.   [*Drawing*
Rom. Gentle Mercutio, put thy rapier up.
Mer. Come, sir, your passado.   [*They fight*
Rom. Draw, Benvolio; beat down their weapons.
Gentlemen, for shame, forbear this outrage!
Tybalt,—Mercutio,—the prince expressly hath
Forbidden bandying in Verona streets,—
Hold, Tybalt!—good Mercutio!

[*Exeunt Tybalt and his Partisans*

Mer.   I am hurt.
A plague o' both your houses! I am sped:
Is he gone, and hath nothing?
Ben.   What! art thou hurt?
Mer. Ay, ay, a scratch, a scratch; marry, 't is enough.
Where is my page?—Go, villain, fetch a surgeon.

[*Exit Page*

Rom. Courage, man; the hurt cannot be much.
Mer. No, 'tis not so deep as a well, nor so wide as a
church-door; but 't is enough, 't will serve: ask for me
to-morrow, and you shall find me a grave man. I am
peppered, I warrant, for this world.—A plague o' both
your houses!—'Zounds! a dog, a rat, a mouse, a cat, to
scratch a man to death! a braggart, a rogue, a villain, that
fights by the book of arithmetic!—Why the devil came
you between us? I was hurt under your arm.
Rom. I thought all for the best.
Mer. Help me into some house, Benvolio,
Or I shall faint.—A plague o' both your houses!

They have made worms' meat of me: I have it,
And soundly too:—your houses!

> [*Exeunt Mercutio and Benvolio*

Rom.   This gentleman, the prince's near ally,
My very friend, hath got this mortal hurt
In my behalf; my reputation stained
With Tybalt's slander,—Tybalt, that an hour
Hath been my cousin: O sweet Juliet!
Thy beauty hath made me effeminate,
And in my temper softened valour's steel!

Re-enter BENVOLIO

Ben.   O Romeo, Romeo, brave Mercutio's dead;
That gallant spirit has aspired the clouds,
Which too untimely here did scorn the earth.
Rom.   This day's black fate on more days doth depend;
This but begins the woe others must end.

Re-enter TYBALT

Ben.   Here comes the furious Tybalt back again.
Rom.   Alive in triumph! and Mercutio slain!
Away to heaven, respective lenity,
And fire-eyed fury be my conduct now!—
Now, Tybalt, take the 'villain' back again
That late thou gav'st me; for Mercutio's soul
Is but a little way above our heads,
Staying for thine to keep him company;
Either thou, or I, or both, must go with him.
Tyb.   Thou, wretched boy, that didst consort him here,
Shalt with him hence.
Rom.   This shall determine that.

> [*They fight; Tybalt falls*

Ben.   Romeo, away, be gone!
The citizens are up, and Tybalt slain:
Stand not amazed: the prince will doom thee death,
If thou art taken.—Hence!—be gone!—away!—
Rom.   O, I am fortune's fool!—
Ben.   Why dost thou stay?   [*Exit Romeo*

Enter Citizens, &c

First Cit.   Which way ran he that killed Mercutio?
Tybalt, that murderer, which way ran he?
Ben.   There lies that Tybalt
First Cit.   Up, sir, go with me;
I charge thee in the prince's name, obey.

Enter PRINCE, *attended;* MONTAGUE, CAPULET,
their Wives, and others

Prin.   Where are the vile beginners of this fray:
Ben.   O noble prince, I can discover all
The unlucky manage of this fatal brawl.
There lies the man, slain by young Romeo,
That slew thy kinsman, brave Mercutio.
La. Cap.   Tybalt, my cousin! O my brother's child!
O prince! O cousin! husband! O, the blood is spilled
Of my dear kinsman!—Prince, as thou art true
For blood of ours, shed blood of Montague.—
O cousin, cousin!
Prin.   Benvolio, who began this bloody fray?
Ben.   Tybalt, here slain, whom Romeo's hand did slay;
Romeo, that spoke him fair, bade him bethink
How nice the quarrel was, and urged withal
Your high displeasure:—all this, utteréd
With gentle breath, calm look, knees humbly bowed,
Could not take truce with the unruly spleen
Of Tybalt deaf to peace, but that he tilts
With piercing steel at bold Mercutio's breast;
Who, all as hot, turns deadly point to point,
And, with a martial scorn, with one hand beats
Cold death aside, and with the other sends
It back to Tybalt, whose dexterity
Retorts it. Romeo he cries aloud,
'Hold, friends! friends, part!' and, swifter than his
            tongue,
His agile arm beats down their fatal points,
And 'twixt them rushes; underneath whose arm
An envious thrust from Tybalt hit the life
Of stout Mercutio, and then Tybalt fled;
But by-and-by comes back to Romeo,
Who had but newly entertained revenge,
And to 't they go like lightning; for, ere I
Could I draw to part them, was stout Tybalt slain;
And as he fell, did Romeo turn and fly.
This is the truth, or let Benvolio die.
La. Cap.   He is a kinsman to the Montague;
Affection makes him false, he speaks not true:
Some twenty of them fought in this black strife,
And all those twenty could but kill one life.
I beg for justice, which thou, prince, must give:
Romeo slew Tybalt, Romeo must not live.
Prin.   Romeo slew him, he slew Mercutio;
Who now the price of his dear blood doth owe?
Mon.   Not Romeo, prince, he was Mercutio's friend;
His fault concludes but what the law should end,

The life of Tybalt.
   Prin.   And for that offence,
Immediately we do exile him hence:
I have an interest in your hate's proceeding,
My blood for your rude brawls doth lie a-bleeding;
But I'll amerce you with so strong a fine,
That you shall all repent the loss of mine.
I will be deaf to pleading and excuses;
Nor tears, nor prayers, shall purchase out abuses;
Therefore use none: let Romeo hence in haste,
Else, when he's found, that hour is his last.
Bear hence this body, and attend our will:
Mercy but murders, pardoning those that kill.

                                   [Exeunt

Scene II.—A Room in Capulet's House

Enter Juliet

   Jul.   Gallop apace, you fiery-footed steeds,
Towards Phœbus' lodging; such a waggoner
As Phæthon would whip you to the west,
And bring in cloudy night immediately.—
Spread thy close curtain, love-performing night,
That runaways' eyes may wink, and Romeo
Leap to these arms, untalked-of, and unseen!—
Lovers can see to do their amorous rites
By their own beauties; or, if love be blind,
It best agrees with night.—Come, civil night,
Thou sober-suited matron, all in black,
And learn me how to lose a winning match,
Played for a pair of stainless maidenhoods:
Hood my unmanned blood bating in my cheeks
With thy black mantle, till strange love grown bold
Think true love acted simple modesty.
Come, night, come, Romeo, come, thou day in night;
For thou wilt lie upon the wings of night
Whiter than new snow on a raven's back.—
Come, gentle night, come, loving, black-browed night,
Give me my Romeo: and, when he shall die,
Take him and cut him out in little stars,
And he will make the face of heaven so fine
That all the world will be in love with night
And pay no worship to the garish sun.—
O, I have bought the mansion of a love,
But not possessed it, and, though I am sold,
Not yet enjoyed.   So tedious is this day
As is the night before some festival

To an impatient child that hath new robes
And may not wear them.   O, here comes my nurse,
And she brings news, and every tongue that speaks
But Romeo's name, speaks heavenly eloquence.

Enter Nurse, with cords

Now, nurse, what news?   What hast thou there?
            the cords
That Romeo bid thee fetch?
   Nurse.   Ay, ay, the cords.
                                   [*Throws them down*
   Jul.   Ay me! what news? why dost thou wring thy
      hands?
   Nurse.   Ah, well-a-day! he's dead, he's dead, he's dead.
We are undone, lady, we are undone.—
Alack the day!—he's gone, he's killed, he's dead!
   Jul.   Can Heaven be so envious!
   Nurse.   Romeo can,
Though Heaven cannot.—O, Romeo, Romeo—
Who ever would have thought it!—Romeo—
   Jul.   What devil art thou, that dost torment me thus?
This torture should be roared in dismal hell.
Hath Romeo slain himself? say thou but *I*,
And that bare vowel, *I*, shall poison more
Than the death-darting eye of cockatrice.
I am not I, if there be such an *I*,
Or those eyes shut, that make thee answer, *I*.
If he be slain, say—*I*; or if not,—no:
Brief sounds determine of my weal or woe.
   Nurse.   I saw the wound, I saw it with mine eyes—
God save the mark!—here on his manly breast:
A piteous corse, a bloody piteous corse;
Pale, pale as ashes, all bedaubed in blood,
All in gore blood;—I swounded at the sight.
   Jul.   O, break, my heart!—poor bankrupt, break at once!
To prison, eyes; ne'er look on liberty!
Vile earth, to earth resign; end motion here,
And thou, and Romeo, press one heavy bier!
   Nurse.   O Tybalt, Tybalt! the best friend I had:
O courteous Tybalt! honest gentleman!
That ever I should live to see thee dead!
   Jul.   What storm is this, that blows so contrary?
Is Romeo slaughtered? and is Tybalt dead?
My dearest cousin, and my dearer lord?—
Then, dreadful trumpet, sound the general doom!
For who is living, if those two are gone?
   Nurse.   Tybalt is gone, and Romeo banishéd;
Romeo, that killed him, he is banishéd.

Jul.   O God!—did Romeo's hand shed Tybalt's blood?
Nurse.   It did, it did: alas the day, it did!
Jul.   O serpent heart, hid with a flowering face!
Did ever dragon keep so fair a cave?
Beautiful tyrant! fiend angelical!
Dove-feathered raven! wolvish-ravening lamb!
Despiséd substance of divinest show.
Just opposite to what thou justly seem'st;
A damnéd saint, an honourable villain!—
O nature, what hadst thou to do in hell,
When thou didst bower the spirit of a fiend
In mortal paradise of such sweet flesh?
Was ever book containing such vile matter
So fairly bound?   O, that deceit should dwell
In such a gorgeous palace!
Nurse.   There's no trust,
No faith, no honesty in men: all perjured,
All forsworn, all naught, all dissemblers.—
Ah! where's my man? give me some *aqua vitæ:*
These griefs, these woes, these sorrows make me old.
Shame come to Romeo!
Jul.   Blistered be thy tongue
For such a wish! he was not born to shame:
Upon his brow Shame is ashamed to sit;
For 't is a throne where Honour may be crowned
Sole monarch of the universal earth.
O, what a beast was I to chide at him!
Nurse.   Will you speak well of him that killed your
            cousin?
Jul.   Shall I speak ill of him that is my husband?
Ah, poor my lord, what tongue shall smooth thy name,
When I, thy three-hours' wife, have mangled it?
But wherefore, villain, didst thou kill my cousin?
That villain cousin would have killed my husband:
Back, foolish tears, back to your native spring;
Your tributary drops belong to woe,
Which you mistaking offer up to joy.
My husband lives, that Tybalt would have slain;
And Tybalt's dead, that would have slain my husband.
All this is comfort; wherefore weep I then?
Some word there was, worser than Tybalt's death,
That murdered me.   I would forget it fain;
But, O, it presses to my memory
Like damnéd guilty deeds to sinners' minds.
'Tybalt is dead, and Romeo banishéd!'
That 'banishéd,' that one word 'banishéd,'
Hath slain ten thousand Tybalts.   Tybalt's death
Was woe enough, if it had ended there:
Or, if sour woe delights in fellowship,

And needly will be ranked with other griefs,
Why followed not, when she said 'Tybalt's dead,'
Thy father, or thy mother, nay, or both,
Which modern lamentation might have moved?
But, with a rearward following Tybalt's death,
'Romeo is banishéd!'—to speak that word,
Is father, mother, Tybalt, Romeo, Juliet,
All slain, all dead: 'Romeo is banishéd!'
There is no end, no limit, measure, bound,
In that word's death; no words can that woe sound.
Where is my father, and my mother, nurse?
   Nurse. Weeping and wailing over Tybalt's corse;
Will you go to them?   I will bring you thither.
   Jul. Wash they his wounds with tears: mine shall be
       spent,
When theirs are dry, for Romeo's banishment.
Take up those cords.   Poor ropes, you are beguiled,
Both you and I, for Romeo is exiled:
He made you for a highway to my bed,
But I, a maid, die maiden-widowéd.
Come, cords; come, nurse; I'll to my wedding bed;
And death, not Romeo, take my maidenhead!
   Nurse. Hie to your chamber; I'll find Romeo
To comfort you:—I wot well where he is.
Hark ye, your Romeo will be here at night:
I'll to him; he is hid at Laurence' cell.
   Jul. O, find him! give this ring to my true knight,
And bid him come to take his last farewell.

                                      [*Exeunt*

SCENE III.—FRIAR LAURENCE's Cell

Enter FRIAR LAURENCE *and* ROMEO

   Fri. Romeo, come forth; come forth, thou fearful man:
Affliction is enamoured of thy parts,
And thou art wedded to calamity.
   Rom. Father, what news? what is the prince's doom?
What sorrow craves acquaintance at my hand,
That I yet know not?
   Fri.   Too familiar
Is my dear son with such sour company:
I bring thee tidings of the prince's doom.
   Rom. What less than doomsday is the prince's doom?
   Fri. A gentler judgment vanished from his lips,
Not body's death, but body's banishment.
   Rom. Ha, banishment! be merciful, say 'death':
For exile hath more terror in his look,
Much more, than death; do not say 'banishment.'

Fri. Here from Verona art thou banishéd;
Be patient, for the world is broad and wide.
    Rom. There is no world without Verona walls
But purgatory, torture, hell itself.
Hence banishéd is banished from the world,
And world's exile is death;—then 'banishéd'
Is death mis-termed.   Calling death banishment,
Thou cutt'st my head off with a golden axe
And smil'st upon the stroke that murders me.
    Fri. O deadly sin! O rude unthankfulness!
Thy fault our law calls death; but the kind prince,
Taking thy part, hath rushed aside the law,
And turned that black word death to banishment;
This is dear mercy, and thou seest it not.
    Rom. 'T is torture, and not mercy: heaven is here,
Where Juliet lives; and every cat and dog
And little mouse, every unworthy thing,
Live here in heaven and may look on her,
But Romeo may not.—More validity,
More honourable state, more courtship lives
In carrion flies than Romeo: they may seize
On the white wonder of dear Juliet's hand,
And steal immortal blessing from her lips;
Who, even in pure and vestal modesty,
Still blush, as thinking their own kisses sin;
But Romeo may not; he is banishéd.
This may flies do, but I from this must fly:
They are free men, but I am banishéd.
And say'st thou yet, that exile is not death?
Hadst thou no poison mixed, no sharp-ground knife,
No sudden mean of death, though ne'er so mean,
But—'banishéd'—to kill me?   'Banishéd'?
O friar! the damnéd use that word in hell;
Howling attends it: how hast thou the heart,
Being a divine, a ghostly confessor,
A sin-absolver, and my friend professed,
To mangle me with that word 'banishéd'?
    Fri. Thou fond mad man, hear me a little speak.
    Rom. O, thou wilt speak again of banishment.
    Fri. I'll give thee armour to keep off that word;
Adversity's sweet milk, philosophy,
To comfort thee, though thou art banishéd.
    Rom. Yet 'banishéd'?—Hang up philosophy!
Unless philosophy can make a Juliet,
Displant a town, reverse a prince's doom,
It helps not, it prevails not: talk no more.
    Fri. O, then I see that madmen have no ears.
    Rom. How should they, when that wise men have no
        eyes?

Fri.   Let me dispute with thee of thy estate.
Rom.   Thou canst not speak of that thou dost not feel.
Wert thou as young as I, Juliet thy love,
An hour but married, Tybalt murderéd,
Doting like me, and like me banishéd,
Then might'st thou speak, then might'st thou tear thy hair,
And fall upon the ground, as I do now,
Taking the measure of an unmade grave.

                                           [*Knocking within*
Fri.   Arise; one knocks; good Romeo, hide thyself.
Rom.   Not I; unless the breath of heart-sick groans,
Mist-like, infold me from the search of eyes.

                                           [*Knocking*
Fri.   Hark, how they knock!—Who's there?—Romeo,
     arise;
Thou wilt be taken.—Stay awhile!—Stand up;

                                           [*Knocking*
Run to my study.—By-and-by.—God's will!
What simpleness is this!—I come, I come.

                                           [*Knocking*
Who knocks so hard? whence come you? what's your
     will?
Nurse.   [*Within*]   Let me come in, and you shall know
     my errand:
I come from Lady Juliet.
Fri.   Welcome then.

Enter NURSE

Nurse.   O holy friar, O, tell me, holy friar,
Where is my lady's lord? where's Romeo?
Fri.   There on the ground, with his own tears made
     drunk.
Nurse.   O! he is even in my mistress' case,
Just in her case!   O woful sympathy!
Piteous predicament!   Even so lies she,
Blubbering and weeping, weeping and blubbering.—
Stand up, stand up; stand, an you be a man:
For Juliet's sake, for her sake, rise and stand;
Why should you fall into so deep an O?
Rom.   Nurse!
Nurse.   Ah sir! ah sir!—Well, death's the end of all.
Rom.   Spak'st thou of Juliet? how is it with her?
Doth she not think me an old murderer,
Now I have stained the childhood of our joy
With blood removed but little from her own?
Where is she? and how doth she? and what says
My concealed lady to our cancelled love?
Nurse.   O, she says nothing, sir, but weeps and weeps;

And now falls on her bed; and then starts up,
And Tybalt calls; and then on Romeo cries,
And then down falls again.
    Rom.   As if that name,
Shot from the deadly level of a gun,
Did murder her; as that name's curséd hand
Murdered her kinsman.—O, tell me, friar, tell me,
In what vile part of this anatomy
Doth my name lodge? tell me, that I may sack
The hateful mansion.   [*Drawing his sword*
    Fri.   Hold thy desperate hand:
Art thou a man? thy form cries out thou art:
Thy tears are womanish; thy wild acts denote
The unreasonable fury of a beast:
Unseemly woman, in a seeming man;
And ill-beseeming beast, in seeming both!
Thou hast amazed me: by my holy order,
I thought thy disposition better tempered.
Hast thou slain Tybalt? wilt thou slay thyself?
And slay thy lady that in thy life lives,
By doing damnéd hate upon thyself?
Why rail'st thou on thy birth, the heaven and earth?
Since birth and heaven and earth, all three do meet
In thee at once, which thou at once wouldst lose.
Fie, fie! thou sham'st thy shape, thy love, thy wit;
Which, like a usurer, abound'st in all,
And usest none in that true use indeed
Which should bedeck thy shape, thy love, thy wit.
Thy noble shape is but a form of wax,
Digressing from the valour of a man;
Thy dear love sworn, but hollow perjury,
Killing that love which thou hast vowed to cherish;
Thy wit, that ornament to shape and love,
Misshapen in the conduct of them both,
Like powder in a skilless soldier's flask,
Is set a-fire by thine own ignorance,
And thou dismembered with thine own defence.
What, rouse thee, man! thy Juliet is alive,
For whose dear sake thou wast but lately dead;
There art thou happy: Tybalt would kill thee,
But thou slew'st Tybalt; there art thou happy too;
The law, that threatened death, becomes thy friend,
And turns it to exile; there art thou happy:
A pack of blessings light upon thy back;
Happiness courts thee in her best array;
But, like a misbehaved and sullen wench,
Thou pout'st upon thy fortune and thy love:
Take heed, take heed, for such die miserable.
Go, get thee to thy love, as was decreed,

Ascend her chamber, hence, and comfort her;
But, look, thou stay not till the watch be set,
For then thou canst not pass to Mantua;
Where thou shalt live till we can find a time
To blaze your marriage, reconcile your friends,
Beg pardon of the prince, and call thee back
With twenty thousand times more joy
Than thou went'st forth in lamentation.—
Go before, nurse: commend me to thy lady,
And bid her hasten all the house to bed,
Which heavy sorrow makes them apt unto:
Romeo is coming.
    Nurse. O Lord! I could have stayed here all the night
To hear good counsel: O, what learning is!—
My lord, I'll tell my lady you will come.
    Rom. Do so, and bid my sweet prepare to chide.
    Nurse. Here, sir, a ring she bid me give you, sir.
Hie you, make haste, for it grows very late.   [*Exit*
    Rom. How well my comfort is revived by this!
    Fri. Go hence; good-night; and here stands all your
        state:
Either be gone before the watch be set,
Or by the break of day, disguised from hence.
Sojourn in Mantua: I'll find out your man,
And he shall signify from time to time
Every good hap to you that chances here.
Give me thy hand; 't is late: farewell: good-night.
    Rom. But that a joy past joy calls out on me,
It were a grief, so brief to part with thee:
Farewell.

                             [*Exeunt*

SCENE IV.—A Room in CAPULET'S House

Enter CAPULET, LADY CAPULET, *and* PARIS

    Cap. Things have fallen out, sir, so unluckily
That we have had no time to move our daughter.
Look you, she loved her kinsman Tybalt dearly,
And so did I:—well, we were born to die.—
'T is very late; she'll not come down to-night:
I promise you, but for your company,
I would have been a-bed an hour ago.
    Par. These times of woe afford no time to woo.—
Madam, good-night: commend me to your daughter.
    La. Cap. I will, and know her mind early to-morrow;
To-night she's mewed up to her heaviness.
    Cap. Sir Paris, I will make a desperate tender

Of my child's love: I think, she will be ruled
In all respects by me; nay more, I doubt it not.
Wife, go you to her ere you go to bed;
Acquaint her here of my son Paris' love
And bid her, mark you me, on Wednesday next—
But, soft: what day is this?
    Par.   Monday, my lord.
    Cap.   Monday? ha! ha! Well, Wednesday is too soon;
O' Thursday let it be:—o' Thursday, tell her,
She shall be married to this noble earl.
Will you be ready? do you like this haste?
We'll keep no great ado:—a friend or two;—
For, hark you, Tybalt being slain so late,
It may be thought we held him carelessly,
Being our kinsman, if we revel much.
Therefore, we'll have some half a dozen friends,
And there an end.   But what say you to Thursday?
    Par.   My lord, I would that Thursday were to-morrow.
    Cap.   Well, get you gone:—o' Thursday be it then.—
Go to your Juliet ere you go to bed,
Prepare her, wife, against this wedding-day.—
Farewell, my lord.—Light to my chamber, ho!
Afore me! 't is so very late, that we
May call it early by-and-by.—Good-night.

                                    [*Exeunt*

Scene V.—Juliet's Chamber

Enter Romeo *and* Juliet

    Jul.   Wilt thou be gone? it is not yet near day:
It was the nightingale, and not the lark,
That pierced the fearful hollow of thine ear;
Nightly she sings on yon pomegranate-tree:
Believe me, love, it was the nightingale.
    Rom. It was the lark, the herald of the morn,
No nightingale: look, love, what envious streaks
Do lace the severing clouds in yonder east.
Night's candles are burnt out, and jocund day
Stands tiptoe on the misty mountain tops:
I must be gone and live, or stay and die.
    Jul.   Yon light is not daylight, I know it, I:
It is some meteor that the sun exhales,
To be to thee this night a torch-bearer,
And light thee on thy way to Mantua:
Therefore stay yet, thou need'st not to be gone.
    Rom. Let me be ta'en, let me be put to death;
I am content, so thou wilt have it so.

I'll say, yon grey is not the morning's eye,
'T is but the pale reflex of Cynthia's brow;
Nor that is not the lark, whose notes do beat
The vaulty heaven so high above our heads:
I have more care to stay than will to go:
Come, death, and welcome! Juliet wills it so.—
How is 't, my soul? let's talk, it is not day.
　　Jul. It is, it is; hie hence, be gone, away!
It is the lark that sings so out of tune,
Straining harsh discords and unpleasing sharps.
Some say, the lark makes sweet division;
This doth not so, for she divideth us:
Some say, the lark and loathéd toad change eyes;
O, now I would they had changed voices too,
Since arm from arm that voice doth us affray,
Hunting thee hence with hunts-up to the day.
O, now be gone: more light and light it grows.
　　Rom. More light and light: more dark and dark our
　　　woes!

Enter Nurse

　　Nurse. Madam!
　　Jul. Nurse?
　　Nurse. Your lady mother is coming to your chamber:
The day is broke; be wary, look about.　　　　[*Exit*
　　Jul. Then, window, let day in, and let life out.
　　Rom. Farewell, farewell! one kiss, and I'll descend.
　　　　　　　　　　　　　　　　　　　[*Descends*
　　Jul. Art thou gone so? love, lord, ay husband, friend!
I must hear from thee every day in the hour,
For in a minute there are many days:
O, by this count I shall be much in years,
Ere I again behold my Romeo.
　　Rom. Farewell! I will omit no opportunity
That may convey my greetings, love, to thee.
　　Jul. O, think'st thou, we shall ever meet again?
　　Rom. I doubt it not; and all these woes shall serve
For sweet discourses in our time to come.
　　Jul. O God! I have an ill-divining soul:
Methinks, I see thee, now thou art so low,
As one dead in the bottom of a tomb:
Either my eyesight fails, or thou look'st pale.
　　Rom. And trust me, love, in my eye so do you:
Dry sorrow drinks our blood. Adieu! adieu!
　　　　　　　　　　　　　　　　　　　　[*Exit*
　　Jul. O fortune, fortune! all men call thee fickle:
If thou art fickle, what dost thou with him
That is renowned for faith? Be fickle, fortune;

For then, I hope, thou will not keep him long,
But send him back.
   La. Cap. [*Within*] Ho, daughter, are you up?
   Jul. Who is 't that calls? is it my lady mother?
Is she not down so late, or up so early?
What unaccustomed cause procures her hither?

Enter LADY CAPULET

   La. Cap. Why, how now, Juliet?
   Jul.   Madam, I am not well.
   La. Cap. Evermore weeping for your cousin's death?
What, wilt thou wash him from his grave with tears?
And if thou couldst, thou couldst not make him live:
Therefore, have done. Some grief shows much of love;
But much of grief shows still some want of wit.
   Jul. Yet let me weep for such a feeling loss.
   La. Cap. So shall you feel the loss but not the friend
Which you so weep for.
   Jul.   Feeling so the loss,
I cannot choose but ever weep the friend.
   La. Cap. Well, girl, thou weep'st not so much for his
       death,
As that the villain lives which slaughtered him.
   Jul. What villain, madam?
   La. Cap.   That same villain, Romeo.
   Jul. Villain and he are many miles asunder.
God pardon him! I do, with all my heart;
And yet no man like he doth grieve my heart.
   La. Cap. This is because the traitor murderer lives.
   Jul. Ay, madam, from the reach of these my hands:
Would, none but I might venge my cousin's death!
   La. Cap. We will have vengeance for it, fear thou not:
Then weep no more. I'll send to one in Mantua,
Where that same banished runagate doth live,
Shall give him such an unaccustomed dram,
That he shall soon keep Tybalt company:
And then, I hope, thou wilt be satisfied.
   Jul. Indeed, I never shall be satisfied
With Romeo, till I behold him—dead—
Is my poor heart so for a kinsman vexed.—
Madam, if you could find out but a man
To bear a poison, I would temper it,
That Romeo should, upon receipt thereof,
Soon sleep in quiet.—O, how my heart abhors
To hear him named, and cannot come to him,
To wreak the love I bore my cousin Tybalt
Upon his body that hath slaughtered him!
   La. Cap. Find thou the means, and I'll find such a man.
60

But now I'll tell thee joyful tidings, girl.
Jul.   And joy comes well in such a needy time.
What are they, I beseech your ladyship?
La. Cap.   Well, well, thou hast a careful father, child;
One who, to put thee from thy heaviness,
Hath sorted out a sudden day of joy,
That thou expect'st not, nor I looked not for.
Jul.   Madam, in happy time, what day is that?
La. Cap.   Marry, my child, early next Thursday morn,
The gallant, young, and noble gentleman,
The County Paris, at Saint Peter's Church,
Shall happily make thee there a joyful bride.
Jul.   Now, by Saint Peter's Church, and Peter too,
He shall not make me there a joyful bride.
I wonder at this haste; that I must wed
Ere he that should be husband comes to woo.
I pray you, tell my lord and father, madam,
I will not marry yet; and, when I do, I swear,
It shall be Romeo, whom you know I hate,
Rather than Paris.   These are news indeed!
La. Cap.   Here comes your father; tell him so yourself,
And see how he will take it at your hands.

Enter CAPULET *and Nurse*

Cap.   When the sun sets, the earth doth drizzle dew;
But for the sunset of my brother's son,
It rains downright.—
How now? a conduit, girl? what, still in tears?
Evermore showering?   In one little body
Thou counterfeit'st a bark, a sea, a wind:
For still thy eyes, which I may call the sea,
Do ebb and flow with tears; the bark thy body is,
Sailing in this salt flood; the winds, thy sighs;
Who, raging with thy tears, and they with them,
Without a sudden calm, will overset
Thy tempest-tosséd body.—How now, wife?
Have you delivered to her our decree?
La. Cap.   Ay sir; but she will none, she gives you thanks.
I would the fool were married to her grave!
Cap.   Soft, take me with you, take me with you, wife.
How! will she none? doth she not give us thanks?
Is she not proud? doth she not count her blessed,
Unworthy as she is, that we have wrought
So worthy a gentleman to be her bridegroom?
Jul.   Not proud, you have, but thankful, that you have:
Proud can I never be of what I hate;
But thankful even for hate that is meant love.
Cap.   How now! how now, chop-logic!   What is this?

'Proud,'—and 'I thank you,'—and 'I thank you not';—
And yet 'not proud;'—mistress minion, you,
Thank me no thankings, nor proud me no prouds,
But fettle your fine joints 'gainst Thursday next,
To go with Paris to Saint Peter's Church,
Or I will drag thee on a hurdle thither.
Out, you green-sickness carrion! out, you baggage!
You tallow-face!
    La. Cap.   Fie, fie! what, are you mad?
    Jul.   Good father, I beseech you on my knees,
Hear me with patience but to speak a word.
    Cap.   Hang thee, young baggage! disobedient wretch
I tell thee what,—get thee to church o' Thursday,
Or never after look me in the face.
Speak not, reply not, do not answer me;
My fingers itch.—Wife, we scarce thought us blest,
That God had lent us but this only child,
But now I see this one is one too much
And that we have a curse in having her:
Out on her, hilding!
    Nurse.   God in heaven bless her!—
You are to blame, my lord, to rate her so.
    Cap.   And why, my lady wisdom? hold your tongue,
Good prudence; smatter with your gossips; go.
    Nurse.   I speak no treason.
    Cap.   O, God ye good den.
    Nurse.   May not one speak?
    Cap.   Peace, you mumbling fool!
Utter your gravity o'er a gossip's bowl,
For here we need it not.
    La. Cap.   You are too hot.
    Cap.   God's bread! it makes me mad:
Day, night, hour, tide, time, work, play,
Alone, in company, still my care hath been
To have her matched; and having now provided
A gentleman of noble parentage,
Of fair demesnes, youthful, and nobly trained,
Stuffed (as they say) with honourable parts,
Proportioned as one's thought would wish a man,—
And then to have a wretched puling fool,
A whining mammet, in her fortune's tender,
To answer—'I'll not wed,'—'I cannot love,'—
'I am too young,'—'I pray you, pardon me.'—
But, an you will not wed, I'll pardon you:
Graze where you will, you shall not house with me:
Look to 't, think on 't, I do not use to jest.
Thursday is near; lay hand on heart, advise.
An you be mine, I'll give you to my friend;
An you be not, hang, beg, starve, die i' the streets,

For, by my soul, I'll ne'er acknowledge thee,
Nor what is mine shall never do thee good.
Trust to 't, bethink you; I'll not be forsworn.   [*Exit*
    Jul.   Is there no pity sitting in the clouds
That sees into the bottom of my grief?—
O, sweet my mother, cast me not away!
Delay this marriage for a month, a week;
Or, if you do not, make the bridal bed
In that dim monument where Tybalt lies.
    La. Cap.   Talk not to me, for I'll not speak a word.
Do as thou wilt, for I have done with thee.   [*Exit*
    Jul.   O God!—O nurse, how shall this be prevented?
My husband is on earth, my faith in heaven:
How shall that faith return again to earth,
Unless that husband send it me from heaven
By leaving earth?—comfort me, counsel me.—
Alack, alack! that Heaven should practise stratagems
Upon so soft a subject as myself!—
What say'st thou? hast thou not a word of joy?
Some comfort, nurse.
    Nurse.   Faith, here 't is.   Romeo
Is banishéd, and all the world to nothing,
That he dares ne'er come back to challenge you;
Or, if he do, it needs must be by stealth.
Then, since the case so stand as now it doth,
I think it best you married with the county.
O, he's a lovely gentleman!
Romeo's a dishclout to him: an eagle, madam,
Hath not so green, so quick, so fair an eye,
As Paris hath.   Beshrew my very heart,
I think you are happy in this second match,
For it excels your first: or if it did not,
Your first is dead, or 't were as good h'e were
As living here and you no use of him.
    Jul.   Speakest thou from thy heart?
    Nurse.   And from my soul too; else beshrew them both.
    Jul.   Amen!
    Nurse.   What?
    Jul.   Well, thou hast comforted me marvellous much.
Go in, and tell my lady I am gone,
Having displeased my father, to Laurence' cell
To make confession and to be absolved.
    Nurse.   Marry, I will; and this is wisely done.

                                          [*Exit*

    Jul.   Ancient damnation!   O most wicked fiend!
Is it more sin to wish me thus forsworn,
Or to dispraise my lord with that same tongue
Which she hath praised him with above compare

So many thousand times?—Go, counsellor;
Thou and my bosom henceforth shall be twain—
I'll to the friar, to know his remedy:
If all else fail, myself have power to die.

[*Exit*

ACT FOUR

Scene I.—Friar Laurence's Cell

Enter Friar Laurence *and* Paris

Fri.   On Thursday, sir? the time is very short.
Par.   My father Capulet will have it so;
And I am nothing slow, to slack his haste.
Fri.   You say you do not know the lady's mind:
Uneven is the course; I like it not.
Par.   Immoderately she weeps for Tybalt's death,
And therefore have I little talked of love,
For Venus smiles not in a house of tears.
Now, sir, her father counts it dangerous
That she doth give her sorrow so much sway,
And in his wisdom hastes our marriage,
To stop the inundation of her tears,
Which, too much minded by herself alone,
May be put from her by society.
Now do you know the reason of this haste.
Fri. [*Aside*] I would I knew not why it should be
      slowed.
Look, sir, here comes the lady towards my cell.

Enter Juliet

Par.   Happily met, my lady, and my wife!
Jul.   That may be, sir, when I may be a wife.
Par.   That 'may be' must be, love, on Thursday next.
Jul.   What must be shall be.
Fri.   That's a certain text.
Par.   Come you to make confession to this father?
Jul.   To answer that, I should confess to you.
Par.   Do not deny to him that you love me.
Jul.   I will confess to you that I love him.
Par.   So will ye, I am sure, that you love me.
Jul.   If I do so, it will be of more price
Being spoken behind your back than to your face.
Par.   Poor soul, thy face is much abused with tears.

Jul. The tears have got small victory by that;
For it was bad enough before their spite.
    Par. Thou wrong'st it, more than tears, with that report.
    Jul. That is no slander, sir, which is a truth;
And what I spake, I spake it to my face.
    Par. Thy face is mine, and thou hast slandered it.
    Jul. It may be so, for it is not mine own.—
Are you at leisure, holy father, now,
Or shall I come to you at evening mass?
    Fri. My leisure serves me, pensive daughter, now.—
My lord, we must entreat the time alone.
    Par. God shield I should disturb devotion!—
Juliet, on Thursday early will I rouse you:
Till then, adieu, and keep this holy kiss.   *[Exit*
    Jul. O, shut the door; and when thou hast done so,
Come weep with me; past hope, past cure, past help.
    Fri. Ah, Juliet, I already know thy grief;
It strains me past the compass of my wits:
I hear thou must, and nothing may prorogue it,
On Thursday next be married to this county.
    Jul. Tell me not, friar, that thou hear'st of this,
Unless thou tell me how I may prevent it:
If in thy wisdom thou canst give no help,
Do thou but call my resolution wise,
And with this knife I'll help it presently.
God joined my heart, and Romeo's, thou our hands;
And ere this hand, by thee to Romeo sealed,
Shall be the label to another deed,
Or my true heart with treacherous revolt
Turn to another, this shall slay them both.
Therefore, out of thy long experienced time,
Give me some present counsel; or, behold,
'Twixt my extremes and me this bloody knife
Shall play the umpire, arbitrating that
Which the commission of thy years and art
Could to no issue of true honour bring.
Be not so long to speak, I long to die,
If what thou speak'st speak not of remedy.
    Fri. Hold, daughter: I do spy a kind of hope,
Which craves as desperate an execution
As that is desperate which we would prevent.
If, rather than to marry County Paris,
Thou hast the strength of will to slay thyself,
Then is it likely thou wilt undertake
A thing like death to chide away this shame,
That cop'st with death himself to 'scape from it;
And, if thou dar'st, I'll give thee remedy.
    Jul. O, bid me leap, rather than marry Paris,
From off the battlements of yonder tower;

Or walk in thievish way; or bid me lurk
Where serpents are; chain me with roaring bears:
Or shut me nightly in a charnel-house,
O'er-covered quite with dead men's rattling bones,
With reeky shanks and yellow chapless skulls:
Or bid me go into a new-made grave
And hide me with a dead man in his shroud;
Things that, to hear them told, have made me tremble;
And I will do it without fear or doubt,
To live an unstained wife to my sweet love.

  Fri. Hold, then: go home, be merry, give consent
To marry Paris. Wednesday is to-morrow;
To-morrow night look that thou lie alone,
Let not thy nurse lie with thee in thy chamber:
Take thou this vial, being then in bed,
And this distilléd liquor drink thou off;
When presently through all thy veins shall run
A cold and drowsy humour; for no pulse
Shall keep his native progress, but surcease:
No warmth, no breath, shall testify thou livest;
The roses in thy lips and cheeks shall fade
To paly ashes; thy eyes' windows fall,
Like death, when he shuts up the day of life;
Each part, deprived of supple government,
Shall, stiff and stark and cold, appear like death:
And in this borrowed likeness of shrunk death
Thou shalt continue two and forty hours,
And then awake as from a pleasant sleep.
Now, when the bridegroom in the morning comes
To rouse thee from thy bed, there art thou dead:
Then, as the manner of our country is,
In thy best robes uncovered on the bier,
Thou shalt be borne to that same ancient vault
Where all the kindred of the Capulets lie.
In the meantime, against thou shalt awake,
Shall Romeo by my letters know our drift;
And hither shall he come: and he and I
Will watch thy waking, and that very night
Shall Romeo bear thee hence to Mantua.
And this shall free thee from this present shame,
If no unconstant toy or womanish fear,
Abate thy valour in the acting it.

  Jul. Give me, give me! O, tell not me of fear!

  Fri. Hold; get you gone: be strong and prosperous
In this resolve. I'll send a friar with speed
To Mantua with my letters to thy lord.

  Jul. Love, give me strength! and strength shall help
   afford.
Farewell, dear father.   *[Exeunt*

Scene II.—A Room in Capulet's House

Enter Capulet, Lady Capulet, *Nurse, and two Servants*

　Cap.　So many guests invite as here are writ.—
　　　　　　　　　　　　　　　　[*Exit First Servant*
Sirrah, go hire me twenty cunning cooks.
　Sec. Serv.　You shall have none ill, sir; for I'll try if
they can lick their fingers.
　Cap.　How canst thou try them so?
　Sec. Serv.　Marry, sir, 't is an ill cook that cannot lick
his own fingers: therefore, he that cannot lick his fingers
goes not with me.
　Cap.　Go, be gone.—　　　　　　[*Exit Sec. Servant*
We shall be much unfurnished for this time.
What, is my daughter gone to Friar Laurence?
　Nurse.　Ay, forsooth.
　Cap.　Well, he may chance to do some good on her:
A peevish self-willed harlotry it is.

Enter Juliet

　Nurse.　See where she comes from shrift with merry look.
　Cap.　How now, my headstrong? where have you been
　　　　　gadding?
　Jul.　Where I have learned me to repent the sin
Of disobedient opposition
To you and your behests; and am enjoined
By holy Laurence to fall prostrate here,
To beg your pardon.—Pardon, I beseech you!
Henceforward I am ever ruled by you.
　Cap.　Send for the county: go tell him of this;
I'll have this knot knit up to-morrow morning.
　Jul.　I met the youthful lord at Laurence' cell;
And gave him what becoméd love I might,
Not stepping o'er the bounds of modesty.
　Cap.　Why, I am glad on 't; this is well: stand up:
This is as 't should be.—Let me see the county;
Ay, marry, go, I say, and fetch him hither.—
Now, afore God, this reverend holy friar,
All our whole city is much bound to him.
　Jul.　Nurse, will you go with me into my closet,
To help me sort such needful ornaments
As you think fit to furnish me to-morrow?
　La. Cap.　No, not till Thursday; there is time enough.
　Cap.　Go, nurse, go with her:—we'll to church to-
　　　　　morrow.
　　　　　　　　　　　　　　　[*Exeunt Juliet and Nurse*

La. Cap. We shall be short in our provision:
'T is now near night.
 Cap.   Tush, I will stir about,
And all things shall be well, I warrant thee, wife.
Go thou to Juliet, help to deck up her:
I'll not to bed to-night;—let me alone;
I'll play the housewife for this once.—What, ho!—
They are all forth: well, I will walk myself
To County Paris, to prepare him up
Against to-morrow. My heart is wondrous light,
Since this same wayward girl is so reclaimed. *[Exeunt*

SCENE III.—JULIET'S Chamber

Enter JULIET *and Nurse*

Jul. Ay, those attires are best: but, gentle nurse,
I pray thee, leave me to myself to-night;
For I have need of many orisons
To move the heaves to smile upon my state,
Which, well thou knowest, is cross and full of sin.

Enter LADY CAPULET.

La. Cap. What, are you busy, ho? need you my help?
Jul. No, madam; we have culled such necessaries
As are behoveful for our state to-morrow:
So please you, let me now be left alone,
And let the nurse this night sit up with you,
For, I am sure, you have your hands full all
In this so sudden business.
 La. Cap.   Good-night:
Get thee to bed, and rest; for thou hast need.
     [Exeunt Lady Capulet and Nurse
 Jul. Farewell!—God knows when we shall meet again.
I have a faint cold fear thrills through my veins,
That almost freezes up the heat of life:
I'll call them back again to comfort me.
Nurse!—What should she do here?
My dismal scene I needs must act alone.—
Come, vial.—
What if this mixture do not work at all?
Shall I be married then to-morrow morning?
No, no;—this shall forbid it:—lie thou there.
      [Laying down a dagger
What if it be a poison, which the friar
Subtly hath ministered to have me dead,

Lest in this marriage he should be dishonoured,
Because he married me before to Romeo?
I fear, it is; and yet, methinks, it should not,
For he hath still been tried a holy man.
How if, when I am laid into the tomb,
I wake before the time that Romeo
Come to redeem me? there's a fearful point!
Shall I not then be stifled in the vault,
To whose foul mouth no healthsome air breathes in,
And there die strangled ere my Romeo comes?
Or, if I live, is it not very like,
The horrible conceit of death and night,
Together with the terror of the place,—
As in a vault, an ancient réceptacle,
Where, for this many hundred years, the bones
Of all my buried ancestors are packed;
Where bloody Tybalt, yet but green in earth,
Lies festering in his shroud; where, as they say,
At some hours in the night spirits resort;—
Alack, alack! is it not like, that I,
So early waking,—what with loathsome smells,
And shrieks like mandrakes' torn out of the earth,
That living mortals hearing them run mad;—
O, if I wake, shall I not be distraught,
Environéd with all these hideous fears,
And madly play with my forefathers' joints,
And pluck the mangled Tybalt from his shroud?
And, in this rage, with some great kinsman's bone,
As with a club, dash out my desperate brains?
O, look! methinks, I see my cousin's ghost
Seeking out Romeo, that did spit his body
Upon a rapier's point:—stay, Tybalt, stay!—
Romeo, I come! this do I drink to thee.

> [*She throws herself on the bed*

Scene IV.—Capulet's Hall

Enter Lady Capulet *and* Nurse

La. Cap.   Hold, take these keys, and fetch more spices,
       nurse.
Nurse.   They call for dates and quinces in the pastry.

Enter Capulet

Cap.   Come, stir, stir, stir! the second cock hath crowed,
The curfew bell hath rung, 't is three o'clock:—
Look to the baked meats, good Angelica:
Spare not for cost.

Nurse.   Go, go, you cot-quean, go;
Get you to bed; 'faith, you'll be sick to-morrow
For this night's watching.
    Cap. No, not a whit. What! I have watched ere now
All night for lesser cause, and ne'er been sick.
    La. Cap. Ay, you have been a mouse-hunt in your time;
But I will watch you from such watching now.
                [Exeunt Lady Capulet and Nurse
    Cap. A jealous-hood, a jealous-hood!—

Enter Servants, with spits, logs, and baskets

                          Now, fellow,
What's there?
    First Serv. Things for the cook, sir; but I know not
        what.
    Cap. Make haste, make haste.   *[Exit First Serv.*
Sirrah, fetch drier logs:
Call Peter, he will show thee where they are.
    Sec. Serv. I have a head, sir, that will find out logs,
And never trouble Peter for the matter.   *[Exit*
    Cap. 'Mass, and well said; a merry whoreson, ha!
Thou shalt be logger-head.—Good faith, 't is day:
The county will be here with music straight,
For so he said he would.—*[Music within]* I hear him
    near.—
Nurse!—Wife!—What, ho!—What, nurse, I say!

Enter Nurse

Go, waken Juliet; go, and trim her up;
I'll go and chat with Paris.—Hie, make haste,
Make haste; the bridegroom he is come already:
Make haste, I say.   *[Exeunt*

SCENE V.—JULIET's Chamber; JULIET on the bed.

Enter Nurse

    Nurse. Mistress!—what, mistress!—Juliet!—fast, I
        warrant her, she:—
Why, lamb!—why, lady!—fie, you slug-a-bed!—
Why, love, I say!—madam! sweet-heart!—why bride!
What, not a word?—you take your pennyworths now;
Sleep for a week; for the next night, I warrant,
The County Paris hath set up his rest
That you shall rest but little.—God forgive me,
Marry, and amen, how sound is she asleep!

I needs must wake her.—Madam, madam, madam!
Ay, let the county take you in your bed;
He'll fright you up, i' faith.   Will it not be?
What, dressed! and in your clothes! and down again!
I must needs wake you.   Lady! lady! lady!
Alas! alas!   Help! help! my lady's dead!
O, well-a-day, that ever I was born!
Some aqua vitæ, ho!   My lord! my lady!

Enter LADY CAPULET

La. Cap.   What noise is here?
Nurse.   O lamentable day!
La Cap.   What is the matter?
Nurse.   Look, look! O heavy day!
La. Cap.   O me!   O me!—my child, my only life,
Revive, look up, or I will die with thee!—
Help, help!—Call help.

Enter CAPULET

Cap.   For shame! bring Juliet forth; her lord is come.
Nurse.   She's dead, deceased, she's dead; alack the day!
La. Cap.   Alack the day, she's dead, she's dead, she's
dead!
Cap.   Ha! let me see her.—Out, alas! she's cold;
Her blood is settled, and her joints are stiff;
Life and these lips have long been separated.
Death lies on her, like an untimely frost
Upon the sweetest flower of all the field.
Nurse.   O lamentable day!
La. Cap.   O woful time!
Cap.   Death, that hath ta'en her hence to make me wail,
Ties up my tongue and will not let me speak.

Enter FRIAR LAURENCE and PARIS, with Musicians

Fri.   Come, is the bride ready to go to church?
Cap.   Ready to go, but never to return.—
O son, the night before thy wedding-day
Hath Death lain with thy wife.   There she lies,
Flower as she was, defloweréd by him.
Death is my son-in-law, Death is my heir;
My daughter he hath wedded.   I will die,
And leave him all; life, living, all is Death's.
Par.   Have I thought long to see this morning's face,
And doth it give me such a sight as this?
La. Cap.   Accursed, unhappy, wretched, hateful day!
Most miserable hour that e'er time saw
In lasting labour of his pilgrimage!

But one, poor one, one poor and loving child,
But one thing to rejoice and solace in,
And cruel death hath catched it from my sight!
   Nurse. O woe! O woful, woful, woful day!
Most lamentable day, most woful day,
That ever, ever, I did yet behold!
O day! O day! O day! O hateful day!
Never was seen so black a day as this:
O woful day, O woful day!
   Par. Beguiled, divorcéd, wrongéd, spited, slain!
Most détestable death, by thee beguiled
By cruel cruel thee quite overthrown!—
O love! O life!—not life, but love in death!
   Cap. Despised, distresséd, hatred, martyred, killed!
Uncomfortable time, why cam'st thou now
To murder, murder our solemnity?—
O child! O child!—my soul, and not my child!
Dead art thou!—Alack, my child is dead!
And with my child my joys are buried.
   Fri. Peace, ho, for shame! confusion's cure lives not
In these confusions. Heaven and yourself
Had part in this fair maid; now Heaven hath all,
And all the better is it for the maid:
Your part in her you could not keep from death,
But Heaven keeps his part in eternal life.
The most you sought was her promotion,
For 't was your heaven she should be advanced:
And weep ye now, seeing she is advanced
Above the clouds, as high as heaven itself?
O, in this love, you love your child so ill,
That you run mad, seeing that she is well:
She's not well married that lives married long,
But she's best married that dies married young.
Dry up your tears, and stick your rosemary
On this fair corse, and, as the custom is,
In all her best array bear her to church;
For though fond nature bids us all lament,
Yet nature's tears are reason's merriment.
   Cap. All things that we ordainéd festival
Turn from their office to black funeral:
Our instruments to melancholy bells;
Our wedding cheer to a sad burial feast;
Our solemn hymns to sullen dirges change;
Our bridal flowers serve for a buried corse,
And all things change them to the contrary.
   Fri. Sir, go you in;—and, madam, go with him;—
And go, Sir Paris:—every one prepare
To follow this fair corse unto her grave.
The heavens do lour upon you for some ill;

Move them no more by crossing their high will.
　　　　[*Exeunt Capulet, Lady Capulet, Paris and Friar*
First Mus.　Faith, we may put up our pipes, and be gone.
Nurse.　Honest good fellows, ah, put up, put up;
For well you know, this is a pitiful case.
First Mus.　Ay, by my troth, the case may be amended.

Enter PETER

Peter.　Musicians, O, musicians! 'Heart's ease,'
'Heart's ease:' O! an you will have me live, play 'Heart's ease.'
First Mus.　Why 'Heart's ease'?
Peter.　O, musicians, because my heart itself plays 'My heart is full of woe.'　O, play me some merry dump, to comfort me.
Sec. Mus.　Not a dump we; 't is no time to play now.
Peter.　You will not then?
Mus.　No.
Peter.　I will then give it you soundly.
First Mus.　What will you give us?
Peter.　No money, on my faith, but the gleek: I will give you the mistrel.
First Mus.　Then will I give you the serving-creature.
Peter.　Then will I lay the serving-creature's dagger on your pate.　I will carry no crotchets: I'll *re* you, I'll *fa* you!　Do you note me?
First Mus.　An you *re* us, and *fa* us, you note us.
Sec. Mus.　Pray you, put up your dagger, and put out your wit.
Peter.　Then have at you with my wit.　I will dry-beat you with an iron wit, and put up my iron dagger.——Answer me like men:

> *When griping grief the heart doth wound,*
> *And doleful dumps the mind oppress,*
> *Then music with her silver sound—*

Why 'silver sound'? why 'music with her silver sound'? What say you, Simon Catling?
First Mus.　Marry, sir, because silver hath a sweet sound.
Peter.　Pretty!—What say you, Hugh Rebeck?
Sec. Mus.　I say—'silver sound,' because musicians sound for silver.
Peter.　Pretty too!—what say you, James Soundpost?
Third Mus.　'Faith, I know not what to say.
Peter.　O, I cry you mercy; you are the singer: I will say for you.　It is 'music with her silver sound,' because musicians have no gold for sounding:—

> *Then music with her silver sound*
> *With speedy help doth lend redress.*

[*Exit*

First Mus. What a pestilent knave is this same!
Sec. Mus. Hang him, Jack! Come, we'll in here;
tarry for the mourners, and stay dinner.   [*Exeunt*

ACT FIVE

SCENE I.—Mantua. A Street

Enter ROMEO

Rom. If I may trust the flattering truth of sleep,
My dreams presage some joyful news at hand:
My bosom's lord sits lightly in his throne;
And all this day an unaccustomed spirit
Lifts me above the ground with cheerful thoughts.
I dreamt, my lady came and found me dead—
Strange dream, that gives a dead man leave to think!—
And breathed such life with kisses in my lips,
That I revived, and was an emperor.
Ah me! how sweet is love itself possessed,
When but love's shadows are so rich in joy!

Enter BALTHASAR

News from Verona!—How now, Balthasar?
Dost thou not bring me letters from the friar?
How doth my lady? Is my father well?
How fares my Juliet? that I ask again;
For nothing can be ill if she be well.
Bal. Then she is well, and nothing can be ill.
Her body sleeps in Capels' monument,
And her immortal part with angels lives.
I saw her laid low in her kindred's vault,
And presently took post to tell it you.
O, pardon me for bringing those ill news,
Since you did leave it for my office, sir.
Rom. Is it e'en so? then, I defy you, stars!
Thou know'st my lodging: get me ink and paper,
And hire post-horses; I will hence to-night.
Bal. I do beseech you, sir, have patience:
Your looks are pale and wild and do import
Some misadventure.
Rom.   Tush, thou art deceived:
Leave me, and do the thing I bid thee do.
Hast thou no letters to me from the friar?

Bal.   No, my good lord.
Rom.   No matter: get thee gone,
And hire those horses; I'll be with thee straight.—
                                            [*Exit Balthasar*
Well, Juliet, I will lie with thee to-night.
Let's see for means:—O mischief, thou art swift
To enter in the thoughts of desperate men!
I do remember an apothecary
And hereabouts 'a dwells, which late I noted
In tattered weeds, with overwhelming brows,
Culling of simples; meagre were his looks,
Sharp misery had worn him to the bones:
And in his needy shop a tortoise hung,
An alligator stuffed, and other skins
Of ill-shaped fishes; and about his shelves
A beggarly account of empty boxes,
Green earthen pots, bladders and musty seeds,
Remnants of packthread and old cakes of roses,
Were thinly scattered to make up a show.
Noting this penury, to myself I said—
And if a man did need a poison now,
Whose sale is present death in Mantua,
Here lives a caitiff wretch would sell it him.
O, this same thought did but forerun my need,
And this same needy man must sell it me.
As I remember, this should be the house:
Being holiday, the beggar's shop is shut.—
What ho! apothecary!

Enter Apothecary

Ap.   Who calls so loud?
Rom.   Come hither, man.—I see, that thou art poor;
Hold, there is forty ducats: let me have
A dram of poison; such soon-speeding gear
As will disperse itself through all the veins,
That the life-weary taker may fall dead,
And that the trunk may be discharged of breath
As violently as hasty powder fired
Doth hurry from the fatal cannon's womb.
Ap.   Such mortal drugs I have; but Mantua's law
Is death to any he that utters them.
Rom.   Art thou so bare and full of wretchedness,
And fear'st to die? famine is in thy cheeks,
Need and oppression starveth in thy eyes,
Contempt and beggary hang upon thy back;
The world is not thy friend, nor the world's law:
The world affords no law to make thee rich:
Then be not poor, but break it, and take this.

Ap.   My poverty, but not my will, consents.
Rom.   I pay thy poverty, and not thy will.
Ap.   Put this in any liquid thing you will,
And drink it off; and, if you had the strength
Of twenty men, it would despatch you straight.
Rom.   There is thy gold, worse poison to men's souls,
Doing more murder in this loathsome world,
Than these poor compounds that thou may'st not sell:
I sell thee poison, thou has sold me none.
Farewell; buy food, and get thyself in flesh.—
Come, cordial and not poison, go with me
To Juliet's grave; for there must I use thee.

                                          [*Exeunt*

SCENE II.—FRIAR LAURENCE'S Cell

Enter FRIAR JOHN

John.   Holy Franciscan friar! brother, ho!

Enter FRIAR LAURENCE

Lau.   This same should be the voice of Friar John.—
Welcome from Mantua: what says Romeo?
Or, if his mind be writ, give me his letter.
John.   Going to find a barefoot brother out,
One of our order, to associate me,
Here in this city visiting the sick,
And finding him, the searchers of the town,
Suspecting that we both were in a house
Where the infectious pestilence did reign,
Sealed up the doors and would not let us forth;
So that my speed to Mantua there was stayed.
Lau.   Who bare my letter then to Romeo?
John.   I could not send it,—here it is again,—
Nor get a messenger to bring it thee,
So fearful were they of infection.
Lau.   Unhappy fortune! by my brotherhood,
The letter was not nice, but full of charge,
Of dear import, and the neglecting it
May do much danger.   Friar John, go hence;
Get me an iron crow, and bring it straight
Unto my cell.
John.   Brother, I'll go and bring it thee.   [*Exit*
Lau.   Now must I to the monument alone;
Within this three hours will fair Juliet wake:
She will beshrew me much, that Romeo
Hath had no notice of these accidents:

But I will write again to Mantua,
And keep her at my cell till Romeo come:
Poor living corse, closed in a dead man's tomb!

[Exit

SCENE III.—A Churchyard; in it a tomb belonging to
the CAPULETS

Enter PARIS, *and his* Page, *bearing flowers and a torch*

    Par.   Give me thy torch, boy: hence, and stand aloof;—
Yet put it out, for I would not be seen.
Under yond yew-trees lay thee all along,
Holding thine ear close to the hollow ground;
So shall no foot upon the churchyard tread,
Being loose, unfirm with digging up of graves,
But thou shalt hear it: whistle then to me,
As signal that thou hear'st something approach.
Give me those flowers.   Do as I bid thee; go.
    Page.   I am almost afraid to stand alone
Here in the churchyard; yet I will adventure.

[Retires

    Par.   Sweet flower, with flowers thy bridal bed I strew.
O woe! thy canopy is dust and stones,
Which with sweet water nightly I will dew,
Or, wanting that, with tears distilled by moans:
The obsequies that I for thee will keep
Nightly shall be to strew thy grave and weep!—

[The Page whistles

The boy gives warning something doth approach.
What cursèd foot wanders this way to-night,
To cross my obsequies and true love's rite?
What, with a torch?—muffle me, night, awhile.   *[Retires*

Enter ROMEO *and* BALTHASAR, *with a torch,
mattock, &c.*

    Rom.   Give me that mattock, and the wrenching iron.
Hold, take this letter: early in the morning
See thou deliver it to my lord and father.
Give me the light.   Upon thy life I charge thee,
Whate'er thou hear'st or seest, stand all aloof
And do not interrupt me in my course.
Why I descend into this bed of death
Is, partly, to behold my lady's face;
But, chiefly, to take thence from her dead finger
A precious ring, a ring that I must use
In dear employment: therefore hence, be gone:

But if thou, jealous, dost return to pry
In what I further shall intend to do,
By Heaven, I will tear thee joint by joint
And strew this hungry churchyard with thy limbs.
The time and my intents are savage-wild,
More fierce and more inexorable far
Than empty tigers, or the roaring sea.
   Bal. I will be gone, sir, and not trouble you.
   Rom. So shalt thou show me friendship. Take thou
      that:
Live, and be prosperous: and farewell, good fellow.
   Bal. For all this same, I'll hide me hereabout:
His looks I fear, and his intents I doubt.

                    [Retires

   Rom. Thou détestable maw, thou womb of death,
Gorged with the dearest morsel of the earth,
Thus I enforce thy rotten jaws to open,
And, in despite, I'll cram thee with more food.
     [Breaking open the door of the tomb

   Par. This is that banished haughty Montague,
That murdered my love's cousin,—with which grief,
It is supposéd, the fair creature died,—
And here is come to do some villainous shame
To the dead bodies: I will apprehend him.

                [Advancing

Stop thy unhallowed toil, vile Montague.
Can vengeance be pursued further than death?
Condemnéd villain, I do apprehend thee:
Obey, and go with me; for thou must die.
   Rom. I must, indeed; and therefore came I hither.
Good gentle youth, tempt not a desperate man;
Fly hence, and leave me: think upon these gone;
Let them affright thee. I beseech thee, youth,
Put not another sin upon my head
By urging me to fury: O, be gone!
By Heaven, I love thee better than myself,
For I come hither armed against myself:
Stay not, be gone; live, and hereafter say,
A madman's mercy bade thee run away.
   Par. I do defy thy conjurations,
And apprehend thee for a felon here.
   Rom. Wilt thou provoke me? then, have at thee,
boy.

                [They fight
   Page. O, Lord, they fight: I will go call the watch.
                [Exit
   Par. O, I am slain. *[Falls]* If thou be merciful,
Open the tomb, lay me with Juliet.   *[Dies*

Rom.   In faith, I will.—Let me peruse this face:
Mercutio's kinsman, noble County Paris!
What said my man, when my betosséd soul
Did not attend him as we rode?   I think
He told me Paris should have married Juliet:
Said he not so? or did I dream it so?
Or am I mad, hearing him talk of Juliet,
To think it was so?—O, give me thy hand,
One writ with me in sour misfortune's book!
I'll bury thee in a triumphant grave.
A grave?   O, no, a lantern, slaughtered youth,
For here lies Juliet, and her beauty makes
This vault a feasting presence full of light.
Death, lie thou there, by a dead man interred.
                     [*Laying Paris in the monument*
How oft, when men are at the point of death,
Have they been merry! which their keepers call
A lightening before death: O, how may I
Call this a lightening?   O my love! my wife!
Death, that hath sucked the honey of thy breath,
Hath had no power yet upon thy beauty:
Thou art not conquered; beauty's ensign yet
Is crimson in thy lips and in thy cheeks,
And death's pale flag is not advancéd there.—
Tybalt, liest thou there in thy bloody sheet?
O, what more favour can I do to thee,
Than with that hand that cut thy youth in twain
To sunder his that was thine enemy?
Forgive me, cousin!—Ah, dear Juliet,
Why art thou yet so fair?   Shall I believe
That unsubstantial death is amourous;
And that the lean abhorréd monster keeps
Thee here in dark to be his paramour?
For fear of that I still will stay with thee,
And never from this palace of dim night
Depart again: here, here will I remain
With worms that are thy chambermaids; O, here
Will I set up my everlasting rest,
And shake the yoke of inauspicious stars
From this world-wearied flesh.—Eyes, look your last!
Arms, take your last embrace! and, lips, O you,
The doors of breath, seal with a righteous kiss
A dateless bargain to engrossing death!
Come, bitter conduct, come, unsavoury guide!
Thou desperate pilot, now at once run on
The dashing rocks thy sea-sick weary bark!
Here's to my love! [*Drinks*]—O true apothecary,
Thy drugs are quick!—Thus with a kiss I die.
                                       [*Dies*

Enter, at the other end of the Churchyard, FRIAR LAURENCE,
with a lantern, crow, and spade

   Fri.   Saint Francis be my speed! how oft to-night
Have my old feet stumbled at graves!—-Who's there?
   Bal.   Here's one, a friend, and one that knows you well.
   Fri.   Bliss be upon you!   Tell me, my good friend,
What torch is yond, that vainly lends his light
To grubs and eyeless skulls? as I discern,
It burneth in the Capels' monument.
   Bal.   It doth so, holy sir; and there's my master,
One that you love.
   Fri.   Who is it?
   Bal.   Romeo.
   Fri.   How long hath he been there?
   Bal.   Full half an hour.
   Fri.   Go with me to the vault.
   Bal.   I dare not, sir.
My master knows not but I am gone hence:
And fearfully did menace me with death,
If I did stay to look on his intents.
   Fri.   Stay then, I'll go alone.—Fear comes upon me;
O, much I fear some ill unlucky thing.
   Bal.   As I did sleep under this yew-tree here,
I dreamt my master and another fought,
And that my master slew him.
   Fri.   Romeo!—
                                [Advances
Alack, alack, what blood is this which stains
The stony embrace of this sepulchre?—
What mean these masterless and gory swords
To lie discoloured by this place of peace?
                          [Enters the tomb
Romeo! O, pale!—Who else? what, Paris too?
And steeped in blood?—Ah! what an unkind hour
Is guilty of this lamentable chance!—
The lady stirs.   *[Juliet wakes*
   Jul.   O comfortable friar! where is my lord?
I do remember well where I should be,
And there I am.—Where is my Romeo?   *[Noise within*
   Fri.   I hear some noise.—Lady, come from that nest
Of death, contagion, and unnatural sleep:
A greater power than we can contradict
Hath thwarted our intents: come, come away.
Thy husband in thy bosom there lies dead;
And Paris too: come, I'll dispose of thee
Among a sisterhood of holy nuns:
Stay not to question, for the watch is coming;

Come, go, good Juliet.—[*Noise again*] I dare no longer
    stay.
  Jul. Go, get thee hence, for I will not away.—
                              [*Exit Friar Laurence*
What's here? a cup closed in my true love's hand?
Poison, I see, hath been his timeless end.
O churl! drunk all, and left no friendly drop,
To help me after?—I will kiss thy lips;
Haply, some poison yet doth hang on them,
To make me die with a restorative.   [*Kisses him*
Thy lips are warm.
  First Watch. [*Within*] Lead, boy:—which way?
  Jul. Yea, noise?—then I'll be brief.—O happy dagger!
                          [*Snatching Romeo's dagger*
This is thy sheath; [*stabs herself*] there rust and let me die.
                  [*Falls on Romeo's body, and dies*

Enter Watch, with Page of PARIS

  Page. This is the place; there, where the torch doth
    burn.
  First Watch. The ground is bloody: search about the
    churchyard.
Go, some of you, whoe'er you find, attach.
                            [*Exeunt some*
Pitiful sight! here lies the county slain;
And Juliet bleeding, warm, and newly dead.
Who here hath lain this two days buriéd.—
Go, tell the prince,—run to the Capulets,—
Raise up the Montagues,—some others search:—
                     [*Exeunt other Watchmen*
We see the ground whereon these woes do lie;
But the true ground of all these piteous woes
We cannot without circumstance descry.

Enter some of the Watch, with BALTHASAR

  Sec. Watch. Here's Romeo's man; we found him in
    the churchyard.
  First Watch. Hold him in safety till the prince come
    hither.

Enter another Watchman, with FRIAR LAURENCE

  Third Watch. Here is a friar, that trembles, sighs, and
    weeps:
We took this mattock and this spade from him,
As he was coming from this churchyard side.
  First Watch. A great suspicion: stay the friar too.

Enter the PRINCE *and Attendants*

Prince.   What misadventure is so early up,
That calls our person from our morning's rest?

Enter CAPULET, LADY CAPULET, *and others*

Cap.   What should it be, that they so shriek abroad?
La. Cap.   The people in the street cry, 'Romeo,'
Some 'Juliet,' and some 'Paris,' and all run
With open outcry toward our monument.
Prince.   What fear is this, which startles in our ears?
First Watch.   Sovereign, here lies the County Paris slain;
And Romeo dead; and Juliet, dead before,
Warm and new killed.
Prince.   Search, seek, and know how this foul murder
      comes.
First Watch.   Here is a friar, and slaughtered Romeo's
      man,
With instruments upon them, fit to open
These dead men's tombs.
Cap.   O Heaven!—O wife, look how our daughter bleeds!
This dagger hath mista'en,—for, lo, his house
Is empty on the back of Montague,
And is mis-sheathéd in my daughter's bosom.
La. Cap.   O, me! this sight of death is as a bell
That warns my old age to a sepulchre.

Enter MONTAGUE *and others*

Prince.   Come, Montague; for thou art early up,
To see thy son and heir more early down.
Mon.   Alas, my liege, my wife is dead to-night,
Grief of my son's exile hath stopped her breath.
What further woe conspires against mine age?
Prince.   Look, and thou shalt see.
Mon.   O thou untaught! what manners is in this,
To press before thy father to a grave?
Prince.   Seal up the mouth of outrage for a while,
Till we can clear these ambiguities,
And know their spring, their head, their true descent
And then will I be general of your woes
And lead you even to death: meantime forbear
And let mischance be slave to patience.—
Bring forth the parties of suspicion.
Fri.   I am the greatest, able to do least,
Yet most suspected, as the time and place
Doth make against me, of this direful murder
And here I stand, both to impeach and purge
Myself condemnéd, and myself excused.

Prince. Then say at once what thou dost know in this.
Fri. I will be brief, for my short date of breath
Is not so long as is a tedious tale.
Romeo, there dead, was husband to that Juliet;
And she, there dead, that Romeo's faithful wife;
I married them; and their stolen marriage day
Was Tybalt's doomsday, whose untimely death
Banished the new made bridegroom from this city;
For whom, and not for Tybalt, Juliet pined.
You, to remove that siege of grief from her,
Betrothed and would have married her perforce,
To County Paris:—then comes she to me,
And, with wild looks, bid me devise some means
To rid her from this second marriage,
Or in my cell there would she kill herself.
Then gave I her, so tutored by my art,
A sleeping potion; which so took effect
As I intended, for it wrought on her
The form of death: meantime, I writ to Romeo,
That he should hither come, as this dire night,
To help to take her from her borrowed grave,
Being the time the potion's force should cease.
But he which bore my letter, Friar John,
Was stayed by accident, and yesternight
Returned my letter back.   Then, all alone,
At the prefixéd hour of her waking,
Came I to take her from her kindred's vault,
Meaning to keep her closely at my cell
Till I conveniently could send to Romeo:
But when I came, some minute ere the time
Of her awakening, here untimely lay
The noble Paris and true Romeo dead.
She wakes; and I entreated her come forth,
And bear this work of Heaven with patience:
But then a noise did scare me from the tomb,
And she, too desperate, would not go with me.
But, as it seems, did violence on herself.
All this I know, and to the marriage
Her nurse is privy; and, if aught in this
Miscarried by my fault, let my old life
Be sacrificed some hour before his time
Unto the rigour of severest law.
    Prince. We still have known thee for a holy man.—
Where's Romeo's man? what can he say to this?
    Bal. I brought my master news of Juliet's death;
And then in post he came from Mantua
To this same place, to this same monument.
This letter he early bid me give his father,
And threatened me with death, going in the vault,

If I departed not, and left him there.
   Prince. Give me the letter, I will look on it.—
Where is the county's page, that raised the watch?—
Sirrah, what made your master in this place?
   Page. He came with flowers to strew his lady's grave,
And bid me stand aloof, and so I did:
Anon comes one with light to ope the tomb.
And, by-and-by, my master drew on him;
And then I ran away to call the watch.
   Prince. This letter doth make good the friar's words,
Their course of love, the tidings of her death:
And here he writes, that he did buy a poison
Of a poor 'pothecary, and therewithal
Came to this vault to die, and lie with Juliet.—
Where be these enemies? Capulet! Montague!
See, what a scourge is laid upon your hate,
That Heaven finds means to kill your joys with love;
And I, for winking at your discords too,
Have lost a brace of kinsmen:—all are punished.
   Cap. O brother Montague! give me thy hand:
This is my daughter's jointure; for no more
Can I demand.
   Mon.   But I can give thee more:
For I will raise her statue in pure gold;
That while Verona by that name is known
There shall no figure at such rate be set
As that of true and faithful Juliet.
   Cap. As rich shall Romeo by his lady lie;
Poor sacrifices of our enmity!
   Prince. A glooming peace this morning with it brings:
The sun for sorrow will not show his head.
Go, hence, to have more talk of these sad things;
   Some shall be pardoned, and some punishèd:
For never was a story of more woe,
Than this of Juliet and her Romeo.

                                       [Exeunt

THE TAMING OF THE SHREW

DRAMATIS PERSONÆ

A Lord
CHRISTOPHER SLY, a tinker
Hostess, Page, Players, Huntsmen and Servants } persons in the Induction

BAPTISTA, a rich gentleman of Padua
VINCENTIO, an old gentleman of Pisa
LUCENTIO, son to Vincentio
PETRUCHIO, a gentleman of Verona, a suitor to Katharina
GREMIO
HORTENSIO } Suitors to Bianca
TRANIO
BIONDELLO } servants to Lucentio
GRUMIO
CURTIS } servants to Petruchio
A Pedant

KATHARINA
BIANCA } daughters to Baptista
Widow

Tailor, Haberdasher, and Servants attending on Baptista and Petruchio

SCENE.—Padua, and Petruchio's House in the country.

THE TAMING OF THE SHREW

INDUCTION

Scene I.—Before an Ale-house on a Heath

Enter Hostess and Sly

Sly. I'll pheese you, in faith.
Host. A pair of stocks, you rogue!
Sly. Y'are a baggage: the Slys are no rogues; look in
the chronicles, we came in with Richard Conqueror. Therefore, *paucas pallabris ;* let the world slide. Sessa!
Host. You will not pay for the glasses you have burst?
Sly. No, not a denier. Go by, Saint Jeronimy: go to
thy cold bed, and warm thee.
Host. I know my remedy: I must go fetch the third-
borough. [*Exit*
Sly. Third, or fourth, or fifth borough, I'll answer him
by law. I'll not budge an inch, boy: let him come, and
kindly.

[*Lies down on the ground, and falls asleep*

*Wind Horns. Enter a Lord from hunting, with Hunts-
men and Servants*

Lord. Huntsman, I charge thee, tender well my hounds:
Brach Merriman, the poor cur, is embossed,
And couple Clowder with the deep mouthed brach.
Saw'st thou not, boy, how Silver made it good
At the hedge-corner, in the coldest fault?
I would not lose the dog for twenty pound.
First Hun. Why, Belman is as good as he, my lord;
He cried upon it at the merest loss,
And twice to day picked out the dullest scent:
Trust me, I take him for the better dog.
Lord. Thou art a fool: if Echo were as fleet,
I would esteem him worth a dozen such,
But sup them well, and look unto them all:
To-morrow I intend to hunt again.
First Hun. I will, my lord.
Lord. What's here? one dead, or drunk? See, doth
   he breathe?
Sec. Hun. He breathes, my lord. Were he not warmed
   with ale,
This were a bed but cold to sleep so soundly.
Lord. O monstrous beast! how like a swine he lies!

Grim death, how foul and loathsome is thine image!
Sirs, I will practise on this drunken man.
What think you, if he were convey'd to bed,
Wrapp'd in sweet clothes, rings put upon his fingers,
A most delicious banquet by his bed,
And brave attendants near him when he wakes,
Would not the beggar then forget himself?
   First Hun.   Believe me, lord, I think he cannot choose.
   Sec. Hun.   It would seem strange unto him when he
    waked.
   Lord.   Even as a flattering dream, or worthless fancy.
Then take him up, and manage well the jest.
Carry him gently to my fairest chamber,
And hang it round with all my wanton pictures;
Balm his foul head with warm distilléd waters,
And burn sweet wood to make the lodging sweet.
Procure me music ready when he wakes
To make a dulcet and a heavenly sound;
And if he chance to speak, be ready straight,
And, with a low submissive reverence,
Say, "What is it your honour will command?"
Let one attend him with a silver basin,
Full of rose-water, and bestrewed with flowers;
Another bear the ewer, the third a diaper,
And say, "Will't please your lordship cool your hands?"
Some one be ready with a costly suit,
And ask him what apparel he will wear;
Another tell him of his hounds and horse,
And that his lady mourns at his disease.
Persuade him that he hath been lunatic;
And, when he says he is —, say, that he dreams,
For he is nothing but a mighty lord.
This do, and do it kindly, gentle sirs:
It will be pastime passing excellent,
If it be husbanded with modesty.
   First Hun.   My lord, I warrant you, we will play our part,
As he shall think, by our true diligence,
He is no less than what we say he is.
   Lord.   Take him up gently, and to bed with him,
And each one to his office when he wakes.—
       [*Sly is borne out. A trumpet sounds*
Sirrah, go see what trumpet 't is that sounds:—
              [*Exit Servant*
Belike, some noble gentleman, that means,
Travelling some journey, to repose him here.—

      Re-enter Servant

How now? who is it?

Serv.   An it please your honour,
Players that offer service to your lordship.
  Lord. Bid them come near.

                    Enter Players

                         Now, fellows, you are welcome.
  Players. We thank your honour.
  Lord. Do you intend to stay with me to night?
  A Play. So please your lordship to accept our duty.
  Lord. With all my heart.—This fellow I remember,
Since once he played a farmer's eldest son:—
'T was where you woo'd the gentlewoman so well.
I have forgot your name: but sure, that part
Was aptly fitted, and naturally performed.
  A Play. I think, 't was Soto that your honour means.
  Lord. 'T is very true: thou didst it excellent.
Well, you are come to me in happy time.
The rather for I have some sport in hand
Wherein your cunning can assist me much.
There is a lord will hear you play to-night;—
But I am doubtful of your modesties,
Lest, over-eyeing of his odd behaviour,
(For yet his honour never heard a play),
You break into some merry passion,
And so offend him; for I tell you, sirs,
If you should smile he grows impatient.
  A Play. Fear not, my lord: we can contain ourselves,
Were he the veriest antick in the world.
  Lord. Go, sirrah, take them to the buttery,
And give them friendly welcome every one:
Let them want nothing that my house affords.—
                         [*Exeunt Servant and Players*
  [*To a Servant*] Sirrah, go you to Bartholomew my page,
And see him dressed in all suits like a lady:
That done, conduct him to the drunkard's chamber;
And call him Madam, do him obeisance:
Tell him from me, as he will win my love,
He bear himself with honourable action
Such as he hath observed in noble ladies
Unto their lords by them accomplishéd;
Such duty to the drunkard let him do,
With soft low tongue, and lowly courtesy;
And say, "What is 't your honour will command,
Wherein your lady and your humble wife,
May show her duty and make know her love?"
And then, with kind embracements, tempting kisses,
And with declining head into his bosom,
Bid him shed tears, as being overjoyed

                         89

To see her noble lord restored to health,
Who, for this seven years, hath esteeméd him
No better than a poor and loathsome beggar.
And if the boy have not a woman's gift,
To rain a shower of commanded tears,
An onion will do well for such a shift,
Which, in a napkin being close conveyed,
Shall in despite enforce a watery eye.
See this despatched with all the haste thou canst:
Anon I'll give thee more instructions.   [*Exit Servant*
I know the boy will well usurp the grace,
Voice, gait, and action of a gentlewoman:
I long to hear him call the drunkard husband,
And how my men will stay themselves from laughter,
When they do homage to this simple peasant.
I'll in to counsel them: haply, my presence
May well abate the over-merry spleen,
Which otherwise would grow into extremes.

[*Exeunt*

SCENE II.—A Bed-chamber in the Lord's house

SLY *is discovered in a rich night-gown, with Attendants;*
some with apparel, others with basin, ewer, and other
appurtenances. Enter Lord, dressed like a servant

 Sly. For God's sake, a pot of small ale!
 First Serv. Will 't please your lordship drink a cup of
  sack?
 Sec. Serv. Will 't please your honour taste of these
  conserves?
 Third Serv. What raiment will your honour wear to
  day?
 Sly. I am Christopher Sly; call not me "honour," nor
"lordship:" I ne'er drank sack in my life; and if you
give me any conserves, give me conserves of beef. Ne'er
ask me what raiment I'll wear, for I have no more doublets
than backs, no more stockings than legs, nor no more shoes
than feet; nay, sometime, more feet than shoes, or such
shoes as my toes look through the overleather.
 Lord. Heaven cease this idle humour in your honour!
O, that a mighty man, of such descent,
Of such possessions, and so high esteem,
Should be infuséd with so foul a spirit!
 Sly. What! would you make me mad? Am not I
Christopher Sly, old Sly's son, of Burton Heath, by birth
a pedlar, by education a card-maker, by transmutation a
bear-herd, and now by present profession a tinker?

Ask Marian Hacket, the fat ale-wife of Wincot, if she
know me not; if she say I am not fourteen pence on the
score for sheer ale, score me up for the lyingest knave
in Christendom. What! I am not bestraught. Here's—

    First Serv. O, this it is that makes your lady mourn.

    Sec. Serv. O, this it is that makes your servants droop!

    Lord. Hence comes it that your kindred shun your house,
As beaten hence by your strange lunacy.
O noble lord, bethink thee of thy birth;
Call home thy ancient thoughts from banishment,
And banish hence these abject lowly dreams.
Look how thy servants do attend on thee,
Each in his office ready at thy beck:
Wilt thou have music? hark! Apollo plays,   [*Music*
And twenty cagéd nightingales do sing:
Or wilt thou sleep? we'll have thee to a couch
Softer and sweeter than the lustful bed
On purpose trimmed up for Semiramis.
Say wilt thou walk, we will bestrew the ground:
Or wilt thou ride, thy horses shall be trapped.
Their harness studded all with gold and pearl.
Dost thou love hawking? thou hast hawks will soar
Above the morning lark: or wilt thou hunt?
Thy hounds shall make the welkin answer them,
And fetch shrill echoes from the hollow earth.

    First Serv. Say thou wilt course, thy greyhounds are as
        swift
As breathéd stags, ay, fleeter than the roe.

    Sec. Serv. Dost thou love pictures? we will fetch thee
        straight
Adonis painted by a running brook,
And Cytherea all in sedges hid,
Which seem to move and wanton with her breath,
Even as the waving sedges play with wind.

    Lord. We'll show thee Io as she was a maid,
And how she was beguiléd and surprised,
As lively painted as the deed was done.

    Third Serv. Or Daphne roaming through a thorny wood,
Scratching her legs, that one shall swear she bleeds;
And at that sight shall sad Apollo weep,
So workmanly the blood and tears are drawn.

    Lord. Thou art a lord, and nothing but a lord:
Thou hast a lady, far more beautiful
Than any woman in this waning age.

    First Serv. And, till the tears that she hath shed for thee,
Like envious floods, o'erran her lovely face,
She was the fairest creature in the world;
And yet she is inferior to none.

    Sly. Am I a lord? and have I such a lady?

Or do I dream? or have I dream'd till now?
I do not sleep; I see, I hear, I speak;
I smell sweet savour, and I feel soft things:
Upon my life, I am a lord indeed,
And not a tinker, nor Christopher Sly.—
Well, bring our lady hither to our sight;
And once again, a pot o' the smallest ale.
   Sec. Serv. Will 't please your mightiness to wash your
      hands?
               [*Servants present a ewer, basin, and napkin*
O, how we joy to see your wit restored!
O, that once more you knew but what you are!
These fifteen years you have been in a dream,
Or, when you waked, so waked as if you slept.
   Sly. These fifteen years! by my fay, a goodly nap,
But did I never speak of all that time?
   Sec. Serv. O, yes, my lord, but very idle words;
For though you lay here in this goodly chamber,
Yet would you say ye were beaten out of door,
And rail upon the hostess of the house,
And say you would present her at the leet,
Because she brought stone jugs and no sealed quarts,
Sometimes you would call out for Cicely Hacket.
   Sly. Ay, the woman's maid of the house.
   Third Serv. Why, sir, you know no house, nor no such
      maid,
Nor no such men, as you have reckoned up,—
As Stephen Sly, and old John Naps of Greece,
And Peter Turf, and Henry Pimpernell,
And twenty more such names and men as these,
Which never were, nor no man ever saw.
   Sly. Now, Lord, be thankéd for my good amends!
   All. Amen.
   Sly. I thank thee; thou shalt not lose by it.

Enter the Page, as a lady, with Attendants

   Page. How fares my noble lord?
   Sly. Marry, I fare well, for here is cheer enough.
Where is my wife?
   Page. Here, noble lord: what is thy will with her?
   Sly. Are you my wife, and will not call me husband?
My men should call me lord: I am your goodman.
   Page. My husband and my lord, my lord and husband;
I am your wife in all obedience.
   Sly. I know it well.—What must I call her?
   Lord. Madam.
   Sly. Al'ce madam, or Joan madam?
   Lord. Madam, and nothing else: so lords call ladies.

Sly. Madam wife, they say that I have dreamed
And slept above some fifteen year or more.
Page. Ay, and the time seems thirty unto me,
Being all this time abandoned from your bed,
Sly. 'T is much.—Servants, leave me and her alone.—
Madam, undress you, and come now to bed.
Page. Thrice noble lord, let me entreat of you
To pardon me yet for a night or two;
Or if not so, until the sun be set:
For your physicians have expressly charg'd,
In peril to incur your former malady,
That I should yet absent me from your bed.
I hope this reason stands for my excuse.
Sly. Ay, it stands so, that I may hardly tarry so
long; but I would be loath to fall into my dreams again:
I will therefore tarry, in despite of the flesh and the blood.

Enter a Servant

Serv. Your honour's players, hearing your amendment,
Are come to play a pleasant comedy;
For so your doctors hold it very meet,
Seeing too much sadness hath congealed your blood,
And melancholy is the nurse of frenzy:
Therefore, they thought it good you hear a play,
And frame your mind to mirth and merriment,
Which bars a thousand harms, and lengthens life.
Sly. Marry, I will; let them play it.   Is not a commonty
a Christmas gambol, or a tumbling trick?
Page. No, my good lord: it is more pleasing stuff.
Sly. What, household stuff?
Page. It is a kind of history.
Sly. Well, we'll see 't.   Come, madam wife, sit by my
    side,
And let the world slip: we shall ne'er be younger.
                          [*They sit down*

ACT ONE

SCENE I.—Padua.   A Public Place

Enter LUCENTIO *and* TRANIO

Luc. Tranio, since for the great desire I had
To see fair Padua, nursery of arts,
I am arrived for fruitful Lombardy,
The pleasant garden of great Italy;
And, by my father's love and leave, am armed
With his good will, and thy good company,

My trusty servant, well approved in all:
Here let us breathe, and haply institute
A course of learning and ingenious studies.
Pisa, renownéd for grave citizens,
Gave me my being, and my father first,
A merchant of great traffic through the world,
Vincentio, come of the Bentivolii.
Vincentio's son, brought up in Florence,
It shall become, to serve all hopes conceived,
To deck his fortune with his virtuous deeds,
And therefore, Tranio, for the time I study,
Virtue and that part of philosophy
Will I apply that treats of happiness
By virtue specially to be achiev'd.—
Tell me thy mind; for I have Pisa left,
And am to Padua come, as he that leaves
A shallow plash to plunge him in the deep,
And with satiety seeks to quench his thirst.
   Tra. *Mi perdonate*, gentle master mine,
I am in all affected as yourself,
Glad that you thus continue your resolve
To suck the sweets of sweet philosophy.
Only, good master, while we do admire
This virtue and this moral discipline,
Let's be no stoics nor no stocks I pray;
Or so devote to Aristotle's checks,
As Ovid be an outcast quite abjured.
Balk logic with acquaintance that you have,
And practise rhetoric in your common talk:
Music and poesy use to quicken you.
The mathematics, and the metaphysics,
Fall to them as you find your stomach serves you.
No profit grows where is no pleasure ta'en.—
In brief, sir, study what you most affect.
   Luc. Gramercies, Tranio; well dost thou advise.
If, Biondello, thou wert come ashore,
We could at once put us in readiness,
And take a lodging fit to entertain
Such friends as time in Padua shall beget.
But stay awhile: what company is this?
   Tra. Master, some show, to welcome us to town.

Enter BAPTISTA, KATHARINA, BIANCA, GREMIO, *and* HOR-
    TENSIO. LUCENTIO *and* TRANIO *stand aside*

   Bap. Gentlemen, importune me no farther,
For how I firmly am resolv'd you know;
That is, not to bestow my youngest daughter,
Before I have a husband for the elder.

If either of you both love Katharina,
Because I know you well, and love you well,
Leave shall you have to court her at your pleasure.
    Gre.   [*Aside*] To cart her rather: she's too rough
       for me.—
There, there, Hortensio, will you any wife?
    Kath. [*To* Bap.] I pray you, sir, is it your will
To make a stale of me amongst these mates?
    Hor. Mates, maid! how mean you that? no mates
       for you,
Unless you were of gentler, milder mould.
    Kath. I' faith, sir, you shall never need to fear:
I wis, it is not half way to her heart:
But if it were, doubt not her care should be
To comb your noddle with a three legged stool,
And paint your face, and use you like a fool.
    Hor. From all such devils, good Lord, deliver us!
    Gre. And me too, good Lord!—
    Tra. Hush, master! here is some good pastime toward:
That wench is stark mad, or wonderful froward.
    Luc. But in the other's silence do I see
Maid's mild behaviour and sobriety.
Peace, Tranio!
    Tra. Well said, master: mum! and gaze your fill.—
    Bap. Gentlemen, that I may soon make good
What I have said,—Bianca, get you in:
And let it not displease thee, good Bianca,
For I will love thee ne'er the less, my girl.
    Kath. A pretty peat! it is best
Put finger in the eye,—and she knew why.
    Bian. Sister, content you in my discontent,—
Sir, to your pleasure humbly I subscribe:
My books and instruments shall be my company,
On them to look and practise by myself.
    Luc. Hark, Tranio! thou may'st hear Minerva speak.
    Hor. Signior Baptista, will you be so strange?
Sorry am I, that your good will effects
Bianca's grief.
    Gre.   Why, will you mew her up,
Signior Baptista, for this fiend of hell,
And make her bear the penance of her tongue?
    Bap. Gentlemen, content ye; I am resolv'd.—
Go in, Bianca.   [*Exit Bianca*
And for I know, she taketh most delight
In music, instruments, and poetry,
Schoolmasters will I keep within my house,
Fit to instruct her youth.—If you, Hortensio,
Or, Signior Gremio, you—know any such,
Prefer them hither; for to cunning men

I will be very kind and liberal
To mine own children in good bringing-up;
And so farewell.   Katharina, you may stay,
For I have more to commune with Bianca.   [*Exit*

    Kath.   Why, and I trust I may go too; may I not?
What! shall I be appointed hours, as though, belike,
I knew not what to take and what to leave?   Ha!
                                             [*Exit*

    Gre.   You may go to the devil's dam; your gifts are
so good, here's none will hold you.   Their love is not
so great, Hortensio, but we may blow our nails together,
and fast it fairly out: our cake's dough on both sides.
Farewell:—yet, for the love I bear my sweet Bianca, if
I can by any means light on a fit man to teach her that
wherein she delights, I will wish him to her father.
    Hor.   So will I, Signior Gremio; but a word, I pray.
Though the nature of our quarrel yet never brook'd parle,
know now, upon advice, it toucheth us both,—that we may
yet again have access to our fair mistress, and be happy
rivals in Bianca's love,—to labour and effect one thing
specially.
    Gre.   What's that, I pray?
    Hor.   Marry, sir, to get a husband for her sister.
    Gre.   A husband! a devil.
    Hor.   I say, a husband.
    Gre.   I say, a devil.   Think'st thou, Hortensio, though
her father be very rich, any man is so very a fool to be
married to hell?
    Hor.   Tush, Gremio! though it pass your patience
and mine, to endure her loud alarums, why, man, there
be good fellows in the world, an a man could light on them,
would take her with all faults, and money enough.
    Gre.   I cannot tell; but I had as lief take her dowry
with this condition,—to be whipped at the high-cross
every morning.
    Hor.   'Faith, as you say, there's small choice in rotten
apples.   But, come; since this bar in law makes us friends,
it shall be so far forth friendly maintained, till by helping
Baptista's eldest daughter to a husband, we set his youngest
free for a husband, and then have to 't afresh.—Sweet
Bianca!—Happy man be his dole!   He that runs fastest
gets the ring.   How say you, Signior Gremio?
    Gre.   I am agreed: and would I had given him the
best horse in Padua to begin his wooing that would
thoroughly woo her, wed her, and bed her, and rid the
house of her.   Come on.
                        [*Exeunt Gremio and Hortensio*

    Tra.   [Advancing] I pray, sir, tell me, is it possible.

That love should of a sudden take such hold?
 Luc. O Tranio! till I found it to be true,
I never thought it possible, or likely;
But see! while idly I stood looking on
I found the effect of love-in-idleness;
And now in plainness do confess to thee,—
(Thou art to me as secret, and as dear
As Anna to the Queen of Carthage was),
Tranio, I burn, I pine; I perish, Tranio,
If I achieve not this young modest girl.
Counsel me, Tranio, for I know thou canst:
Assist me, Tranio, for I know thou wilt.
 Tra. Master, it is no time to chide you now;
Affection is not rated from the heart:
If love have touch'd you, nought remains but so,—
Redime te captum, quam queas minimo.
 Luc. Gramercies, lad; go forward; this contents;
The rest will comfort, for thy counsel's sound.
 Tra. Master, you look'd so longly on the maid,
Perhaps you mark'd not what's the pith of all.
 Luc. O! yes, I saw sweet beauty in her face,
Such as the daughter of Agenor had,
That made great Jove to humble him to her hand
When with his knees he kiss'd the Cretan strand.
 Tra. Saw you no more? mark'd you not, how her sister
Began to scold, and raise up such a storm
That mortal ears might hardly endure the din?
 Luc. Tranio, I saw her coral lips to move,
And with her breath she did perfume the air:
Sacred, and sweet was all I saw in her.
 Tra. Nay, then, 't is time to stir him from his trance.
I pray, awake, sir: if you love the maid,
Bend thoughts and wits to achieve her. Thus it stands:
Her elder sister is so curst and shrewd,
That till the father rid his hands of her,
Master, your love must live a maid at home;
And therefore has he closely mew'd her up,
Because she will not be annoyed with suitors.
 Luc. Ah, Tranio, what a cruel father's he!
But art thou not advised, he took some care
To get her cunning schoolmasters to instruct her?
 Tra. Ay, marry am I, sir; and now 't is plotted.
 Luc. I have it Tranio.
 Tra.   Master, for my hand,
Both our inventions meet and jump in one.
 Luc. Tell me thine first.
 Tra.   You will be schoolmaster,
And undertake the teaching of the maid:
That's your device.

Luc.   It is: may it be done?
Tra.   Not possible; for who shall bear your part,
And be in Padua, here, Vincentio's son,
Keep house, and ply his book, welcome his friends,
Visit his countrymen, and banquet them?
Luc. Basta, content thee; for I have it full.
We have not yet been seen in any house,
Nor can we be distinguished by our faces,
For man or master: then, it follows thus:—
Thou shalt be master, Tranio, in my stead,
Keep house, and port, and servants, as I should.
I will some other be; some Florentine,
Some Neapolitan, or meaner man of Pisa.
'T is hatched, and shall be so.—Tranio, at once
Uncase thee, take my coloured hat and cloak:
When Biondello comes, he waits on thee,
But I will charm him first to keep his tongue.
Tra.   So had you need.   [*They exchange habits*
In brief, sir, sith it your own pleasure is,
And I am tied to be obedient
(For so your father charged me at our parting;
"Be serviceable to my son," quoth he,
Although I think 't was in another sense),
I am content to be Lucentio,
Because so well I love Lucentio.
Luc.   Tranio, be so, because Lucentio loves,
And let me be a slave, to achieve that maid
Whose sudden sight hath thralled my wounded eye.

Enter BIONDELLO

Here comes the rogue.—Sirrah, where have you been?
Bion.   Where have I been? Nay, how now? where
          are you?
Master, has my fellow Tranio stolen your clothes,
Or you stolen his, or both? pray, what's the news?
Luc.   Sirrah, come hither: 't is no time to jest,
And therefore frame your manners to the time.
Your fellow Tranio here, to save my life,
Puts my apparel and my countenance on,
And I for my escape have put on his;
For in a quarrel, since I came ashore,
I kill'd a man, and fear I was descried.
Wait you on him, I charge you, as becomes,
While I make way from hence to save my life.
You understand me?
Bion.   I, sir? ne'er a whit.
Luc.   And not a jot of Tranio in your mouth:
Tranio is changed into Lucentio.

Bion.   The better for him; would I were so too!
Tra.   So could I, 'faith, boy, to have the next wish after,
That Lucentio indeed had Baptista's youngest daughter.
But, sirrah, not for my sake, but your master's, I advise
You use your manners discreetly in all kind of companies:
When I am alone, why, then I am Tranio;
But in all places else, your master, Lucentio.
Luc.   Tranio, let's go.—
One thing more rests, that thyself execute;
To make one among these wooers: if thou ask me why,
Sufficeth, my reasons are both good and weighty.
                                                    [*Exeunt*

First Serv.   My lord, you nod; you do not mind the
play.
Sly.   Yes, by Saint Anne, do I.   A good matter, surely:
comes there any more of it?
Page.   My lord, 't is but begun.
Sly.   'T is a very excellent piece of work, madam lady:
would 't were done!

SCENE II.—Padua.   Before HORTENSIO's
house

Enter PETRUCHIO *and* GRUMIO

Pet.   Verona, for a while I take my leave,
To see my friends in Padua; but, of all,
My best beloved and approved friend,
Hortensio; and, I trow, this is his house,—
Here, sirrah Grumio! knock, I say.
Gru.   Knock, sir, whom should I knock? is there any
man has rebused your worship?
Pet.   Villain, I say, knock me here soundly.
Gru.   Knock you here, sir? why, sir, what am I, sir,
that I should knock you here, sir?
Pet.   Villain, I say, knock me at this gate;
And rap me well, or, I'll knock your knave's pate.
Gru.   My master is grown quarrelsome.—I should
                    knock you first,
And then I know after who comes by the worst.
Pet.   Will it not be?
'Faith, sirrah, an you'll not knock, I'll wring it:
I'll try how you can *sol, fa,* and sing it,
                                    [*He wrings* GRUMIO *by the ears*
Gru.   Help, masters, help! my master is mad.
Pet.   Now, knock when I bid you: sirrah! villain!

Enter HORTENSIO

Hor. How now? what's the matter?—My old friend
Grumio, and my good friend Petruchio!—How do you all
at Verona?
Pet. Signior Hortensio, come you to part the fray?
Con tutto il cuore ben trovato, may I say.
*Hor. Alla nostra casa ben venuto; molto honorato signor
mio Petruchio.*
Rise, Grumio, rise: we will compound this quarrel.
Gru. Nay, 't is no matter, sir, what he 'leges in Latin.
If this be not a lawful cause for me to leave his service,
look you, sir,—he bid me knock him, and rap him soundly,
sir: well, was it fit for a servant to use his master so;
being, perhaps, (for aught I see) two-and-thirty,—a pip out?
Whom, would to God, I had well knock'd at first,
Then had not Grumio come by the worst.
Pet. A senseless villain!—Good Hortensio,
I bade the rascal knock upon your gate,
And could not get him for my heart to do it.
Gru. Knock at the gate?—O heavens!
Spake you not these words plain,—"Sirrah, knock me here,
Rap me here, knock me well, and knock me soundly?"
And come you now with knocking at the gate?
Pet. Sirrah, be gone, or talk not, I advise you.
Hor. Petruchio, patience; I am Grumio's pledge.
Why, this is a heavy chance 'twixt him and you,
Your ancient, trusty, pleasant servant Grumio.
And tell me now, sweet friend, what happy gale
Blows you to Padua here, from old Verona?
Pet. Such wind as scatters young men through the
                                                world,
To seek their fortunes further than at home,
Where small experience grows. But, in a few,
Signior Hortensio, thus it stands with me:
Antonio, my father, is deceased,
And I have thrust myself into this maze,
Haply to wive and thrive as best I may.
Crowns in my purse I have, and goods at home,
And so am come abroad to see the world.
Hor. Petruchio, shall I then come roundly to thee,
And wish thee to a shrewd ill-favoured wife?
Thou'dst thank me but a little for my counsel;
And yet I'll promise thee she shall be rich,
And very rich:—but thou'rt too much my friend,
And I'll not wish thee to her.
Pet. Signior Hortensio, 'twixt such friends as we
Few words suffice; and therefore, if thou know
One rich enough to be Petruchio's wife

100

(As wealth is burthen of my wooing dance),
Be she as foul as was Florentius' love,
As old as Sibyl, and as curst and shrewd
As Socrates' Xanthippe, or a worse:
She moves me not, or not removes, at least,
Affection's edge in me,—were she as rough
As are the swelling Adriatic seas:
I come to wive it wealthily in Padua;
If wealthily, then happily in Padua.

   Gru. Nay, look you, sir, he tells you flatly what his
mind is: why, give him gold enough and marry him to a
puppet, or an aglet baby; or an old trot with ne'er a
tooth in her head, though she have as many diseases as
two-and-fifty horses: why, nothing comes amiss, so
money comes withal.

   Hor. Petruchio, since we are stepped thus far in,
I will continue that I broached in jest.
I can, Petruchio, help thee to a wife
With wealth enough, and young, and beauteous,
Brought up as best becomes a gentlewoman:
Her only fault, and that is faults enough,
Is, that she is intolerable curst,
And shrewd and froward; so beyond all measure,
That were my state far worser than it is,
I would not wed her for a mine of gold.

   Pet. Hortensio, peace! thou know'st not gold's effect.—
Tell me her father's name, and 't is enough;
For I will board her, though she chide as loud
As thunder, when the clouds in autumn crack.

   Hor. Her father is Baptista Minola,
An affable and courteous gentleman;
Her name is Katharina Minola,
Renown'd in Padua for her scolding tongue.

   Pet. I know her father, though I know not her,
And he knew my deceased father well.
I will not sleep, Hortensio, till I see her;
And therefore let me be thus bold with you
To give you over at this first encounter,
Unless you will accompany me thither.

   Gru. I pray you, sir, let him go while the humour lasts.
O' my word, an she knew him as well as I do, she would
think scolding would do little good upon him. She may,
perhaps, call him half a score knaves or so; why, that's
nothing: an he begin once, he'll rail in his ropetricks.
I'll tell you what, sir,—an she stand him but little, he
will throw a figure in her face, and so disfigure her with it,
that she shall have no more eyes to see withal than a cat.
You know him not, sir.

   Hor. Tarry, Petruchio, I must go with thee,

For in Baptista's keep my treasure is:
He hath the jewel of my life in hold,
His youngest daughter, beautiful Bianca,
And her withholds from me and other more
Suitors to her and rivals in my love;
Supposing it a thing impossible,
For those defects I have before rehearsed,
That ever Katharina will be woo'd:
Therefore this order hath Baptista ta'en,
That none shall have access unto Bianca,
Till Katharine the curst have got a husband.
 Gru. Katharine the curst!
A title for a maid of all titles the worst.
 Hor. Now shall my friend Petruchio do me grace,
And offer me, disguised in sober robes,
To old Baptista as a schoolmaster
Well seen in music, to instruct Bianca;
That so I may by this device at least
Have leave and leisure to make love to her,
And unsuspected court her by herself.

   Enter Gremio, *and* Lucentio *disguised*

 Gru. Here's no knavery! See, to beguile the old
folks, how the young folks lay their heads together!
Master, master, look about you: who goes there? ha!
 Hor. Peace, Grumio: 't is the rival of my love.
Petruchio, stand by awhile.
 Gru. A proper stripling, and an amorous!
            [They retire
 Gre. O! very well; I have perused the note.
Hark you, sir; I'll have them very fairly bound:
All books of love, see that, at any hand;
And see you read no other lectures to her.
You understand me.—Over and beside
Signior Baptista's liberality,
I'll mend it with a largess.—Take your papers, too,
And let me have them very well perfumed,
For she is sweeter than perfume itself
To whom they go to. What will you read to her?
 Luc. Whate'er I read to her, I'll plead for you
As for my patron, stand you so assured,
As firmly as yourself were still in place;
Yea, and perhaps with more successful words
Than you, unless you were a scholar, sir.
 Gre. O, this learning! what a thing it is!
 Gru. O, this woodcock! what an ass it is!
 Pet. Peace, sirrah!
        102

Hor. Grumio, mum!—[*Coming forward*] God save
you, Signior Gremio!
Gre. And you're well met, Signior Hortensio.   Trow you
Whither I am going?—To Baptista Minola.
I promised to inquire carefully
About a schoolmaster for fair Bianca;
And, by good fortune, I have lighted well
On this young man; for learning, and behaviour,
Fit for her turn; well read in poetry,
And other books,—good ones, I warrant ye.
Hor. 'T is well: and I have met a gentleman,
Hath promised me to help me to another,
A fine musician to instruct our mistress:
So shall I no whit be behind in duty
To fair Bianca, so beloved of me.
Gre. Beloved of me; and that my deeds shall prove.
Gru. And that his bags shall prove.—
Hor. Gremio, 't is now no time to vent our love.
Listen to me, and if you speak me fair,
I'll tell you news indifferent good for either.
Here is a gentleman whom by chance I met,
Upon agreement from us to his liking,
Will undertake to woo curst Katharine;
Yea, and to marry her, if her dowry please.
Gre. So said, so done, is well.—
Hortensio, have you told him all her faults?
Pet. I know she is an irksome, brawling scold:
If that be all, masters, I hear no harm.
Gre. No, say'st me so, friend? What countryman?
Pet. Born in Verona, old Antonio's son:
My father dead, my fortune lives for me;
And I do hope good days and long to see.
Gre. O, sir, such a life, with such a wife, were strange;
But if you have a stomach, to 't o' God's name:
You shall have me assisting you in all.
But will you woo this wild cat?
Pet.   Will I live?
Gru. Will he woo her? ay, or I'll hang her.
Pet. Why came I hither, but to that intent?
Think you, a little din can daunt mine ears?
Have I not in my time heard lions roar?
Have I not heard the sea, puff'd up with winds,
Rage like an angry boar, chafed with sweat?
Have I not heard great ordnance in the field,
And Heaven's artillery thunder in the skies?
Have I not in a pitchéd battle heard
Loud 'larums, neighing steeds, and trumpets' clang?
And do you tell me of a woman's tongue,
That gives not half so great a blow to hear

As will a chestnut in a farmer's fire?
Tush! tush! fear boys with bugs.
    Gru.   **For he fears none.**
    Gre.   Hortensio, hark.
This gentleman is happily arrived,
My mind presumes, for his own good and ours.
    Hor.   I promised we would be contributors,
And bear his charge of wooing, whatsoe'er.
    Gre.   And so we will, provided that he win her.
    Gru.   I would I were as sure of a good dinner.

Enter TRANIO, *bravely apparelled; and* BIONDELLO

    Tra.   Gentlemen, God save you! If I may be bold,
Tell me, I beseech you, which is the readiest way
To the house of Signior Baptista Minola?
    Gre.   He that has the two fair daughters:—is 't he
          you mean?
    Tra.   Even he,—Biondello!
    Gre.   Hark you, sir: you mean not her too?
    Tra.   Perhaps, him and her, sir: what have you to do?
    Pet.   Not her that chides, sir, at any hand, I pray.
    Tra.   I love no chiders, sir.—Biondello, let's away.
    Luc.   [*Aside*] Well begun, Tranio.
    Hor.   Sir, a word ere you go.
Are you a suitor to the maid you talk of, yea or no?
    Tra.   An if I be, sir, is it any offence?
    Gre.   No; if without more words you will get you
          hence.
    Tra.   Why, sir, I pray, are not the streets as free
For me as for you?
    Gre.   But so is not she.
    Tra.   For what reason, I beseech you?
    Gre.   For this reason, if you'll know,
That she's the choice love of Signior Gremio.
    Hor.   That she's the chosen of Signior Hortensio.
    Tra.   Softly, my masters! if you be gentlemen,
Do me this right; hear me with patience.
Baptista is a noble gentleman,
To whom my father is not all unknown;
And were his daughter fairer than she is,
She may more suitors have, and me for one.
Fair Leda's daughter had a thousand wooers;
Then well one more may fair Bianca have,
And so she shall. Lucentio shall make one,
Though Paris came in hope to speed alone.
    Gre.   What! this gentleman will out-talk us all.
    Luc.   Sir, give him head; I know, he'll prove a jade.
    Pet.   Hortensio, to what end are all these words?

Hor.   Sir, let me be so bold as ask you,
Did you yet ever see Baptista's daughter?
Tra.   No, sir; but hear I do that he hath two,
The one as famous for a scolding tongue
As is the other for beauteous modesty.
Pet.   Sir, sir, the first 's for me; let her go by.
Gre.   Yea, leave that labour to great Hercules,
And let it be more than Alcides' twelve.
Pet.   Sir, understand you this of me: in sooth,
The youngest daughter, whom you hearken for,
Her father keeps from all access of suitors
And will not promise her to any man
Until the elder sister first be wed;
The younger then is free, and not before.
Tra.   If it be so, sir, that you are the man
Must stead us all, and me among the rest;
And if you break the ice, and do this feat,
Achieve the elder, set the younger free
For our access,—whose hap shall be to have her
Will not so graceless be to be ingrate.
Hor.   Sir, you say well, and well you do conceive;
And since you do profess to be a suitor,
You must, as we do, gratify this gentleman,
To whom we all rest generally beholding.
Tra.   Sir, I shall not be slack: in sign whereof,
Please ye we may contrive this afternoon,
And quaff carouses to our mistress' health;
And do as adversaries do in law,
Strive mightily, but eat and drink as friends.
Gru., Bion.   O excellent motion! Fellows, let's be gone.
Hor.   The motion 's good indeed, and be it so.—
Petruchio, I shall be your *ben venuto.*

[*Exeunt*

ACT TWO

Scene I.—Padua.   A Room in Baptista's House

Enter Katharina *and* Bianca

Bian.   Good sister, wrong me not, nor wrong yourself,
To make a bondmaid and a slave of me:
That I disdain; but for these other goods,
Unbind my hands, I'll pull them off myself.
Yea, all my raiment, to my petticoat;
Or what you will command me will I do,
So well I know my duty to my elders.
Kath.   Of all thy suitors, here I charge thee, tell
Whom thou lov'st best: see thou dissemble not.

Bian.   Believe me, sister, of all men alive,
I never yet beheld that special face
Which I could fancy more than any other.
   Kath.   Minion, thou liest. Is 't not Hortensio?
   Bian.   If you affect him, sister, here I swear,
I'll plead for you myself, but you shall have him.
   Kath.   O, then, belike, you fancy riches more;
You will have Gremio to keep you fair.
   Bian.   Is it for him you do envy me so?
Nay, then you jest; and now I well perceive,
You have but jested with me all this while.
I pr'ythee, sister Kate, untie my hands.
   Kath.   If that be jest, then all the rest was so.
                                        [*Striking her*

                    Enter BAPTISTA

   Bap.   Why, how now, dame! whence grows this in-
                solence?—
Bianca, stand aside:—poor girl! she weeps.
Go ply thy needle; meddle not with her.
For shame, thou hilding of a devilish spirit,
Why dost thou wrong her that did ne'er wrong thee?
When did she cross thee with a bitter word?
   Kath.   Her silence flouts me, and I'll be revenged.
                                 [*Flies after Bianca*
   Bap.   What! in my sight?—Bianca, get thee in.
                                        [*Exit Bianca*
   Kath.   What! will you not suffer me? Nay, now I see,
She is your treasure, she must have a husband;
I must dance bare-foot on her wedding-day,
And, for your love to her, lead apes in hell.
Talk not to me: I will go sit and weep,
Till I can find occasion of revenge.   [*Exit*
   Bap.   Was ever gentleman thus grieved as I?—
But who comes here?

Enter GREMIO, *with* LUCENTIO *in a mean habit;* PETRUCHIO,
   with HORTENSIO *as a musician; and* TRANIO, *with*
   BIONDELLO *bearing a lute and books*

   Gre.   Good morrow, neighbour Baptista.
   Bap.   Good morrow, neighbour Gremio.
God save you, gentlemen.
   Pet.   And you, good sir. Pray, have you not a daughter,
Call'd Katharina, fair, and virtuous?
   Bap.   I have a daughter, sir, called Katharina.
   Gre.   You are too blunt: go to it orderly.
   Bap.   You wrong me, Signior Gremio: give me leave:—
I am a gentleman of Verona, sir,

That, hearing of her beauty, and her wit,
Her affability, and bashful modesty,
Her wondrous qualities, and mild behaviour,
Am bold to show myself a forward guest
Within your house, to make mine eye the witness
Of that report which I so oft have heard.
And, for an entrance to my entertainment,
I do present you with a man of mine,
                    [*Presenting* HORTENSIO
Cunning in music and the mathematics,
To instruct her fully in those sciences,
Whereof, I know, she is not ignorant.
Accept of him, or else you do me wrong:
His name is Licio, born in Mantua.
    Bap.   You're welcome, sir; and he, for your good sake.
But for my daughter Katherine, this I know,
She is not for your turn, the more my grief.
    Pet.   I see, you do not mean to part with her,
Or else you like not of my company.
    Bap.   Mistake me not; I speak but as I find.
Whence are you, sir? what may I call your name?
    Pet.   Petruchio is my name, Antonio's son;
A man well known throughout all Italy.
    Bap.   I know him well: you are welcome for his sake.
    Gre.   Saving your tale, Petruchio, I pray,
Let us, that are poor petitioners, speak too.
Backare! you are marvellous forward.
    Pet.   O! pardon me, Signior Gremio; I would fain
        be doing.
    Gre.   I doubt it not, sir; but you'll curse your
        wooing.—
Neighbour, this is a gift very grateful, I am sure of it.
To express the like kindness, myself that have been more
kindly beholding to you than any, freely give unto you
this young scholar [*presenting* LUCENTIO] that hath
been long studying at Rheims; as cunning in Greek,
Latin, and other languages, as the other in music and
mathematics. His name is Cambio: pray accept his
service.
    Bap.   A thousand thanks, Signior Gremio; welcome,
good Cambio.—[*To* TRANIO.]   But, gentle sir, methinks,
you walk like a stranger: may I be so bold to know the
cause of your coming?
    Tra.   Pardon me, sir, the boldness is mine own,
That, being a stranger in this city here,
Do make myself a suitor to your daughter,
Unto Bianca, fair and virtuous.
Nor is your firm resolve unknown to me,
In the preferment of the eldest sister.

This liberty is all that I request,—
That, upon knowledge of my parentage,
I may have welcome 'mongst the rest that woo,
And free access and favour as the rest.
And, toward the education of your daughters,
I here bestow a simple instrument,
And this small packet of Greek and Latin books:
If you accept them, then their worth is great.

    Bap.   Lucentio is your name? of whence, I pray?

    Tra.   Of Pisa, sir; son to Vincentio.

    Bap.   A mighty man of Pisa; by report
I know him well: you are very welcome, sir.—
[*To* Hor.] Take you the lute, [*to* Luc.] and you the set
      of books;
You shall go see your pupils presently.
Holla, within!

Enter a Servant

                Sirrah, lead these gentlemen
To my daughters; and tell them both,
These are their tutors: bid them use them well.
    [*Exit Servant, with Hortensio, Lucentio, and Bion-*
              dello
We will go walk a little in the orchard,
And then to dinner. You are passing welcome,
And so I pray you all to think yourselves.

    Pet.   Signior Baptista, my business asketh haste,
And every day I cannot come to woo.
You knew my father well, and in him, me,
Left solely heir to all his lands and goods,
Which I have bettered rather than decreased:
Then tell me,—if I get your daughter's love,
What dowry shall I have with her to wife?

    Bap.   After my death, the one half of my lands;
And in possession twenty thousand crowns.

    Pet.   And, for that dowry, I'll assure her of
Her widowhood, be it that she survive me,
In all my lands and leases whatsoever.
Let specialties be therefore drawn between us,
That covenants may be kept on either hand.

    Bap.   Ay, when the special thing is well obtained,
That is, her love; for that is all in all.

    Pet.   Why, that is nothing; for I tell you, father,
I am as peremptory as she proud-minded;
And where two raging fires meet together,
They do consume the thing that feeds their fury:
Though little fire grows great with little wind,
Yet extreme gusts will blow out fire and all;

So I to her, and so she yields to me,
For I am rough, and woo not like a babe.
  Bap. Well may'st thou woo, and happy be thy speed!
But be thou armed for some unhappy words.
  Pet. Ay, to the proof, as mountains are for winds,
That shake not, though they blow perpetually.

      Re-enter HORTENSIO, *with his head broken*

  Bap. How now, my friend? why dost thou look so
      pale?
  Hor. For fear, I promise you, if I look pale.
  Bap. What, will my daughter prove a good musician?
  Hor. I think, she'll sooner prove a soldier:
Iron may hold with her, but never lutes.
  Bap. Why, then, thou canst not break her to the lute?
  Hor. Why, no, for she hath broke the lute to me.
I did but tell her she mistook her frets,
And bow'd her hand to teach her fingering,
When, with a most impatient, devilish spirit,
"Frets call you these?" quoth she; "I'll fume with
      them:"
And with that word she struck me on the head,
And through the instrument my pate made way;
And there I stood amazéd for a while,
As on a pillory, looking through the lute,
While she did call me "rascal fiddler,"
And "twangling Jack," with twenty such vile terms,
As had she studied to misuse me so.
  Pet. Now, by the world, it is a lusty wench!
I love her ten times more than e'er I did:
O, how I long to have some chat with her!
  Bap. Well, go with me, and be not so discomfited:
Proceed in practice with my younger daughter;
She's apt to learn, and thankful for good turns.—
Signior Petruchio, will you go with us,
Or shall I send my daughter Kate to you?
  Pet. I pray you do: I will attend her here,
      [*Exeunt Baptista, Gremio, Tranio, and Hortensio*
And woo her with some spirit when she comes.
Say, that she rail; why, then I'll tell her plain,
She sings as sweetly as a nightingale;
Say, that she frown; I'll say, she looks as clear
As morning roses newly washed with dew:
Say, she be mute, and will not speak a word;
Then I'll commend her volubility,
And say, she uttereth piercing eloquence:
If she do bid me pack, I'll give her thanks,
As though she bid me stay by her a week:

If she deny to wed, I'll crave the day
When I shall ask the banns, and when be married.—
But here she comes; and now, Petruchio, speak.

Enter KATHARINA

Good morrow, Kate, for that's your name, I hear.
    Kath. Well have you heard, but something hard **of**
        hearing:
They call me Katharine, that do talk of me.
    Pet. You lie, in faith; for you are call'd plain Kate,
And bonny Kate, and sometimes Kate the curst;
But Kate, the prettiest Kate in Christendom;
Kate of Kate Hall, my super-dainty Kate,
For dainties are all cates: and therefore, Kate,
Take this of me, Kate of my consolation:—
Hearing thy mildness praised in every town,
Thy virtues spoke of, and thy beauty sounded,
Yet not so deeply as to thee belongs,
Myself am mov'd to woo thee for my wife.
    Kath. Moved! in good time: let him that **moved you**
        hither,
Remove you hence. I knew you at the first,
You were a movable.
    Pet.   Why, what's a movable?
    Kath. A joint-stool.
    Pet.   Thou hast hit it: come, sit **on me.**
    Kath. Asses are made to bear, and so are you.
    Pet. Women are made to bear, and so are you.
    Kath. No such jade as bear you, if me you mean.
    Pet. Alas, good Kate! I will not burden thee;
For, knowing thee to be but young and light,—
    Kath. Too light for such a swain as you to catch,
And yet as heavy as my weight should be.
    Pet. Should be? should buz.
    Kath.   Well ta'en, and like a buzzard,
    Pet. O slow-wing'd turtle! shall a buzzard **take thee?**
    Kath. Ay, for a turtle, as he takes a buzzard.
    Pet. Come, come, you wasp; i' faith, you **are too**
        angry.
    Kath. If I be waspish, best beware my sting.
    Pet. My remedy is then, to pluck it out.
    Kath. Ay, if the fool could find it where it lies.
    Pet. Who knows not where a wasp does **wear his**
        sting?
In his tail.
    Kath. In his tongue.
    Pet.   Whose tongue?
    Kath. Yours, if you talk of tails; **and so farewell.**—

Pet. What! with my tongue in your tail? nay, come
   again:
Good Kate, I am a gentleman.
 Kath.   That I'll try. [*Striking him*
 Pet. I swear I'll cuff you, if you strike again.
 Kath. So may you lose your arms.
If you strike me, you are no gentleman,
And if no gentleman, why, then no arms.
 Pet. A herald, Kate? O, put me in thy books.
 Kath. What is your crest? a coxcomb?
 Pet. A combless cock, so Kate will be my hen.
 Kath. No cock of mine; you crow too like a craven.
 Pet. Nay, come, Kate, come; you must not look so
   sour.
 Kath. It is my fashion when I see a crab.
 Pet. Why, here's no crab, and therefore look not sour.
 Kath. There is, there is.
 Pet. Then show it me.
 Kath.   Had I a glass, I would.
 Pet. What, you mean my face?
 Kath.   Well aimed of such a young one.
 Pet. Now, by Saint George, I am too young for you.
 Kath. Yet you are withered.
 Pet.   'Tis with cares.
 Kath.   I care not.
 Pet. Nay, hear you, Kate: in sooth, you 'scape not so.
 Kath. I chafe you, if I tarry: let me go.
 Pet. No, not a whit: I find you passing gentle.
'T was told me, you were rough, and coy, and sullen,
And now I find report a very liar;
For thou art pleasant, gamesome, passing courteous,
But slow in speech, yet sweet as spring-time flowers.
Thou canst not frown, thou canst not look askance,
Nor bite the lip, as angry wenches will;
Nor hast thou pleasure to be cross in talk;
But thou with mildness entertain'st thy wooers,
With gentle conference, soft and affable.
Why does the world report that Kate doth limp?
O slanderous world! Kate, like the hazel-twig,
Is straight, and slender; and as brown in hue
As hazel-nuts, and sweeter than the kernels.
O, let me see thee walk: thou dost not halt.
 Kath. Go, fool, and whom thou keep'st command.
 Pet. Did ever Dian so become a grove,
As Kate this chamber with her princely gait?
O, be thou Dian, and let her be Kate,
And then let Kate be chaste, and Dian sportful.
 Kath. Where did you study all this goodly speech?
 Pet. It is extempore, from my mother-wit.

Kath. A witty mother! witless else her son.
Pet. Am I not wise?
Kath.   Yes; keep you warm.
Pet. Marry, so I mean, sweet Katharine, in thy bed.
And therefore, setting all this chat aside,
Thus in plain terms:—your father hath consented
That you shall be my wife; your dowry 'greed on;
And, will you nill you, I will marry you.
Now, Kate, I am a husband for your turn;
For, by this light, whereby I see thy beauty;
Thy beauty that doth make me like thee well,
Thou must be married to no man but me:
For I am he am born to tame you, Kate,
And bring you from a wild Kate to a Kate
Conformable, as other household Kates.
Here comes your father: never make denial;
I must and will have Katharine to my wife.

Re-enter BAPTISTA, GREMIO, *and* TRANIO

Bap. Now, Signior Petruchio, how speed you with my
          daughter?
Pet. How but well, sir? how but well?
It were impossible I should speed amiss.
Bap. Why, how now, daughter Katharine? in your
          dumps?
Kath. Call you me daughter? now, I promise you,
You have showed a tender fatherly regard,
To wish me wed to one half lunatic;
A mad-cap ruffian, and a swearing Jack,
That thinks with oaths to face the matter out.
Pet. Father, 't is thus:—yourself and all the world,
That talked of her, have talked amiss of her.
If she be curst, it is for policy,
For she's not froward, but modest as the dove;
She is not hot, but temperate as the morn;
For patience she will prove a second Grissel,
And Roman Lucrece for her chastity;
And to conclude,—we have 'greed so well together,
That upon Sunday is the wedding-day.
Kath. I'll see thee hanged on Sunday first.
Gre. Hark, Petruchio: she says she'll see thee hanged
          first.
Tra. Is this your speeding? nay then, good night
          our part.
Pet. Be patient, gentlemen, I choose her for myself:
If she and I be pleased, what's that to you?
'Tis bargained 'twixt us twain, being alone,
That she shall still be curst in company.

I tell you, 't is incredible to believe
How much she loves me.   O, the kindest Kate!
She hung about my neck, and kiss on kiss
She vied so fast, protesting oath on oath,
That in a twink she won me to her love.
O, you are novices: 't is a world to see,
How tame, when men and women are alone,
A meacock wretch can make the curstest shrew.—
Give me thy hand, Kate: I will unto Venice,
To buy apparel 'gainst the wedding-day.—
Provide the feast, father, and bid the guests;
I will be sure, my Katharine shall be fine.
    Bap.   I know not what to say; but give me your hands:
God send you joy, Petruchio! 't is a match.
    Gre., Tra.   Amen, say we: we will be witnesses.
    Pet.   Father, and wife, and gentlemen, adieu.
I will to Venice; Sunday comes apace.
We will have rings, and things, and fine array;
And kiss me, Kate, we will be married o' Sunday.

        [Exeunt Petruchio and Katharina, severally

    Gre.   Was ever match clapped up so suddenly?
    Bap.   'Faith, gentlemen, now I play a merchant's part,
And venture madly on a desperate mart.
    Tra.   'T was a commodity lay fretting by you:
'T will bring you gain, or perish on the seas.
    Bap.   The gain I seek is quiet in the match.
    Gre.   No doubt but he hath got a quiet catch.—
But now, Baptista, to your younger daughter.
Now is the day we long have looked for:
I am your neighbour, and was suitor first,
    Tra.   And I am one, that love Bianca more
Than words can witness, or your thoughts can guess.
    Gre.   Youngling, thou canst not love so dear as I.
    Tra.   Grey-beard, thy love doth freeze.
    Gre.   But thine doth fry.
Skipper stand back: 't is age that nourisheth.
    Tra.   But youth in ladies' eyes that flourisheth.
    Bap.   Content you, gentlemen; I'll compound this
        strife:
'T is deeds must win the prize; and he, of both,
That can assure my daughter greatest dower,
Shall have Bianca's love.—
Say, Signior Gremio, what can you assure her?
    Gre.   First, as you know, my house within the city
Is richly furnishéd with plate and gold:
Basins, and ewers, to lave her dainty hands;
My hangings all of Tyrian tapestry;
In ivory coffers I have stuffed my crowns;

In cypress chests my arras, counterpoints,
Costly apparel, tents and canopies,
Fine linen, Turkey cushions bossed with pearl,
Valance of Venice gold in needlework,
Pewter or brass, and all things that belong
To house or housekeeping; then, at my farm,
I have a hundred milch-kine to the pail,
Sixscore fat oxen standing in my stalls,
And all things answerable to this portion.
Myself am struck in years, I must confess:
And if I die to-morrow, this is hers,
If whilst I live she will be only mine.
   Tra. That "only" came well in.—Sir, list to me.
I am my father's heir and only son:
If I may have your daughter to my wife,
I'll leave her houses three or four as good,
Within rich Pisa walls, as any one
Old Signior Gremio has in Padua;
Besides two thousand ducats by the year
Of fruitful land, all which shall be her jointure.—
What, have I pinched you, Signor Gremio?
   Gre. Two thousand ducats by the year of land!
My land amounts not to so much in all:
That she shall have; besides an argosy,
That now is lying in Marseilles' road.—
What, have I choked you with an argosy?
   Tra. Gremio, 't is known, my father hath no less
Than three great argosies, besides two galliasses,
And twelve tight galleys: these I will assure her,
And twice as much, whate'er thou offer'st next.
   Gre. Nay, I have offered all, I have no more;
And she can have no more than all I have:—
If you like me, she shall have me and mine.
   Tra. Why, then the maid is mine from all the world,
By your firm promise. Gremio is out-vied.
   Bap. I must confess, your offer is the best;
And, let your father make her the assurance,
She is your own; else you must pardon me:
If you should die before him, where's her dower?
   Tra. That's but a cavil: he is old, I young.
   Gre. And may not young men die, as well as old?
   Bap. Well, gentlemen,
I am thus resolv'd.—On Sunday next, you know,
My daughter Katharine is to be married:
Now, on the Sunday following shall Bianca
Be bride to you, if you make this assurance;
If not, to Signior Gremio:
And so I take my leave, and thank you both.   [*Exit*
   Gre. Adieu, good neighbour.—Now I fear thee not:

Sirrah, young gamester, your father were a fool
To give thee all, and, in his waning age,
Set foot under thy table.   Tut! a toy!
An old Italian fox is not so kind, my boy.   [*Exit*
   Tra.   A vengeance on your crafty wither'd hide!
Yet I have faced it with a card of ten.
'T is in my head to do my master good:—
I see no reason, but supposed Lucentio
Must get a father, called—supposed Vincentio;
And that's a wonder: fathers, commonly,
Do get their children; but in this case of wooing,
A child shall get a sire, if I fail not of my cunning.

                                                    [*Exit*

ACT THREE

Scene I.—A Room in Baptista's House

Enter Lucentio, Hortensio, *and* Bianca

   Luc.   Fiddler, forbear: you grow too forward, sir.
Have you so soon forgot the entertainment
Her sister Katharine welcom'd you withal?
   Hor.   But, wrangling pedant, this is
The patroness of heavenly harmony:
Then give me leave to have prerogative;
And when in music we have spent an hour,
Your lecture shall have leisure for as much.
   Luc.   Preposterous ass, that never read so far
To know the cause why music was ordain'd!
Was it not to refresh the mind of man,
After his studies, or his usual pain?
Then give me leave to read philosophy,
And while I pause serve in your harmony,
   Hor.   Sirrah, I will not bear these braves of thine.
   Bian.   Why, gentlemen, you do me double wrong,
To strive for that which resteth in my choice.
I am no breeching scholar in the schools;
I'll not be tied to hours, nor 'pointed times;
But learn my lessons as I please myself.
And, to cut off all strife, here sit we down:—
Take you your instrument, play you the whiles;
His lecture will be done ere you have tuned.
   Hor.   You'll leave his lecture, when I am in tune?
                                                    [*Retires*
   Luc.   That will be never:—tune your instrument.
   Bian.   Where left we last?
   Luc.   Here, madam:—

Hic ibat Simois; hic est Sigeia tellus;
Hic steterat Priami regia celsa senis.

Bian. Construe them.

Luc. *Hic ibat,* as I told you before,—*Simois,* I am
Lucentio,—*hic est,* son unto Vincentio of Pisa,—*Sigeia*
tellus, disguised thus to get your love;—*Hic steterat,*
and that Lucentio that comes a-wooing,—*Priami,* is my
man Tranio,—*regia,* bearing my port,—*celsa sensis,* that
we might beguile the old pantaloon.

Hor. [*Returning*] Madam, my instrument 's in tune.

Bian. Let's hear. [*Hor. plays*] O fie! the treble jars.

Luc. Spit in the hole, man, and tune again.

Bian. Now let me see if I can construe it:
Hic ibat Simois, I know you not;—*Hic est Sigeia tellus,*
I trust you not;—*Hic steterat Priami,* take heed he hear us
not;—*regia,* presume not;—*celsa senis,* despair not.

Hor. Madam, 't is now in tune.

Luc.   All but the base.

Hor. The base is right; 't is the base knave that jars.
How fiery and forward our pedant is!
Now, for my life, the knave doth court my love,
Pedascule, I'll watch you better yet.

Bian. In time I may believe, yet I mistrust.

Luc. Mistrust it not: for sure, Æacides
Was Ajax, called so from his grandfather.

Bian. I must believe my master; else, I promise you
I should be arguing still upon that doubt:
But let it rest.—Now, Licio, to you.
Good masters, take it not unkindly, pray,
That I have been thus pleasant with you both.

Hor. [*To* LUCENTIO] You may go walk, and give me
          leave awhile:
My lessons make no music in three parts.

Luc. Are you so formal, sir? [*Aside*] Well, I must
          wait.
And watch withal; for, but I be deceiv'd,
Our fine musician groweth amorous.

Hor. Madam, before you touch the instrument,
To learn the order of my fingering,
I must begin with rudiments of art;
To teach you gamut in a briefer sort,
More pleasant, pithy, and effectual,
Than hath been taught by any of my trade;
And there it is in writing, fairly drawn.

Bian. Why, I am past my gamut long ago.

Hor. Yet read the gamut of Hortensio.

Bian. [*Reads*]
     "'Gamut' I am, the ground of all accord,
     A re, to plead Hortensio's passion;

116

'B mi,' *Bianca, take him for thy lord,*
'C faut,' *that loves with all affection:*
'D sol re,' *one cliff, two notes have I;*
'E la mi,' *show pity, or I die."*
Call you this gamut? tut! I like it not:
Old fashions please me best; I am not so nice,
To change true rules for odd inventions.

Enter a Servant

Serv.   Mistress, your father prays you leave your books,
And help to dress your sister's chamber up:
You know, to-morrow is the wedding-day.
   Bian.   Farewell, sweet masters both: I must be gone.
                                        [*Exeunt Bianca and Servant*
   Luc.   'Faith, mistress, then I have no cause to stay.
                                        [*Exit*

   Hor.   But I have cause to pry into this pedant:
Methinks, he looks as though he were in love.—
Yet if thy thoughts, Bianca, be so humble,
To cast thy wandering eyes on every stale,
Seize thee that list: if once I find thee ranging,
Hortensio will be quit with thee by changing.   [*Exit*

SCENE II.—Padua.   Before BAPTISTA's House

Enter BAPTISTA, GREMIO, TRANIO, KATHARINA,
BIANCO, LUCENTIO, *and Attendants*

Bap.   Signior Lucentio, this is the 'pointed day,
That Katharine and Petruchio should be married,
And yet we hear not of our son-in-law.
What will be said? what mockery will it be,
To want the bridegroom, when the priest attends
To speak the ceremonial rites of marriage!
What says Lucentio to this shame of ours?
   Kath.   No shame but mine: I must, forsooth, be forced
To give my hand, opposed against my heart,
Unto a mad-brain rudesby, full of spleen,
Who woo'd in haste, and means to wed at leisure.
I told you, I, he was a frantic fool,
Hiding his bitter jests in blunt behaviour;
And to be noted for a merry man,
He'll woo a thousand, 'point the day of marriage,
Make friends, invite them, and proclaim the banns;
Yet never means to wed where he hath woo'd.
Now must the world point at poor Katharine,

117

And say,—"Lo, there is mad Petruchio's wife,
If it would please him come and marry her."
    Tra. Patience, good Katharine, and Baptista too.
Upon my life, Petruchio means but well,
Whatever fortune stays him from his word:
Though he be blunt, I know him passing wise;
Though he be merry, yet withal he's honest.
    Kath. Would Katharine had never seen him though!
        [*Exit, weeping, followed by Bianca and others*
    Bap. Go, girl; I cannot blame thee now to weep;
For such injury would vex a very saint,
Much more a shrew of thy impatient humour.

Enter BIONDELLO

    Bion. Master, master! old news, and such news as
you never heard of!
    Bap. Is it new and old too? how may that be?
    Bion. Why, is it not news to hear of Petruchio's coming?
    Bap. Is he come?
    Bion. Why, no, sir?
    Bap. What then?
    Bion. He is coming.
    Bap. When will he be here?
    Bion. When he stands where I am, and sees you there.
    Tra. But, say, what to thine old news?
    Bion. Why, Petruchio is coming, in a new hat, and
an old jerkin; a pair of old breeches thrice turned; a
pair of boots that have been candle-cases, one buckled,
another laced; an old rusty sword ta'en out of the town-
armoury, with a broken hilt, and chapeless; with two
broken points: his horse hipped, with an old mothy
saddle, and stirrups of no kindred; besides, possessed with
the glanders, and like to mose in the chine; troubled
with the lampass, infected with the fashions, full of wind-
galls, sped with spavins, rayed with the yellows, past cure
of the fives, stark spoiled with the staggers, begnawn with
the bots, swayed in the back, and shoulder-shotten; ne'er
legged before, and with a half-checked bit, and a head-
stall of sheep's leather; which, being restrained to keep
him from stumbling, hath been often burst, and now
repaired with knots; one girth six times pieced, and a
woman's crupper of velure, which hath two letters for
her name fairly set down in studs, and here and there
pieced with packthread.
    Bap. Who comes with him?
    Bion. O, sir! his lackey, for all the world caparisoned
like the horse; with a linen stock on one leg, and a kersey
boot-hose on the other, gartered with a red and blue list;

an old hat, and the humour of forty fancies pricked in
't for a feather: a monster, a very monster in apparel,
and not like a Christian footboy, or a gentleman's lackey.

Tra.   'T is some odd humour pricks him to this fashion;
Yet oftentimes he goes but mean-apparelled.

Bap.   I am glad he is come, howsoe'er he comes.

Bion.   Why, sir, he comes not.

Bap.   Didst thou not say, he comes?

Bion.   Who? that Petruchio came?

Bap.   Ay, that Petruchio came.

Bion.   No, sir; I say, his horse comes with him on
his back.

Bap.   Why, that 's all one.

Bion.   Nay, by Saint Jamy,
          I hold you a penny,
          A horse and a man,
          Is more than one,
          And yet not many.

Enter PETRUCHIO *and* GRUMIO

Pet.   Come, where be these gallants?   who's   at
home?

Bap.   You are welcome, sir.

Pet.   And yet I come not well.

Bap.   And yet you halt not.

Tra.   Not so well apparelled,
As I wish you were.

Pet.   Were it better, I should rush in thus.
But where is Kate? where is my lovely bride?—
How does my father?—Gentles, methinks you frown:
And wherefore gaze this goodly company,
As if they saw some wondrous monument,
Some comet, or unusual prodigy?

Bap.   Why, sir, you know, this is your wedding-day.
First were we sad, fearing you would not come;
Now sadder, that you come so unprovided,
Fie! doff this habit, shame to your estate,
An eyesore to our solemn festival.

Tra.   And tell us what occasion of import
Hath all so long detained you from your wife,
And sent you hither so unlike yourself?

Pet.   Tedious it were to tell, and harsh to hear:
Sufficeth, I am come to keep my word,
Though in some part enforcéd to digress;
Which, at more leisure, I will so excuse
As you shall well be satisfied withal.
But, where is Kate? I stay too long from her:
The morning wears, 't is time we were at church.

Tra. See not your bride in these unreverent robes.
Go to my chamber: put on clothes of mine.
   Pet. Not I, believe me: thus I'll visit her.
   Bap. But thus, I trust, you will not marry her.
   Pet. Good sooth, even thus; therefore ha' done with
      words:
To me she 's married, not unto my clothes.
Could I repair what she will wear in me,
As I can change these poor accoutrements,
'T were well for Kate, and better for myself,
But what a fool am I to chat with you,
When I should bid good-morrow to my bride,
And seal the title with a lovely kiss!
        [*Exeunt Petruchio, Grumio, and Biondello*
   Tra. He hath some meaning in his mad attire.
We will persuade him, be it possible,
To put on better ere he go to church.
   Bap. I'll after him, and see the event of this.   [*Exit*
   Tra. But to her love concerneth us to add
Her father's liking: which to bring to pass,
As I before imparted to your worship,
I am to get a man,—whate'er he be,
It skills not much, we'll fit him to our turn,—
And he shall be Vincentio of Pisa,
And make assurance, here in Padua,
Of greater sums than I have promiséd.
So shall you quietly enjoy your hope,
And marry sweet Bianca with consent.
   Luc. Were it not that my fellow-schoolmaster
Doth watch Bianca's steps so narrowly,
'T were good, methinks, to steal our marriage;
Which once perform'd, let all the world say no,
I'll keep mine own, despite of all the world.
   Tra. That by degrees we mean to look into,
And watch our vantage in this business,
We'll over-reach the grey-beard, Gremio,
The narrow-prying father, Minola,
The quaint musician, amorous Licio;
All for my master's sake, Lucentio.

Re-enter GREMIO

Signior Gremio, came you from the church?
   Gre. As willingly as e'er I came from school.
   Tra. And is the bride and bridegroom coming home?
   Gre. A bridegroom say you? 't is a groom indeed,
A grumbling groom, and that the girl shall find.
   Tra. Curster than she? why, 't is impossible.
   Gre. Why, he's a devil, a devil, a very fiend.

Tra.   Why, she 's a devil, a devil, the devil's dam.
Gre.   Tut! she 's a lamb, a dove, a fool to him.
I'll tell you, Sir Lucentio: when the priest
Should ask, if Katharine should be his wife,
"Ay, by gogs-wouns," quoth he: and swore so loud,
That, all amaz'd, the priest let fall the book;
And, as he stoop'd again to take it up,
This mad-brain'd bridegroom took him such a cuff,
That down fell priest and book, and book and priest:
"Now take them up," quoth he, "if any list."
Tra.   What said the wench, when he arose again?
Gre.   Trembled and shook; for why, he stamped and
          swore,
As if the vicar meant to cozen him.
But after many ceremonies done,
He calls for wine:—"A health!" quoth he; as if
He had been aboard, carousing to his mates
After a storm:—quaffed off the muscadel,
And threw the sops all in the sexton's face;
Having no other reason,
But that his beard grew thin and hungerly,
And seemed to ask him sops as he was drinking.
This done, he took the bride about the neck,
And kiss'd her lips with such a clamorous smack,
That, at the parting, all the church did echo,
And I, seeing this, came thence for very shame;
And after me, I know, the rout is coming:
Such a mad marriage never was before.
Hark, hark! I hear the minstrels play.   [*Music*

Enter PETRUCHIO, KATHARINA, BIANCA, BAPTISTA,
      HORTENSIO, GRUMIO, *and* Train

Pet.   Gentlemen and friends, I thank you for your pains.
I know you think to dine with me to-day,
And have prepar'd great store of wedding-cheer;
But, so it is, my haste doth call me hence,
And therefore here I mean to take my leave.
Bap.   Is 't possible you will away to-night?
Pet.   I must away to-day, before night come.
Make it no wonder: if you knew my business,
You would entreat me rather go than stay.
And, honest company, I thank you all,
That have beheld me give away myself
To this most patient, sweet, and virtuous wife.
Dine with my father, drink a health to me,
For I must hence: and farewell to you all.
Tra.   Let us entreat you stay till after dinner.
Pet.   It may not be.

121

Gre.   Let me entreat you.
Pet.   It cannot be.
Kath.   Let me entreat you.
Pet.   I am content.
Kath.   Are you content to stay?
Pet.   I am content you shall entreat me stay,
But yet not stay, entreat me how you can.
Kath.   Now, if you love me, stay.
Pet.   Grumio, my horse!
Gru.   Ay, sir, they be ready: the oats have eaten
the horses.
Kath.   Nay, then,
Do what thou canst, I will not go to-day;
No, nor to-morrow, nor till I please myself.
The door is open, sir, there lies your way,
You may be jogging whiles your boots are green;
For me, I'll not be gone, till I please myself.
'T is like you'll prove a jolly surly groom,
That take it on you at the first so roundly.
Pet.   O, Kate! content thee: pr'ythee, be not angry.
Kath.   I will be angry.   What hast thou to do?—
Father, be quiet; he shall stay my leisure.
Gre.   Ay, marry, sir, now it begins to work.
Kath.   Gentlemen, forward to the bridal dinner.
I see, a woman may be made a fool,
If she had not a spirit to resist.
Pet.   They shall go forward, Kate, at thy command.—
Obey the bride, you that attend on her:
Go to the feast, revel and domineer,
Carouse full measure to her maidenhead,
Be mad and merry, or go hang yourselves.
But for my bonny Kate, she must with me.
Nay, look not big, nor stamp nor stare, nor fret;
I will be master of what is mine own.
She is my goods, my chattels; she is my house,
My household stuff, my field, my barn,
My horse, my ox, my ass, my anything;
And here she stands; touch her whoever dare,
I'll bring mine action on the proudest he
That stops my way in Padua.—Grumio,
Draw forth thy weapon; we're beset with thieves:
Rescue thy mistress, if thou be a man.—
Fear not, sweet wench; they shall not touch thee, Kate:
I'll buckler thee against a million.

          [*Exeunt Petruchio, Katharina, and Grumio*

Bap.   Nay, let them go, a couple of quiet ones.
Gre.   Went they not quickly, I should die with laughing.
Tra.   Of all mad matches never was the like!

Luc.   Mistress, what's your opinion of your sister?
Bian. That, being mad herself, she's madly mated.
Gre.   I warrant him, Petruchio is Kated.
Bap.   Neighbours and friends, though bride and bride-
                groom wants
For to supply the places at the table,
You know, there wants no junkets at the feast.—
Lucentio shall supply the bridegroom's place,
And let Bianca take her sister's room.
Tra.   Shall sweet Bianca practise how to bride it?
Bap.   She shall, Lucentio.—Come, gentlemen, let's go.
                                                    [*Exeunt*

ACT FOUR

Scene I.—A Hall in Petruchio's Country House

Enter Grumio

Gru.   Fie, fie, on all tired jades, on all mad masters,
and all foul ways! Was ever man so beaten? was ever
man so rayed? was ever man so weary? I am sent before
to make a fire, and they are coming after to warm them.
Now, were not I a little pot, and soon hot, my very lips
might freeze to my teeth, my tongue to the roof of my
mouth, my heart in my belly, ere I should come by a fire
to thaw me; but I, with blowing the fire, shall warm myself
for, considering the weather, a taller man than I will take
cold. Holloa, hoa! Curtis!

Enter Curtis

Curt. Who is that, calls so coldly?
Gru.   A piece of ice: if thou doubt it, thou may'st slide
from my shoulder to my heel, with no greater a run but
my head and my neck. A fire, good Curtis.
Curt. Is my master and his wife coming, Grumio?
Gru.   O! ay, Curtis, ay; and therefore fire, fire; cast
on no water.
Curt. Is she so hot a shrew as she's reported?
Gru.   She was, good Curtis, before this frost; but, thou
know'st, winter tames man, woman, and beast, for it hath
tamed my old master, and my new mistress, and myself,
fellow Curtis.
Curt. Away, you three-inch fool! I am no beast.
Gru.   Am I but three inches? why, thy horn is a foot;
and so long am I at the least. But wilt thou make a fire,
or shall I complain on thee to our mistress, whose hand (she
being now at hand) thou shalt soon feel, to thy cold comfort
for being slow in thy hot office.

Curt. I pr'ythee, good Grumio, tell me, how goes the world?

Gru. A cold world, Curtis, in every office but thine; and, therefore, fire. Do thy duty, and have thy duty, for my master and mistress are almost frozen to death.

Curt. There's fire ready; and, therefore, good Grumio, the news.

Gru. Why, "Jack, boy! ho, boy!" and as much news as thou wilt.

Curt. Come, you are so full of cony-catching.

Gru. Why, therefore, fire: for I have caught extreme cold. Where's the cook? is supper ready, the house trimmed, rushes strewed, cobwebs swept; the serving-men in their new fustian, their white stockings, and every officer his wedding-garment on? Be the Jacks fair within, the Jills fair without, the carpets laid, and everything in order?

Curt. All ready; and therefore, I pray thee, news.

Gru. First, know, my horse is tired; my master and mistress fallen out.

Curt. How?

Gru. Out of their saddles into the dirt; and thereby hangs a tale.

Curt. Let's ha't, good Grumio.

Gru. Lend thine ear.

Curt. Here.

Gru. There.   [*Striking him*

Curt. This is to feel a tale, not to hear a tale.

Gru. And therefore 't is called a sensible tale; and this cuff was but to knock at your ear, and beseech listening. Now I begin: *Imprimis*, we came down a foul hill, my master riding behind my mistress,—

Curt. Both of one horse?

Gru. What's that to thee?

Curt. Why, a horse.

Gru. Tell thou the tale:—but hadst thou not crossed me, thou shouldst have heard how her horse fell, and she under her horse; thou shouldst have heard, in how miry a place; how she was bemoiled; how he left her with the horse upon her; how he beat me because her horse stumbled; how she waded through the dirt to pluck him off me; how he swore; how she prayed, that never prayed before; how I cried; how the horses ran away; how her bridle was burst; how I lost my crupper;—with many things of worthy memory which now shall die in oblivion, and thou return unexperienced to thy grave.

Curt. By this reckoning he is more shrew than she.

Gru. Ay: and that thou and the proudest of you all shall find, when he comes home. But what talk I of this?—

Call forth Nathaniel, Joseph, Nicholas, Philip, Walter, Sugarsop, and the rest: let their heads be sleekly combed, their blue coats brushed, and their garters of an indifferent knit; let them courtsy with their left legs, and not presume to touch a hair of my master's horsetail, till they kiss their hands. Are they all ready?

Curt. They are.

Gru. Call them forth.

Curt. Do you hear, ho! you must meet my master, to countenance my mistress.

Gru. Why, she hath a face of her own.

Curt. Who knows not that?

Gru. Thou, it seems, that callest for company to countenance her.

Curt. I call them forth to credit her.

Gru. Why, she comes to borrow nothing of them.

Enter Several Servants

Nath. Welcome home, Grumio.

Phil. How now, Grumio?

Jos. What, Grumio!

Nich. Fellow Grumio!

Nath. How now, old lad?

Gru. Welcome, you;—how now, you:—what, you; —fellow, you;—and thus much for greeting. Now, my spruce companions, is all ready and all things neat?

Nath. All things is ready. How near is our master?

Gru. E'en at hand, alighted by this; and therefore be not—Cock's passion, silence!—I hear my master.

Enter PETRUCHIO *and* KATHARINA

Pet. Where be these knaves? What! no man at door
To hold my stirrup, nor to take my horse?
Where is Nathaniel, Gregory, Philip?

All Serv. Here, here, sir; here, sir.

Pet. Here, sir! here, sir! here, sir! here, sir!
You logger-headed and unpolished grooms!
What, no attendance? no regard? no duty?
Where is the foolish knave I sent before?

Gru. Here, sir; as foolish as I was before.

Pet. You peasant swain! you whoreson malt-horse
        drudge!
Did I not bid thee meet me in the park,
And bring along these rascal knaves with thee?

Gru. Nathaniel's coat, sir, was not fully made,
And Gabriel's pumps were all unpinked i' the heel;
There was no link to colour Peter's hat,

And Walter's dagger was not come from sheathing:
There were none fine, but Adam, Ralph, and Gregory;
The rest were ragged, old, and beggarly;
Yet, as they are, here are they come to meet you.
    Pet. Go, rascals, go, and fetch my supper in.
                                        [Exeunt Servants
[Sings] Where is the life that late I led—
Where are those—? Sit down, Kate, and welcome,
Soud, soud, soud, soud!

Re-enter Servants with Supper

Why, when I say?—Nay, good sweet Kate, be merry,
Off with my boots, you rogues, you villains! When?
[Sings] It was the friar of orders grey,
      As he forth walkéd on his way:—
Out, you rogue! you pluck my foot awry:
Take that, and mend the plucking of the other.—
                                      [Strikes him
Be merry, Kate.—Some water, here: what, ho!—
Where's my spaniel Troilus?—Sirrah, get you hence,
And bid my cousin Ferdinand come hither:
                                      [Exit Servant
One, Kate, that you must kiss, and be acquainted with.—
Where are my slippers?—Shall I have some water?

Enter a Servant with a basin and ewer

Come, Kate, and wash, and welcome heartily.—
You whoreson villain! will you let it fall?
                                      [Strikes him
    Kath.   Patience, I pray you; 't was a fault unwilling.
    Pet. A whoreson, beetle-headed, flap-eared knave!
Come, Kate, sit down; I know you have a stomach.
Will you give thanks, sweet Kate, or else shall I?
What's this? mutton?
    First Serv.   Ay.
    Pet.   Who brought it?
    First Serv.   I.
    Pet. 'T is burnt; and so is all the meat.
What dogs are these!—Where is the rascal cook?
How durst you, villains, bring it from the dresser,
And serve it thus to me that love it not?
There, take it to you, trenchers, cups, and all.
                [Throws the meat, &c., at them
You heedless joltheads, and unmannered slaves!
What! do you grumble? I'll be with you straight.
    Kath. I pray you, husband, be not so disquiet:
The meat was well, if you were so contented.

Pet.   I tell thee, Kate, 't was burnt and dried away,
And I expressly am forbid to touch it,
For it engenders choler, planteth anger;
And better 't were that both of us did fast,—
Since, of ourselves, ourselves are choleric,—
Than feed it with such over-roasted flesh.
Be patient, to-morrow 't shall be mended,
And for this night we'll fast for company.
Come, I will bring thee to thy bridal chamber.

                    [*Exeunt Petruchio, Katharina, and Curtis*

Nath.   Peter, didst ever see the like?
Peter.   He kills her in her own humour.

Re-enter CURTIS

Gru.   Where is he?
Curt.   In her chamber,
Making a sermon of continency to her;
And rails, and swears, and rates, that she, poor soul,
Knows not which way to stand, to look, to speak,
And sits as one new-risen from a dream.
Away, away! for he is coming hither.   [*Exeunt*

Re-enter PETRUCHIO

Pet.   Thus have I politicly begun my reign,
And 't is my hope to end successfully.
My falcon now is sharp, and passing empty,
And, till she stoop she must not be full-gorged,
For then she never looks upon her lure,
Another way I have to man my haggard,
To make her come, and know her keeper's call;
That is, to watch her, as we watch these kites,
That bate and beat and will not be obedient.
She ate no meat to-day, nor none shall eat;
Last night she slept not, nor to-night she shall not:
As with the meat, some undeservéd fault
I'll find about the making of the bed;
And here I'll fling the pillow, there the bolster,
This way the coverlet, another way the sheets:—
Ay, and amid this hurly, I intend
That all is done in reverent care of her;
And, in conclusion, she shall watch all night:
And if she chance to nod, I'll rail and brawl,
And with the clamour keep her still awake.
This is a way to kill a wife with kindness;
And thus I'll curb her mad and headstrong humour.
He that knows better how to tame a shrew,
Now let him speak: 't is charity to show.   [*Exit*

127

SCENE II.—Padua. Before BAPTISTA'S House

Enter TRANIO *and* HORTENSIO

Tra. Is't possible, friend Licio, that Mistress Bianca
Doth fancy any other but Lucentio?
I tell you, sir, she bears me fair in hand.
Hor. Sir, to satisfy you in what I have said,
Stand by, and mark the manner of his teaching.
                                        [*They stand aside*

Enter BIANCA *and* LUCENTIO

Luc. Now, mistress, profit you in what you read?
Bian. What, master, read you? first resolve me that.
Luc. I read that I profess, the Art to Love.
Bian. And may you prove, sir, master of your art!
Luc. While you, sweet dear, prove mistress of my
            heart.   [*They retire*
Hor. [*Coming forward*] Quick proceeders, marry!
            Now tell me, I pray,
You that durst swear that your Mistress Bianca
Loved none in the world so well as Lucentio.
Tra. O despiteful love! unconstant womankind!
I tell thee, Licio, this is wonderful.—
Hor. Mistake no more; I am not Licio,
Nor a musician, as I seem to be,
But one that scorns to live in this disguise
For such a one, as leaves a gentleman
And makes a god of such a cullion,
Know, sir, that I am called Hortensio.
Tra. Signior Hortensio, I have often heard
Of your entire affection to Bianca;
And since mine eyes are witness of her lightness,
I will with you, if you be so contented,
Forswear Bianca and her love for ever.
Hor. See, how they kiss and court!—Signior Lucentio,
Here is my hand, and here I firmly vow
Never to woo her more; but do forswear her,
As one unworthy all the former favours
That I have fondly flattered her withal.
Tra. And here I take the like unfeignéd oath,
Never to marry with her, though she would entreat.
Fie on her! see, how beastly she doth court him.
Hor. Would all the world but he had quite forsworn!
For me, that I may surely keep mine oath,
I will be married to a wealthy widow,
Ere three days pass, which hath as long loved me,
As I have loved this proud disdainful haggard.

128

And so farewell, Signior Lucentio.—
Kindness in women, not their beauteous looks,
Shall win my love:—and so I take my leave,
In resolution as I swore before.

[Exit Hortensio.—Lucentio and Bianca advance

Tra.   Mistress Bianca, bless you with such grace,
As longeth to a lover's bléssed case!
Nay, I have ta'en you napping, gentle love,
And have forsworn you, with Hortensio.
  Bian.   Tranio, you jest.   But have you both forsworn
          me?
  Tra.   Mistress, we have.
  Luc.   Then we are rid of Licio.
  Tra.   I' faith, he'll have a lusty widow now,
That shall be woo'd and wedded in a day.
  Bian.   God give him joy!
  Tra.   Ay, and he'll tame her.
  Bian.   He says so, Tranio.
  Tra.   'Faith, he is gone unto the taming-school.
  Bian.   The taming-school!   what, is there such a
place?
  Tra.   Ay, mistress, and Petruchio is the master;
That teacheth tricks, eleven and twenty long,
To tame a shrew and charm her chattering tongue.

Enter BIONDELLO, *running*

  Bion.   O master, master! I have watched so long
That I'm dog-weary; but at last I spied
An ancient angel coming down the hill,
Will serve the turn.
  Tra.   What is he, Biondello?
  Bion.   Master, a mercatant, or a pedant,
I know not what; but formal in apparel,
In gait and countenance surely like a father.
  Luc.   And what of him, Tranio?
  Tra.   If he be credulous, and trust my tale,
I'll make him glad to seem Vincentio,
And give assurance to Baptista Minola,
As if he were the right Vincentio,
Take in your love, and then let me alone.

[Exeunt Lucentio and Bianca

Enter a Pedant

  Ped.   God save you, sir!
  Tra.   And you, sir! you are welcome.
Travel you far on, or are you at the farthest?
  Ped.   Sir, at the farthest for a week or two;

129

But then up farther, and as far as Rome,
And so to Tripoli, if God lend me life.
    Tra.   What countryman, I pray?
    Ped.   Of Mantua.
    Tra.   Of Mantua, sir?—marry, God forbid!
And come to Padua, careless of your life?
    Ped.   My life, sir! how, I pray? for that goes hard.
    Tra.   'T is death for any one in Mantua
To come to Padua.   Know you not the cause?
Your ships are stayed at Venice; and the duke,
For private quarrel 'twixt your duke and him,
Hath published and proclaimed it openly.
'T is marvel; but that you are but newly come,
You might have heard it else proclaimed about.
    Ped.   Alas, sir! it is worse for me than so;
For I have bills for money by exchange
From Florence, and must here deliver them.
    Tra.   Well, sir, to do you courtesy,
This will I do, and this I will advise you.—
First, tell me, have you ever been at Pisa?
    Ped.   Ay, sir, in Pisa have I often been;
Pisa, renownéd for grave citizens.
    Tra.   Among them, know you one Vincentio?
    Ped.   I know him not, but I have heard of him:
A merchant of incomparable wealth.
    Tra.   He is my father, sir; and, sooth to say,
In countenance somewhat doth resemble you.
    Bion. [*Aside*] As much as an apple doth an oyster,
              and all one.
    Tra.   To save your life in this extremity,
This favour will I do you for his sake;
And think it not the worst of all your fortunes,
That you are like to Sir Vincentio.
His name and credit shall you undertake,
And in my house you shall be friendly lodged,
Look, that you take upon you as you should!
You understand me, sir;—so shall you stay
Till you have done your business in the city.
If this be courtesy, sir, accept of it.
    Ped.   O! sir, I do; and will repute you ever
The patron of my life and liberty.
    Tra.   Then go with me, to make the matter good.
This by the way I let you understand;
My father is here looked for every day
To pass assurance of a dower in marriage
'Twixt me and one Baptista's daughter here:
In all these circumstances I'll instruct you.
Go with me, to clothe you as becomes you.

                                      [*Exeunt*

SCENE III.—A Room in PETRUCHIO'S House

Enter KATHARINA *and* GRUMIO

   Gru.   No, no, forsooth; I dare not, for my life.
   Kath.   The more my wrong, the more his spite appears.
What, did he marry me to famish me?
Beggars that come unto my father's door,
Upon entreaty, have a present alms;
If not, elsewhere they meet with charity:
But I, who never knew how to entreat,
Nor never needed that I should entreat,
Am starved for meat, giddy for lack of sleep;
With oaths kept waking, and with brawling fed.
And that which spites me more than all these wants,
He does it under name of perfect love;
As who should say, if I should sleep, or eat,
'T were deadly sickness, or else present death.
I pr'ythee go, and get me some repast;
I care not what, so it be wholesome food.
   Gru.   What say you to a neat's foot?
   Kath.   'T is passing good: I pr'ythee let me have it.
   Gru.   I fear, it is too choleric a meat.
How say you to a fat tripe, finely broiled?
   Kath.   I like it well; good Grumio, fetch it me.
   Gru.   I cannot tell; I fear, 't is choleric,
What say you to a piece of beef, and mustard?
   Kath.   A dish that I do love to feed upon.
   Gru.   Ay, but the mustard is too hot a little,
   Kath.   Why, then, the beef, and let the mustard rest.
   Gru.   Nay, then, I will not; you shall have the mustard,
Or else you get no beef of Grumio.
   Kath.   Then both, or one, or anything thou wilt.
   Gru.   Why, then, the mustard without the beef.
   Kath.   Go, get thee gone, thou false deluding slave,
                               [*Beats him*
That feed'st me with the very name of meat.
Sorrow on thee and all the pack of you
That triumph thus upon my misery!
Go, get thee gone, I say.

Enter PETRUCHIO, *with a dish of meat, and* HORTENSIO.

   Pet.   How fares my Kate? What, sweeting, all amort?
   Hor.   Mistress, what cheer?
   Kath.   'Faith, as cold as can be.
   Pet.   Pluck up thy spirits, look cheerfully upon me.
Here, love; thou seest how diligent I am,

131

To dress thy meat myself, and bring it thee:
                    [*Sets the dish on a table*
I am sure, sweet Kate, this kindness merits thanks,
What! not a word? Nay then, thou lov'st it not,
And all my pains is sorted to no proof.—
Here, take away this dish.
    Kath.   I pray you, let it stand.
    Pet. The poorest service is repaid with thanks.
And so shall mine, before you touch the meat.
    Kath. I thank you, sir.
    Hor. Signior Petruchio, fie! you are to blame.
Come, Mistress Kate, I'll bear you company.
    Pet. [*Aside*] Eat it all up, Hortensio, if thou lov'st
      me.—
Much good do it unto thy gentle heart!
Kate, eat apace.—And now, my honey love,
Will we return unto thy father's house,
And revel it as bravely as the best,
With silken coats, and caps, and golden rings,
With ruffs, and cuffs, and farthingales, and things;
With scarfs, and fans, and double change of bravery,
With amber bracelets, beads and all this knavery.
What, hast thou dined? The tailor stays thy leisure,
To deck thy body with his ruffling treasure.

Enter Tailor

Come, tailor, let us see these ornaments;
Lay forth the gown.—

Enter Haberdasher

               What news with you, sir?
    Hab. Here is the cap your worship did bespeak.
    Pet. Why, this was moulded on a porringer;
A velvet dish:—fie, fie! 't is lewd and filthy.
Why, 't is a cockle or a walnut-shell,
A knack, a toy, a trick, a baby's cap:
Away with it! come, let me have a bigger.
    Kath. I'll have no bigger: this doth fit the time,
And gentlewomen wear such caps as these.
    Pet. When you are gentle, you shall have one too;
And not till then.
    Hor. [*Aside*] That will not be in haste.
    Kath. Why, sir, I trust, I may have leave to speak,
And speak I will; I am no child, no babe:
Your betters have endured me say my mind,
And, if you cannot, best you stop your ears.
My tongue will tell the anger of my heart;
Or else my heart, concealing it, will break;

And, rather than it shall, I will be free
Even to the uttermost, as I please, in words.
    Pet.   Why, thou say'st true: it is a paltry cap,
A custard-coffin, a bauble, a silken pie.
I love thee well, in that thou lik'st it not.
    Kath.   Love me or love me not, I like the cap,
And it I will have, or I will have none.

                                    [*Exit Haberdasher*

    Pet.   Thy gown? why, ay:—come, tailor, let us see 't.
O, mercy, God! what masking stuff is here!
What's this? a sleeve? 't is like a demi-cannon:
What! up and down, carved like an apple-tart?
Here's snip, and nip, and cut, and slish, and slash,
Like to a censer in a barber's shop.—
Why, what, a devil's name, tailor, call'st thou this?
    Hor.   [*Aside*]   I see, she's like to have neither cap nor
            gown.
    Tai.   You bid me make it orderly and well,
According to the fashion and the time.
    Pet.   Marry, and did: but if you be remembered,
I did not bid you mar it to the time.
Go, hop me over every kennel home,
For you shall hop without my custom, sir.
I'll none of it: hence! make your best of it.
    Kath.   I never saw a better fashioned gown,
More quaint, more pleasing, nor more commendable.
Belike, you mean to make a puppet of me.
    Pet.   Why, true; he means to make a puppet of thee.
    Tai.   She says, your worship means to make a puppet
            of her.
    Pet.   O monstrous arrogance! Thou liest, thou thread,
Thou thimble,
Thou yard, three-quarters, half-yard, quarter, nail!
Thou flea, thou nit, thou winter-cricket thou!—
Braved in mine own house with a skein of thread?
Away! thou rag, thou quantity, thou remnant,
Or I shall so be-mete thee with thy yard
As thou shalt think on prating whilst thou liv'st!
I tell thee, I, that thou hast marred her gown.
    Tai.   Your worship is deceived; the gown is made
Just as my master had direction.
Grumio gave order how it should be done.
    Gru.   I gave him no order; I gave him the stuff.
    Tai.   But how did you desire it should be made?
    Gru.   Marry, sir, with needle and thread.
    Tai.   But did you not request to have it cut?
    Gru.   Thou hast faced many things.
    Tai.   I have.

                            133

Gru. Face not me; thou hast braved many men;
brave not me; I will neither be faced nor braved. I say
unto thee,—I bid thy master cut out the gown; but I did
not bid him cut it to pieces: *ergo,* thou liest.
Tai. Why, here is the note of the fashion to testify.
Pet. Read it.
Gru. The note lies in's throat, if he say I said so.
Tai. "*Imprimis,* a loose-bodied gown."
Gru. Master, if ever I said loose-bodied gown, sew
me in the skirts of it, and beat me to death with a bottom
of brown thread. I said, a gown.
Pet. Proceed.
Tai. "With a small compassed cape."
Gru. I confess the cape.
Tai. "With a trunk sleeve."
Gru. I confess two sleeves.
Tai. "The sleeves curiously cut."
Pet. Ay, there's the villainy.
Gru. Error i' the bill, sir; error i' the bill. I com-
manded the sleeves should be cut out, and sewed up again;
and that I'll prove upon thee, though thy little finger
be armed in a thimble.
Tai. This is true, that I say: an I had thee in place
where, thou shouldst know it.
Gru. I am for thee straight: take thou the bill, give
me thy mete-yard, and spare not me.
Hor. God-a-mercy, Grumio, then he shall have no
odds.
Pet. Well, sir, in brief, the gown is not for me.
Gru. You are i' the right, sir: 't is for my mistress.
Pet. Go, take it up unto thy master's use.
Gru. Villain, not for thy life! Take up my mistress'
gown for thy master's use!
Pet. Why, sir, what's your conceit in that?
Gru. O, sir, the conceit is deeper than you think for.
Take up my mistress' gown to his master's use!
O, fie, fie, fie!
Pet. [*Aside*] Hortensio, say thou wilt see the tailor
paid.—Go take it hence; be gone, and say no more.
Hor. Tailor, I'll pay thee for thy gown to-morrow:
Take no unkindness of his hasty words.
Away, I say: commend me to thy master.

[*Exit Tailor*

Pet. Well, come, my Kate; we will unto your father's,
Even in these honest mean habiliments.
Our purses shall be proud, our garments poor:
For 't is the mind that makes the body rich;
And as the sun breaks through the darkest clouds,

So honour peereth in the meanest habit.
What, is the jay more precious than the lark,
Because his feathers are more beautiful?
Or is the adder better than the eel,
Because his painted skin contents the eye?
O! no, good Kate; neither art thou the worse
For this poor furniture, and mean array.
If thou account'st it shame, lay it on me;
And therefore frolic; we will hence forthwith,
To feast and sport us at thy father's house.
Go, call my men, and let us straight to him;
And bring our horses unto Long Lane end;
There we will mount, and thither walk on foot.—
Let's see; I think, 't is now some seven o'clock,
And well we may come there by dinner-time.
　　Kath.　I dare assure you, sir, 't is almost two,
And 't will be supper-time, ere you come there.
　　Pet.　It shall be seven, ere I go to horse,
Look, what I speak, or do, or think to do,
You are still crossing it.—Sirs, let 't alone;
I will not go to-day; and ere I do,
It shall be what o'clock I say it is.
　　Hor.　Why, so this gallant will command the sun.
　　　　　　　　　　　　　　　　　　　　　　　[Exeunt

Scene IV.—Padua.　Before Baptista's House

Enter Tranio, *and the Pedant dressed like* Vincentio

　　Tra.　Sir, this is the house: please it you that I call?
　　Ped.　Ay, what else? and, but I be deceived,
Signior Baptista may remember me,
Near twenty years ago in Genoa,
Where we were lodgers at the Pegasus.
　　Tra.　'T is well; and hold your own, in any case,
With such austerity as 'longeth to a father.

Enter Biondello

　　Ped.　I warrant you.　But sir, here comes your boy;
'T were good he were school'd.
　　Tra.　Fear you not him.　Sirrah Biondello,
Now do your duty thoroughly, I advise you:
Imagine 't were the right Vincentio.
　　Bion.　Tut! fear not me.
　　Tra.　But hast thou done thy errand to Baptista?
　　Bion.　I told him that your father was at Venice,
And that you looked for him this day in Padua.

Tra. Thou'rt a tall fellow: hold thee that to drink.
Here comes Baptista.—Set your countenance, sir.

Enter BAPTISTA *and* LUCENTIO

Signior Baptista, you are happily met.
Sir, this is the gentleman I told you of.
I pray you stand good father to me now,
Give me Bianca for my patrimony.
    Ped. Soft, son!—
Sir, by your leave: having come to Padua
To gather in some debts, my son Lucentio
Made me acquainted with a weighty cause
Of love between your daughter and himself:
And, for the good report I hear of you,
And for the love he beareth to your daughter
And she to him,—to stay him not too long,
I am content, in a good father's care,
To have him match'd; and, if you please to like
No worse than I, sir, upon some agreement
Me shall you find most ready and most willing
With one consent to have her so bestowed;
For curious I cannot be with you,
Signior Baptista, of whom I hear so well.
    Bap. Sir, pardon me in what I have to say:
Your plainness, and your shortness please me well.
Right true is it, your son Lucentio here
Doth love my daughter, and she loveth him,
Or both dissemble deeply their affections;
And, therefore, if you say no more than this,
That like a father you will deal with him
And pass my daughter a sufficient dower,
The match is made at once, and all is done;
Your son shall have my daughter with consent.
    Tra. I thank you, sir. Where then do you know best
We be affied, and such assurance ta'en
As shall with either part's agreement stand?
    Bap. Not in my house, Lucentio; for, you know,
Pitchers have ears, and I have many servants.
Besides, old Gremio is hearkening still,
And, happily, we might be interrupted.
    Tra. Then at my lodging, an it like you, sir:
There doth my father lie, and there this night
We'll pass the business privately and well.
Send for your daughter by your servant here;
My boy shall fetch the scrivener presently.
The worst is this,—That, at so slender warning,
You're like to have a thin and slender pittance.
    Bap. It likes me well;—Cambio, hie you home,

And bid Bianca make her ready straight;
And, if you will, tell what hath happenéd:
Lucentio's father is arrived in Padua,
And how she's like to be Lucentio's wife.
    Luc. I pray the gods she may, with all my heart!
    Tra. Dally not with the gods, but get thee gone.—
Signior Baptista, shall I lead the way?
Welcome: one mess is like to be your cheer.
Come, sir; we will better it in Pisa.
    Bap. I follow you.

             [*Exeunt Tranio, Pedant, and Baptista*

    Bion. Cambio!—
    Luc. What say'st thou, Biondello?
    Bion. You saw my master wink and laugh upon you?
    Luc. Biondello, what of that?
    Bion. 'Faith, nothing; but he has left me here behind, to expound the meaning or moral of his signs and tokens.
    Luc. I pray thee, moralise them.
    Bion. Then thus. Baptista is safe, talking with the deceiving father of a deceitful son.
    Luc. And what of him?
    Bion. His daughter is to be brought by you to the supper.
    Luc. And then?—
    Bion. The old priest of Saint Luke's Church is at your command at all hours.
    Luc. And what of all this?
    Bion. I cannot tell, except they are busied about a counterfeit assurance; take you assurance of her, *cum privilegio ad imprimendum solum.* To the church!—take the priest, clerk, and some sufficient honest witnesses. If this be not that you look for, I have no more to say, But bid Bianca farewell for ever and a day.
    Luc. Hear'st thou, Biondello?
    Bion. I cannot tarry: I knew a wench married in an afternoon as she went to the garden for parsley to stuff a rabbit; and so may you, sir; and so adieu, sir. My master hath appointed me to go to Saint Luke's, to bid the priest be ready to come against you come with your appendix.

                        [*Exit*

    Luc. I may, and will, if she be so contented:
She will be pleased, then wherefore should I doubt?
Hap what hap may, I'll roundly go about her;
It shall go hard, if Cambio go without her.

                        [*Exit*

SCENE V.—A Public Road

Enter PETRUCHIO, KATHARINA, *and* HORTENSIO

Pet.   Come on, o' God's name; once more toward our
     father's.
Good Lord, how bright and goodly shines the moon!
   Kath.   The moon! the sun: it is not moonlight now.
   Pet.   I say, it is the moon that shines so bright.
   Kath.   I know, it is the sun that shines so bright.
   Pet.   Now, by my mother's son, and that 's myself,
It shall be moon, or star, or what I list,
Or ere I journey to your father's house.—
Go on, and fetch our horses back again.—
Evermore crossed, and crossed; nothing but crossed!
   Hor.   Say as he says, or we shall never go.
   Kath.   Forward, I pray, since we have come so far,
And be it moon, or sun, or what you please.
And if you please to call it a rush-candle,
Henceforth, I vow, it shall be so for me.
   Pet.   I say, it is the moon.
   Kath.   I know, it is the moon.
   Pet.   Nay, then you lie; it is the blessèd sun.
   Kath.   Then, God be bless'd, it is the blessèd sun;
But sun it is not, when you say it is not,
And the moon changes even as your mind.
What you will have it named, even that it is;
And so it shall be so for Katharine.
   Hor.   Petruchio, go thy ways; the field is won.
   Pet.   Well, forward, forward! thus the bowl should run,
And not unluckily against the bias.—
But soft; what company is coming here?

Enter VINCENTIO, *in a travelling dress*

[TO VINCENTIO]   Good morrow, gentle mistress; where
          away?—
Tell me, sweet Kate, and tell me truly too,
Hast thou beheld a fresher gentlewoman?
Such war of white and red within her cheeks!
What stars do spangle heaven with such beauty
As those two eyes become that heavenly face?—
Fair lovely maid, once more good day to thee.—
Sweet Kate, embrace her for her beauty's sake.
   Hor.   'A will make the man mad, to make a woman
of him.
   Kath.   Young budding virgin, fair and fresh and sweet,
Whither away, or where is thy abode?
Happy the parents of so fair a child;
Happier the man, whom favourable stars

138

Allot thee for his lovely bedfellow!

Pet. Why, how now, Kate? I hope thou art not mad:
This is a man, old, wrinkled, faded, withered,
And not a maiden, as thou say'st he is.

Kath. Pardon, old father, my mistaking eyes,
That have been so bedazzled with the sun,
That everything I look on seemeth green;
Now I perceive thou art a reverend father;
Pardon, I pray thee, for my mad mistaking.

Pet. Do, good old grandsire; and, withal, make known
Which way thou travellest; if along with us,
We shall be joyful of thy company.

Vin. Fair sir, and you my merry mistress,
That with your strange encounter much amaz'd me,
My name 's Vincentio; my dwelling, Pisa;
And bound I am to Padua, there to visit
A son of mine, which long I have not seen.

Pet. What is his name?

Vin.   Lucentio, gentle sir.

Pet. Happily met; the happier for thy son.
And now by law, as well as reverend age,
I may entitle thee—my loving father:
The sister to my wife, this gentlewoman,
Thy son by this hath married.   Wonder not,
Nor be not grieved; she is of good esteem,
Her dowry wealthy, and of worthy birth
Beside, so qualified as may beseem
The spouse of any noble gentleman.
Let me embrace with old Vincentio;
And wander we to see thy honest son,
Who will of thy arrival be full joyous.

Vin. But is this true? or is it else your pleasure,
Like pleasant travellers, to break a jest
Upon the company you overtake?

Hor. I do assure thee, father, so it is.

Pet. Come, go along, and see the truth hereof;
For our first merriment hath made thee jealous.

            [*Exeunt Petruchio, Katharina, and Vincentio*

Hor. Well, Petruchio, this has put me in heart.
Have to my widow; and if she be froward,
Then hast thou taught Hortensio to be untoward.   [*Exit*

139

ACT FIVE

Scene I.—Padua. Before Lucentio's House

Enter on one side Biondello, Lucentio, *and* Bianca;
Gremio *walking on the other side*

Bion. Softly and swiftly, sir, for the priest is ready.
Luc. I fly, Biondello; but they may chance to need
thee at home: therefore leave us.
Bion. Nay, 'faith, I'll see the church o' your back;
and then come back to my master as soon as I can.
                [*Exeunt Lucentio, Bianca, and Biondello*
Gre. I marvel Cambio comes not all this while.

Enter Petruchio, Katharina, Vincentio, *and
Attendants*

Pet. Sir, here's the door, this is Lucentio's house:
My father's bears more toward the market-place;
Thither must I, and here I leave you, sir.
Vin. You shall not choose but drink before you go.
I think I shall command your welcome here,
And, by all likelihood, some cheer is toward.   [*Knocks*
Gre. They're busy within; you were best knock
louder.

Enter Pedant above, at a window

Ped. What 's he, that knocks as he would beat down
the gate?
Vin. Is Signior Lucentio within, sir?
Ped. He's within, sir, but not to be spoken withal.
Vin. What, if a man bring him a hundred pound or two,
to make merry withal?
Ped. Keep your hundred pounds to yourself: he shall
need none, so long as I live.
Pet. Nay, I told you, your son was well beloved in
Padua.—Do you hear, sir?—to leave frivolous circum-
stances,—I pray you, tell Signior Lucentio, that his father
is come from Pisa, and is here at the door to speak with him.
Ped. Thou liest; his father is come from Pisa, and here
looking out of the window.
Vin. Art thou his father?
Ped. Ay, sir; so his mother says, if I may believe her.
Pet. [To Vincentio] Why, how now, gentleman!
Why, this is flat knavery, to take upon you another man's
name.

Ped. Lay hands on the villain. I believe, 'a means to cozen somebody in this city under my countenance.

Re-enter BIONDELLO

Bion. I have seen them in the church together: God send 'em good shipping!—But who is here? mine old master, Vincentio! now we are undone, and brought to nothing.

Vin. [*Seeing* BIONDELLO] Come hither, crack-hemp.

Bion. I hope I may choose, sir.

Vin. Come hither, you rogue. What, have you forgot me?

Bion. Forgot you? no, sir: I could not forget you, for I never saw you before in all my life.

Vin. What, you notorious villain, didst thou never see thy master's father, Vincentio?

Bion. What, my old, worshipful old master? yes, marry, sir; see where he looks out of the window.

Vin. Is 't so, indeed?   [*Beats* BIONDELLO

Bion. Help, help, help! here's a madman will murder me.   [*Exit*

Ped. Help, son! help, Signior Baptista!
        [*Exit from the window*

Pet. Pr'ythee, Kate, let's stand aside, and see the end of this controversy.   [*They retire*

Re-enter Pedant below; BAPTISTA, TRANIO, *and Servants*

Tra. Sir, what are you, that offer to beat my servant?

Vin. What am I, sir? nay, what are you, sir?—O immortal gods! O fine villain! a silken doublet! a velvet hose! a scarlet cloak! and a copatain hat!—O, I am undone! I am undone! while I play the good husband at home, my son and my servant spend all at the university.

Tra. How now? what 's the matter?

Bap. What, is the man lunatic?

Tra. Sir, you seem a sober ancient gentleman by your habit, but your words show you a madman. Why, sir, what 'cerns it you if I wear pearl and gold? I thank my good father, I am able to maintain it.

Vin. Thy father? O villain! he is a sail-maker in Bergamo.

Bap. You mistake, sir: you mistake, sir. Pray, what do you think is his name?

Vin. His name? as if I knew not his name; I have brought him up ever since he was three years old, and his name is Tranio.

Ped. Away, away, mad ass! his name is Lucentio;
and he is mine only son, and heir to the lands of me, Signior
Vincentio.

Vin. Lucentio! O! he hath murdered his master!
Lay hold on him, I charge you, in the duke's name.—
O, my son, my son!—Tell me, thou villain, where is my
son Lucentio?

Tra. Call forth an officer.

Enter one with an Officer

Carry this mad knave to the gaol.—Father Baptista, I
charge you see that he be forthcoming.

Vin. Carry me to the gaol!

Gre. Stay, officer; he shall not go in prison.

Bap. Talk not, Signior Gremio. I say, he shall go to
prison.

Gre. Take heed, Signior Baptista, lest you be cony-
catched in this business. I dare swear this is the right
Vincentio.

Ped. Swear, if thou darest.

Gre. Nay, I dare not swear it.

Tra. Then thou wert best say, that I am not Lucentio.

Gre. Yes, I know thee to be Signior Lucentio.

Bap. Away with the dotard! to the gaol with him!

Vin. Thus strangers may be haled and abused.—
O monstrous villain!

Re-enter BIONDELLO, *with* LUCENTIO *and* BIANCA

Bion. O, we are spoiled! and yonder he is! deny him,
Forswear him, or else we are all undone.

Luc. Pardon, sweet father.   [*Kneeling*

Vin.   Lives my sweet son!
                    [*Biondello, Tranio and Pedant run out*

Bion. Pardon, dear father.   [*Kneeling*

Bap.   How hast thou offended?
Where is Lucentio?

Luc.   Here's Lucentio,
Right son to the right Vincentio;
That have by marriage made thy daughter mine.
While counterfeit supposes blear'd thine eyne.

Gre. Here's packing with a witness, to deceive us all!

Vin. Where is that damnéd villain, Tranio,
That faced and braved me in this matter so?

Bap. Why, tell me, is not this my Cambio!

Bion. Cambio is changed into Lucentio.

Luc. Love wrought these miracles. Bianca's love
Made me exchange my state with Tranio,
While he did bear my countenance in the town;

And happily I have arrived at the last
Unto the wishéd haven of my bliss.
What Tranio did, myself ·enforced him to;
Then pardon him, sweet father, for my sake.
    Vin. I'll slit the villain's nose, that would have sent
me to the gaol.
    Bap. [To LUCENTIO] But do you hear, sir? Have
you married my daughter without asking my good will?
    Vin. Fear not, Baptista; we will content you: go to;
but I will in, to be revenged for this villainy.   [*Exit*
    Bap. And I, to sound the depth of this knavery.
                                     [*Exit*
    Luc. Look not pale, Bianca; thy father will not frown.
                     [*Exeunt Lucentio and Bianca*
    Gre. My cake is dough; but I'll in among the rest,
Out of hope of all but my share of the feast.   [*Exit*

PETRUCHIO *and* KATHARINA *advance*

    Kath. Husband, let's follow, to see the end of this ado.
    Pet. First kiss me, Kate, and we will.
    Kath. What, in the midst of the street?
    Pet. What! art thou ashamed of me?
    Kath. No, sir, God forbid; but ashamed to kiss.
    Pet. Why, then let's home again.—Come, sirrah, let's
        away.
    Kath. Nay, I will give thee a kiss: now pray thee, love,
        stay.
    Pet. Is not this well?—Come, my sweet Kate:
Better once than never, for never too late.   [*Exeunt*

SCENE II.—A Room in LUCENTIO'S House

A Banquet set out. Enter BAPTISTA, VINCENTIO, GREMIO,
the Pedant, LUCENTIO, BIANCA, PETRUCHIO, KATHARINA,
HORTENSIO, *and Widow;* TRANIO, BIONDELLO, GRUMIO,
and others, attending

    Luc. At last, though long, our jarring notes agree:
And time it is, when raging war is done,
To smile at scapes and perils overblown.—
My fair Bianca, bid my father welcome,
While I with selfsame kindness welcome thine.—
Brother Petruchio,—sister Katharina,—
And thou, Hortensio, with thy loving widow,
Feast with the best, and welcome to my house:
My banquet is to close our stomachs up,

After our great good cheer.   Pray you, sit down:
For now we sit to chat, as well as eat.
                                    [*They sit at table*
  Pet. Nothing but sit and sit, and eat and eat!
  Bap. Padua affords this kindness, son Petruchio.
  Pet. Padua affords nothing but what is kind.
  Hor. For both our sakes I would that word were true.
  Pet. Now, for my life, Hortensio fears his widow.
  Wid. Then never trust me, if I be afeard.
  Pet. You are very sensible, and yet you miss my sense;
I mean, Hortensio is afeard of you.
  Wid. He that is giddy thinks the world turns round.
  Pet. Roundly replied.
  Kath.   Mistress, how mean you that?
  Wid. Thus I conceive by him.
  Pet. Conceives by me!—How likes Hortensio that?
  Hor. My widow says, thus she conceives her tale.
  Pet. Very well mended. Kiss him for that, good
widow.
  Kath. He that is giddy thinks the world turns round:—
I pray you, tell me what you meant by that.
  Wid. Your husband, being troubled with a shrew,
Measures my husband's sorrow by his woe:
And now you know my meaning.
  Kath. A very mean meaning.
  Wid.   Right, I mean you.
  Kath. And I am mean, indeed, respecting you.
  Pet. To her, Kate!
  Hor. To her, widow!
  Pet. A hundred marks, my Kate does put her down.
  Hor. That's my office.
  Pet. Spoke like an officer.—Ha' to thee, lad.
                                    [*Drinks* to HORTENSIO
  Bap. How likes Gremio these quick-witted folks?
  Gre. Believe me, sir, they butt together well.
  Bian. Head and butt? and hasty-witted body
Would say, your head and butt were head and horn.
  Vin. Ay, mistress bride, hath that awakened you?
  Bian. Ay, but not frighted me; therefore, I'll sleep
again.
  Pet. Nay, that thou shalt not; since you have begun,
Have at you for a bitter jest or two.
  Bian. Am I your bird? I mean to shift my bush,
And then pursue me as you draw your bow.—
You are welcome all.
                    [*Exeunt Bianca, Katharina, and Widow*
  Pet. She hath prevented me.—Here, Signior Tranio;
This bird you aimed at, though you hit her not:
Therefore, a health to all that shot and missed.

Tra. O sir! Lucentio slipp'd me, like his greyhound,
Which runs himself, and catches for his master.
    Pet. A good swift simile, but something currish.
    Tra. 'T is well, sir, that you hunted for yourself:
'T is thought, your deer does hold you at a bay.
    Bap. O ho, Petruchio! Tranio hits you now.
    Luc. I thank thee for that gird, good Tranio.
    Hor. Confess, confess, hath he not hit you here?
    Pet. 'A has a little galled me, I confess;
And, as the jest did glance away from me,
'T is ten to one it maimed you two outright.
    Bap. Now, in good sadness, son Petruchio,
I think thou hast the veriest shrew of all.
    Pet. Well, I say no; and therefore, for assurance,
Let's each one send unto his wife;
And he, whose wife is most obedient
To come at first when he doth send for her,
Shall win the wager which we will propose.
    Hor. Content. What is the wager?
    Luc.   Twenty crowns.
    Pet. Twenty crowns!
I'll venture so much on my hawk or hound,
But twenty times so much upon my wife.
    Luc. A hundred then.
    Hor.   Content.
    Pet.   A match! 't is done.
    Hor. Who shall begin?
    Luc.   That will I.
Go, Biondello, bid your mistress come to me.
    Bion. I go.   *[Exit*
    Bap. Son, I will be your half, Bianca comes.
    Luc. I'll have no halves; I'll bear it all myself.

Re-enter BIONDELLO

How now! what news?
    Bion.   Sir, my mistress sends you word,
That she is busy, and she cannot come.
    Pet. How! she is busy, and she cannot come!
Is that an answer?
    Gre.   Ay, and a kind one too:
Pray God, sir, your wife send you not a worse.
    Pet. I hope, better.
    Hor. Sirrah Biondello, go, and entreat my wife
To come to me forthwith.   *[Exit Bion.*
    Pet.   O ho! entreat her!
Nay, then she must needs come.
    Hor.   I am afraid, sir,
Do what you can, yours will not be entreated.

Re-enter BIONDELLO

Now, where's my wife?
   Bion. She says, you have some goodly jest in hand;
She will not come: she bids you come to her.
   Pet. Worse and worse: she will not come? O vile,
Intolerable, not to be endured!
Sirrah, Grumio, go to your mistress; say,
I command her come to me.   *[Exit Grumio*
   Hor.   I know her answer.
   Pet. What?
   Hor. She will not.
   Pet. The fouler fortune mine, and there an end.

Enter KATHARINA

   Bap. Now, by my halidome, here comes Katharina!
   Kath. What is your will, sir, that you send for me.
   Pet. Where is your sister, and Hortensio's wife?
   Kath. They sit conferring by the parlour fire.
   Pet. Go, fetch them hither: if they deny to come,
Swinge me them soundly forth unto their husbands.
Away, I say, and bring them hither straight.
        [Exit Katharina
   Luc. Here is a wonder, if you talk of a wonder.
   Hor. And so it is. I wonder what it bodes.
   Pet. Marry, peace it bodes, and love, and quiet life,
An awful rule, and right supremacy;
And, to be short, what not that's sweet and happy?
   Bap. Now fair befall thee, good Petruchio!
The wager thou hast won; and I will add
Unto their losses twenty thousand crowns;—
Another dowry to another daughter,
For she is changed, as she had never been.
   Pet. Nay, I will win my wager better yet,
And show more sign of her obedience,
Her new-built virtue and obedience.
See, where she comes, and brings your froward wives
As prisoners to her womanly persuasion.—

Re-enter KATHARINA *with* BIANCA *and* Widow

Katharine, that cap of yours becomes you not:
Off with that bauble, throw it under foot.
      *[*KATHARINA *pulls off her cap, and throws it down*
   Wid. Lord! let me never have a cause to sigh,
Till I be brought to such a silly pass!
   Bian. Fie! what a foolish duty call you this?
   Luc. I would, your duty were as foolish too:
The wisdom of your duty, fair Bianca,

Hath cost me an hundred crowns since supper-time.
    Bian. The more fool you for laying on my duty.
    Pet. Katharine, I charge thee, tell these headstrong women
What duty they do owe their lords and husbands.
    Wid. Come, come, you're mocking: we will have no telling.
    Pet. Come on, I say; and first begin with her.
    Wid. She shall not.
    Pet. I say she shall:—and first begin with her.
    Kath. Fie, fie! unknit that threatening unkind brow,
And dart not scornful glances from those eyes
To wound thy lord, thy king, thy governor:
It blots thy beauty, as frosts do bite the meads,
Confounds thy fame as whirlwinds shake fair buds,
And in no sense is meet or amiable.
A woman moved is like a fountain troubled,
Muddy, ill-seeming, thick, bereft of beauty;
And, while it is so, none so dry or thirsty
Will deign to sip, or touch one drop of it.
Thy husband is thy lord, thy life, thy keeper,
Thy head, thy sovereign; one that cares for thee,
And for thy maintenance; commits his body
To painful labour, both by sea and land,
To watch the night in storms, the day in cold,
Whilst thou liest warm at home, secure and safe;
And craves no other tribute at thy hands,
But love, fair looks, and true obedience,
Too little payment for so great a debt.
Such duty as the subject owes the prince,
Even such a woman oweth to her husband;
And when she's froward, peevish, sullen, sour,
And not obedient to his honest will,
What is she but a foul contending rebel,
And graceless traitor to her loving lord?
I am ashamed, that women are so simple
To offer war, where they should kneel for peace;
Or seek for rule, supremacy, and sway,
When they are bound to serve, love and obey.
Why are our bodies soft, and weak, and smooth,
Unapt to toil and trouble in the world,
But that our soft conditions, and our hearts,
Should well agree with our external parts?
Come, come, you froward and unable worms,
My mind hath been as big as one of yours,
My heart as great, my reason, haply, more
To bandy word for word, and frown for frown;
But now I see, our lances are but straws,
Our strength as weak, our weakness past compare,—

That seeming to be most, which we indeed least are.
Then vail your stomachs, for it is no boot,
And place your hands below your husband's foot:
In token of which duty, if he please,
My hand is ready; may it do him ease.

    Pet.   Why, there's a wench!—Come on, and kiss me, Kate.

    Luc.   Well, go thy ways, old lad, for thou shalt ha't.

    Vin.   'T is a good hearing, when children are toward.

    Luc.   But a harsh hearing, when women are froward.

    Pet.   Come, Kate, we'll to bed.—

We three are married, but you two are sped.
'T was I won the wager, though you hit the white;
And being a winner, God give you good night.

                          [*Exeunt Petruchio and Katharina*

    Hor.   Now go thy ways, thou hast tamed a curst shrew.

    Luc.   'T is a wonder, by your leave, she will be tamed so.

                                 [*Exeunt*

THE TEMPEST

DRAMATIS PERSONÆ

ALONSO, *king of Naples*
SEBASTIAN, *his brother*
PROSPERO, *the rightful Duke of Milan*
ANTONIO, *his brother, the usurping Duke of Milan*
FERDINAND, *son to the King of Naples*
GONZALO, *an honest old Counsellor*
ADRIAN, } *Lords*
FRANCISCO, }
CALIBAN, *a savage and deformed Slave*
TRINCULO, *a Jester*
STEPHANO, *a drunken Butler*
Master of a Ship
Boatswain
Mariners

MIRANDA, *daughter to Prospero*

ARIEL, *an airy Spirit*
IRIS,
CERES,
JUNO, } *Spirits*
Nymphs,
Reapers,

Other Spirits attending on Prospero

SCENE.—*The Sea, with a Ship: an Island*

150

THE TEMPEST

ACT ONE

SCENE I.—On a Ship at Sea. A tempestuous noise of
Thunder and Lightning heard

Enter a Ship-Master and a Boatswain

Mast. Boatswain!

Boats. Here, master: what cheer?

Mast. Good, speak to the mariners: fall to 't yarely,
or we run ourselves aground: bestir, bestir.   [*Exit*

Enter Mariners

Boats. Heigh, my hearts! cheerly, cheerly, my hearts!
yare, yare. Take in the topsail; tend to the master's
whistle.—Blow, till thou burst thy wind, if room enough.

Enter ALONSO, SEBASTIAN, ANTONIO, FERDINAND,
GONZALO, *and others*

Alon. Good boatswain, have care. Where's the master?
Play the men.

Boats. I pray now, keep below.

Ant. Where is the master, boatswain?

Boats. Do you not hear him? You mar our labour.
Keep your cabins; you do assist the storm.

Gon. Nay, good, be patient.

Boats. When the sea is. Hence! What care these
roarers for the name of king? To cabin: silence! trouble
us not.

Gon. Good, yet remember whom thou hast aboard.

Boats. None that I more love than myself. You are
a counsellor: if you can command these elements to silence,
and work the peace of the present, we will not hand a
rope more; use your authority: if you cannot, give
thanks you have lived so long, and make yourself ready
in your cabin for the mischance of the hour, if it so hap.—
Cheerly, good hearts!—Out of our way, I say.   [*Exit*

Gon. I have great comfort from this fellow: methinks,
he hath no drowning mark upon him; his complexion is
perfect gallows. Stand fast, good Fate, to his hanging!
make the rope of his destiny our cable, for our own doth

Act I Sc i

little advantage! If he be not born to be hanged, our case is miserable. *[Exeunt*

Re-enter Boatswain

Boats. Down with the topmast: yare; lower, lower. Bring her to try with main-course. [*A cry within*]. A plague upon this howling! they are louder than the weather, or our office.—

Re-enter SEBASTIAN, ANTONIO, *and* GONZALO

Yet again! what do you here? Shall we give o'er, and drown? Have you a mind to sink?
Seb. A pox o' your throat, you bawling, blasphemous, incharitable dog!
Boats. Work you, then.
Ant. Hang, cur, hang, you whoreson, insolent noisemaker, we are less afraid to be drowned than thou art.
Gon. I'll warrant him for drowning, though the ship were no stronger than a nutshell, and as leaky as an unstanched wench.
Boats. Lay her a-hold, a-hold! Set her two courses off to sea again; lay her off.

Enter Mariners, wet

Mar. All lost! to prayers, to prayers! all lost!
[Exeunt
Boats. What, must our mouths be cold?
Gon. The king and prince at prayers; let's assist them, For our case is as theirs.
Seb. I am out of patience.
Ant. We are merely cheated of our lives by drunkards.—
This wide-chopp'd rascal,—'would, thou might'st lie drowning,
The washing of ten tides!
Gon. He'll be hang'd yet,
Though every drop of water swear against it,
And gape at wid'st to glut him.
[*A confused noise within*] Mercy on us!—
We split, we split!—Farewell, my wife and children!—
Farewell, brother!—We split, we split, we split!—
Ant. Let's all sink with the king. *[Exit*
Seb. Let's take leave of him. *[Exit*
Gon. Now would I give a thousand furlongs of sea for an acre of barren ground; long heath, brown furze, anything. The wills above be done, but I would fain die a dry death. *[Exit*

SCENE II.—The Island: before the Cell of PROSPERO

Enter PROSPERO *and* MIRANDA

Mira.   If by your art, my dearest father, you have
Put the wild waters in this roar, allay them.
The sky, it seems, would pour down stinking pitch,
But that the sea, mounting to the welkin's cheek,
Dashes the fire out.   Oh! I have suffered
With those that I saw suffer: a brave vessel,
Who had no doubt some noble creatures in her,
Dashed all to pieces.   Oh! the cry did knock
Against my very heart.   Poor souls, they perished.
Had I been any god of power, I would
Have sunk the sea within the earth, or ere
It should the good ship so have swallowed, and
The fraughting souls within her.

    Pro.   Be collected:
No more amazement.   Tell your piteous heart
There's no harm done.

    Mira.   O, woe the day!

    Pro.   No harm.
I have done nothing but in care of thee
(Of thee, my dear one! thee, my daughter), who
Art ignorant of what thou art, nought knowing
Of whence I am; nor that I am more better
Than Prospero, master of a full poor cell,
And thy no greater father.

    Mira.   More to know
Did never meddle with my thoughts.

    Pro.   'T is time
I should inform thee further.   Lend thy hand
And pluck my magic garment from me.—So:
                    [*Lays down his mantle*
Lie there, my art.—Wipe thou thine eyes; have comfort.
The direful spectacle of the wreck, which touched
The very virtue of compassion in thee,
I have with such provision in mine art
So safely ordered, that there is no soul—
No, not so much perdition as an hair,
Betid to any creature in the vessel
Which thou heard'st cry, which thou saw'st sink.   Sit
        down;
For thou must now know farther.

    Mira.   You have often
Begun to tell me what I am; but stopped,
And left me to a bootless inquisition,
Concluding, "Stay, not yet."

Pro.   The hour's now come,
The very minute bids thee ope thine ear;
Obey, and be attentive.   Canst thou remember
A time before we came unto this cell?
I do not think thou canst, for then thou wast not
Out three years old.
    Mira.   Certainly, sir, I can.
    Pro.   By what? by any other house, or person?
Of anything the image, tell me, that
Hath kept with thy remembrance.
    Mira.   'T is far off;
And rather like a dream, than an assurance
That my remembrance warrants: had I not
Four or five women once, that tended me?
    Pro.   Thou hadst, and more, Miranda.   But how is it,
That this lives in thy mind?   What seest thou else
In the dark backward and abysm of time?
If thou remember'st aught ere thou cam'st here,
How thou cam'st here thou may'st.
    Mira.   But that I do not.
    Pro.   Twelve year since, Miranda, twelve year since,
Thy father was the Duke of Milan, and
A prince of power.
    Mira.   Sir, are not you my father?
    Pro.   Thy mother was a piece of virtue, and
She said—thou wast my daughter; and thy father
Was Duke of Milan, and his only heir
A princess;—no worse issued.
    Mira.   O, the heavens!
What foul play had we, that we came from thence?
Or blessèd was 't, we did?
    Pro.   Both, both, my girl:
By foul play, as thou say'st, were we heaved thence;
But blessedly holp hither.
    Mira.   O! my heart bleeds
To think o' the teen that I have turn'd you to,
Which is from my remembrance.   Please you, farther.
    Pro.   My brother, and thy uncle, called Antonio,—
I pray thee, mark me,—that a brother should
Be so perfidious!—he whom, next thyself,
Of all the world I loved, and to him put
The manage of my state, as, at that time,
Through all the signiories it was the first,
And Prospero the prime duke; being so reputed
In dignity, and for the liberal arts,
Without a parallel: those being all my study,
The government I cast upon my brother,
And to my state grew stranger, being transported,
And rapt in secret studies.   Thy false uncle—

Dost thou attend me?
   Mira.   Sir, most heedfully.
   Pro.   Being once perfected how to grant suits,
How to deny them, who to advance, and who
To trash for over-topping, new created
The creatures that were mine, I say, or changed them,
Or else new formed them: having both the key
Of officer and office, set all hearts i' the state
To what tune pleased his ear; that now he was
The ivy, which had hid my princely trunk,
And sucked my verdure out on 't.—Thou attend'st not.
   Mira.   O, good sir, I do.
   Pro.   I pray thee, mark me.—
I, thus neglecting worldly ends, all dedicated
To closeness and the bettering of my mind
With that which, but by being so retired,
O'er-prized all popular rate, in my false brother
Awakened an evil nature, and my trust,
Like a good parent, did beget of him
A falsehood, in its contrary as great
As my trust was, which had, indeed, no limit,
A confidence sans bound. He being thus lorded,
Not only with what my revenue yielded,
But what my power might else exact,—like one,
Who having, unto truth, by telling of it,
Made such a sinner of his memory,
To credit his own lie,—he did believe
He was indeed the duke; out o' the substitution,
And executing the outward face of royalty,
With all prerogative: hence his ambition growing,—
Dost thou hear?
   Mira.   Your tale, sir, would cure deafness.—
   Pro.   To have no screen between this part he played,
And him he played it for, he needs will be
Absolute Milan. Me, poor man, my library
Was dukedom large enough: of temporal royalties
He thinks me now incapable; confederates
(So dry he was for sway) with the King of Naples,
To give him annual tribute, do him homage,
Subject his coronet to his crown, and bend
The dukedom, yet unbowed, (alas, poor Milan!)
To most ignoble stooping.
   Mira.   O the heavens!
   Pro.   Mark his condition, and the event, then tell me
If this might be a brother.
   Mira.   I should sin
To think but nobly of my grandmother:
Good wombs have borne bad sons.
   Pro.   Now the condition.

This King of Naples, being an enemy
To me inveterate, hearkens my brother's suit;
Which was, that he in lieu o' the premises,
Of homage, and I know not how much tribute,
Should presently extirpate me and mine
Out of the dukedom, and confer fair Milan,
With all the honours, on my brother: whereon,
A treacherous army levied, one midnight
Fated to the purpose, did Antonio open
The gates of Milan; and, i' the dead of darkness,
The ministers for the purpose hurried thence
Me, and thy crying self.
   Mira.   Alack, for pity!
I, not remembering how I cried out then,
Will cry it o'er again: it is a hint,
That wrings mine eyes to 't.
   Pro.   Hear a little further,
And then I'll bring thee to the present business
Which now 's upon 's: without the which this story
Were most impertinent.
   Mira.   Wherefore did they not
That hour destroy us?
   Pro.   Well demanded, wench:
My tale provokes that question.   Dear, they durst not,
So dear the love my people bore me, nor set
A mark so bloody on the business; but
With colours fairer painted their foul ends.
In few, they hurried us aboard a bark,
Bore us some leagues to sea; where they prepared
A rotten carcass of a boat, not rigg'd,
Nor tackle, sail, nor mast; the very rats
Instinctively had quit it, there they hoist us,
To cry to the sea that roared to us: to sigh
To the winds, whose pity, sighing back again,
Did us but loving wrong.
   Mira.   Alack! what trouble
Was I then to you!
   Pro.   O, a cherubin
Thou wast, that did preserve me.   Thou didst smile,
Infuséd with a fortitude from heaven,
When I have decked the sea with drops full salt,
Under my burden groaned; which raised in me
An undergoing stomach, to bear up
Against what should ensue.
   Mira.   How came we ashore?
   Pro. By Providence divine.
Some food we had, and some fresh water, that
A noble Neapolitan, Gonzalo,
Out of his charity (who being then appointed

Master of this design) did give us, with
Rich garments, linens, stuffs, and necessaries,
Which since have steaded much: so, of his gentleness,
Knowing I loved my books, he furnished me,
From my own library, with volumes that
I prize above my dukedom.
    Mira.   Would I might
But ever see that man!
    Pro.   Now I arise.
Sit still, and hear the last of our sea-sorrow.
Here in this island we arrived; and here
Have I, thy schoolmaster, made thee more profit
Than other princess' can, that have more time
For vainer hours, and tutors not so careful.
    Mira. Heavens thank you for 't! And now I pray
you, sir,
For still 'tis beating in my mind, your reason
For raising this sea-storm?
    Pro.   Know thus far forth.—
By accident most strange, bountiful Fortune,
Now my dear lady, hath mine enemies
Brought to this shore; and by my prescience
I find my zenith doth depend upon
A most auspicious star, whose influence
If now I court not, but omit, my fortunes
Will ever after droop. Here cease more questions.
Thou art inclined to sleep; 'tis a good dulness,
And give it way:—I know thou canst not choose.—
                        [MIRANDA *sleeps*
Come away, servant, come! I am ready now.
Approach, my Ariel: come!

Enter ARIEL

    Ari. All hail, great master; grave sir, hail! I come
To answer thy best pleasure; be 't to fly,
To swim, to dive into the fire, to ride
On the curled clouds: to thy strong bidding, task
Ariel, and all his quality.
    Pro.   Hast thou, spirit,
Performed to point the Tempest that I bade thee?
    Ari. To every article.
I boarded the king's ship; now on the beak,
Now in the waist, the deck, in every cabin,
I flamed amazement: sometimes, I'd divide,
And burn in many places; on the topmast,
The yards and bowsprit, would I flame distinctly,
Then meet and join. Jove's lightnings, the precursors
O' the dreadful thunder-claps, more momentary

And sight-outrunning were not: the fire, and cracks
Of sulphurous roaring the most mighty Neptune
Seem to besiege, and make his bold waves tremble,
Yes, his dread trident shake.
 Pro.   My brave spirit!
Who was so firm, so constant, that this coil
Would not infect his reason?
 Ari.   Not a soul
But felt a fever of the mad, and played
Some tricks of desperation. All, but mariners,
Plung'd in the foaming brine, and quit the vessel,
Then all a-fire with me: the king's son, Ferdinand,
With hair up-staring (then like reeds, not hair),
Was the first man that leap'd; cried, "Hell is empty,
And all the devils are here."
 Pro.   Why, that's my spirit!
But was not this nigh shore?
 Ari.   Close by, my master.
 Pro. But are they, Ariel, safe?
 Ari.   Not a hair perish'd;
On their sustaining garments not a blemish,
But fresher than before; and, as thou bad'st me,
In troops I have dispersed them 'bout the isle.
The king's son have I landed by himself,
Whom I left cooling of the air with sighs,
In an odd angle of the isle, and sitting,
His arms in this sad knot.
 Pro.   Of the king's ship
The mariners, say how thou hast disposed,
And all the rest o' the Fleet?
 Ari.   Safely in harbour
Is the King's ship; in the deep nook, where once
Thou call'dst me up at midnight to fetch dew
From the still-vext Bermoothes; there she's hid:
The mariners all under hatches stowed,
Whom, with a charm joined to their suffered labour,
I have left asleep: and for the rest o' the Fleet
Which I dispersed, they all have met again,
And are upon the Mediterranean flote,
Bound sadly home for Naples,
Supposing that they saw the King's ship wrecked,
And his great person perish.
 Pro.   Ariel, thy charge
Exactly is performed; but there's more work.
What is the time o' the day?
 Ari.   Past the mid season.
 Pro. At least two glasses. The time 'twixt six and
  now
Must by us both be spent most preciously.

Ari. Is there more toil? Since thou dost give me
        pains,
Let me remember thee what thou hast promised,
Which is not yet performed me.
    Pro.   How now? moody?
What is 't thou canst demand?
    Ari.   My liberty.
    Pro. Before the time be out? no more!
    Ari.   I pr'ythee,
Remember, I have done thee worthy service;
Told thee no lies, made no mistakings, served
Without or grudge, or grumblings. Thou didst promise
To bate me a full year.
    Pro.   Dost thou forget
From what a torment I did free thee?
    Ari.   No.
    Pro. Thou dost; and think'st it much, to tread the
        ooze
Of the salt deep,
To run upon the sharp wind of the north,
To do me business in the veins o' th' earth,
When it is bak'd with frost.
    Ari.   I do not, sir.
    Pro. Thou liest, malignant thing! Hast thou forgot
The foul witch Sycorax, who, with age and envy,
Was grown into a hoop? hast thou forgot her?
    Ari. No, sir.
    Pro. Thou hast. Where was she born? speak; tell
        me.
    Ari. Sir, in Argier.
    Pro.   O! was she so? I must,
Once in a month, recount what thou hast been,
Which thou forgett'st. This damn'd witch, Sycorax,
For mischiefs manifold, and sorceries terrible
To enter human hearing, from Argier,
Thou know'st, was banished: for one thing she did,
They would not take her life. Is not this true?
    Ari. Ay, sir.
    Pro. This blue-eyed hag was hither brought with child,
And here was left by the sailors: thou, my slave
As thou report'st thyself, was then her servant:
And, for thou wast a spirit too delicate
To act her earthy and abhorred commands,
Refusing her grand hests, she did confine thee,
By help of her more potent ministers,
And in her most unmitigable rage,
Into a cloven pine; within which rift
Imprison'd, thou didst painfully remain
A dozen years; within which space she died,

And left thee there, where thou didst vent thy groans
As fast as mill-wheels strike.   Then was this island
(Save for the son which she did litter here,
A freckled whelp, hag-born) not honoured with
A human shape.
    Ari.   Yes; Caliban, her son.
    Pro.   Dull thing, I say so; he, that Caliban,
Whom now I keep in service.   Thou best know'st
What torment I did find thee in: thy groans
Did make wolves howl, and penetrate the breasts
Of ever-angry bears.   It was a torment
To lay upon the damned, which Sycorax
Could not again undo: it was mine art,
When I arrived and heard thee, that made gape
The pine, and let thee out.
    Ari.   I thank thee, master.
    Pro.   If thou more murmur'st, I will rend an oak
And peg thee in his knotty entrails, till
Thou hast howled away twelve winters.
    Ari.   Pardon, master;
I will be correspondent to command,
And do my spiriting gently.
    Pro.   Do so, and
After two days I will discharge thee.
    Ari.   That's
My noble master! What shall I do? say what?
What shall I do?
    Pro.   Go, make thyself like a nymph o' the sea;
Be subject to no sight but thine and mine;
Invisible to every eye-ball else.
Go, take this shape, and hither come in it.
Go; hence with diligence!

                             [Exit Ariel
Awake, dear heart, awake! thou hast slept well;
Awake!
    Mira.   The strangeness of your story put
Heaviness in me.
    Pro.   Shake it off.   Come on;
We'll visit Caliban, my slave, who never
Yields us kind answer.
    Mira.   'Tis a villain, sir,
I do not love to look on.
    Pro.   But, as 't is,
We cannot miss him: he does make our fire,
Fetch in our wood, and serves in offices
That profit us.—What ho! slave! Caliban!
Thou earth, thou! speak.
    Cal.   [*Within*]   There's wood enough within.
    Pro.   Come forth, I say, there 's other business for thee:

Come, thou tortoise! when!

Re-enter ARIEL, *like a water-nymph*

Fine apparition! My quaint Ariel,
Hark in thine ear.
    Ari.   My lord, it shall be done.   [*Exit*
    Pro.   Thou poisonous slave, got by the devil himself
Upon thy wicked dam, come forth!

Enter CALIBAN

    Cal.   As wicked dew as e'er my mother brushed
With raven's feather from unwholesome fen,
Drop on you both! a south-west blow on ye,
And blister you all o'er!
    Pro.   For this, be sure, to-night thou shalt have cramps,
Side-stitches that shall pen thy breath up; urchins
Shall forth, at vast of night, that they may work
All exercise on thee: thou shalt be pinched
As thick as honey-comb, each pinch more stinging
Than bees that made them.
    Cal.   I must eat my dinner.
This island's mine, by Sycorax my mother,
Which thou tak'st from me. When thou camest first,
Thou strok'dst me, and mad'st much of me; wouldst
    give me
Water with berries in 't; and teach me how
To name the bigger light, and how the less,
That burn by day and night: and then I loved thee,
And showed thee all the qualities o' th' isle,
The fresh springs, brine-pits, barren place, and fertile.
Curséd be I that did so!—All the charms
Of Sycorax, toads, beetles, bats, light on you!
For I am all the subjects that you have,
Which first was mine own king; and here you sty me
In this hard rock, whiles you do keep from me
The rest o' the island.
    Pro.   Thou most lying slave,
Whom stripes may move, not kindness: I have used thee,
Filth as thou art, with human care; and lodged thee
In mine own cell, till thou didst seek to violate
The honour of my child.
    Cal.   O ho! O ho!—I would it had been done!
Thou didst prevent me; I had peopled else
This isle with Calibans.
    Pro.   Abhorréd slave,
Which any print of goodness wilt not take,
Being capable of all ill,—I pitied thee,
Took pains to make thee speak, taught thee each hour

One thing or other: when thou didst not, savage,
Know thine own meaning, but wouldst gabble like
A thing most brutish, I endow'd thy purposes
With words that made them known; but thy vile race,
Though thou didst learn, had that in't which good natures
Could not abide to be with: therefore wast thou
Deservedly confined into this rock,
Who hadst deserved more than a prison.
   Cal.   You,
You taught me language: and my profit on't
Is, I know how to curse.   The red plague rid you
For learning me your language!
   Pro.   Hag-seed, hence!
Fetch us in fuel; and be quick, thou'rt best,
To answer other business.   Shrugg'st thou, malice?
If thou neglect'st, or dost unwillingly
What I command, I'll rack thee with old cramps;
Fill all thy bones with aches; make thee roar,
That beasts shall tremble at thy din.
   Cal.   No, 'pray thee!—
  [*Aside*]   I must obey; his art is of such power,
It would control my dam's god, Setebos,
And make a vassal of him.
   Pro.   So, slave; hence! [*Exit Caliban*

Re-enter ARIEL, *invisible, playing and singing;*
      FERDINAND *following him.*

ARIEL'S SONG

Come unto these yellow sands,
    And then take hands;
Court'sied when you have, and kissed,—
    The wild waves whist,—
Foot it featly here and there;
And, sweet sprites, the burden bear,
    Hark! hark!

Burden.   Bowgh, wowgh,   [*Dispersedly*
    The watch-dogs bark:
Burden.   Bowgh, wowgh,
    Hark, hark! I hear
The strain of strutting chanticleer
Cry, Cock-a-doodle-doo.

   Fer.   Where should this music be? i' the air, or the
      earth?—
It sounds no more:—and sure, it waits upon
Some god o' the island.   Sitting on a bank,

Weeping again the king my father's wreck,
This music crept by me upon the waters,
Allaying both their fury, and my passion,
With its sweet air: thence I have followed it,
Or it hath drawn me rather: but 't is gone.—
No, it begins again.

ARIEL *sings*

Full fathom five thy father lies:
    Of his bones are coral made,
Those are pearls that were his eyes:
    Nothing of him that doth fade,
But doth suffer a sea-change,
    Into something rich and strange.
Sea-nymphs hourly ring his knell:
                        [*Burden.*   Ding-dong
Hark! now I hear them,—ding-dong, bell.

Fer.   The ditty does remember my drowned father.—
This is no mortal business, nor no sound
That the earth owes.—I hear it now above me.
    Pro.   The fringéd curtains of thine eye advance,
And say, what thou seest yond.
    Mira.   What is 't? a spirit?
Lord, how it looks about!   Believe me, sir,
It carries a brave form:—but 't is a spirit.
    Pro.   No, wench: it eats and sleeps, and hath such senses
As we have, such.   This gallant, which thou seest,
Was in the wreck; and but he's something stained
With grief, that's beauty's canker, thou might 'st call him
A goodly person.   He hath lost his fellows,
And strays about to find them.
    Mira.   I might call him
A thing divine, for nothing natural
I ever saw so noble.—
    Pro.   [*Aside*]   It goes on, I see,
As my soul prompts it.—Spirit, fine spirit! I'll free thee
Within two days for this.
    Fer.   Most sure, the goddess
On whom these airs attend!—Vouchsafe, my prayer
May know if you remain upon this island,
And that you will some good instructions give,
How I may bear me here; my prime request,
Which I do last pronounce is, O you wonder!
If you be maid, or no?
    Mira.   No wonder, sir;

But certainly a maid.
    Fer.   My language! heavens!—
I am the best of them that speak this speech,
Were I but where 't is spoken.
    Pro.   How! the best?
What wert thou, if the King of Naples heard thee?
    Fer. A single thing, as I am now, that wonders
To hear thee speak of Naples. He does hear me,
And that he does I weep: myself am Naples;
Who with mine eyes, ne'er since at ebb, beheld
The king, my father, wrecked.
    Mira.   Alack, for mercy!
    Fer. Yes, faith, and all his lords; the Duke of Milan,
And his brave son, being twain.
    Pro.   The Duke of Milan,
And his more braver daughter could control thee,
If now 't were fit to do 't.—[*Aside*] At the first sight
They have changed eyes:—delicate Ariel,
I'll set thee free for this!—[*To him*] A word, good sir;
I fear you have done yourself some wrong: a word.
    Mira. Why speaks my father so ungently? This
Is the third man that e'er I saw; the first
That e'er I sighed for. Pity move my father
To be inclined my way!
    Fer.   O! if a virgin,
And your affection not gone forth, I'll make you
The Queen of Naples.
    Pro.   Soft, sir: one word more.—
[*Aside*] They are both in either's powers; but this swift
           business
I must uneasy make, lest too light winning
Make the prize light. [*To him*] One word more: I charge
           thee,
That thou attend me. Thou dost here usurp
The name thou ow'st not; and hast put thyself
Upon this island as a spy, to win it
From me, the lord on 't.
    Fer.   No, as I am a man.
    Mira. There's nothing ill can dwell in such a temple;
If the ill spirit have so fair a house,
Good things will strive to dwell with 't.
    Pro. [*To* FERD.] Follow me.—
Speak not you for him; he's a traitor.—Come.
I'll manacle thy neck and feet together;
Sea-water shalt thou drink, thy food shall be
The fresh-brook mussels, withered roots, and husks
Wherein the acorn cradled. Follow.
    Fer.   No;
I will resist such entertainment, till

Mine enemy has more power.
                    [*He draws and is charmed from moving*
    Mira.   O, dear father,
Make not too rash a trial of him, for
He's gentle, and not fearful.
    Pro.   What! I say:
My foot my tutor?—Put thy sword up, traitor;
Who mak'st a show, but dar'st not strike, thy conscience
Is so possessed with guilt; come from thy ward,
For I can here disarm thee with this stick,
And make thy weapon drop.
    Mira.   Beseech you, father!
    Pro.   Hence; hang not on my garments!
    Mira.   Sir, have pity.
I'll be his surety.
    Pro.   Silence! one word more
Shall make me chide thee, if not hate thee.   What!
An advocate for an impostor? hush!
Thou think'st there is no more such shapes as he,
Having seen but him and Caliban; foolish wench!
To the most of men this is a Caliban,
And they to him are angels.
    Mira.   My affections
Are then most humble: I have no ambition
To see a goodlier man.
    Pro. [*To* Ferd.]   Come on; obey:
Thy nerves are in their infancy again,
And have no vigour in them.
    Fer.   So they are:
My spirits, as in a dream, are all bound up.
My father's loss, the weakness which I feel,
The wreck of all my friends, nor this man's threats,
To whom I am subdued, are but light to me,
Might I but through my prison once a day
Behold this maid: all corners else o' the earth
Let liberty make use of; space enough
Have I in such a prison.—
    Pro.   It works.—Come on.—
Thou hast done well, fine Ariel!—[*To* Ferd.] Follow me.—
[*To* Ariel] Hark, what thou else shalt do me.
    Mira.   Be of comfort.
My father's of a better nature, sir,
Than he appears by speech; this is unwonted,
Which now came from him.—
    Pro.   Thou shalt be as free
As mountain winds; but then exactly do
All points of my command.
    Ari.   To the syllable.
    Pro.   Come, follow.—Speak not for him.   [*Exeunt*

ACT TWO

Scene I.—Another Part of the Island

Enter Alonso, Sebastian, Antonio, Gonzalo, Adrian,
Francisco, *and others*

    Gon. Beseech you, sir, be merry; you have cause
(So have we all) of joy; for our escape
Is much beyond our loss. Our hint of woe
Is common; every day, some sailor's wife,
The master of some merchant, and the merchant,
Have just our theme of woe: but for the miracle,
I mean our preservation, few in millions
Can speak like us: then wisely, good sir, weigh
Our sorrow with our comfort.
    Alon.   Pr'ythee, peace.
    Seb. He receives comfort like cold porridge.
    Ant. The visitor will not give him o'er so.
    Seb. Look; he's winding up the watch of his wit:
by-and-by it will strike.
    Gon. Sir,—
    Seb. One:—tell.
    Gon. When every grief is entertained, that's offered,
Comes to the entertainer—
    Seb. A dollar.
    Gon. Dolour comes to him, indeed: you have spoke
truer than you purposed.
    Seb. You have taken it wiselier than I meant you
should.
    Gon. Therefore, my lord,—
    Ant. Fie, what a spendthrift is he of his tongue!
    Alon. I pr'ythee, spare.
    Gon.   Well, I have done. But yet—
    Seb. He will be talking.
    Ant.   Which he or Adrian,
For a good wager, first begins to crow?
    Seb. The old cock.
    Ant. The cockrel.
    Seb. Done. The wager?
    Ant. A laughter.
    Seb. A match!
    Adr. Though this island seem to be desert,—
    Seb. Ha, ha, ha! So, you're paid.
    Adr. Uninhabitable, and almost inaccessible,—
    Seb. Yet—
    Adr. Yet—
    Ant. He could not miss it.

Adr. It must needs be of subtle, tender, and delicate temperance.

Ant. Temperance was a delicate wench.

Seb. Ay, and a subtle, as he most learnedly delivered.

Adr. The air breathes upon us here most sweetly.

Seb. As if it had lungs, and rotten ones.

Ant. Or as 't were perfumed by a fen.

Gon. Here is everything advantageous to life.

Ant. True; save means to live.

Seb. Of that there's none, or little.

Gon. How lush and lusty the grass looks! how green!

Ant. The ground, indeed, is tawny.

Seb. With an eye of green in 't.

Ant. He misses not much.

Seb. No, he doth but mistake the truth totally.

Gon. But the rarity of it is, which is indeed almost beyond credit—

Seb. As many vouched rarities are.

Gon. That our garments, being, as they were, drenched, in the sea, hold, notwithstanding, their freshness and glosses; being rather new-dyed, than stained with salt water.

Ant. If but one of his pockets could speak; would it not say, he lies?

Seb. Ay, or very falsely pocket up his report.

Gon. Methinks, our garments are now as fresh as when we put them on first in Afric, at the marriage of the king's fair daughter Claribel to the King of Tunis.

Seb. 'T was a sweet marriage, and we prosper well in our return.

Adr. Tunis was never graced before with such a paragon to their queen.

Gon. Not since Widow Dido's time.

Ant. Widow? a pox o' that! How came that widow in? Widow Dido!

Seb. What if he had said, Widower Æneas too? Good Lord, how you take it!

Adr. Widow Dido, said you? you make me study of that; she was of Carthage; not of Tunis.

Gon. This Tunis, sir, was Carthage.

Adr. Carthage?

Gon. I assure you, Carthage.

Ant. His word is more than the miraculous harp.

Seb. He hath raised the wall, and houses too.

Ant. What impossible matter will he make easy next?

Seb. I think he will carry this island home in his pocket and give it his son for an apple.

Ant. And sowing the kernels of it in the sea, bring forth more islands.

Gon. Ay?
Ant. Why, in good time.
Gon. Sir, we were talking, that our garments seem now
as fresh as when we were at Tunis at the marriage of your
daughter, who is now queen.
  Ant. And the rarest that e'er came there.
  Seb. Bate, I beseech you, Widow Dido.
  Ant. O, Widow Dido; ay, Widow Dido.
  Gon. Is not, sir, my doublet as fresh as the first day I
wore it? I mean, in a sort.
  Ant. That sort was well fished for.
  Gon. When I wore it at your daughter's marriage?
  Alon. You cram these words into mine ears, against
The stomach of my sense. Would I had never
Married my daughter there! for, coming thence,
My son is lost; and, in my rate, she too,
Who is so far from Italy removed,
I ne'er again shall see her. O thou, mine heir
Of Naples and of Milan! what strange fish
Hath made his meal on thee?
  Fran.   Sir, he may live.
I saw him beat the surges under him,
And ride upon their backs; he trod the water,
Whose enmity he flung aside, and breasted
The surge most swoln that met him; his bold head
'Bove the contentious waves he kept, and oared
Himself with his good arms in lusty stroke
To the shore, that o'er his wave-worn basis bowed,
As stooping to relieve him. I not doubt,
He came alive to land.
  Alon.   No, no; he's gone.
  Seb. Sir, you may thank yourself for this great loss
That would not bless our Europe with your daughter,
But rather lose her to an African,
Where she, at least, is banished from your eye,
Who hath cause to wet the grief on 't.
  Alon.   Pr'ythee, peace.
  Seb. You were kneeled to, and importuned otherwise
By all of us; and the fair soul herself
Weighed, between lothness and obedience, at
Which end o' the beam she'd bow. We have lost your son,
I fear, for ever; Milan and Naples have
More widows in them, of this business' making,
Than we bring men to comfort them;
The fault 's your own.
  Alon. So is the dear'st of th' loss.
  Gon.   My Lord Sebastian,
The truth you speak doth lack some gentleness,
And time to speak it in; you rub the sore,

When you should bring the plaster.
 Seb.   Very well.
 Ant. And most chirurgeonly.
 Gon. It is foul weather in us all, good sir.
When you are cloudy.
 Seb.   Foul weather?
 Ant.   Very foul.
 Gon. Had I plantation of this isle, my lord,—
 Ant. He'd sow 't with nettle-seed.
 Seb.   Or docks, or mallows.
 Gon. And were the king on 't, what would I do?
 Seb. Scape being drunk, for want of wine.
 Gon. I' the commonwealth I would by contraries
Execute all things, for no kind of traffic
Would I admit; no name of magistrate;
Letters should not be known; riches, poverty,
And use of service, none; contract, succession,
Bourn, bound of land, tilth, vineyard, none;
No use of metal, corn, or wine, or oil:
No occupation, all men idle, all:
And women too, but innocent and pure;
No sovereignty:—
 Seb. Yet he would be king on 't.
 Ant. The latter end of his commonwealth forgets the
beginning.
 Gon. All things in common nature should produce,
Without sweat or endeavour: treason, felony,
Sword, pike, knife, gun, or need of any engine,
Would I not have; but nature should bring forth,
Of its own kind, all foison, all abundance,
To feed my innocent people.
 Seb. No marrying 'mong his subjects?
 Ant. None, man; all idle; whores, and knaves.
 Gon. I would with such perfection govern, sir,
To excel the golden age.
 Seb.   'Save his Majesty!
 Ant. Long Live Gonzalo!
 Gon.   And, do you mark me, sir?—
 Alon. Pr'ythee; no more: thou dost talk nothing to me.
 Gon. I do well believe your highness; and did it to
minister occasion to these gentlemen, who are of such
sensible and nimble lungs, that they always use to laugh
at nothing.
 Ant. 'T was you we laughed at.
 Gon. Who, in this kind of merry fooling, am nothing
to you; so you may continue, and laugh at nothing still.
 Ant. What a blow was there given!
 Seb. An it had not fallen flat-long.
 Gon. You are gentlemen of brave mettle; you would

lift the moon out of her sphere, if she would continue in it
five weeks without changing.

Enter ARIEL, *invisible; solemn music playing*

Seb.   We would so, and then go a bat-fowling.
Ant.   Nay, good my lord, be not angry.
Gon.   No, I warrant you; I will not adventure my
discretion so weakly.   Will you laugh me asleep, for I am
very heavy?
Ant.   Go sleep, and hear us.
                              [*All sleep but Alon, Seb., and Ant.*
Alon.   What! all so soon asleep? I wish mine eyes
Would, with themselves, shut up my thoughts; I find,
They are inclined to do so.
Seb.   Please you, sir,
Do not omit the heavy offer of it;
It seldom visits sorrow; when it doth,
It is a comforter.
Ant.   We two, my lord,
Will guard your person while you take your rest,
And watch your safety.
Alon.   Thank you. Wondrous heavy.—
                              [*Alonso sleeps.   Exit Ariel*
Seb.   What a strange drowsiness possesses them!
Ant.   It is the quality o' the climate.
Seb.   Why
Doth it not then our eyelids sink? I find not
Myself disposed to sleep.
Ant.   Nor I: my spirits are nimble.
They fell together all, as by consent;
They dropped as by a thunder-stroke.   What might,
Worthy Sebastian—O! what might—no more:—
And yet, methinks, I see it in thy face,
What thou shouldst be. The occasion speaks thee, and
My strong imagination sees a crown
Dropping upon thy head.
Seb.   What! art thou waking?
Ant.   Do you not hear me speak?
Seb.   I do; and, surely,
It is a sleepy language, and thou speak'st
Out of thy sleep.   What is it thou didst say?
This is a strange repose, to be asleep
With eyes wide open; standing, speaking, moving,
And yet so fast asleep.
Ant.   Noble Sebastian,
Thou let'st thy fortune sleep, die rather; wink'st
Whiles thou art waking.
Seb.   Thou dost snore distinctly:

There's meaning in thy snores,
 Ant. I am more serious than my custom: you
Must be so too, if heed me; which to do,
Trebles thee o'er.
  Seb.   Well: I am standing water.
  Ant. I'll teach you how to flow.
  Seb.   Do so: to ebb
Hereditary sloth instructs me.
  Ant.   O!
If you but knew, how you the purpose cherish,
Whiles thus you mock it! how, in stripping it,
You more invest it! ebbing men, indeed,
Most often do so near the bottom run
By their own fear, or sloth.
  Seb.   Pr'ythee, say on.
The setting of thine eye and cheek proclaim
A matter from thee, and a birth, indeed,
Which throes thee much to yield.
  Ant.   Thus, sir:
Although this lord of weak remembrance, this,
(Who shall be of as little memory,
When he is earthed) hath here almost persuaded
(For he's a spirit of persuasion, only
Professes to persuade) the king, his son's alive,
'T is as impossible that he's undrowned,
As he that sleeps here, swims.
  Seb.   I have no hope
That he's undrowned.
  Ant.   O, out of that no hope,
What great hope have you? no hope that way, is
Another way so high a hope, that even
Ambition cannot pierce a wink beyond,
But doubts discovery there. Will you grant with me,
That Ferdinand is drowned?
  Seb.   He's gone.
  Ant.   Then, tell me,
Who's the next heir of Naples?
  Seb.   Claribel.
  Ant. She that is Queen of Tunis; she that dwells
Ten leagues beyond man's life; she that from Naples
Can have no note, unless the sun were post,
(The man i' the moon 's too slow) till new-born chins
Be rough and razorable; she, from whom
We all were sea-swallowed, though some cast again;
And by that destiny to perform an act,
Whereof what 's past is prologue, what to come,
In yours and my discharge.
  Seb.   What stuff is this?—How say you?
'T is true, my brother's daughter 's Queen of Tunis;

So is she heir of Naples; 'twixt which regions
There is some space.
    Ant.   A space whose every cubit
Seems to cry out, "How shall that Claribel
Measure us back to Naples? Keep in Tunis,
And let Sebastian wake!"—Say, this were death
That now hath seized them; why, they were no worse
Than now they are. There be that can rule Naples.
As well as he that sleeps; lords that can prate
As amply and unnecessarily,
As this Gonzalo; I myself could make
A chough of as deep chat. O, that you bore
The mind that I do! What a sleep were this
For your advancement! Do you understand me?
    Seb.   Methinks, I do.
    Ant.   And how does your content
Tender your own good fortune.
    Seb.   I remember,
You did supplant your brother Prospero.
    Ant.   True:
And look how well my garments sit upon me;
Much feater than before. My brother's servants
Were then my fellows, now they are my men.
    Seb.   But, for your conscience—
    Ant.   Ay, sir; where lies that? If it were a kibe,
'T would put me to my slipper; but I feel not
This deity in my bosom: twenty consciences.
That stand 'twixt me and Milan, candied be they,
And melt ere they molest. Here lies your brother,—
No better than the earth he lies upon,
If he were that which now he 's like, that 's dead,—
Whom I, with this obedient steel, three inches of it,
Can lay to bed for ever; whiles you, doing thus,
To the perpetual wink for aye might put
This ancient morsel, this Sir Prudence, who
Should not upbraid our course; for all the rest,
They'll take suggestion as a cat laps milk;
They'll tell the clock to any business that
We say befits the hour.
    Seb.   Thy case, dear friend,
Shall be my precedent: as thou got'st Milan,
I'll come by Naples. Draw thy sword; one stroke
Shall free thee from the tribute which thou pay'st,
And I the king shall love thee.
    Ant.   Draw together;
And when I rear my hand, do you the like,
To fall it on Gonzalo.
    Seb.   O, but one word.
                        [They converse apart.

Music. Re-enter ARIEL, *invisible*

Ari. My master through his art forsees the danger
That you, his friend, are in; and sends me forth
(For else his project dies) to keep them living.
                              [*Sings in Gonzalo's ear*

> *While you here do snoring lie,*
> *Open-eyed Conspiracy,*
>   *His time doth take.*
> *If of life you keep a care,*
> *Shake off slumber, and beware:*
>   *Awake!   Awake!*

Ant. Then let us both be sudden.
Gon.   Now, good angels,
Preserve the king.   [*They wake*
  Alon. Why, how now, ho! awake! Why are you
        drawn?
Wherefore this ghastly looking?
Gon.   What 's the matter?
  Seb. Whiles we stood here securing your repose,
Even now we heard a hollow burst of bellowing
Like bulls, or rather lions; did it not wake you?
It struck mine ear most terribly.
  Alon.   I heard nothing.
  Ant. O! 't was a din to fright a monster's ear,
To make an earthquake: sure, it was the roar
Of a whole herd of lions.
  Alon.   Heard you this, Gonzalo?
  Gon. Upon mine honour, sir, I heard a humming,
And that a strange one too, which did awake me.
I shaked you, sir, and cried; as mine eyes opened,
I saw their weapons drawn.—There was a noise,
That's verily; 't is best we stand upon our guard,
Or that we quit this place. Let 's draw our weapons.
  Alon. Lead off this ground, and let 's make further
        search
For my poor son.
  Gon.   Heavens keep him from these beasts,
For he is, sure, i' the island.
  Alon.   Lead away.   [*Exeunt*
  Ari. Prospero, my lord, shall know what I have done;
So, king, go safely on to seek thy son.   [*Exit*

SCENE II.—*Another Part of the Island*

Enter CALIBAN, *with a burden of wood. A noise*
of Thunder heard

  Cal. All the infections that the sun sucks up
173

From bogs, fens, flats, on Prosper fall, and make him
By inch-meal a disease! His spirits hear me,
And yet I needs much curse; but they 'll nor pinch,
Fright me with urchin-shows, pitch me i' the mire,
Nor lead me, like a firebrand, in the dark
Out of my way, unless he bid 'em; but
For every trifle are they set upon me:
Sometime like apes, that moe and chatter at me,
And after, bite me; then like hedge-hogs, which
Lie tumbling in my bare-foot way, and mount
Their pricks at my foot-fall; sometime am I
All wound with adders, who with cloven tongues
Do hiss me into madness.—Lo, now, lo,
Here comes a spirit of his, and to torment me
For bringing wood in slowly; I 'll fall flat.
Perchance, he will not mind me.

Enter TRINCULO

Trin. Here 's neither bush nor shrub to bear off any
weather at all, and another storm brewing; I hear it sing
i' the wind: yond same black cloud, yond huge one, looks
like a foul bombard that would shed his liquor. If it
should thunder, as it did before, I know not where to hide
my head; yond same cloud cannot choose but fall by pail-
fuls.—What have we here? a man or a fish? Dead or
alive? A fish: he smells like a fish; a very ancient and
fish-like smell; a kind of, not of the newest, Poor-John.
A strange fish! Were I in England now (as once I was),
and had but this fish painted, not a holiday fool there but
would give a piece of silver: there would this monster
make a man: any strange beast there makes a man.
When they will not give a doit to relieve a lame beggar.
they will lay out ten to see a dead Indian. Legged like a
man; and his fins like arms. Warm; o' my troth! I do
now let loose my opinion, hold it no longer; this is no fish,
but an islander, that hath lately suffered by a thunder-bolt.
[*Thunder*] Alas! the storm is come again; my best way
is to creep under his gaberdine; there is no other shelter
hereabout: misery acquaints a man with strange bed-
fellows. I will here shroud, till the dregs of the storm be
past.

Enter STEPHANO, *singing: a bottle in his hand*

Ste.   *I shall no more to sea, to sea,*
                 Here shall I die a-shore.—

This is a very scurvy tune to sing at a man's funeral.
Well, here 's my comfort.   [*Drinks*

The master, the swabber, the boatswain, and I,
  The gunner, and his mate,
Lov'd Mall, Meg, and Marian, and Margery,
  But none of us cared for Kate ;
  For she had a tongue with a tang,
    Would cry to a sailor, Go hang.
She loved not the savour of tar, nor of pitch,
Yet a tailor might scratch her where-e'er she did itch :
  Then to sea, boys, and let her go hang.

This is a scurvy tune too; but here 's my comfort.

                                        [*Drinks*

Cal. Do not torment me: Oh!

Ste. What 's the matter? Have we devils here? Do
you put tricks upon us with savages, and men of Inde?
Ha! I have not scaped drowning to be afeard now of
your four legs; for it hath been said: As proper a man
as ever went on four legs cannot make him give ground;
and it shall be said so again, while Stephano breathes at
nostrils.

Cal. The spirit torments me: Oh!

Ste. This is some monster of the isle, with four legs,
who hath got, as I take it, an ague. Where the devil
should he learn our language? I will give him some
relief, if it be but for that: if I can recover him, and keep
him tame, and get to Naples with him, he 's a present for
any emperor that ever trod on neat's-leather.

Cal. Do not torment me, pr'ythee: I 'll bring my wood
home faster.

Ste. He 's in his fit now, and does not talk after the
wisest. He shall taste of my bottle: if he have never
drunk wine afore, it will go near to remove his fit. If I
can recover him, and keep him tame, I will not take too
much for him: he shall pay for him that hath him, and
that soundly.

Cal. Thou dost me yet but little hurt: thou wilt anon,
I know it by thy trembling; now Prosper works upon
thee.

Ste. Come on your ways: open your mouth: here is
that which will give language to you, cat. Open your
mouth: this will shake your shaking, I can tell you, and
that soundly—you cannot tell who 's your friend: open
your chaps again.

Trin. I should know that voice. It should be—but
he is drowned, and these are devils. O! defend me!—

Ste. Four legs, and two voices! a most delicate monster. His forward voice, now, is to speak well of his friend
his backward voice is to utter foul speeches and to detract.
If all the wine in my bottle will recover him, I will help

his ague. Come.—Amen! I will pour some in thy other
mouth.

Trin. Stephano!

Ste. Doth thy other mouth call me! Mercy! mercy!
This is a devil, and no monster: I will leave him: I have
no long spoon.

Trin. Stephano!—if thou beest Stephano, touch me,
and speak to me, for I am Trinculo!—be not afeard,—
thy good friend Trinculo.

Ste. If you beest Trinculo, come forth. I 'll pull thee
by the lesser legs: if any be Trinculo's legs, these are they.
Thou art very Trinculo indeed! How cam'st thou to be
the siege of this moon-calf? Can he vent Trinculos?

Trin. I took him to be killed with a thunder-stroke.
—But art thou not drowned, Stephano? I hope now,
thou art not drowned. Is the storm overblown? I hid
me under the dead moon-calf's gaberdine for fear of the
storm. And art thou living, Stephano? O Stephano! two
Neapolitans scaped.

Ste. Pr'ythee, do not turn me about: my stomach is
not constant.

Cal. These be fine things, an if they be not sprites.
That 's a brave god, and bears celestial liquor:
I will kneel to him.

Ste. How didst thou 'scape? How cam'st thou hither?
swear by this bottle, how thou cam'st hither. I escaped
upon a butt of sack, which the sailors heaved overboard,
by this bottle! which I made of the bark of a tree, with
mine own hands, since I was cast a-shore.

Cal. I 'll swear, upon that bottle, to be thy true subject,
for the liquor is not earthly.

Ste. Here: swear then how thou escap'dst.—

Trin. Swam a-shore, man, like a duck. I can swim
like a duck, I 'll be sworn.

Ste. Here, kiss the book. Though thou canst swim
like a duck, thou art made like a goose.

Trin. O Stephano! hast any more of this?

Ste. The whole butt, man: my cellar is in a rock by
the sea-side, where my wine is hid. How now, moon-calf?
How does thine ague?

Cal. Hast thou not dropped from heaven?

Ste. Out o' the moon, I do assure thee: I was the man
in the moon, when time was.

Cal. I have seen thee in her, and I do adore thee:
My mistress showed me thee, and thy dog, and thy bush.

Ste. Come, swear to that; kiss the book; I will furnish
it anon with new contents: swear.

Trin. By this good light, this is a very shallow monster:
—I afeard of him!—a very weak monster.—The man i' the

moon?—a most poor credulous monster.—Well drawn, monster, in good sooth.

Cal. I 'll show thee every fertile inch o' the island, And I will kiss thy foot. I pr'ythee, be my god.

Trin. By this light, a most perfidious and drunken monster: when his god 's asleep, he 'll rob his bottle.

Cal. I 'll kiss thy foot: I 'll swear myself thy subject.

Ste. Come on, then; down, and swear.

Trin. I shall laugh myself to death at this puppy-headed monster. A most scurvy monster: I could find in my heart to beat him,—

Ste. Come, kiss.

Trin. —but that the poor monster 's in drink. An abominable monster!

Cal. I 'll show thee the best springs: I 'll pluck thee
      berries;
I 'll fish for thee, and get thee wood enough.
A plague upon the tyrant that I serve!
I 'll bear him no more sticks, but follow thee,
Thou wondrous man.

Trin. A most ridiculous monster, to make a wonder of a poor drunkard!

Cal. I pr'ythee, let me bring thee where crabs grow;
And I with my long nails will dig thee pig-nuts;
Show thee a jay's nest, and instruct thee how
To snare the nimble marmoset; I 'll bring thee
To clustering filberts, and sometimes I 'll get thee
Young scamels from the rock. Wilt thou go with me?

Ste. I pr'ythee now, lead the way, without any more talking.—Trinculo the king and all our company else being drowned, we will inherit here.—Here; bear my bottle.—Fellow Trinculo, we 'll fill him by-and-by again.

Cal. [*Sings drunkenly*]

    Farewell, master ; farewell, farewell!

Trin. A howling monster, a drunken monster.

Cal. *No more dams I 'll make for fish :*
    Nor fetch in firing
    At requiring ;
  Nor scrape trencher, nor wash dish :
    'Ban, 'Ban, Ca—Caliban
    Has a new master—get a new man.

Freedom, hey-day! hey-day, freedom! freedom! hey-day, freedom!

Ste. O brave monster! lead the way.   [*Exeunt*

ACT THREE

SCENE I.—Before PROSPERO'S Cell

Enter FERDINAND, *bearing a log*

There be some sports are painful, and their labour
Delight in them sets off; some kinds of baseness
Are nobly undergone; and most poor matters
Point to rich ends. This my mean task
Would be as heavy to me as odious; but
The mistress which I serve quickens what 's dead,
And makes my labours pleasures; O, she is
Ten times more gentle than her father's crabbed;
And he 's composed of harshness. I must remove
Some thousands of these logs, and pile them up,
Upon a sore injunction; my sweet mistress
Weeps when she sees me work; and says, such baseness
Had never like executor. I forget:
But these sweet thoughts do even refresh my labours,
Most busy left when I do it.

Enter MIRANDA; *and* PROSPERO *at a distance*

   Mira.   Alas, now, pray you,
Work not so hard: I would, the lightning had
Burnt up those logs that you are enjoined to pile.
Pray, set it down, and rest you: when this burns,
'T will weep for having wearied you. My father
Is hard at study; pray now, rest yourself:
He 's safe for these three hours.
   Fer.   O most dear mistress!
The sun will set, before I shall discharge
What I must strive to do.
   Mira.   If you 'll sit down,
I 'll bear your logs the while. Pray, give me that:
I 'll carry it to the pile.
   Fer.   No, precious creature:
I had rather crack my sinews, break my back,
Than you should such dishonour undergo,
While I sit lazy by.
   Mira.   It would become me
As well as it does you; and I should do it
With much more ease, for my good will is to it,
And yours it is against.—

Pro.   Poor worm! thou art infected:
This visitation shows it.—
   Mira.   You look wearily.
   Fer. No, noble mistress; 't is fresh morning with me
When you are by, at night.   I do beseech you,
Chiefly that I might set it in my prayers,
What is your name?
   Mira.   Miranda—O my father!
I have broke your hest to say so.
   Fer.   Admired Miranda,
Indeed the top of admiration; worth
What 's dearest to the world!   Full many a lady
I have eyed with best regard, and many a time
The harmony of their tongues hath into bondage
Brought my too diligent ear; for several virtues
Have I liked several women; never any
With so full soul, but some defect in her
Did quarrel with the noblest grace she owed,
And put it to the foil: but you, O you,
So perfect, and so peerless, are created
Of every creature's best.
   Mira.   I do not know
One of my sex; no woman's face remember,
Save, from my glass, mine own; nor have I seen
More that I may call men, than thou, good friend,
And my dear father: how features are, abroad,
I am skill-less of; but, by my modesty
(The jewel in my dower), I would not wish
Any companion in the world but you;
Nor can imagination form a shape,
Besides yourself, to like of.   But I prattle
Something too wildly, and my father's precepts
I therein do forget.
   Fer.   I am, in my condition,
A prince, Miranda; I do think, a king;
(I would, not so!) and would no more endure
This wooden slavery, than to suffer
The flesh-fly blow my mouth.—Hear my soul speak:
The very instant that I saw you, did
My heart fly to your service; there resides,
To make me slave to it; and for your sake,
Am I this patient log-man.
   Mira.   Do you love me?
   Fer. O heaven! O earth! bear witness to this sound,
And crown what I profess with kind event,
If I speak true; if hollowly, invert
What best is boded me, to mischief! I,
Beyond all limit of what else i' the world,
Do love, prize, honour you.

Mira.   I am a fool,
To weep at what I am glad of.—
  Pro.   Fair encounter
Of two most rare affections! Heavens rain grace
On that which breeds between them!—
  Fer.   Wherefore weep you?
  Mira. At mine unworthiness, that dare not offer
What I desire to give; and much less take
What I shall die to want. But this is trifling;
And all the more it seeks to hide itself,
The bigger bulk it shows. Hence, bashful cunning,
And prompt me, plain and holy innocence!
I am your wife, if you will marry me;
If not, I 'll die your maid: to be your fellow
You may deny me; but I 'll be your servant,
Whether you will or no.
  Fer.   My mistress, dearest;
And I thus humble ever.
  Mira.   My husband, then?
  Fer. Ay, with a heart as willing
As bondage e'er of freedom: here 's my hand.
  Mira. And mine, with my heart in 't: and now fare-
          well,
Till half an hour hence.
  Fer.   A thousand thousand!
                          [*Exeunt Ferd. and Mira.*

  Pro. So glad of this as they I cannot be,
Who are surprised withal; but my rejoicing
At nothing can be more. I 'll to my book;
For yet, ere supper-time, must I perform
Much business appertaining.

                                                    [*Exit*

SCENE II.—Another Part of the Island

Enter CALIBAN *with a bottle;* STEPHANO *and* TRINCULO
                        following

  Ste. Tell not me:—when the butt is out, we will drink
water; not a drop before; therefore bear up and board
'em.—Servant-monster, drink to me.
  Trin. Servant-monster? the folly of this island!
They say, there 's but five upon this isle: we are three
of them; if the other two be brained like us, the state
totters.
  Ste. Drink, servant-monster, when I bid thee: thy eyes
are almost set in thy head.

                              180

Trin. Where should they be set else? he were a brave monster indeed, if they were set in his tail.

Ste. My man-monster hath drowned his tongue in sack. For my part, the sea cannot drown me: I swam, ere I could recover the shore, five-and-thirty leagues, off and on, by this light.—Thou shalt be my lieutenant, monster, or my standard.

Trin. Your lieutenant, if you list; he 's no standard.

Ste. We 'll not run, monsieur monster.

Trin. Nor go neither; but you 'll lie, like dogs, and yet say nothing neither.

Ste. Moon-calf, speak once in thy life, if thou beest a good moon-calf.

Cal. How does thy honour? Let me lick thy shoe. I 'll not serve him, he is not valiant.

Trin. Thou liest, most ignorant monster: I am in case to justle a constable. Why, thou deboshed fish, thou, was there ever man a coward, that hath drunk so much sack as I to-day? Wilt thou tell a monstrous lie, being but half a fish, and half a monster?

Cal. Lo, how he mocks me! will thou let him, my lord?

Trin. Lord, quoth he!—that a monster should be such a natural!

Cal. Lo, lo, again! bite him to death, I pr'ythee.

Ste. Trinculo, keep a good tongue in your head: if you prove a mutineer, the next tree!—The poor monster's my subject, and he shall not suffer indignity.

Cal. I thank my noble lord. Wilt thou be pleased to hearken once again to the suit I made to thee?

Ste. Marry will I; kneel and repeat it; I will stand, and so shall Trinculo.

Enter ARIEL, *invisible*

Cal. As I told thee before, I am subject to a tyrant: a sorcerer, that by his cunning hath cheated me of the island.

Ari. Thou liest.

Cal. Thou liest, thou jesting monkey, thou! I would, my valiant master would destroy thee: I do not lie.

Ste. Trinculo, if you trouble him any more in his tale, by this hand, I will supplant some of your teeth.

Trin. Why, I said nothing.

Ste. Mum then, and no more.—[*To Cal.*] Proceed.

Cal. I say, by sorcery he got this isle;
From me he got it: if thy greatness will,
Revenge it on him—for, I know, thou dar'st;
But this thing dare not.

Ste. That 's most certain.

Cal. Thou shalt be lord of it, and I 'll serve thee.

Ste. How now shall this be compassed? Canst **thou**
bring me to the party?

Cal. Yea, yea, my lord: I 'll yield him thee **asleep,**
Where thou may'st knock a nail into his head.

Ari. Thou liest; thou canst not.

Cal. What a pied ninny 's this! Thou scurvy patch!—
I do beseech thy greatness, give him blows,
And take his bottle from him: when that 's gone,
He shall drink nought but brine; for I 'll not show **him**
Where the quick freshes are.

Ste. Trinculo, run into no further danger; **interrupt**
the monster one word further, and, by this hand, I **'ll**
turn my mercy out of doors, and make a stock-fish **of**
thee.

Trin. Why, what did I? I did nothing. I 'll **go**
further off.

Ste. Didst thou not say he lied?

Ari. Thou liest.

Ste. Do I so? take thou that. [*Strikes him*] As **you**
like this, give me the lie another time.

Trin. I did not give the lie.—Out o' your wits, **and**
hearing too?—A pox o' your bottle! this can sack **and**
drinking do.—A murrain on your monster, and the **devil**
take your fingers!

Cal. Ha, ha, ha!

Ste. Now, forward with your tale. Pry'thee, **stand**
farther off.

Cal. Beat him enough: after a little time,
I 'll beat him too.

Ste.   Stand farther.—Come, proceed.

Cal. Why, as I told thee, 't is a custom with him
I' the afternoon to sleep: there thou may'st brain **him,**
Having first seized his books; or with a log
Batter his skull, or paunch him with a stake,
Or cut his wezand with thy knife. Remember,
First to possess his books; for without them
He 's but a sot, as I am, nor hath not
One spirit to command: they all do hate him
As rootedly as I. Burn but his books;
He has brave utensils (for so he calls them),
Which, when he has a house, he 'll deck withal:
And that most deeply to consider is
The beauty of his daughter; he himself
Calls her a nonpareil: I never saw a woman,
But only Sycorax my dam, and she;
But she as far surpasseth Sycorax,
As great'st does least.

Ste.   Is it so brave a lass?
Cal. Ay, lord; she will become thy bed, I warrant,
And bring thee forth brave brood.
Ste. Monster, I will kill this man. His daughter and I
will be king and queen; (save our graces!) and Trinculo
and thyself shall be viceroys.—Dost thou like the plot,
Trinculo?
Trin. Excellent.
Ste. Give me thy hand: I am sorry I beat thee; but,
while thou livest, keep a good tongue in thy head.
Cal. Within this half-hour will he be asleep;
Wilt thou destroy him then?
Ste.   Ay, on mine honour.
Ari. This will I tell my master.
Cal. Thou mak'st me merry: I am full of pleasure.
Let us be jocund: will you troll the catch
You taught me but while-ere?
Ste. At thy request, monster, I will do reason, any
reason. Come on, Trinculo, let us sing.   [*Sings*
    Flout 'em, and scout 'em ; and scout 'em, and flout 'em ;
    Thought is free.
Cal. That 's not the tune.

[*Ariel plays the tune on a tabor and pipe*

Ste. What is this same?
Trin. This is the tune of our catch, played by the
picture of Nobody.
Ste. If thou beest a man, show thyself in thy likeness;
if thou beest a devil, take 't as thou list.
Trin. O, forgive me my sins!
Ste. He that dies, pays all debts: I defy thee.—Mercy
upon us.
Cal. Art thou afeard?
Ste. No, monster, not I.
Cal. Be not afeard; the isle is full of noises,
Sounds, and sweet airs, that give delight, and hurt not.
Sometimes a thousand twangling instruments
Will hum about mine ears; and sometime voices,
That, if I then had waked after long sleep,
Will make me sleep again: and then, in dreaming,
The clouds, methought, would open, and show riches
Ready to drop upon me, that when I waked
I cried to dream again.
Ste. This will prove a brave kingdom to me, where I
shall have my music for nothing.
Cal. When Prospero is destroyed.
Ste. That shall be by-and-by: I remember the story.
Trin. The sound is going away: let 's follow it, and
after do our work.

183

Ste. Lead, monster; we 'll follow.—I would, I could
see this taborer: he lays it on.
  Trin. Wilt come? I 'll follow, Stephano.   [*Exeunt*

SCENE III.—Another Part of the Island

Enter ALONSO, SEBASTIAN, ANTONIO, GONZALO, ADRIAN,
        FRANCISCO, *and others*

  Gon.   By 'r lakin, I can go no farther, sir;
My old bones ache: here 's a maze trod, indeed,
Through forth-rights and meanders! By your patience.
I needs must rest me.
  Alon.   Old lord, I cannot blame thee,
Who am myself attached with weariness,
To the dulling of my spirits.   Sit down, and rest.
Even here I will put off my hope, and keep it
No longer for my flatterer: he is drowned.
Whom thus we stray to find, and the sea mocks
Our frustrate search on land.   Well, let him go.
  Ant.   [*Aside to Seb.*]   I am right glad that he 's so out
      of hope.
Do not, for one repulse, forgo the purpose
That you resolved to effect.
  Seb.   [*Aside to Ant.*]   The next advantage
Will we take throughly.
  Ant.   [*Aside to Seb.*]   Let it be to-night;
For, now they are oppress'd with travel, they
Will not, nor cannot, use such vigilance,
As when they are fresh.
  Seb.   [*Aside to Ant.*]   I say, to-night: no more.

Solemn and strange music; and PROSPERO *above, invisible.
  Enter several strange Shapes bringing in a banquet:
  they dance about it with gentle actions of salutation, and
  inviting the King, &c., to eat, they depart.*

  Alon.   What harmony is this? my good friends, hark!
  Gon.   Marvellous sweet music!
  Alon.   Give us kind keepers, heavens!   What were
these.
  Seb.   A living drollery.   Now, I will believe
That there are unicorns: that in Arabia
There is one tree, the phœnix' throne; one phœnix
At this hour reigning there.
  Ant.   I 'll believe both;
And what does else want credit, come to me,

And I 'll be sworn 't is true: travellers ne'er did lie,
Though fools at home condemn them.
    Gon.   If in Naples
I should report this now, would they believe me?
If I should say, I saw such islanders
(For, certes, there are people of the island),
Who, though they are of monstrous shape, yet, note,
Their manners are more gentle-kind than of
Our human generation you shall find
Many, nay, almost any.
    Pro. [*Aside*]   Honest lord,
Thou hast said well, for some of you there present
Are worse than devils.
    Alon.   I cannot too much muse,
Such shapes, such gesture, and such sound, expressing
(Although they want the use of tongue) a kind
Of excellent dumb discourse.
    Pro. [*Aside*]   Praise in departing.
    Fran.   They vanished strangely.
    Seb.   No matter, since
They have left their viands behind, for we have stomachs.
Will 't please you taste of what is here?
    Alon.   Not I.
    Gon.   Faith, sir, you need not fear.   When we were boys,
Who would believe that there were mountaineers
Dew-lapped like bulls, whose throats had hanging at them
Wallets of flesh? or that there were such men,
Whose heads stood in their breasts? which now we find
Each putter-out of five for one will bring us
Good warrant of.
    Alon.   I will stand to, and feed,
Although my last: no matter, since I feel
The best is past.—Brother, my lord the duke,
Stand to, and do as we.

Thunder and lightning. Enter ARIEL *like a harpy, claps
his wings upon the table, and, with a quaint device, the
banquet vanishes.*

    Ari. You are three men of sin, whom Destiny
(That hath to instrument this lower world,
And what is in 't) the never-surfeited sea
Hath caused to belch up you, and on this island
Where man doth not inhabit; you 'mongst men
Being most unfit to live. I have made you mad;
And even with such like valour men hang and drown
Their proper selves.
             [*Seeing Alon., Seb., &c., draw their swords*
             You fools! I and my fellows

Are ministers of Fate: the elements,
Of whom your swords are tempered, may as well
Wound the loud winds, or with bemocked-at stabs
Kill the still-closing waters, as diminish
One dowle that 's in my plume; my fellow-ministers
Are like invulnerable.   If you could hurt,
Your swords are now too massy for your strengths,
And will not be uplifted.   But remember
(For that 's my business to you) that you three
From Milan did supplant good Prospero;
Exposed unto the sea (which hath requit it)
Him, and his innocent child: for which foul deed
The powers, delaying, not forgetting, have
Incensed the seas and shores, yea, all the creatures,
Against your peace.   Thee of thy son, Alonso,
They have bereft; and do pronounce by me,
Lingering perdition, worse than any death
Can be at once, shall step by step attend
You, and your ways; whose wraths to guard you from,
Which here, in this most desolate isle, else falls
Upon your heads, is nothing, but heart's sorrow,
And a clear life ensuing.

*He vanishes in thunder : then, to soft music, enter the Shapes
again, and dance with mocks and mows, and carry out
the table.*

    Pro. [*Aside*] Bravely the figure of this harpy hast thou
Performed, my Ariel; a grace it had, devouring.
Of my instruction hast thou nothing bated
In what thou hadst to say: so, with good life
And observation strange, my meaner ministers
Their several kinds have done.   My high charms work,
And these, mine enemies, are all knit up
In their distractions; they now are in my power;
And in these fits I leave them, while I visit
Young Ferdinand whom they suppose is drowned,
And his and my loved darling.   [*Exit Prospero*
    Gon. I' the name of something holy, sir, why stand you
In this strange stare?
    Alon.   O, it is monstrous! monstrous!
Methought, the billows spoke, and told me of it;
The winds did sing it to me; and the thunder,
That deep and dreadful organ-pipe, pronounced
The name of Prosper: it did bass my trespass.
Therefore my son i' the ooze is bedded; and
I 'll seek him deeper than e'er plummet sounded,
And with him there lie mudded.   [*Exit*
    Seb.   But one fiend at a time.
I 'll fight their legions o'er.

Ant.   I 'll be thy second.

> [*Exeunt Seb. and Ant.*

Gon. All three of them are desperate; their great
    guilt,
Like poison given to work a great time after,
Now 'gins to bite the spirits.—I do beseech you,
That are of suppler joints, follow them swiftly,
And hinder them from what this ecstasy
May now provoke them to.

Adr.   Follow, I pray you.   [*Exeunt*

ACT FOUR

Scene I.—Before Prospero's Cell

Enter Prospero, Ferdinand, *and* Miranda

Pro. If I have too austerely punished you,
Your compensation makes amends; for I
Have given you here a thread of mine own life,
Or that for which I live; whom once again
I tender to thy hand.   All thy vexations
Were but my trials of thy love, and thou
Hast strangely stood the test: here, afore Heaven,
I ratify this my rich gift.   O Ferdinand,
Do not smile at me that I boast her off,
For thou shalt find she will outstrip all praise
And make it halt behind her.

Fer.   I do believe it,
Against an oracle.

Pro. Then, as my gift, and thine own acquisition
Worthily purchased, take my daughter: but
If thou dost break her virgin-knot before
All sanctimonious ceremonies may
With full and holy rite be ministered,
No sweet aspersion shall the heavens let fall
To make this contract grow, but barren hate,
Sour-eyed disdain, and discord, shall bestrew
The union of your bed with weeds so loathly,
That you shall hate it both: therefore, take heed,
As Hymen's lamps shall light you.

Fer.   As I hope
For quiet days, fair issue, and long life,
With such love as 't is now,—the murkiest den,
The most opportune place, the strong'st suggestion
Our worser Genius can, shall never melt
Mine honour into lust, to take away
The edge of that day's celebration,

When I shall think, or Phœbus' steeds are foundered,
Or night kept chained below.
    Pro.   Fairly spoken.
Sit, then, and talk with her; she is thine own.—
What, Ariel, my industrious servant Ariel!

Enter ARIEL

    Ari.   What would my potent master? here I am.
    Pro.   Thou and thy meaner fellows your last service
Did worthily perform, and I must use you
In such another trick.   Go, bring the rabble,
O'er whom I give thee power, here, to this place:
Incite them to quick motion; for I must
Bestow upon the eyes of this young couple
Some vanity of mine art: it is my promise
And they expect it from me.
    Ari.   Presently?
    Pro.   Ay, with a twink,
    Ari.   Before you can say, "come," and "go,"
And breathe twice, and cry, "so so,"
Each one, tripping on his toe,
Will be here with mop and mow.
Do you love me, master?—no?
    Pro.   Dearly, my delicate Ariel. Do not approach,
Till thou dost hear me call.
    Ari.   Well:—I conceive.   [*Exit*
    Pro.   Look thou be true. Do not give dalliance
Too much the rein: the strongest oaths are straw
To the fire i' the blood. Be more abstemious,
Or else good night your vow.
    Fer.   I warrant you, sir;
The white-cold virgin snow upon my heart
Abates the ardour of my liver.
    Pro.   Well.—
Now come, my Ariel! bring a corollary,
Rather than want a spirit: appear, and pertly.—
No tongue, all eyes; be silent.   [*Soft music*

Enter IRIS

    Iris.   Ceres, most bounteous lady, thy rich leas
Of wheat, rye, barley, vetches, oats, and pease;
Thy turfy mountains, where live nibbling sheep,
And flat meads thatched with stover, them to keep;
Thy banks with pionéd and twilléd brims,
Which spongy April at thy hest betrims,
To make cold nymphs chaste crowns; and thy broom-
        groves,

Whose shadow the dismisséd bachelor loves,
Being lass-lorn; thy pole-clipt vineyard;
And thy sea-marge, sterile, and rocky-hard,
Where thou thyself dost air; the queen o' the sky,
Whose watery arch and messenger am I,
Bids thee leave these, and with her sovereign grace,
Here on this grass-plot, in this very place,
To come and sport: her peacocks fly amain:
Approach, rich Ceres, her to entertain.

Enter CERES

    Cer. Hail, many-coloured messenger, that ne'er
Dost disobey the wife of Jupiter;
Who with thy saffron wings upon my flowers
Diffuseth honey-drops, refreshing showers;
And with each end of thy blue bow dost crown
My bosky acres, and my unshrubbed down,
Rich scarf to my proud earth; why hath thy queen
Summoned me hither, to this short-grassed green?
    Iris. A contract of true love to celebrate,
And some donation freely to estate
On the blessed lovers.
    Cer.   Tell me, heavenly bow,
If Venus, or her son, as thou dost know,
Do now attend the queen?   Since they did plot
The means that dusky Dis my daughter got,
Her and her blind boy's scandaled company
I have forsworn.
    Iris.   Of her society
Be not afraid: I met her deity
Cutting the clouds towards Paphos, and her son
Dove-drawn with her.   Here thought they to have done
Some wanton charm upon this man and maid,
Whose vows are, that no bed-rite shall be paid
Till Hymen's torch be lighted; but in vain:
Mars's hot minion is returned again;
Her waspish-headed son has broke his arrows,
Swears he will shoot no more, but play with sparrows,
And be a boy right out.
    Cer.   Highest queen of state,
Great Juno comes: I know her by her gait.

Enter JUNO

    Juno. How does my bounteous sister?   Go with me
To bless this twain, that they may prosperous be
And honour'd in their issue.

Song

Juno. *Honour, riches, marriage-blessing,*
Long continuance, and increasing,
Hourly joys be still upon you !
Juno sings her blessings on you.

Cer. *Earth's increase, foison plenty,*
Barns and garners never empty ;
Vines with clustering bunches growing ;
Plants with goodly burden bowing.

Spring come to you, at the farthest,
In the very end of harvest !
Scarcity and want shall shun you ;
Ceres' blessing so is on you.

Fer. This is a most majestic vision, and
Harmonious charmingly.   May I be bold
To think these spirits?
Pro.   Spirits, which by mine art
I have from their confines called, to enact
My present fancies.
Fer.   Let me live here ever:
So rare a wondered father and a wife
Makes this place Paradise.

[*Juno and Ceres whisper, and send*
Iris on employment

Pro.   Sweet, now, silence:
Juno and Ceres whisper seriously,
There's something else to do.   Hush, and be mute,
Or else our spell is marred.
Iris. You nymphs, called Naiads, of the wandering
brooks,
With your sedged crowns, and ever-harmless looks,
Leave your crisp channels, and on this green land
Answer your summons: Juno does command.
Come, temperate nymphs, and help to celebrate
A contract of true love: be not too late.

Enter certain Nymphs

You sun-burnt sicklemen, of August weary,
Come hither from the furrow, and be merry.
Make holiday: your rye-straw hats put on,
And these fresh nymphs encounter every one
In country footing.

Enter certain Reapers, properly habited : they join with the
Nymphs in a graceful dance ; towards the end whereof
PROSPERO *starts suddenly, and speaks ; after which, to a*
strange, hollow, and confused noise, they heavily vanish.

190

Pro. [*Aside*] I had forgot that foul conspiracy
Of the beast Caliban, and his confederates
Against my life; the minute of their plot
Is almost come.—[*To the Spirits*] Well done.—Avoid:
       —no more.
   Fer. This is strange: your father 's in some passion
That works him strongly.
   Mira.   Never till this day,
Saw I him touched with anger so distempered.
   Pro. You do look, my son, in a moved sort,
As if you were dismayed: be cheerful, sir.
Our revels now are ended. These our actors,
As I foretold you, were all spirits, and
Are melted into air, into thin air:
And, like the baseless fabric of this vision,
The cloud-capped towers, the gorgeous palaces,
The solemn temples, the great globe itself,
Yea, all which it inherit, shall dissolve,
And, like this insubstantial pageant faded,
Leave not a rack behind. We are such stuff
As dreams are made of, and our little life
Is rounded with a sleep.—Sir, I am vexed,
Bear with my weakness, my old brain is troubled:
Be not disturbed with my infirmity.
If you be pleas'd, retire into my cell,
And there repose: a turn or two I'll walk,
To still my beating mind.
   Fer., Mira.   We wish your peace. [*Exeunt*
   Pro. Come with a thought;—I thank thee, Ariel,
       come!

Enter ARIEL

   Ari. Thy thoughts I cleave to. What 's thy pleasure?
   Pro.   Spirit,
We must prepare to meet with Caliban.
   Ari. Ay, my commander: when I presented Ceres,
I thought to have told thee of it, but I feared,
Lest I might anger thee.
   Pro. Say again, where didst thou leave these varlets?
   Ari. I told you, sir, they were red-hot with drinking;
So full of valour, that they smote the air
For breathing in their faces; beat the ground
For kissing of their feet; yet always bending
Towards their project. Then I beat my tabor,
At which, like unbacked colts, they pricked their ears,
Advanced their eyelids, lifted up their noses,
As they smelt music. So I charmed their ears,

That, calf-like, they my lowing followed, through
Toothed briers, sharp furzes, pricking goss, and thorns,
Which entered their frail shins.   At last I left them
I' the filthy-mantled pool beyond your cell,
There dancing up to the chins, that the foul lake
O'erstunk their feet.
  Pro.   This was well done, my bird.
Thy shape invisible retain thou still:
The trumpery in my house, go, bring it hither,
For stale to catch these thieves.
  Ari.   I go, I go.   [*Exit*
  Pro. A devil, a born devil, on whose nature
Nurture can never stick; on whom my pains,
Humanely taken, all, all lost, quite lost;
And as with age his body uglier grows,
So his mind cankers.   I will plague them all
Even to roaring.

   Re-enter ARIEL, *loaden with glistering apparel,* &c.

       Come, hang them on this line.

PROSPERO *and* ARIEL *remain invisible.   Enter* CALIBAN,
   STEPHANO, *and* TRINCULO, *all wet*

  Cal. Pray you, tread softly, that the blind mole may
    not
Hear a foot fall; we now are near his cell.
  Ste. Monster, your fairy, which, you say, is a harmless
fairy, has done little better than played the Jack with us.
  Trin. Monster, I do smell all horse-p—, at which my
nose is in great indignation.
  Ste. So is mine.   Do you hear, monster?   If I should
take a displeasure against you, look you,—
  Trin. Thou wert but a lost monster.
  Cal. Good, my lord, give me thy favour still.
Be patient, for the prize I'll bring thee to
Shall hoodwink this mischance: therefore, speak softly;
All 's hushed as midnight yet.
  Trin. Ay, but to lose our bottles in the pool,—
  Ste. There is not only disgrace and dishonour in that,
monster, but an infinite loss.
  Trin. That 's more to me than my wetting: yet this
is your harmless fairy, monster.
  Ste. I will fetch off my bottle, though I be o'er ears for
my labour.
  Cal. Pr'ythee, my king, be quiet.   Seest thou here,
This is the mouth o' the cell: no noise, and enter:
Do that good mischief, which may make this island

Thine own for ever, and I, thy Caliban,
For aye thy foot-licker.
    Ste. Give me thy hand. I do begin to have bloody
thoughts.
    Trin. O King Stephano! O peer! O worthy Stephano!
look, what a wardrobe here is for thee!
    Cal. Let it alone, thou fool: it is but trash.
    Trin. O, ho, monster! we know what belongs to a
frippery;—O King Stephano!
    Ste. Put off that gown, Trinculo, by this hand, I'll
have that gown.
    Trin. Thy grace shall have it.
    Cal. The dropsy drown this fool! what do you mean,
To dote thus on such luggage? Let's along,
And do the murder first: if he awake,
From toe to crown he'll fill our skins with pinches;
Make us strange stuff.
    Ste. Be you quiet, monster.—Mistress line, is not this
my jerkin? Now is the jerkin under the line: now, jerkin,
you are like to lose your hair, and prove a bald jerkin.
    Trin. Do, do: we steal by line and level, an 't like
your grace.
    Ste. I thank thee for that jest; here 's a garment for 't:
wit shall not go unrewarded, while I am king of this country. "Steal by line and level" is an excellent pass of pate;
there's another garment for 't.
    Trin. Monster, come, put some lime upon your fingers,
and away with the rest.
    Cal. I will have none on 't: we shall lose our time
And all be turned to barnacles, or to apes
With foreheads villainous low.
    Ste. Monster, lay-to your fingers: help to bear this
away where my hogshead of wine is, or I 'll turn you out
of my kingdom. Go to; carry this.
    Trin. And this.
    Ste. Ay, and this.

*A noise of hunters heard. Enter divers Spirits, in shape
  of hounds, and hunt them about:* PROSPERO *and* ARIEL
  setting them on.

    Pro. Hey, Mountain, hey!
    Ari. Silver, there it goes, Silver!
    Pro. Fury, Fury! there, Tyrant, there! hark, hark!
                [Cal., Ste., and Trin. are driven out
Go, charge my goblins that they grind their joints
With dry convulsions; shorten up their sinews
With agéd cramps, and more pinch-spotted make them.
Than pard or cat o' mountain.

Ari.   Hark! they roar.
Pro.   Let them be hunted soundly.   At this hour
Lie at my mercy all mine enemies:
Shortly shall all my labours end, and thou
Shalt have the air at freedom: for a little
Follow, and do me service.

                                        [*Exeunt*

ACT FIVE

Scene I.—Before the Cell of Prospero

Enter Prospero *in his magic robes; and* Ariel

Pro.   Now does my project gather to a head:
My charms crack not, my spirits obey, and time
Goes upright with his carriage.   How 's the day?
Ari.   On the sixth hour; at which time, my lord,
You said our work should cease.
Pro.   I did say so,
When first I raised the Tempest.   Say, my spirit,
How fares the King and 's followers?
Ari.   Confined together
In the same fashion as you gave in charge;
Just as you left them: all are prisoners, sir,
In the line-grove which weather-fends your cell;
They cannot budge till your release.   The king,
His brother, and yours, abide all three distracted,
And the remainder mourning over them,
Brimful of sorrow and dismay; but chiefly
Him that you termed the good old lord, Gonzalo:
His tears run down his beard, like winter's drops
From eaves of reeds.   Your charm so strongly works them,
That if you now beheld them, your affections
Would become tender.
Pro.   Dost thou think so, spirit?
Ari.   Mine would, sir, were I human.
Pro.   And mine shall.
Hast thou, which art but air, a touch, a feeling
Of their afflictions, and shall not myself,
One of their kind, that relish all as sharply
Passion as they, be kindlier moved than thou art?
Though with their high wrongs I am struck to the quick,
Yet, with my nobler reason, 'gainst my fury
Do I take part.   The rarer action is
In virtue than in vengeance: they being penitent,
The sole drift of my purpose doth extend
Not a frown further.   Go, release them, Ariel.

My charms I'll break, their senses I'll restore,
And they shall be themselves.
   Ari.   I'll fetch them, sir.   [*Exit*
   Pro. Ye elves of hills, brooks, standing lakes, and
       groves,
And ye that on the sands with printless foot
Do chase the ebbing Neptune, and do fly him
When he comes back; you demi-puppets that
By moonshine do the green-sour ringlets make,
Whereof the ewe not bites; and you whose pastime
Is to make midnight mushrooms; that rejoice
To hear the solemn curfew; by whose aid
(Weak masters though ye be) I have bedimmed
The noontide sun, called forth the mutinous winds,
And 'twixt the green sea and the azured vault
Set roaring war: to the dread rattling thunder
Have I given fire, and rifted Jove's stout oak
With his own bolt: the strong-based promontory
Have I made shake; and by the spurs plucked up
The pine and cedar. Graves, at my command,
Have waked their sleepers, oped, and let them forth
By my so potent art. But this rough magic
I here abjure; and, when I have required
Some heavenly music (which even now I do),
To work mine end upon their senses that
This airy charm is for, I'll break my staff,
Bury it certain fathoms in the earth,
And deeper than did ever plummet sound
I'll drown my book.   [*Solemn music*

Re-enter ARIEL: *after him,* ALONSO, *with a frantic gesture,
attended by* GONZALO; SEBASTIAN *and* ANTONIO *in like
manner, attended by* ADRIAN *and* FRANCISCO. *They all
enter the circle which* PROSPERO *had made, and there
stand charmed; which* PROSPERO *observing, speaks:*

A solemn air, and the best comforter
To an unsettled fancy, cure thy brains,
Now useless, boiled within thy skull! There stand,
For you are spell-stopped.—
Holy Gonzalo, honourable man,
Mine eyes, even sociable to the show of thine,
Fall fellowly drops.—The charm dissolves apace;
And as the morning steals upon the night,
Melting the darkness, so their rising senses
Begin to chase the ignorant fumes that mantle
Their clearer reason.—O good Gonzalo,
My true preserver, and a loyal sir
To him thou follow'st, I will pay thy graces

Home, both in word and deed.—Most cruelly
Didst thou, Alonso, use me and my daughter:
Thy brother was a furtherer in the act;—
Thou'rt pinched for 't now, Sebastian.—Flesh and blood,
You brother mine, that entertained ambition,
Expelled remorse and nature; who, with Sebastian
(Whose inward pinches therefore are most strong),
Would here have killed your king; I do forgive thee,
Unnatural though thou art.—Their understanding
Begins to swell, and the approaching tide
Will shortly fill the reasonable shores,
That now lie foul and muddy.—Not one of them,
That yet looks on me, or would know me.   Ariel,
Fetch me the hat and rapier in my cell;   [Exit Ariel
I will discase me, and myself present,
As I was sometime Milan.—Quickly, spirit;
Thou shalt ere long be free.

ARIEL sings, and helps to attire him

Ari.   *Where the bee sucks, there suck I,*
         In a cowslip's bell I lie;
         There I couch when owls do cry.
         On the bat's back I do fly
         After summer merrily.
         Merrily, merrily, shall I live now,
         Under the blossom that hangs on the bough.

Pro.   Why, that 's my dainty Ariel!   I shall miss
         thee;
But yet thou shalt have freedom:—so, so, so.—
To the king's ship, invisible as thou art:
There shalt thou find the mariners asleep
Under the hatches; the master, and the boatswain,
Being awake, enforce them to this place,
And presently, I pr'ythee.
     Ari.   I drink the air before me, and return
Or e'er your pulse twice beat.   [Exit Ariel
     Gon.   All torment, trouble, wonder and amazement
Inhabits here: some heavenly power guide us
Out of this fearful country!—
     Pro.   Behold, Sir King.
The wrongéd Duke of Milan, Prospero.
For more assurance that a living prince
Does now speak to thee, I embrace thy body;
And to thee, and thy company, I bid
A hearty welcome.
     Alon.   Whe'r thou beest he or no
Or some enchanted trifle to abuse me,

196

As late I have been, I not know: thy pulse
Beats as of flesh and blood; and, since I saw thee,
The affliction of my mind amends, with which,
I fear, a madness held me.   This must crave
(An if this be at all) a most strange story.
Thy dukedom I resign; and do entreat
Thou pardon me my wrongs.—But how should Prospero
Be living, and be here?—
    Pro.   First, noble friend,
Let me embrace thine age, whose honour cannot
Be measured, or confined.
    Gon.   Whether this be,
Or be not, I'll not swear.
    Pro.   You do yet taste
Some subtleties o' the isle, that will not let you
Believe things certain.—Welcome, my friends all.—
[*Aside to Seb. and Ant.*]   But you, my brace of lords, were
            I so minded,
I here could pluck his highness' frown upon you,
And justify you traitors: at this time
I will tell no tales.
    Seb.   [*Aside*]   The devil speaks in him.
    Pro.   No.—
For you, most wicked sir, whom to call brother
Would even infect my mouth, I do forgive
Thy rankest fault; all of them; and require
My dukedom of thee, which perforce, I know,
Thou must restore.—
    Alon.   If thou beest Prospero,
Give us particulars of thy preservation:
How thou hast met us here, who three hours since
Were wrecked upon this shore; where I have lost
(How sharp the point of this remembrance is!)
My dear son Ferdinand.
    Pro.   I am woe for 't, sir.
    Alon.   Irreparable is the loss, and patience
Says it is past her cure.
    Pro.   I rather think,
You have not sought her help; of whose soft grace,
For the like loss I have her sovereign aid,
And rest myself content.
    Alon.   You the like loss?
    Pro.   As great to me, as late; and, supportable
To make the dear loss, have I means much weaker
Than you may call to comfort you, for I
Have lost my daughter.
    Alon.   A daughter?
O heavens! that they were living both in Naples,
The king and queen there! that they were, I wish

Myself were mudded in that oozy bed
Where my son lies.   When did you lose your daughter?
    Pro.   In this last Tempest.   I perceive, these lords
At this encounter do so much admire,
That they devour their reason, and scarce think
Their eyes do offices of truth, their words
Are natural breath: but, howsoe'er you have
Been justled from your senses, know for certain,
That I am Prospero, and that very duke
Which was thrust forth of Milan; who most strangely
Upon this shore, where you were wrecked, was landed,
To be the lord on 't.   No more yet of this;
For 't is a chronicle of day by day,
Not a relation for a breakfast, nor
Befitting this first meeting.   Welcome, sir;
This cell 's my court: here have I few attendants,
And subjects none abroad: pray you, look in.
My dukedom since you have given me again,
I will requite you with as good a thing;
At least, bring forth a wonder, to content ye
As much as me my dukedom.—

The entrance of the cell opens, and discovers FERDINAND
and MIRANDA *playing at chess*

    Mira.   Sweet lord, you play me false.
    Fer.   No, my dearest love,
I would not for the world.
    Mira.   Yes, for a score of kingdoms you should wrangle,
And I would call it fair play.
    Alon.   If this prove
A vision of the island, one dear son
Shall I twice lose.
    Seb.   A most high miracle!—
    Fer.   Though the seas threaten, they are merciful:
I have cursed them without cause.

                            [*Ferd. kneels to Alon.*
    Alon.   Now, all the blessing
Of a glad father compass thee about!
Arise, and say how thou cam'st here.
    Mira.   O wonder!
How many goodly creatures are there here!
How beauteous mankind is!   O brave new world,
That has such people in 't!
    Pro.   'T is new to thee.
    Alon.   What is this maid, with whom thou wast at play?
Your eld'st acquaintance cannot be three hours:
Is she the goddess that hath severed us,
And brought us thus together?

Fer.   Sir, she is mortal:
But, my immortal Providence, she 's mine:
I chose her when I could not ask my father
For his advice, nor thought I had one.   She
Is daughter to this famous Duke of Milan,
Of whom so often I have heard renown,
But never saw before; of whom I have
Received a second life; and second father
This lady makes him to me.
    Alon.   I am hers,
But O, how oddly will it sound, that I
Must ask my child forgiveness.
    Pro.   There, sir, stop:
Let us not burden our remembrance with
A heaviness that 's gone.
    Gon.   I have inly wept,
Or should have spoke ere this.   Look down, you gods,
And on this couple drop a blessèd crown,
For it is you that have chalked the way
Which brought us hither!
    Alon.   I say, Amen, Gonzalo.
    Gon.   Was Milan thrust from Milan, that his issue
Should become kings of Naples?   O, rejoice
Beyond a common joy, and set it down
With gold on lasting pillars.   In one voyage
Did Claribel her husband find at Tunis;
And Ferdinand, her brother, found a wife,
Where he himself was lost; Prospero his dukedom,
In a poor isle; and all of us, ourselves,
When no man was his own.
    Alon.   [*To Ferd. and Mir.*]   Give me your hands:
Let grief and sorrow still embrace his heart,
That doth not wish you joy!
    Gon.   Be it so: Amen.

Re-enter ARIEL, *with the Master and Boatswain
amazedly following*

O look, sir, look, sir, here is more of us.
I prophesied, if a gallows were on land,
This fellow could not drown.—Now, blasphemy,
That swear'st grace o'erboard,.not an oath on shore?
Hast thou no mouth by land?   What is the news?
    Boats.   The best news is, that we have safely found
Our king, and company: the next, our ship,
Which but three glasses since we gave out split,
Is tight and yare, and bravely rigged as when
We first put out to sea.

Ari. [*Aside to Pro.*]   Sir, all this service
Have I done since I went.
Pro. [*Aside to Ari.*]   My tricksy spirit!
Alon.   These are not natural events; they strengthen
From strange to stranger. Say, how came you hither?
Boats. If I did think, sir, I were well awake,
I'd strive to tell you. We were dead of sleep,
And (how, we know not) all clapped under hatches,
Where, but even now, with strange and several noises
Of roaring, shrieking, howling, jingling chains,
And more diversity of sounds, all horrible,
We were awaked; straightway, at liberty:
Where we, in all her trim, freshly beheld
Our royal, good, and gallant ship; our master
Capering to eye her. On a trice, so please you,
Even in a dream, were we divided from them,
And were brought moping hither.
Ari. [*Aside to Pro.*]   Was 't well done?
Pro. [*Aside to Ari.*]   Bravely my diligence! Thou shalt
    be free.
Alon. This is as strange a maze as e'er men trod;
And there is in this business more than nature
Was ever conduct of; some oracle
Must rectify our knowledge.
Pro.   Sir, my liege,
Do not infest your mind with beating on
The strangeness of this business: at picked leisure,
Which shall be shortly, single I'll resolve you
(Which to you shall seem probable) of every
These happened accidents; till when, be cheerful,
And think of each thing well.—[*Aside to Ari.*] Come
    hither, spirit:
Set Caliban and his companions free;
Untie the spell. [*Exit Ariel*]—How fares my gracious
    sir?
There are yet missing of your company
Some few odd lads, that you remember not.

Re-enter ARIEL, *driving in* CALIBAN, STEPHANO, *and*
TRINCULO, *in their stolen apparel*

Ste. Every man shift for all the rest, and let no man
take care for himself, for all is but fortune.—Coragio,
bully-monster, Coragio!
Trin. If these be true spies which I wear in my head,
here's a goodly sight.
Cal. O Setebos! these be brave spirits, indeed.
How fine my master is! I am afraid
He will chastise me.

Seb.   Ha, ha!
What things are these, my Lord Antonio?
Will money buy them!
   Ant.   Very like: one of them
Is a plain fish, and, no doubt, marketable.
   Pro.   Mark but the badges of these men, my lords,
Then say, if they be true.—This misshapen knave,
His mother was a witch: and one so strong
That could control the moon, make flows and ebbs,
And deal in her command, without her power.
These three have robb'd me; and this demi-devil
(For he 's a bastard one) had plotted with them
To take my life: two of these fellows you
Must know, and own; this thing of darkness I
Acknowledge mine.
   Cal.   I shall be pinched to death.
   Alon.   Is not this Stephano, my drunken butler?
   Seb.   He is drunk now: where had he wine?
   Alon.   And Trinculo is reeling ripe: where should they
Find this grand liquor that hath gilded 'em?
How cam'st thou in this pickle?
   Trin.   I have been in such a pickle, since I saw you
last, that, I fear me, will never out of my bones: I shall
not fear fly-blowing.
   Seb.   Why, how now, Stephano?
   Ste.   O! touch me not: I am not Stephano, but a cramp.
   Pro.   You 'd be king of the isle, sirrah?
   Ste.   I should have been a sore one, then.
   Alon.   [*Pointing to Cal.*] This is a strange thing as
     e'er I look'd on.
   Pro.   He is as disproportioned in his manners
As in his shape.—Go, sirrah, to my cell;
Take with you your companions; as you look
To have my pardon, trim it handsomely.
   Cal.   Ay, that I will; and I'll be wise hereafter,
And seek for grace. What a thrice-double ass
Was I, to take this drunkard for a god,
And worship this dull fool!
   Pro.   Go to; away!
   Alon.   Hence, and bestow your luggage where you
     found it.
   Seb.   Or stole it, rather.   [*Exeunt Cal., Ste., and Trin.*
   Pro.   Sir, I invite your highness, and your train,
To my poor cell, where you shall take your rest
For this one night; which, part of it, I'll waste
With such discourse as, I not doubt, shall make it
Go quick away; the story of my life,
And the particular accidents gone by,
Since I came to this isle: and in the morn,

I 'll bring you to your ship, and so to Naples,
Where I have hope to see the nuptial
Of these our dear-belovéd solemnised:—
And thence retire me to my Milan, where
Every third thought shall be my grave.
 Alon.   I long
To hear the story of your life, which must
Take the ear strangely.
 Pro.   I 'll deliver all;
And promise you calm seas, auspicious gales,
And sail so expeditious, that shall catch
Your royal fleet far off.—My Ariel,—chick,—
That is thy charge; then to the elements!
Be free, and fare thou well!—Please you, draw near.
                 [*Exeunt*

EPILOGUE

Spoken by Prospero

Now my charms are all o'erthrown,
And what strength I have 's mine own;
Which is most faint: now, 't is true,
I must be here confined by you,
Or sent to Naples.   Let me not,
Since I have my dukedom got,
And pardoned the deceiver, dwell
In this bare island, by your spell;
But release me from my bands,
With the help of your good hands.
Gentle breath of yours my sails
Must fill, or else my project fails,
Which was to please.   Now I want
Spirits to enforce, art to enchant;
And my ending is despair
Unless I be relieved by prayer,
Which pierces so, that it assaults.
Mercy itself, and frees all faults.
As you from crimes would pardoned be,
Let your indulgence set me free.

TIMON OF ATHENS

DRAMATIS PERSONÆ

TIMON, *a noble Athenian*
LUCIUS ⎫
LUCULLUS ⎬ *flattering lords*
SEMPRONIUS ⎭
VENTIDIUS, *one of Timon's false friends*
APEMANTUS, *a churlish philosopher*
ALCIBIADES, *an Athenian captain*
FLAVIUS, *steward to Timon*
FLAMINIUS ⎫
LUCILIUS ⎬ *servants to Timon*
SERVILIUS ⎭
CAPHIS ⎫
PHILOTUS ⎟
TITUS ⎟
LUCIUS ⎬ *servants to Timon's creditors*
HORTENSIUS ⎟
And others ⎭
Three Strangers. A Page. A Fool
Poet, Painter, Jeweller, and Merchant
An Old Athenian

PHRYNIA ⎫ *mistresses to Alcibiades*
TIMANDRA ⎭

Cupid and Maskers
Lords, Senators, Officers, Soldiers, Thieves, and Attendants

SCENE.—*Athens and the neighbouring woods.*

TIMON OF ATHENS

ACT ONE

Scene I.—Athens. A Hall in Timon's House

*Enter Poet, Painter, Jeweller, Merchant, Mercer, and others,
at several doors*

Poet. Good day, sir.
Pain.   I am glad you're well.
Poet. I have not seen you long. How goes the world?
Pain. It wears, sir, as it grows.
Poet.   Ay, that 's well known;
But what particular rarity? what strange,
Which manifold record not matches? See,
Magic of Bounty, all these spirits thy power
Hath conjured to attend! I know the merchant.
Pain. I know them both: th' other 's a jeweller.
Mer. O! 't is a worthy lord!
Jew.   Nay, that 's most fixed.
Mer. A most incomparable man; breathed, as it were,
To an untirable and continuate goodness:
He passes.
Jew. I have a jewel here—
Mer. O, pray, let 's see 't: for the Lord Timon, sir?
Jew. If he will touch the estimate: but, for that—
Poet. "When we for recompense have praised the vile,
It stains the glory in that happy verse,
Which aptly sings the good."
Mer.   'T is a good form.
Jew. And rich: here is a water, look ye.
Pain. You are rapt, sir, in some work, some dedication
To the great lord.
Poet.   A thing slipped idly from me.
Our poesy is as a gum, which oozes
From whence 't is nourished: the fire i' the flint
Shows not, till it be struck; our gentle flame
Provokes itself, and, like the current, flies
Each bound it chafes.—What have you there?
Pain. A picture, sir.—When comes your book forth?
Poet. Upon the heels of my presentment, sir.
Let 's see your piece.
Pain.   'T is a good piece.
Poet.   So 't is:
This comes off well and excellent.
Pain.   Indifferent.

Poet.   Admirable.   How this grace
Speaks his own standing! what a mental power
This eye shoots forth! how big imagination
Moves in this lip! to the dumbness of the gesture
One might interpret.
    Pain.   It is a pretty mocking of the life.
Here is a touch; is 't good?
    Poet.   I'll say of it,
It tutors nature: artificial strife
Lives in these touches, livelier than life.

Enter certain Senators, who pass over the stage

    Pain.   How this lord is followed!
    Poet.   The senators of Athens:—happy man!
    Pain.   Look,—more!
    Poet.   You see this confluence, this great flood of visi-
        tors.
I have, in this rough work, shaped out a man
Whom this beneath-world doth embrace and hug
With amplest entertainment: my free drift
Halts not particularly, but moves itself
In a wide sea of wax: no levelled malice
Infects one comma in the course I hold;
But flies an eagle flight, bold and forth on,
Leaving no tract behind.
    Pain.   How shall I understand you?
    Poet.   I'll unbolt to you.
You see how all conditions, how all minds,—
As well of glib and slippery creatures as
Of grave and austere quality—tender down
Their services to Lord Timon: his large fortune,
Upon his good and gracious nature hanging,
Subdues and properties to his love and tendance
All sorts of hearts; yea, from the glass-faced flatterer
To Apemantus, that few things loves better
Than to abhor himself: even he drops down
The knee before him, and returns in peace
Most rich in Timon's nod.
    Pain.   I saw them speak together.
    Poet.   Sir, I have upon a high and pleasant hill
Feigned Fortune to be throned; the base o' the mount
Is ranked with all deserts, all kinds of natures
That labour on the bosom of this sphere
To propagate their states; amongst them all
Whose eyes are on this sovereign lady fixed,
One do I personate of Lord Timon's frame,
Whom Fortune with her ivory hand wafts to her,
Whose present grace to present slaves and servants

Translates his rivals.
    Pain.   'T is conceived to scope,
This throne, this Fortune, and this bill, methinks,
With one man beckoned from the rest below,
Bowing his head against the steepy mount
To climb his happiness, would be well expressed
In our condition.
    Poet.   Nay, sir, but hear me on.
All those which were his fellows but of late
Some better than his value—on the moment
Follow his strides, his lobbies filled with tendance,
Rain sacrificial whisperings in his ear.
Make sacred even his stirrup, and through him
Drink the free air.
    Pain.   Ay, marry, what of these?
    Poet. When Fortune, in her shift and change of
        mood,
Spurns down her late beloved, all his dependants,
Which laboured after him to the mountain's top,
Even on their knees and hands, let him slip down,
Not one accompanying his declining foot.
    Pain. 'T is common.
A thousand moral paintings I can show,
That shall demonstrate these quick blows of Fortune's
More pregnantly than words. Yet you do well
To show Lord Timon that mean eyes have seen
The foot above the head.

Trumpets sound. Enter TIMON, *attended; the Servant
   of* VENTIDIUS *talking with him;* LUCILIUS *and
       other attendants following*

    Tim.   Imprisoned is he, say you?
    Ven. Serv. Ay, my good lord: five talents is his debt,
His means most short, his creditors most strait:
Your honourable letter he desires
To those have shut him up; which failing him
Periods his comfort.
    Tim.   Noble Ventidius!—Well;
I am not of that feather, to shake off
My friend when he must need me. I do know him
A gentleman that well deserves a help,—
Which he shall have: I'll pay the debt, and free him.
    Ven. Serv. Your lordship ever binds him.
    Tim. Commend me to him; I will send his ransom;
And, being enfranchised, bid him come to me.
'T is not enough to help the feeble up,
But to support him after.—Fare you well.
    Ven. Serv. All happiness to your honour!   [*Exit*

Enter an Old Athenian,

Old Ath. Lord Timon, hear me speak.
Tim.   Freely, good father.
Old Ath. Thou hast a servant named Lucilius.
Tim. I have so: what of him?
Old Ath. Most noble Timon, call the man before thee.
Tim. Attends he here, or no?—Lucilius!
Luc. [*coming forward*] Here, at your lordship's service.
Old Ath. This fellow here, Lord Timon, this thy creature
By night frequents my house.   I am a man
That from my first have been inclined to thrift,
And my estate deserves an heir more raised
Than one which holds a trencher.
Tim.   Well; what further?
Old Ath. One only daughter have I, no kin else,
On whom I may confer what I have got:
The maid is fair, o' the youngest for a bride,
And I have bred her at my dearest cost,
In qualities of the best.   This man of thine
Attempts her love: I pr'ythee, noble lord,
Join with me to forbid him her resort;
Myself have spoke in vain.
Tim.   The man is honest.
Old Ath. Therefore he will be, Timon:
His honesty rewards him in itself,
It must not bear my daughter.
Tim.   Does she love him?
Old Ath. She is young, and apt:
Our own precedent passions do instruct us
What levity 's in youth.
Tim. [*To Lucilius*] Love you the maid?
Luc. Ay, my good lord: and she accepts of it.
Old Ath. If in her marriage my consent be missing,
I call the gods to witness, I will choose
Mine heir from forth the beggars of the world,
And dispossess her all.
Tim.   How shall she be endowed,
If she be mated with an equal husband?
Old Ath. Three talents on the present; in future, all.
Tim. This gentleman of mine hath served me long;
To build his fortune, I will strain a little,
For 't is a bond in men.   Give him thy daughter;
What you bestow, in him I'll counterpoise,
And make him weigh with her.
Old Ath.   Most noble lord,
Pawn me to this your honour, she is his.
Tim. My hand to thee: mine honour on my promise.
Luc. Humbly I thank your lordship.   Never may

That state or fortune fall into my keeping,
Which is not owed to you!
                                    [*Exeunt Lucilius and Old Athenian*
  Poet.   Vouchsafe my labour, and long live your lordship!
  Tim.   I thank you; you shall hear from me anon:
Go not away.—What have you there, my friend?
  Pain.   A piece of painting, which I do beseech
Your lordship to accept.
  Tim.   Painting is welcome.
The painting is almost the natural man;
For since dishonour traffics with man's nature,
He 's but outside: these pencilled figures are
Even such as they give out.   I like your work;
And you shall find like it: wait attendance
Till you hear further from me.
  Pain.   The gods preserve ye!
  Tim.   Well fare you, gentleman: give me your
           hand;
We must needs dine together.—Sir, your jewel
Hath suffered under praise.
  Jew.   What, my lord! dispraise?
  Tim.   A mere satiety of commendations.
If I should pay you for 't as 't is extolled,
It would unclew me quite.
  Jew.   My lord, 't is rated
As those which sell would give: but you well know,
Things of like value, differing in the owners,
Are prizéd by their masters.   Believe 't, dear lord,
You mend the jewel by the wearing it.
  Tim.   Well mocked.
  Mer.   No, my good lord; he speaks the common tongue,
Which all men speak with him.
  Tim.   Look, who comes here:
Will you be chid?

                        Enter APEMANTUS

  Jew.   We 'll bear, with your lordship.
  Mer.   He'll spare none.
  Tim.   Good morrow to thee, gentle Apemantus.
  Apem.   Till I be gentle, stay thou for thy good morrow;
When thou art Timon's dog, and these knaves honest.
  Tim.   Why dost thou call them knaves? thou know'st
           them not.
  Apem.   Are they not Athenians?
  Tim.   Yes.
  Apem.   Then I repent not.
  Jew.   You know me, Apemantus?
  Apem.   Thou know'st I do; I called thee by thy name.

Tim. Thou art proud, Apemantus.

Apem. Of nothing so much as that I am not like Timon.

Tim. Whither art going?

Apem. To knock out an honest Athenian's brains.

Tim. That 's a deed thou 'lt die for.

Apem. Right, if doing nothing be death by the law.

Tim. How likest thou this picture, Apemantus?

Apem. The best, for the innocence.

Tim. Wrought he not well that painted it?

Apem. He wrought better that made the painter; and yet he 's but a filthy piece of work.

Pain. You are a dog.

Apem. Thy mother 's of my generation: what 's she, if I be a dog?

Tim. Wilt dine with me, Apemantus?

Apem. No; I eat not lords.

Tim. An thou shouldst, thou 'dst anger ladies.

Apem. O, they eat lords; so they come by great bellies.

Tim. That 's a lascivious apprehension.

Apem. So thou apprehendest it; take it for thy labour.

Tim. How dost thou like this jewel, Apemantus?

Apem. Not so well as plain-dealing, which will not cost a man a doit.

Tim. What dost thou think 't is worth?

Apem. Not worth my thinking.—How now, poet?

Poet. How now, philosopher?

Apem. Thou liest.

Poet. Art not one?

Apem. Yes.

Poet. Then I lie not.

Apem. Art not a poet?

Poet. Yes.

Apem. Then thou liest: look in thy last work, where thou hast feigned him a worthy fellow.

Poet. That 's not feigned, he is so.

Apem. Yes, he is worthy of thee, and to pay thee for thy labour: he that loves to be flattered is worthy o' the flatterer. Heavens, that I were a lord!

Tim. What wouldst do then, Apemantus?

Apem. Even as Apemantus does now, hate a lord with my heart.

Tim. What, thyself?

Apem. Ay.

Tim. Wherefore?

Apem. That I had no angry wit to be a lord.—Art not thou a merchant?

Mer. Ay, Apemantus.

Apem. Traffic confound thee, if the gods will not!

Mer. If traffic do it, the gods do it.

Apem.   Traffic's thy god; aud thy god confound thee!

Trumpets sound.   Enter a Servant

Tim.   What trumpet's that?
Serv.   'T is Alcibiades, and some twenty horse,
All of companionship.
Tim.   Pray, entertain them; give them guide to us.—
                         [*Exeunt some Attendants*
You must needs dine with me.—Go not you hence,
Till I have thanked you; and, when dinner 's done,
Show me this piece.—I am joyful of your sights.—

Enter ALCIBIADES, *with his Company*

Most welcome, sir!
Apem.   So, so; there!—
Achés contract and starve your supple joints!—
That there should be small love 'mongst these sweet
         knaves,
And all this courtesy!   The strain of man's bred out
Into baboon and monkey.
Alcib.   Sir, you have saved my longing, and I feed
Most hungerly on your sight.
Tim.   Right welcome, sir:
Ere we depart, we 'll share a bounteous time
In different pleasures.   Pray you, let us in.
                         [*Exeunt all but Apemantus*

Enter two Lords

First Lord.   What time o' day is 't, Apemantus?
Apem.   Time to be honest.
First Lord.   That time serves still.
Apem.   The most accursèd thou, that still omitt'st it.
Second Lord.   Thou art going to Lord Timon's feast.
Apem.   Ay; to see meat fill knaves, and wine **heat**
fools.
Second Lord.   Fare thee well, fare thee well.
Apem.   Thou art a fool to bid me farewell twice.
Second Lord.   Why, Apemantus?
Apem.   Shouldst have kept one to thyself, **for I mean to**
give thee none.
First Lord.   Hang thyself.
Apem.   No, I will do nothing at thy bidding: make
thy requests to thy friend.
Second Lord.   Away, unpeaceable dog, or I'll spurn thee
hence!
Apem.   I will fly, like a dog, the heels o' the àss.   [*Exit*

First Lord.   He's opposite to humanity.   Come, shall we
      in
And taste Lord Timon's bounty? he outgoes
The very heart of kindness.
      Second Lord.   He pours it out; Plutus, the god of gold,
Is but his steward: no meed but he repays
Seven-fold above itself; no gift to him
But breeds the giver a return exceeding
All use of quittance.
      First Lord.   The noblest mind he carries
That ever governed man.
      Second Lord.   Long may he live in fortunes! Shall
      we in?
      First Lord.   I'll keep you company.   [*Exeunt*

SCENE II.—Athens.   A Room of State in TIMON'S
                    House

Hautboys playing loud music.   A great banquet served in;
    FLAVIUS *and others attending: then enter* TIMON, ALCIBIA-
    DES, LUCIUS, LUCULLUS, SEMPRONIUS, *and other Ath-*
    enian Senators, with VENTIDIUS, *whom Timon released*
    from prison, and Attendants.   Then comes, dropping
    after all, APEMANTUS, *discontentedly, like himself*

      Ven.   Most honoured Timon.
It hath pleased the gods to remember my father's age,
And call him to long peace.
He is gone happy, and has left me rich:
Then, as in grateful virtue I am bound
To your free heart, I do return those talents,
Doubled with thanks and service, from whose help
I derived liberty.
      Tim.   O, by no means,
Honest Ventidius: you mistake my love:
I gave it freely ever; and there 's none
Can truly say he gives, if he receives:
If our betters play at that game we must not dare
To imitate them: faults that are rich are fair.
      Ven.   A noble spirit.
      Tim.   Nay, my lords,
Ceremony was but devised at first
To set a gloss on faint deeds, hollow welcomes
Recanting goodness, sorry ere 't is shown;
But where there is true friendship, there needs none.
Pray, sit; more welcome are ye to my fortunes
                    212

Than my fortunes to me.   [*They sit*
  First Lord. My lord, we always have confessed it—
  Apem. Ho, ho, confessed it? hanged it, have you
not?
  Tim. O, Apemantus,—you are welcome.
  Apem. No, you shall not make me welcome;
I come to have thee thrust me out of doors.
  Tim. Fie, thou 'rt a churl; ye 've got a humour there
Does not become a man, 't is much to blame.—
They say, my lords, *Ira furor brevis est*,
But yond man, he is ever angry.
Go, let him have a table by himself;
For he does neither affect company
Nor is he fit for it, indeed.
  Apem. Let me stay at thine apperil, Timon:
I come to observe; I give thee warning on 't.
  Tim. I take no heed of thee; thou 'rt an Athenian;
therefore, welcome. I myself would have no power;
pr'ythee, let my meat make thee silent.
  Apem. I scorn thy meat; 't would choke me, for I
should ne'er flatter thee.—O you gods! what a number
of men eat Timon, and he sees 'em not!
It grieves me to see
So many dip their meat in one man's blood;
And all the madness is, he cheers them up too.
I wonder, men dare trust themselves with men;
Methinks, they should invite them without knives;
Good for their meat, and safer for their lives.
There 's much example for 't; the fellow, that sits next
him now, parts bread with him, and pledges the breath
of him in a divided draught, is the readiest man to kill him;
it has been proved.
If I were a huge man, I should fear to drink at meals,
Lest they should spy my wind-pipe's dangerous notes:
Great men should drink with harness on their throats.
  Tim. [*to a Lord who drinks to him*] My lord, in heart;
        and let the health go round.
  Second Lord. Let it flow this way, my good lord.
  Apem. Flow this way! A brave fellow!—he keeps
his tides well. Those healths will make thee and thy state
look ill, Timon.
Here 's that, which is too weak to be a sinner,
Honest water, which ne'er left man i' the mire:
This and my food are equals: there 's no odds:
Feasts are too proud to give thanks to the gods.
        Immortal gods, I crave no pelf
        I pray for no man but myself.
        Grant I may never prove so fond
        To trust man on his oath or bond;

Or a harlot for her weeping;
Or a dog that seems a-sleeping;
Or a keeper with my freedom;
Or my friends, if I should need 'em.
Amen.   So fall to 't:
Rich men sin, and I eat root.

[*Eats and drinks*
Much good dich thy good heart, Apemantus!

Tim.   Captain Alcibiades, your heart 's in the field now.

Alcib.   My heart is ever at your service, my lord.

Tim.   You had rather be at a breakfast of enemies, than a dinner of friends.

Alcib.   So they were bleeding-new, my lord, there 's no meat like 'em: I could wish my best friend at such a feast.—

Apem.   Would all those flatterers were thine enemies then, that then thou mightst kill 'em, and bid me to 'em.—

First Lord.   Might we but have that happiness, my lord, that you would once use our hearts, whereby we might express some part of our zeals, we should think ourselves for ever perfect.

Tim.   O, no doubt, my good friends, but the gods themselves have provided that I shall have much help from you: how had you been my friends else? why have you that charitable title from thousands, did you not chiefly belong to my heart? I have told more of you to myself than you can with modesty speak in your own behalf; and thus far I confirm you. O you gods, think I, what need we have any friends, if we should ne'er have need of 'em? they were the most needless creatures living, should we ne'er have use for 'em; and would most resemble sweet instruments hung up in cases, that keep their sounds to themselves. Why, I have often wished myself poorer, that I might come nearer to you. We are born to do benefits; and what better or properer can we call our own, than the riches of our friends? O, what a precious comfort 't is, to have so many, like brothers, commanding one another's fortunes! O joy, e'en made away ere 't can be born! Mine eyes cannot hold out water, methinks: to forget their faults, I drink to you.

Apem.   Thou weep'st to make them drink, Timon.

Second Lord.   Joy had the like conception in our eyes. And, at that instant, like a babe, sprung up.

Apem.   Ho, ho! I laugh to think that babe a bastard.

Third Lord.   I promise you, my lord, you moved me much.

Apem.   Much!   [*Tucket sounded*
Tim.   What means that trump?

Enter a Servant

Tim.   How now?
Serv. Please you, my lord, there are certain ladies
most desirous of admittance.
Tim. Ladies! What are their wills?
Serv. There comes with them a forerunner, my lord,
which bears that office to signify their pleasures.
Tim. I pray, let them be admitted.

Enter CUPID

Cup. Hail to thee, worthy Timon; and to all
That of his bounties taste!—The five best senses
Acknowledge thee their patron, and are come
Freely to gratulate thy plenteous bosom.
Th' ear, taste, touch, smell, pleased from thy table rise;
They only now come but to feast thine eyes.
Tim. They 're welcome all: let 'em have kind ad-
          mittance:
Music, make their welcome!
                                        [*Exit Cupid*
First Lord. You see, my lord, how ample you're be-
lov'd.

Music. Re-enter CUPID, *with a masque of Ladies as Amazons,
          with lutes in their hands, dancing and playing*

Apem. Hoy-day, what a sweep of vanity comes this
          way!
They dance! they are mad women.
Like madness is the glory of this life,
As this pomp shows to a little oil and root.
We make ourselves fools to disport ourselves;
And spend our flatteries to drink those men
Upon whose age we void it up again
With poisonous spite and envy.
Who lives, that 's not depravèd, or depraves?
Who dies, that bears not one spurn to their graves
Of their friend's gift?
I should fear, those that dance before me now
Would one day stamp upon me: 't has been done;
Men shut their doors against a setting sun.

The Lords rise from table, with much adoring of TIMON;
*and, to show their loves, each singles out an Amazon, and all
dance, men with women, a lofty strain or two to the hautboys, and cease.*

Tim. You have done our pleasures much grace, fair
          ladies.

Set a fair fashion on our entertainment,
Which was not half so beautiful and kind;
You've added worth unto 't, and lively lustre,
And entertained me with mine own device;
I am to thank you for 't.
  First Lady. My lord, you take us even at the best.
  Apem. 'Faith, for the worst is filthy; and would not
hold taking, I doubt me.
  Tim. Ladies, there is an idle banquet
Attends you: please you to dispose yourselves.
  All Lad. Most thankfully, my lord.
                          [*Exeunt Cupid and Ladies*
  Tim. Flavius!
  Flav. My lord.
  Tim. The little casket bring me hither.
  Flav. Yes, my lord. [*Aside*] More jewels yet!
There is no crossing him in 's humour;
Else I should tell him well, i' faith, I should,
When all 's spent, he 'd be crossed then, an he could.
'T is pity bounty had not eyes behind,
That man might ne'er be wretched for his mind.   [*Exit*
  First Lord. Where be our men?
  Serv. Here, my lord, in readiness.
  Second Lord. Our horses!

       Re-enter FLAVIUS, *with the casket*
  Tim. O my friends, I have one word to say to you.
Look you, my good lord,
I must entreat you, honour me so much,
As to advance this jewel; accept and wear it,
Kind my lord.
  First Lord. I am so far already in your gifts,—
  All. So are we all.

            Enter a Servant
  Serv. My lord, there are certain nobles of the senate
Newly alighted, and come to visit you.
  Tim. They 're fairly welcome.
  Flav.   I beseech your honour,
Vouchsafe me a word: it does concern you near.
  Tim. Near? why, then, another time I'll hear thee.
I pr'ythee,
Let 's be provided to show them entertainment.
  Flav. [*Aside*] I scarce know how.

          Enter another Servant
  Second Servant. May it please your honour, Lord
Lucius,

                    216

Out of his free love, hath presented to you
Four milk-white horses, trapped in silver.
    Tim. I shall accept them fairly: let the presents
be worthily entertained.

Enter a third Servant

                          How now, what news?
    Third Servant. Please you, my lord, that honourable
gentleman, Lord Lucullus, entreats your company to-
morrow to hunt with him; and has sent your honour two
brace of greyhounds.
    Tim. I'll hunt with him; and let them be received,
Not without fair reward.
    Flav. [*Aside*]   What will this come to?
He commands us to provide and give great gifts,
And all out of an empty coffer;
Nor will he know his purse; or yield me this,
To show him what a beggar his heart is,
Being of no power to make his wishes good.
His promises fly so beyond his state,
That what he speaks is all in debt, he owes
For every word: he's so kind, that he now
Pays interest for 't; his land's put to their books.
Well, would I were gently put out of office,
Before I were forced out!
Happier is he that has no friend to feed
Than such as do even enemies exceed.
I bleed inwardly for my lord.   [*Exit*
    Tim.   You do yourselves
Much wrong, you bate too much of your own merits:
Here, my lord, a trifle of our love.
    Second Lord. With more than common thanks I will
           receive it.
    Third Lord. O, he's the very soul of bounty.
    Tim. And now I remember, my lord, you gave
Good words the other day of a bay courser
I rode on; it is yours, because you liked it.
    Third Lord. O, I beseech you, pardon me, my lord,
In that.
    Tim. You may take my word, my lord, I know, no man
Can justly praise but what he does affect:
I weigh my friend's affection with mine own;
I'll tell you true.—I'll call to you.
    All Lords.   O, none so welcome.
    Tim. I take all and your several visitations
So kind to heart, 't is not enough to give:
Methinks, I could deal kingdoms to my friends,
And ne'er be weary.—Alcibiades,

Thou art a soldier, therefore seldom rich:
It comes in charity to thee; for all thy living
Is 'mongst the dead, and all the lands thou hast
Lie in a pitched field.
    Alcib.   Ay, defiléd land, my lord.
    First Lord. We are so virtuously bound—
    Tim. And so am I to you.
    Second Lord. So infinitely endeared—
    Tim. All to you.—Lights, more lights!
    First Lord.   The best of happiness,
Honour and fortunes, keep with you, Lord Timon!
    Tim. Ready for his friends.
                    [Exeunt Alcibiades, Lords, &c.
    Apem.   What a coil 's here:
Serving of becks, and jutting-out of bums!
I doubt whether their legs be worth the sums
That are given for 'em.   Friendship 's full of dregs:
Methinks, false hearts should never have sound legs.
Thus honest fools lay out their wealth on court'sies.
    Tim. Now, Apemantus, if thou wert not sullen, I
would be good to thee.
    Apem. No, I'll nothing: for if I should be bribed too,
there would be none left to rail upon thee; and then thou
wouldst sin the faster.   Thou giv'st so long, Timon, I fear
me, thou wilt give away thyself in paper shortly: what
need these feasts, pomps, and vain-glories?
    Tim. Nay, an you begin to rail on society once, I am
sworn not to give regard to you.   Farewell; and come
with better music.   *[Exit*
    Apem. So thou wilt not hear me now,—
Thou shalt not then,—I'll lock thy heaven from thee.
O, that men's ears should be
To counsel deaf, but not to flattery!

                           [Exit

ACT TWO

SCENE I.—Athens.   A Room in a Senator's House

Enter a Senator, with papers in his hand

    Sen. And late, five thousand: to Varro and to Isidore
He owes nine thousand;—besides my former sum,
Which makes it five-and-twenty.—Still in motion
Of raging waste?   It cannot hold; it will not.
If I want gold, steal but a beggar's dog
And give it Timon, why, the dog coins gold.

If I would sell my horse, and buy ten more
Better than he, why, give my horse to Timon,
Ask nothing, give it him, it foals me, straight,
Ten able horses.   No porter at his gate;
But rather one that smiles, and still invites
All that pass by.   It cannot hold; no reason
Can found his state in safety.   Caphis, ho!
Caphis, I say!

Enter CAPHIS

   Caph.   Here, sir: what is your pleasure?
   Sen. Get on your cloak, and haste you to Lord Timon;
Importune him for my moneys; be not ceased
With slight denial; nor then silenced, when—
'Commend me to your master'—and the cap
Plays in the right hand, thus:—but tell him, sirrah,
My uses cry to me; I must serve my turn
Out of mine own; his days and times are past,
And my reliances on 's fracted dates
Have smit my credit.   I love and honour him;
But must not break my back to heal his finger:
Immediate are my needs; and my relief
Must not be tossed and turned to me in words,
But find supply immediate.   Get you gone.
Put on a most importunate aspéct,
A visage of demand; for, I do fear,
When every feather sticks in his own wing,
Lord Timon will be left a naked gull,
Which flashes now a phœnix.   Get you gone.
   Caph. I go, sir.
   Sen. Take the bonds along with you,
And have the dates in compt.
   Caph.   I will, sir.
   Sen.   Go.   [*Exeunt*

SCENE II.—Athens.   A Hall in TIMON'S House

Enter FLAVIUS, *with many bills in his hand*

   Flav. No care, no stop! so senseless of expense
That he will neither know how to maintain it
Nor cease his flow of riot: takes no account
How things go from him, nor resumes no care
Of what is to continue.   Never mind
Was to be so unwise, to be so kind.
What shall be done?   He will not hear, till feel.
I must be round with him, now he comes from hunting.
Fie, fie, fie, fie!

219

Enter CAPHIS, *and the Servants of* ISIDORE *and* VARRO

Caph.   Good even, Varro.   What,
You come for money?
Var. Serv.   Is 't not your business too?
Caph.   It is;—and yours too, Isidore?
Isid. Serv.   It is so.
Caph.   Would we were all discharged!
Var. Serv.   I fear it.
Caph.   Here comes the lord.

Enter TIMON, ALCIBIADES, *and Lords, &c.*

Tim.   So soon as dinner 's done, we 'll forth again,
My Alcibiades,—With me? what is your will?
Caph.   My lord, here is a note of certain dues.
Tim.   Dues!   Whence are you?
Caph.   Of Athens here, my lord.
Tim.   Go to my steward.
Caph.   Please it your lordship, he hath put me off
To the succession of new days this month:
My master is awaked by great occasion
To call upon his own; and humbly prays you
That with your other noble parts you'll suit
In giving him his right.
Tim.   Mine honest friend,
I pr'ythee, but repair to me next morning.
Caph.   Nay, good my lord,—
Tim.   Contain thyself, good friend.
Var. Serv.   One Varro's servant, my good lord,—
Isid. Serv.   From Isidore;
He humbly prays your speedy payment,—
Caph.   If you did know, my lord, my master's wants,—
Var. Serv.   'T was due on forfeiture, my lord, six weeks
And past,—
Isid. Serv.   Your steward puts me off, my lord;
And I am sent expressly to your lordship.
Tim.   Give me breath.—
I do beseech you, good my lords, keep on;
I'll wait upon you instantly.—
                              [*Exeunt Alcibiades and Lords*
[*To Flavius*]   Come hither: pray you,
How goes the world, that I am thus encountered
With clamorous demands of date-broke bonds,
And the detention of long-since-due debts,
Against my honour?
Flav.   Please you, gentlemen,
The time is unagreeable to this business:
Your importunity cease till after dinner,

That I may make his lordship understand
Wherefore you are not paid.
    Tim.   Do so, my friends.—
See them well entertained.   *[Exit*
    Flav.   Pray, draw near.   *[Exit*

Enter APEMANTUS *and Fool*

    Caph.   Stay, stay; here comes the fool with Apemantus:
let 's ha' some sport with 'em.
    Var. Serv.   Hang him, he 'll abuse us.
    Isid. Serv.   A plague upon him, dog!
    Var. Serv.   How dost, fool?
    Apem.   Dost dialogue with thy shadow?
    Var. Serv.   I speak not to thee.
    Apem.   No; 't is to thyself.—[*To the Fool*] Come
away.
    Isid. Serv.   [*To Var. Serv.*] There 's the fool hangs on
your back already.
    Apem.   No, thou stand'st single; thou 'rt not on him
yet.
    Caph.   Where 's the fool now?
    Apem.   He last asked the question.—Poor rogues, and
usurers' men! bawds between gold and want!
    All Serv.   What are we, Apemantus?
    Apem.   Asses.
    All Serv.   Why?
    Apem.   That you ask me what you are, and do not
know yourselves.—Speak to 'em, fool.
    Fool.   How do you, gentlemen?
    All Serv.   Gramercies, good fool. How does your
mistress?
    Fool.   She 's e'en setting on water to scald such chickens
as you are. Would we could see you at Corinth!
    Apem.   Good! gramercy.

Enter Page

    Fool.   Look you, here comes my mistress' page.
    Page.   [*To the Fool*] Why, how now, captain? what do
you in this wise company?—How dost thou, Apemantus?
    Apem.   Would I had a rod in my mouth, that I might
answer thee profitably.
    Page.   Pr'ythee, Apemantus, read me the superscrip-
tion of these letters: I know not which is which.
    Apem.   Canst not read?
    Page.   No.
    Apem.   There will little learning die then, that day
thou art hanged. This is to Lord Timon; this to

Alcibiades. Go; thou wast born a bastard, and thou 'lt die a bawd.

Page. Thou wast whelped a dog, and thou shalt famish, a dog's death. Answer not; I am gone.

                                             [*Exit*

Apem. Even so thou outrunn'st grace. Fool, I will go with you to Lord Timon's.

Fool. Will you leave me there?

Apem. If Timon stay at home.—You three serve three usurers?

All Serv. Ay; would they served us!

Apem. So would I,—as good a trick as ever hangman served thief.

Fool. Are you three usurers' men?

All Serv. Ay, fool.

Fool. I think, no usurer but has a fool to his servant: my mistress is one, and I am her fool. When men come to borrow of your masters, they approach sadly, and go away merry; but they enter my mistress' house merrily, and go away sadly. The reason of this?

Var. Serv. I could render one.

Apem. Do it then, that we may account thee a whoremaster and a knave; which notwithstanding, thou shalt be no less esteemed.

Var. Serv. What is a whoremaster, fool?

Fool. A fool in good clothes, and something like thee. 'T is a spirit: sometime it appears like a lord; sometime like a lawyer; sometime like a philosopher, with two stones more than 's artificial one. He is very often like a knight; and generally in all shapes that man goes up and down in from fourscore to thirteen this spirit walks in.

Var. Serv. Thou art not altogether a fool.

Fool. Nor thou altogether a wise man: as much foolery as I have, so much wit thou lackest.

Apem. That answer might have become Apemantus.

All Serv. Aside, aside: here comes Lord Timon.

Re-enter TIMON *and* FLAVIUS

Apem. Come with me, fool, come.

Fool. I do not always follow lover, elder brother, and woman;—sometime, the philosopher.

                    [*Exeunt Apemantus and Fool*

Flav. Pray you, walk near: I'll speak with you, anon.

                              [*Exeunt Servants*

Tim. You make me marvel: wherefore, ere this time, Had you not fully laid my state before me,

That I might so have rated my expense
As I have leave of means?
  Flav.   You would not hear me,
At many leisures I proposed.
  Tim.   Go to:
Perchance some single vantages you took
When my indisposition put you back;
And that unaptness made your minister
Thus to excuse yourself.
  Flav.   O my good lord,
At many times I brought in my accounts,
Laid them before you: you would throw them off,
And say you found them in mine honesty.
When for some trifling present you have bid me
Return so much, I have shook my head, and wept;
Yea, 'gainst the authority of manners, prayed you
To hold your hand more close: I did endure
Not seldom nor so slight checks, when I have
Prompted you, in the ebb of your estate
And your great flow of debts. My loved lord,
Though you hear now—too late—yet now 's a time
The greatest of your having lacks a half
To pay your present debts.
  Tim.   Let all my land be sold.
  Flav. 'T is all engaged, some forfeited and gone;
And what remains will hardly stop the mouth
Of present dues. The future comes apace:
What shall defend the interim? and at length
How goes our reckoning?
  Tim. To Lacedæmon did my land extend.
  Flav. O my good lord, the world is but a word:
Were it all yours to give it in a breath,
How quickly were it gone!
  Tim.   You tell me true.
  Flav. If you suspect my husbandry, or falsehood,
Call me before the exactest auditors
And set me on the proof. So the gods bless me,
When all our offices have been oppressed
With riotous feeders, when our vaults have wept
With drunken spilth of wine, when every room
Hath blazed with lights, and brayed with minstrelsy,
I have retired me to a wasteful cock
And set mine eyes at flow.
  Tim.   Pr'ythee no more,
  Flav. Heavens, have I said, the bounty of this lord!
How many prodigal bits have slaves and peasants
This night englutted! Who is not Lord Timon's?
What heart, head, sword, force, means, but is Lord Timon's?
Great Timon, noble, worthy, royal Timon!

Ah, when the means are gone that buy this praise,
The breath is gone whereof this praise is made.
Feast-won, fast-lost; one cloud of winter showers,
These flies are couched.
    Tim.   Come, sermon me no further:
No villainous bounty yet hath passed my heart;
Unwisely, not ignobly, have I given.
Why dost thou weep? Canst thou the conscience lack
To think I shall lack friends? Secure thy heart;
If I would broach the vessels of my love,
And try the argument of hearts by borrowing,
Men and men's fortunes could I frankly use
As I can bid thee speak.
    Flav.   Assurance bless your thoughts!
    Tim.   And, in some sort, these wants of mine are
        crowned,
That I account them blessings; for by these
Shall I try friends. You shall perceive how you
Mistake my fortunes. I am wealthy in my friends.—
Within there! Flaminius! Servilius!

    Enter FLAMINIUS, SERVILIUS, *and other Servants*

    Servants. My lord? my lord?
    Tim. I will despatch you severally.—You [*to Servilius*]
to Lord Lucius;—[*to Flaminius*] to Lord Lucullus you;
I hunted with his honour to-day;—[*to another*] you, to
Sempronius. Commend me to their loves; and, I am
proud, say, that my occasions have found time to use them
toward a supply of money: let the request be fifty talents.
    Flam. As you have said, my lord.
    Flav. [*Aside*] Lord Lucius and Lucullus? humph!
    Tim. [*To another Servant*] Go you, sir, to the senators,—
Of whom, even to the state's best health, I have
Deserved this hearing,—bid 'em send o' the instant
A thousand talents to me.
    Flav.   I have been bold,
For that I knew it the most general way,
To them to use your signet and your name;
But they do shake their heads, and I am here
No richer in return.
    Tim.   Is 't true? can 't be?
    Flav. They answer, in a joint and corporate voice,
That now they are at fall, want treasure, cannot
Do what they would; are sorry—you are honourable—
But yet they could have wished—they know not—
Something hath been amiss—a noble nature
May catch a wrench—would all were well—'tis pity;—

And so, intending other serious matters,
After distasteful looks and these hard fractions,
With certain half-caps and cold moving nods
They froze me into silence.
    Tim.   You gods, reward them!—
Pr'ythee, man, look cheerily. These old fellows
Have their ingratitude in them hereditary:
Their blood is caked, 't is cold, it seldom flows;
'T is lack of kindly warmth they are not kind;
And nature, as it grows again toward earth,
Is fashioned for the journey, dull and heavy.
[*To another Servant*] Go to Ventidius.—[*To Flavius*]
    'Pr'ythee, be not sad;
Thou art true and honest: ingeniously I speak;
No blame belongs to thee.—[*To that other Servant*] Ven-
    tidius lately
Buried his father; by whose death he 's stepped
Into a great estate: when he was poor,
Imprisoned, and in scarcity of friends,
I cleared him with five talents: greet him from me;
Bid him suppose some good necessity
Touches his friend, which craves to be remembered
With those five talents.   [*Exit Servant*
[*To Flavius*]   That had, give 't these fellows
To whom 't is instant due. Ne'er speak, or think
That Timon's fortunes 'mong his friends can sink.
    Flav. I would I could not think it: that thought is
        bounty's foe,
Being free itself, it thinks all others so.   [*Exeunt*

ACT THREE

SCENE I.—Athens. A Room in the House of
LUCULLUS

FLAMINIUS *waiting. Enter a Servant to him*

    Serv. I have told my lord of you; he is coming down
    to you.
    Flam. I thank you, sir.

Enter LUCULLUS
    Serv. Here 's my lord.
    Lucul. [*Aside*] One of Lord Timon's men? a gift, I
warrant. Why, this hits right; I dreamt of a silver basin
and ewer to-night. Flaminius, honest Flaminius, you
are very respectively welcome, sir.—Fill me some wine.

[Exit Servant]—And how does that honourable, complete,
free-hearted gentleman of Athens, thy very bountiful good
lord and master?

Flam. His health is well, sir.

Lucul. I am right glad that his health is well, sir.
And what hast thou there under thy cloak, pretty Flaminius?

Flam. Faith, nothing but an empty box, sir, which,
in my lord's behalf, I come to entreat your honour to
supply; who, having great and instant occasion to use
fifty talents, hath sent to your lordship to furnish him,
nothing doubting your present assistance therein.

Lucul. La, la, la, la,—"nothing doubting," says he?
alas, good lord! a noble gentleman 't is, if he would not
keep so good a house. Many a time and often I have
dined with him, and told him on 't; and come again to
supper to him, of purpose to have him spend less: and
yet he would embrace no counsel, take no warning by
my coming. Every man has his fault, and honesty is his:
I have told him on 't, but I could ne'er get him from 't.

Re-enter Servant with wine

Serv. Please your lordship, here is the wine.

Lucul. Flaminius, I have noted thee always wise.
Here 's to thee.

Flam. Your lordship speaks your pleasure.

Lucul. I have observed thee always for a towardly
prompt spirit,—give thee thy due,—and one that knows
what belongs to reason; and canst use the time well, if
the time use thee well; good parts in thee.—*[To the Servant]*
Get you gone, sirrah. *[Exit Servant]*—Draw nearer,
honest Flaminius. Thy lord 's a bountiful gentleman;
but thou art wise, and thou knowest well enough, although
thou comest to me, that this is no time to lend money,
especially upon bare friendship, without security. Here 's
three solidares for thee: good boy, wink at me, and say
thou saw'st me not. Fare thee well.

Flam. Is 't possible, the world should so much differ,
And we alive that lived? Fly, damnéd baseness,
To him that worships thee.

                              [Throwing the money away

Lucul. Ha! now I see thou art a fool, and fit for thy
master.   *[Exit*

Flam. May these add to the number that may scald
     thee!
Let molten coin be thy damnation,
Thou disease of a friend, and not himself!
Has friendship such a faint and milky heart,

It turns in less than two nights? O you gods,
I feel my master's passion! This slave
Unto his honour has my lord's meat in him:
Why should it thrive, and turn to nutriment,
When he is turned to poison?
May disease only work upon 't, and when
He 's sick to death, let not that part of nature
Which my lord paid for be of any power!
To expel sickness, but prolong his hour!   [*Exit*

SCENE II.—Athens. A Public Place

Enter LUCIUS, *with three Strangers*

Luc. Who? the Lord Timon? he is my very good
friend, and an honourable gentleman.

First Strang. We know him for no less, though we are
but strangers to him. But I can tell you one thing, my
lord, and which I hear from common rumours: now Lord
Timon's happy hours are done and past, and his estate
shrinks from him.

Luc. Fie, no, do not believe it; he cannot want for
money.

Second Strang. But believe you this, my lord, that not
long ago, one of his men was with the Lord Lucullus, to
borrow so many talents; nay, urged extremely for 't, and
showed what necessity belonged to 't, and yet was denied.

Luc. How!

Second Strang. I tell you, denied, my lord.

Luc. What strange case was that! now, before the
gods, I am ashamed on 't. Denied that honourable man!
there was very little honour shown in 't. For my own
part, I must needs confess, I have received some small
kindnesses from him, as money, plate, jewels, and such-
like trifles, nothing comparing to his; yet, had he mistook
him, and sent to me, I should ne'er have denied his occasion
so many talents.

Enter SERVILIUS

Ser. See, by good hap, yonder 's my lord; I have
sweat to see his honour.—[*To Lucius*] My honoured
lord,—

Luc. Servilius! you are kindly met, sir. Fare thee
well. Commend me to thy honourable virtuous lord,
my very exquisite friend.

Ser. May it please your honour, my lord hath sent—

Luc. Ha! what has he sent? I am so much endeared

to that lord; he 's ever sending: how shall I thank him,
thinkest thou? And what has he sent now?

Ser. He has only sent his present occasion, now, my
lord: requesting your lordship to supply his instant use
with so many talents.

Luc. I know, his lordship is but merry with me:
He cannot want fifty-five hundred talents.

Ser. But in the meantime he wants less, my lord.
If his occasion were not virtuous,
I should not urge it half so faithfully.

Luc. Dost thou speak seriously, Servilius?

Ser. Upon my soul, 't is true, sir.

Luc. What a wicked beast was I, to disfurnish myself
against such a good time, when I might ha' shown myself
honourable! how unluckily it happened that I should
purchase the day before for a little part, and undo a great
deal of honour!—Servilius, now, before the gods, I am
not able to do; the more beast, I say.—I was sending to
use Lord Timon myself, these gentlemen can witness;
but I would not, for the wealth of Athens, I had done it
now. Commend me bountifully to his good lordship; and
I hope his honour will conceive the fairest of me, because
I have no power to be kind:—and tell him this from me,
I count it one of my greatest afflictions, say, that I cannot
pleasure such an honourable gentleman. Good Servilius,
will you befriend me so far, as to use mine own words
to him?

Ser. Yes, sir, I shall.

Luc. I 'll look you out a good turn, Servilius.—

[*Exit Servilius*

True, as you said, Timon is shrunk, indeed;
And he that 's once denied will hardly speed.   [*Exit*

First Strang. Do you observe this, Hostilius?

Second Strang. Ay, too well.

First Strang.   Why, this
Is the world's soul; and just of the same piece
Is every flatterer's sport. Who can call him
His friend that dips in the same dish? for, in
My knowing, Timon has been this lord's father,
And Timon kept his credit with his purse,
Supported his estate; nay, Timon's money,
Has paid his men their wages; he ne'er drinks,
But Timon's silver treads upon his lip;
And yet—O, see the monstrousness of man
When he looks out in an ungrateful shape!—
He does deny him, in respect of his,
What charitable men afford to beggars.

Third Strang. Religion groans at it.

228

First Strang.   For mine own part,
I never tasted Timon in my life,
Nor came any of his bounties over me
To mark me for his friend; yet, I protest,
For his right noble mind, illustrious virtue,
And for his honourable carriage,
Had his necessity made use of me
I would have put my wealth into donation
And the best half should have returned to him,
So much I love his heart.   But, I perceive,
Men must learn now with pity to dispense;
For policy sits above conscience.   [*Exeunt*

SCENE III.—Athens.   A Room in SEMPRONIUS's House

Enter SEMPRONIUS, *and a Servant of* TIMON's

Sem.   Must he needs trouble me in 't?   Hum! 'bove
all others?
He might have tried Lord Lucius, or Lucullus;
And now Ventidius is wealthy too,
Whom he redeemed from prison: all these three
Owe their estates unto him.
Serv.   My lord, they
Have all been touched, and found base metal; for
They 've all denied him.
Sem.   How! have they denied him?
Have Ventidius and Lucullus denied him?
And does he send to me?   Three? hum!—
It shows but little love or judgment in him:
Must I be his last refuge?   His friends, like physicians,
Thrice give him over: must I take the cure upon me?
He has much disgraced me in 't: I'm angry at him,
That might have known my place.   I see no sense for 't,
But his occasions might have woo'd me first;
For, in my conscience, I was the first man
That e'er received gift from him:
And does he think so backwardly of me now,
That I'll requite it last?   No:
So it may prove an argument of laughter
To the rest, and I 'mongst lords be thought a fool.
I'd rather than the worth of thrice the sum,
He had sent to me first, but for my mind's sake;
I'd such courage to do him good.   But now
Return,
And with their faint reply this answer join:
Who bates mine honour, shall not know my coin.
                                                  [*Exit*

Serv. Excellent! Your lordship 's a goodly villain.
The devil knew not what he did, when he made man politic,
—he crossed himself by 't: and I cannot think, but, in the
end, the villainies of man will set him clear. How fairly this
lord strives to appear foul! takes virtuous copies to be
wicked; like those that, under hot, ardent zeal, would set
whole realms on fire.
Of such a nature is his politic love
This was my lord's last hope; now all are fled,
Save the gods only. Now his friends are dead,
Doors, that were ne'er acquainted with their wards
Many a bounteous year, must be employed
Now to guard sure their master:
And this is all a liberal course allows;
Who cannot keep his wealth must keep his house.

[Exit

Scene IV.—Athens. A Hall in Timon's House

Enter Two Servants of Varro, *and the Servant of* Lucius,
meeting Titus, Hortensius, *and other Servants to*
Timon's *creditors, waiting his coming out*

First Var. Serv. Well met; good morrow, Titus and
            Hortensius.
Tit. The like to you, kind Varro.
Hor.   Lucius!
What, do we meet together?
Luc. Serv.   Ay, and I think,
One business does command us all; for mine
Is money.
Tit.   So is theirs, and ours.

Enter Philotus

Luc. Serv.   And Sir Philotus too!
Phi. Good day at once.
Luc. Serv.   Welcome, good brother.
What do you think the hour?
Phi.   Labouring for nine.
Luc. Serv. So much?
Phi.   Is not my lord seen yet?
Luc. Serv.   Not yet.
Phi. I wonder on 't: he was wont to shine at seven.
Luc. Serv. Ay, but the days are waxed shorter with
            him;
You must consider, that a prodigal course
Is like the sun's;

But not, like his, recoverable.   I fear,
'T is deepest winter in Lord Timon's purse;
That is, one may reach deep enough, and yet
Find little.
    Phi.   I am of your fear for that.
    Tit.   I'll show you how to observe a strange event.
Your lord sends now for money.
    Hor.   True, he does.
    Tit.   And he wears jewels now of Timon's gift.
For which I wait for money.
    Hor.   It is against my heart.
    Luc. Serv.   Mark, how strange it shows,
Timon in this should pay more than he owes:
And e'en as if your lord should wear rich jewels,
And send for money for 'em.
    Hor.   I'm weary of this charge, the gods can witness:
I know my lord hath sent of Timon's wealth,
And now ingratitude makes it worse than stealth.
    First Var. Serv.   Yes, mine's three thousand crowns.
              What's yours?
    Luc. Serv.   Five thousand, mine.
    First Var. Serv.   'T is much deep: and it should seem
              by the sum
Your master's confidence was above mine;
Else, surely, his had equalled.

Enter FLAMINIUS

    Tit.   One of Lord Timon's men.
    Luc. Serv.   Flaminius,—Sir, a word.   Pray, is my lord
              ready to come forth?
    Flam.   No, indeed, he is not.
    Tit.   We attend his lordship: pray, signify so much.
    Flam.   I need not tell him that; he knows you are too
              diligent.   [*Exit*

Enter FLAVIUS *in a cloak, muffled*

    Luc. Serv.   Ha! is not that his steward muffled so?
He goes away in a cloud: call him, call him.
    Tit.   Do you hear, sir?
    First Var. Serv.   By your leave, sir,—
    Flav.   What do you ask of me, my friend?
    Tit.   We wait for certain money here, sir.
    Flav.   Ay,
If money were as certain as your waiting,
'T were sure enough.   Why then preferred you not
Your sums and bills when your false masters ate
Of my lord's meat?   Then they could smile, and fawn
Upon his debts, and take down the interest

231

Into their gluttonous maws.
You do yourselves but wrong to stir me up;
Let me pass quietly:
Believe 't, my lord and I have made an end;
I have no more to reckon, he to spend.
   Luc. Serv.   Ay, but this answer will not serve.
   Flav.   If 't will not serve, 't is not so base as you;
For you serve knaves.

                                  [Exit
   First Var. Serv.   How! what does his cashiered worship
mutter?
   Second Var. Serv.   No matter what; he 's poor, and
that 's revenge enough. Who can speak broader than he
that has no house to put his head in? such may rail against
great buildings.

Enter SERVILIUS

   Tit.   O, here 's Servilius; now we shall know some
answer.
   Ser.   If I might beseech you, gentlemen, to repair some
other hour, I should derive much from 't; for, take it
on my soul, my lord leans wondrously to discontent.
His comfortable temper has forsook him; he 's much out
of health, and keeps his chamber.
   Luc. Serv.   Many do keep their chambers are not sick:
And if it be so far beyond his health,
Methinks he should the sooner pay his debts,
And make a clear way to the gods.
   Ser.   Good gods!
   Tit.   We cannot take this for an answer, sir.
   Flam.   [*Within*]   Servilius, help!—my lord! my lord!

Enter TIMON, *in a rage;* FLAMINIUS *following*

   Tim.   What! are my doors opposed against my passage?
Have I been ever free, and must my house
Be my retentive enemy, my gaol?
The place which I have feasted, does it now,
Like all mankind, show me an iron heart?
   Luc. Serv.   Put in now, Titus.
   Tit.   My lord, here is my bill.
   Luc. Serv.   Here 's mine.
   Hor.   And mine, my lord.
   Both Var. Serv.   And ours, my lord.
   Phi.   All our bills.
   Tim.   Knock me down with 'em: cleave me to the
        girdle.
   Luc. Serv.   Alas! my lord,—

Tim. Cut my heart in sums.
Tit. Mine, fifty talents.
Tim. Tell out my blood.
Luc. Serv. Five thousand crowns, my lord.
Tim. Five thousand drops pays that.—What yours?—
  and yours?
First Var. Serv. My lord,—
Second Var. Serv. My lord,—
Tim. Tear me, take me; and the gods fall upon you!
                                                [*Exit*
Hor. 'Faith, I perceive our masters may throw their
caps at their money: these debts may well be called des-
perate ones, for a madman owes 'em.
                                              [*Exeunt*

                Re-enter TIMON *and* FLAVIUS

Tim. They have e'en put my breath from me, the
     slaves:
Creditors!—devils.
Flav. My dear lord,—
Tim. What if it should be so?
Flav. My lord,—
Tim. I'll have it so.—My steward!
Flav. Here, my lord.
Tim. So fitly? Go, bid all my friends again,
Lucius, Lucullus, and Sempronius; all:
I'll once more feast the rascals.
Flav.   O my lord,
You only speak from your distracted soul:
There is not so much left to furnish out
A moderate table.
Tim. Be 't not in thy care: go
I charge thee; invite them all: let in the tide
Of knaves once more; my cook and I'll provide.
                                              [*Exeunt*

            SCENE V.—Athens. The Senate-House

                    The Senate sitting

First Sen. My lord, you have my voice to it: the
     fault 's
Bloody; 't is necessary he should die:
Nothing emboldens sin so much as mercy.
Second Sen. Most true; the law shall bruise him.

                Enter ALCIBIADES, *attended*

Alcib. Honour, health, and compassion to the senate!
                        233

First Sen. Now, captain?
Alcib. I am an humble suitor to your virtues;
For pity is the virtue of the law,
And none but tyrants use it cruelly.
It pleases time and fortune to lie heavy
Upon a friend of mine who, in hot blood,
Hath stepped into the law, which is past depth
To those that without heed do plunge into 't.
He is a man, setting his fate aside,
Of comely virtues:
Nor did he soil the fact with cowardice,—
An honour in him, which buys out his fault,—
But, with a noble fury and fair spirit,
Seeing his reputation touched to death,
He did oppose his foe;
And with such sober and unnoted passion
He did behave his anger, ere 't was spent,
As if he had but proved an argument.
First Sen. You undergo too strict a paradox,
Striving to make an ugly deed look fair:
Your words have took such pains, as if they laboured
To bring manslaughter into form, and set
Quarrelling upon the head of valour: which
Indeed is valour misbegot, and came
Into the world when sects and factions
Were newly born. He 's truly valiant
That wisely can suffer the worst that man
Can breathe, and make his wrongs but his outsides,
To wear them like his raiment, carelessly,
And ne'er prefer his injuries to his heart,
To bring it into danger.
If wrongs be evils, and enforce us kill,
What folly 't is to hazard life for ill!
Alcib. My lord,—
First Sen. You cannot make gross sins look clear:
To revenge is no valour, but to bear.
Alcib. My lords, then, under favour, pardon me,
If I speak like a captain.—
Why do fond men expose themselves to battle,
And not endure all threats? not sleep upon 't,
And let the foes quietly cut their throats,
Without repugnancy? For if there be
Such valour in the bearing, what make we
Abroad? why, women are more valiant
That stay at home, if bearing carry it;
And the ass more captain than the lion; the felon
Loaden with irons wiser than the judge,
If wisdom be in suffering. O my lords!
As you are great, be pitifully good.

Who cannot condemn rashness, in cold blood?
To kill, I grant, is sin's extremest gust;
But in defence, by mercy, 't is most just.
To be in anger, is impiety;
But who is man that is not angry?
Weigh but the crime with this.
    Second Sen. You breathe in vain.
    Alcib.   In vain! His service done
At Lacedæmon and Byzantium,
Were a sufficient briber for his life.
    First Sen. What 's that?
    Alcib. Why, I say, my lords, h' as done fair service,
And slain in fight many of your enemies.
How full of valour did he bear himself
In the last conflict, and made plenteous wounds!
    Second Sen. He has made too much plenty with 'em; he
Is a sworn rioter: he has a sin, that often
Drowns him, and takes his valour prisoner:
If there were no more foes, that were enough
To overcome him: in that beastly fury
He has been known to commit outrages
And cherish factions. 'T is inferred to us,
His days are foul, and his drink dangerous.
    First Sen. He dies.
    Alcib. Hard fate! he might have died in war.
My lords, if not for any parts in him,—
Though his right arm might purchase his own time,
And be in debt to none,—yet, more to move you,
Take my deserts to his, and join 'em both:
And, for I know, your reverend ages love
Security, I'll pawn my victories, all
My honour to you, upon his good returns.
If by this crime he owes the law his life,
Why, let the war receive 't in valiant gore;
For law is strict, and war is nothing more.
    First Sen. We are for law,—he dies; urge it no more,
On height of our displeasure. Friend or brother,
He forfeits his own blood that spills another.
    Alcib. Must it be so? it must not be. My lords,
I do beseech you, know me.
    Second Sen. How!
    Alcib. Call me to your remembrances.
    Third Sen.   What!
    Alcib. I cannot think, but your age has forgot me;
It could not else be I should prove so base
To sue, and be denied such common grace.
My wounds ache at you.
    First Sen.   Do you dare our anger?
'T is in few words, but spacious in effect;

We banish thee for ever.
    Alcib.   Banish me!
Banish your dotage; banish usury,
That makes the senate ugly.
    First Sen. If, after two days' shine, Athens contain
        thee,
Attend our weightier judgment. And, not to swell our
        spirit,
He shall be executed presently.   *[Exeunt Senators*
    Alcib. Now the gods keep you old; that you may live
Only in bone, that none may look on you!
I'm worse than mad: I have kept back their foes,
While they have told their money, and let out
Their coin upon large interest; I myself,
Rich only in large hurts·—all those, for this?
Is this the balsam that the usuring senate
Pours into captains' wounds? Ha, banishment?
It comes not ill; I hate not to be banished:
It is a cause worthy my spleen and fury,
That I may strike at Athens. I'll cheer up
My discontented troops, and lay for hearts.
'T is honour with most lands to be at odds;
Soldiers should brook as little wrongs as gods.

                                    [Exit

SCENE VI.—A Banquet-hall in TIMON'S House

Music. Tables set out: Servants attending. Enter at several doors divers Lords, LUCIUS, LUCULLUS, SEMPRO-NIUS, *Senators and* VENTIDIUS

    First Lord. The good time of day to you, sir.
    Second Lord. I also wish it to you. I think, this honourable lord did but try us this other day.
    First Lord. Upon that were my thoughts tiring when we encountered. I hope it is not so low with him as he made it seem in the trial of his several friends.
    Second Lord. It should not be, by the persuasion of his new feasting.
    First Lord. I should think so. He hath sent me an earnest inviting, which many my near occasions did urge me to put off; but he hath conjured me beyond them, and I must needs appear.
    Second Lord. In like manner was I in debt to my importunate business, but he would not hear my excuse. I am sorry, when he sent to borrow of me, that my provision was out.

First Lord. I am sick of that grief too, as I understand
how all things go.

Second Lord. Every man here 's so. What would he
have borrowed of you?

First Lord. A thousand pieces.

Second Lord. A thousand pieces!

First Lord. What of you?

Third Lord. He sent to me, sir,—Here he comes.

Enter TIMON *and Attendants*

Tim. With all my heart, gentlemen both:—and how
        fare you?

First Lord. Ever at the best, hearing well of your
lordship.

Second Lord. The swallow follows not summer more
willing than we your lordship.

Tim. [*Aside*] Nor more willingly leaves winter; such
summer-birds are men.—[*To them*] Gentlemen, our dinner
will not recompense this long stay: feast your ears with
the music awhile, if they will fare so harshly. O, the
trumpets sound; we shall to 't presently.

First Lord. I hope it remains not unkindly with your
lordship, that I returned you an empty messenger.

Tim. O, sir, let it not trouble you.

Second Lord. My noble lord,—

Tim. Ah! my good friend,—what cheer?

Second Lord. My most honourable lord, I am e'en sick
of shame, that, when your lordship this other day sent
to me, I was so unfortunate a beggar.

Tim. Think not on 't, sir.

Second Lord. If you had sent but two hours before,—

Tim. Let it not cumber your better remembrance.—
Come, bring in all together.

                              [*The banquet brought in*

Second Lord. All covered dishes!

First Lord. Royal cheer, I warrant you.

Third Lord. Doubt not that, if money and the season
can yield it.

First Lord. How do you? What 's the news?

Third Lord. Alcibiades banished: hear you of it?

First & Second Lord. Alcibiades banished!

Third Lord. 'T is so, be sure of it.

First Lord. How? how?

Second Lord. I pray you, upon what?

Tim. My worthy friends, will you draw near?

Third Lord. I'll tell you more anon. Here 's a noble
feast toward.

Second Lord. This is the old man still.

Third Lord.   Will 't hold? will 't hold?
Second Lord.   It does; but time will—and so—
Third Lord.   I do conceive.
Tim.   Each man to his stool, with that spur as he
would to the lip of his mistress: your diet shall be in all
places alike.   Make not a city feast of it, to let the meat
cool ere we can agree upon the first plaçe: sit, sit.   The
gods require our thanks.—
You great benefactors, sprinkle our society with thank-
fulness.   For your own gifts make yourselves praised:
but reserve still to give, lest your dieties be despised.
Lend to each man enough, that one need not lend to another:
for, were your godheads to borrow of men, men would for-
sake the gods.   Make the meat be beloved, more than the
man that gives it.   Let no assembly of twenty be without
a score of villains: if there sit twelve women at the table
let a dozen of them be—as they are.—The rest of your
foes, O gods,—the senators of Athens, together with the
common lag of people,—what is amiss in them, you gods,
make suitable for destruction.   For these, my present
friends,—as they are to me nothing, so in nothing bless
them, and to nothing are they welcome.
Uncover, dogs, and lap.

> [*The dishes are uncovered, and seen to be full
> of warm water*

Some speak.   What does his lordship mean?
Some other.   I know not.
Tim.   May you a better feast never behold,
You knot of mouth-friends! smoke, and luke-warm water,
Is your perfection.   This is Timon's last,
Who, stuck and spangled with your flatteries,
Washes it off, and sprinkles in your faces.

> [*Throwing water in their faces*

Your reeking villainy.   Live loathed and long,
Most smiling, smooth, detested parasites,
Courteous destroyers, affable wolves, meek bears,
You fools of fortune, trencher-friends, time's flies,
Cap-and-knee slaves, vapours, and minute-jacks!
Of man and beast the infinite malady.
Crust you quite o'er!—What, dost thou go?
Soft, take thy physic first.—thou too,—and thou:—

> [*Throws the dishes at them*

Stay, I will lend thee money, borrow none,—
What, all in motion?   Henceforth be no feast
Whereat a villain 's not a welcome guest.
Burn, house! sink, Athens! henceforth hated be
Of Timon, man and all humanity!

> [*Exit*

Re-enter the Lords, with other Lords, and Senators

First Lord. How now, my lords?
Second Lord. Know you the quality of Lord Timon's
  fury?
Third Lord. Push! did you see my cap?
Fourth Lord. I have lost my gown.
Third Lord. He 's but a mad lord, and nought but
humour sways him. He gave me a jewel the other day,
and now he has beat it out of my hat:—did you see my
jewel?
Fourth Lord. Did you see my cap?
Second Lord. Here 't is.
Fourth Lord. Here lies my gown.
First Lord. Let 's make no stay.
Second Lord. Lord Timon 's mad.
Third Lord.   I feel 't upon my bones.
Fourth Lord. One day he gives us diamonds, next
  day stones.   [*Exeunt*

ACT FOUR

Scene I.—Without the Walls of Athens

Enter Timon

Tim. Let me look back upon thee, O thou wall
That girdlest in those wolves, dive in the earth
And fence not Athens! Matrons turn incontinent!
Obedience fail in children! Slaves and fools
Pluck the grave wrinkled senate from the bench,
And minister in their steads! To general filths
Convert o' the instant, green virginity!
Do 't in your parents' eyes! Bankrupts, hold fast:
Rather than render back, out with your knives,
And cut your trusters' throats! Bound servants,
    steal!
Large handed robbers your grave masters are,
And pill by law. Maid, to thy master's bed;
Thy mistress is o' the brothel! Son of sixteen,
Pluck the lined crutch from thy old limping sire,
With it beat out his brains! Piety, and fear,
Religion to the gods, peace, justice, truth,
Domestic awe, night-rest, and neighbourhood,
Instruction, manners, mysteries, and trades,
Degrees, observances, customs, and laws,
Decline to your confounding contraries,
And let confusion live!—Plagues incident to men,

239

Your potent and infectious feyers heap
On Athens, ripe for stroke! Thou cold sciatica,
Cripple our senators, that their linbs may halt
As lamely as their manners! Lust and liberty,
Creep in the minds and marrows of our youth,
That 'gainst the stream of virtue they may strive,
And drown themselves in riot. Itches, blains.
Sow all the Athenian bosoms, and their crop
Be general leprosy! Breath infect breath,
That their society, as their friendship, may
Be merely poison! Nothing I'll bear from thee
But nakedness, thou detestable town!
Take thou that too, with multiplying bans!
Timon will to the woods; where he shall find
The unkindest beast more kinder than mankind.
The gods confound—hear me, you good gods all—
The Athenians both within and out that wall!
And grant, as Timon grows, his hate may grow
To the whole race of mankind, high and low!
Amen.   [*Exit*

SCENE II.—Athens. A Room in TIMON's House

Enter FLAVIUS, *with two or three Servants*

First Serv. Hear you, master steward,—where 's our
       master?
Are we undone? cast off? nothing remaining?
   Flav. Alack! my fellows, what should I say to you?
Let me be recorded by the righteous gods,
I am as poor as you.
   First Serv.   Such a house broke!
So noble a master fallen! All gone! and not
One friend to take his fortune by the arm,
And go along with him!
   Second Serv.   As we do turn our backs
From our companion thrown into his grave,
So his familiars from his buried fortunes
Slink all away; leave their false vows with him,
Like empty purses picked; and his poor self,
A dedicated beggar to the air,
With his disease of all-shunned poverty,
Walks, like contempt, alone.—More of our fellows.

Enter other Servants

   Flav. All broken implements of a ruined house.
   Third Serv. Yet do our hearts wear Timon's livery.
That see I by our faces; we are fellows still,

Serving alike in sorrow.   Leaked is our bark;
And we, poor mates, stand on the dying deck,
Hearing the surges threat: we must all part
Into this sea of air.
   Flav.   Good fellows all,
The latest of my wealth I'll share amongst you.
Wherever we shall meet, for Timon's sake,
Let 's yet be fellows; let 's shake our heads, and say,
As 't were a knell unto our master's fortunes,
'We have seen better days.'   Let each take some;
                          [Giving them money
Nay, put out all your hands.   Not one word more:
Thus part we rich in sorrow, parting poor.
                [They embrace, and part several ways
O, the fierce wretchedness that glory brings us!
Who would not wish to be from wealth exempt,
Since riches point to misery and contempt?
Who'd be so mocked with glory? or so live
But in a dream of friendship?
To have his pomp, and all what state compounds,
But only painted, like his varnished friends?
Poor honest lord, brought low by his own heart,
Undone by goodness.   Strange, unusual blood,
When man's worst sin is, he does too much good!
Who then dares to be half so kind again?
For bounty, that makes gods, does still mar men.
My dearest lord,—blessed, to be most accursed,
Rich, only to be wretched,—thy great fortunes
Are made thy chief afflictions.   Alas, kind lord!
He 's flung in rage from this ingrateful seat
Of monstrous friends;
Nor has he with him to supply his life,
Or that which can command it.
I 'll follow, and inquire him out:
I 'll ever serve his mind with my best will;
Whilst I have gold, I 'll be his steward still.   *[Exit*

SCENE III.—The Woods.   Before TIMON's Cave

Enter TIMON

   Tim.   O blessèd breeding sun, draw from the earth
Rotten humidity!
Below thy sister's orb infect the air!
Twinned brothers of one womb,
Whose procreation, residence, and birth,
Scarce is dividant,—touch them with several fortunes,
The greater scorns the lesser: not his nature
To whom all sores lay siege, can bear great fortune

But by contempt of nature.
Raise me this beggar, and deny 't that lord,—
The senator shall bear contempt hereditary,
The beggar native honour.
It is the pasture lards the brother's sides,
The want that makes him lean. Who dares, who dares,
In purity of manhood stand upright,
And say 'This man 's a flatterer?'   If one be,
So are they all; for every grise of fortune
Is smoothed by that below: the learnéd pate
Ducks to the golden fool.   All is oblique;
There 's nothing level in our curséd natures,
But direct villainy.   Therefore, be abhorred
All feasts, societies, and throngs of men!
His semblable, yea, himself, Timon disdains:
Destruction fang mankind!—Earth, yield me roots!
                                              [*Digging*
Who seeks for better of thee, sauce his palate
With thy most operant poison!—What is here?
Gold? yellow, glittering, precious gold?   No, gods,
I am no idle votarist.   Roots, you clear heavens!—
Thus much of this will make black, white; foul, fair;
Wrong, right; base, noble; old, young; coward, valiant.
Ha, you gods, why, this—what this, you gods?—
          why, this
Will lug your priests and servants from your sides,
Pluck stout men's pillows from below their heads.
This yellow slave
Will knit and break religions; bless the accursed;
Make the hoar leprosy adored; place thieves,
And give them title, knee, and approbation
With senators on the bench: this, this is it,
That makes the wappened widow wed again;
She whom the spital-house and ulcerous sores
Would cast the gorge at, this embalms and spices
To the April day again.   Come, damnéd earth,
Thou common whore of mankind, that putt'st odds
Among the rout of nations, I will make thee
Do thy right nature.—[*March afar off*] Ha! a drum?—
          Thou 'rt quick,
But yet I'll bury thee: thou 'lt go, strong thief,
When gouty keepers of thee cannot stand:—
Nay, stay thou out for earnest.
                              [*Keeping back some gold*

Enter ALCIBIADES, *with drum and fife in warlike manner;*
          PHRYNIA *and* TIMANDRA

Alcib.   What art thou there? speak.
                    242

Tim.   A beast, as thou art.—The canker gnaw thy heart
For showing me again the eyes of man!
    Alcib.   What is thy name?   Is man so hateful to thee,
That art thyself a man?
    Tim.   I am Misanthropos, and hate mankind.
For thy part, I do wish thou wert a dog,
That I might love thee something.
    Alcib.   I know thee well;
But in thy fortunes am unlearned and strange.
    Tim.   I know thee too; and more than that I know
thee,
I not desire to know.   Follow thy drum:
With man's blood paint the ground, gules, gules:
Religious canons, civil laws are cruel;
Then what should war be?   This fell whore of thine
Hath in her more destruction than thy sword,
For all her cherubin look.
    Phry.   Thy lips rot off!
    Tim.   I will not kiss thee; then the rot returns
To thine own lips again.
    Alcib.   How came the noble Timon to this change?
    Tim.   As the moon does, by wanting light to give:
But then, renew I could not, like the moon;
There were no suns to borrow of.
    Alcib.   Noble Timon, what friendship may I do thee?
    Tim.   None, but to maintain my opinion.
    Alcib.   What is it, Timon?
    Tim.   Promise me friendship, but perform none: if
thou wilt not promise, the gods plague thee, for thou art
a man! if thou dost perform, confound thee, for thou art
a man!
    Alcib.   I've heard in some sort of thy miseries.
    Tim.   Thou saw'st them when I had prosperity.
    Alcib.   I see them now: then was a blessèd time.
    Tim.   As thine is now, held with a brace of harlots.
    Timan.   Is this the Athenian minion, whom the world
Voiced so regardfully?
    Tim.   Art thou Timandra?
    Timan.   Yes.
    Tim.   Be a whore still: they love thee not that use thee;
Give them diseases, leaving with thee their lust.
Make use of thy salt hours; season the slaves
For tubs and baths; bring down rose-cheekèd youth
To the tub-fast and the diet.
    Timan.   Hang thee, monster!
    Alcib.   Pardon him, sweet Timandra, for his wits
Are drowned and lost in his calamities.—
I have but little gold of late, brave Timon,
The want whereof doth daily make revolt

In my penurious band: I have heard and grieved
How cursèd Athens, mindless of thy worth,
Forgetting thy great deeds, when neighbour states,
But for thy sword and fortune, trod upon them,—
   Tim. I pr'ythee, beat thy drum, and get thee gone.
   Alcib. I am thy friend, and pity thee, dear Timon.
   Tim. How dost thou pity him whom you dost trouble?
I had rather be alone.
   Alcib.   Why, fare thee well:
Here is some gold for thee.
   Tim.   Keep it, I cannot eat it.
   Alcib. When I have laid proud Athens on a heap,—
   Tim. Warr'st thou 'gainst Athens?
   Alcib.   Ay, Timon, and have cause.
   Tim. The gods confound them all in thy conquest;
and thee after, when thou hast conquered!
   Alcib. Why me, Timon?
   Tim. That, by killing of villains, thou wast born to
       conquer my country.
Put up thy gold: go on,—here's gold,—go on;
Be as a planetary plague, when Jove
Will o'er some high-viced city hang his poison
In the sick air, let not thy sword skip one.
Pity not honoured age for his white beard:
He is an usurer. Strike me the counterfeit matron;
It is her habit only that is honest,
Herself 's a bawd. Let not the virgin's cheek
Make soft thy trenchant sword; for those milkpaps,
That through the window-bars bore at men's eyes,
Are not within the leaf of pity writ,
But set down horrible traitors. Spare not the babe
Whose dimpled smiles from fools exhaust their mercy:
Think it a bastard, whom the oracle
Hath doubtfully pronounced thy throat shall cut,
And mince it sans remorse. Swear against objects;
Put armour on thine ears, and on thine eyes,
Whose proof nor yells of mothers, maids, nor babes,
Nor sight of priests in holy vestments bleeding,
Shall pierce a jot. There 's gold to pay thy soldiers;
Make large confusion; and, thy fury spent,
Confounded be thyself! Speak not, be gone.
   Alcib. Hast thou gold yet? I'll take the gold thou
       giv'st me,
Not all thy counsel.
   Tim. Dost thou, or dost thou not, heaven's curse
       upon thee!
   Phr. & Timan. Give us some gold, good Timon: hast
       thou more?
   Tim. Enough to make a whore forswear her trade,

And, to make whores, a bawd.   Hold up, you sluts,
Your aprons mountant: you are not oathable,—
Although, I know, you'll swear, terribly swear
Into strong shudders and to heavenly agues
The immortal gods that hear you,—spare your oaths,
I'll trust to your conditions: be whores still;
And he whose pious breath seeks to convert you,
Be strong in whore, allure him, burn him up;
Let your close fire predominate his smoke,
And be no turncoats: yet may your pains, six
   months,
Be quite contrary.   Thatch your poor thin roofs
With burdens of the dead:—some that were hanged,
No matter:—wear them, betray with them.   Whore
   still;
Paint till a horse may mire upon your face.
A pox of wrinkles!
  Phr. & Timan.   Well, more gold.—What then?—
Believe 't, that we 'll do anything for gold.
  Tim.   Consumptions sow
In hollow bones of man! strike their sharp shins,
And mar men's spurring.   Crack the lawyer's voice,
That he may never more false title plead,
Nor sound his quillets shrilly: hoar the flamen,
That scolds against the quality of flesh,
And not believes himself: down with the nose,
Down with it flat; take the bridge quite away
Of him that, his particular to foresee,
Smells from the general weal: make curled-pate ruffians
   bald;
And let the unscarred braggarts of the war
Derive some pain from you.   Plague all,
That your activity may defeat and quell
The source of all erection.—There 's more gold:
Do you damn others, and let this damn you,
And ditches grave you all!
  Phr. & Timan.   More counsel with more money, boun-
  teous Timon.
  Tim.   More whore, more mischief first; I have given
  you earnest.
  Alcib.   Strike up the drum towards Athens! Farewell
  Timon:
If I thrive well, I'll visit thee again.
  Tim.   If I hope well, I 'll never see thee more.
  Alcib.   I never did thee harm.
  Tim.   Yes, thou spok'st well of me.
  Alcib.   Call'st thou that harm?
  Tim.   Men daily find it.   Get thee away, and take
Thy beagles with thee.

Alcib. We but offend him.—Strike!

> [*Drum beats. Exeunt Alcibiades, Phrynia, and Timandra*

Tim. That nature, being sick of man's unkindness,
Should yet be hungry!—Common mother, thou,

> [*Digging*

Whose womb unmeasurable, and infinite breast,
Teems, and feeds all; whose selfsame mettle,
Whereof thy proud child, arrogant man, is puffed,
Engenders the black toad and adder blue,
The gilded newt and eyeless venomed worm,
With all the abhorréd births below crisp heaven
Whereon Hyperion's quickening fire doth shine;
Yield him who all thy human sons doth hate,
From forth thy plenteous bosom, one poor root!
Ensear thy fertile and conceptious womb,
Let it no more bring out ingrateful man!
Go great with tigers, dragons, wolves, and bears;
Teem with new monsters, whom thy upward face
Hath to the marbled mansion all above
Never presented!—O, a root,—dear thanks!—
Dry up thy marrows, vines, and plough-torn leas;
Whereof ingrateful man, with liquorish draughts
And morsels unctuous, greases his pure mind,
That from it all consideration slips!

Enter APEMANTUS

More man? Plague! plague!

Apem. I was directed hither: men report,
Thou dost affect my manners, and dost use them.

Tim. 'T is then, because thou dost not keep a dog,
Whom I would imitate. Consumption catch thee!

Apem. This is in thee a nature but infected;
A poor unmanly melancholy, sprung
From change of fortune. Why this spade? this place?
This slave-like habit? and these looks of care?
Thy flatterers yet wear silk, drink wine, lie soft,
Hug their diseased perfumes, and have forgot
That ever Timon was. Shame not these woods
By putting on the cunning of a carper.
Be thou a flatterer now, and seek to thrive
By that which has undone thee: hinge thy knee,
And let his very breath, whom thou 'lt observe,
Blow off thy cap; praise his most vicious strain
And call it excellent. Thou wast told thus;
Thou gav'st thine ear, like tapsters that bid welcome
To knaves and all approachers: 't is most just
That thou turn rascal; hadst thou wealth again,

Rascals should have 't. Do not assume my likeness.
   Tim. Were I like thee I 'd throw away myself.
   Apem. Thou hast cast away thyself, being like thyself;
A madman so long, now a fool. What! think'st
That the bleak air, thy boisterous chamberlain,
Will put thy shirt on warm? Will these mossed trees,
That have outlived the eagle, page thy heels,
And skip where thou point'st out? Will the cold brook
Candied with ice, caudle thy morning taste
To cure thy o'er-night's surfeit? Call the creatures,—
Whose naked natures live in all the spite
Of wreakful heaven, whose bare unhoused trunks,
To the conflicting elements exposed,
Answer mere nature,—bid them flatter thee;
O, thou shalt find—
   Tim.   A fool of thee. Depart.
   Apem. I love thee better now than e'er I did.
   Tim. I hate thee worse.
   Apem.   Why?
   Tim.   Thou flatter'st misery.
   Apem. I flatter not: but say thou art a caitiff.
   Tim. Why dost thou seek me out?
   Apem.   To vex thee.
   Tim. Always a villain's office, or a fool's.
Dost please thyself in 't?
   Apem.   Ay.
   Tim.   What! a knave too?
   Apem. If thou didst put this sour-cold habit on
To castigate thy pride, 't were well; but thou
Dost it enforcedly: thou'dst courtier be again,
Wert thou not beggar. Willing misery
Outlives incertain pomp, is crowned before;
The one is filling still, never complete;
The other, at high wish: best state, contentless,
Hath a distracted and most wretched being,
Worse than the worst content,
Thou shouldst desire to die, being miserable.
   Tim. Not by his breath that is more miserable
Thou art a slave, whom Fortune's tender arm
With favour never clasped, but bred a dog.
Hadst thou, like us, from our first swath, proceeded
The sweet degrees that this brief world affords
To such as may the passive drudges of it
Freely command, thou wouldst have plunged thyself
In general riot; melted down thy youth
In different beds of lust; and never learned
The icy precepts of respect, but followed
The sugared game before thee. But myself,
Who had the world as my confectionary;

The mouths, the tongues, the eyes, and hearts of men
At duty, more than I could frame employment;
That numberless upon me stuck, as leaves
Do on the oak, have with one winter's brush
Fell from their boughs, and left me open, bare
For every storm that blows;—I, to bear this,
That never knew but better, is some burden:
Thy nature did commence in sufferance, time
Hath made thee hard in 't.   Why shouldst thou hate men?
They never flattered thee: what hast thou given?
If thou wilt curse,—thy father, that poor rag,
Must be thy subject; who, in spite, put stuff
To some she beggar, and compounded thee
Poor rogue hereditary.   Hence! be gone!—
If thou hadst not been born the worst of men,
Thou hadst been a knave and flatterer.

    Apem.   Art thou proud yet?
    Tim.   Ay, that I am not thee.
    Apem.   I, that I was no prodigal.
    Tim.   I, that I am one now:
Were all the wealth I have shut up in thee,
I'd give thee leave to hang it.   Get thee gone.—
That the whole life of Athens were in this!
Thus would I eat it.   [*Eating a root*
    Apem.   Here; I'll mend thy feast.
              [*Offering him something*
    Tim.   First mend my company, take away thyself.
    Apem.   So I shall mend mine own, by the lack of thine.
    Tim.   'T is not well mended so, it is but botched;
If not, I would it were.
    Apem.   What wouldst thou have to Athens?
    Tim.   Thee thither in a whirlwind.   If thou wilt,
Tell them there I have gold; look, so I have.
    Apem.   Here is no use for gold.
    Tim.   The best and truest;
For here it sleeps, and does no hiréd harm.
    Apem.   Where liest o' nights, Timon?
    Tim.   Under that 's above me.
Where feed'st thou o' days, Apemantus
    Apem.   Where my stomach finds meat; or, rather, where
I eat it.
    Tim.   Would poison were obedient, and knew my mind!
    Apem.   Where wouldst thou send it?
    Tim.   To sauce thy dishes.
    Apem.   The middle of humanity thou never knewest,
but the extremity of both ends.   When thou wast in thy
gilt and thy perfume they mocked thee for too much
curiosity; in thy rags thou knowest none, but art despised
for the contrary.   There 's a medlar for thee; eat it.

Tim. On what I hate I feed not.

Apem. Dost hate a medlar?

Tim. Ay, though it look like thee.

Apem. An thou hadst hated meddlers sooner, thou shouldst have loved thyself better now. What man didst thou ever know unthrift that was beloved after his means?

Tim. Who, without those means thou talkest of, didst thou ever know beloved?

Apem. Myself.

Tim. I understand thee: thou hadst some means to keep a dog.

Apem. What things in the world canst thou nearest compare to thy flatterers?

Tim. Women nearest; but men, men are the things themselves. What wouldst thou do with the world, Apemantus, if it lay in thy power?

Apem. Give it the beasts, to be rid of the men.

Tim. Wouldst thou have thyself fall in the confusion of men, and remain a beast with the beasts?

Apem. Ay, Timon.

Tim. A beastly ambition, which the gods grant thee to attain to. If thou wert the lion, the fox would beguile thee: if thou wert the lamb, the fox would eat thee: if thou wert the fox, the lion would suspect thee, when, peradventure, thou wert accused by the ass: if thou wert the ass, thy dulness would torment thee, and still thou livedst but as a breakfast to the wolf: if thou wert the wolf, thy greediness would afflict thee, and oft thou shouldst hazard thy life for thy dinner: wert thou the unicorn, pride and wrath would confound thee, and make thine own self the conquest of thy fury: wert thou a bear, thou wouldst be killed by the horse: wert thou a horse, thou wouldst be seized by the leopard: wert thou a leopard, thou wert german to the lion, and the spots of thy kindred were jurors on thy life; all thy safety were remotion, and thy defence, absence. What beast couldst thou be, that were not subject to a beast? and what a beast art thou already, that seest not thy loss in transformation!

Apem. If thou couldst please me with speaking to me, thou might'st have hit upon it here: the commonwealth of Athens is become a forest of beasts.

Tim. How has the ass broke the wall, that thou art out of the city?

Apem. Yonder comes a poet and a painter. The plague of company light upon thee! I will fear to catch it, and give away. When I know not what else to do, I'll see thee again.

Tim. When there is nothing living but thee, thou

shalt be welcome.   I had rather be a beggar's dog than
Apemantus.
 Apem. Thou art the cap of all the fools alive.
 Tim. Would thou wert clean enough to spit upon.
 Apem. A plague on thee, thou art too bad to
   curse.
 Tim. All villains that do stand by thee are pure.
 Apem. There is no leprosy but what thou speak'st.
 Tim. If I name thee.—
I 'll beat thee, but I should infect my hands.
 Apem. I would my tongue could rot them off!
 Tim. Away, thou issue of a mangy dog!
Choler does kill me that thou art alive;
I swoon to see thee.
 Apem. Would thou wouldst burst!
 Tim.   Away, thou tedious rogue!
I am sorry I shall lose a stone by thee.
         [*Throws a stone at him*
 Apem. Beast!
 Tim. Slave!
 Apem. Toad!
 Tim. Rogue, rogue, rogue!
      [Apemantus *retreats backward, as going*
I am sick of this false world, and will love naught
But even the mere necessities upon 't.
Then, Timon, presently prepare thy grave:
Lie where the light foam of the sea may beat
Thy grave-stone daily: make thine epitaph,
That death in me at others' lives may laugh.
[*Looking on the gold*] O thou sweet king-killer, and dear
    divorce
'Twixt natural son and sire! thou bright defiler
Of Hymen's purest bed! thou valiant Mars!
Thou ever young, fresh, loved, and delicate wooer,
Whose blush doth thaw the consecrated snow
That lies on Dian's lap! thou visible god,
That solder'st close impossibilities,
And mak'st them kiss! that speak'st with every tongue,
To every purpose! O thou touch of hearts!
Think, thy slave man rebels; and by thy virtue
Set them into confounding odds, that beasts
May have the world in empire!
 Apem.   'Would 't were so;
But not till I am dead!—I'll say, thou'st gold:
Thou wilt be thronged to shortly.
 Tim.   Thronged to?
 Apem.   Ay.
 Tim. Thy back, I pr'ythee.
 Apem.   Live and love thy misery!

Tim. Long live so, and so die!—I am quit.—

[*Exit Apemantus*

More things like men?—Eat, Timon, and abhor them.

Enter Thieves

First Thief. Where should he have this gold? It is some fragment, some slender ort of his remainder. The mere want of gold, and the falling-from of his friends, drove him into this melancholy.

Second Thief. It is noised he hath a mass of treasure.

Third Thief. Let us make the assay upon him: if he care not for 't, he will supply us easily; if he covetously reserve it, how shall 's get it?

Second Thief. True; for he bears it not about him, 't is hid.

First Thief. Is not this he?

All. Where?

Second Thief. 'T is his description.

Third Thief. He; I know him.

All. Save thee, Timon.

Tim. Now, thieves?

All. Soldiers, not thieves.

Tim. Both too; and women's sons.

All. We are not thieves, but men that much do want.

Tim. Your greatest want is, you want much of meat.
Why should you want? Behold, the earth hath roots;
Within this mile break forth a hundred springs;
The oaks bear mast, the briers scarlet hips;
The bounteous housewife, Nature, on each bush
Lays her full mess before you. Want! why want?

First Thief. We cannot live on grass, on berries, water.
As beasts, and birds, and fishes.

Tim. Nor on the beasts themselves, the birds, and
    fishes;
You must eat men. Yet thanks I must you con,
That you are thieves professed, that you work not
In holier shape; for there is boundless theft
In limited professions. Rascal thieves,
Here 's gold. Go, suck the subtle blood o' the grape,
Till the high fever seethe your blood to froth,
And so 'scape hanging. Trust not the physician;
His antidotes are poison, and he slays
More than you rob. Take wealth and lives together;
Do villainy, do, since you protest to do 't,
Like workmen. I 'll example you with thievery:
The sun 's a thief, and with his great attention
Robs the vast sea; the moon 's an arrant thief,
And her pale fire she snatches from the sun;

The sea 's a thief, whose liquid surge resolves
The moon into salt tears; the earth 's a thief,
That feeds and breeds by a composture stolen
From general excrement; each thing 's a thief;
The laws, your curb and whip, in their rough power
Have unchecked theft.   Love not yourselves; away!
Rob one another.   There 's more gold: cut throats;
All that you meet are thieves.   To Athens, go:
Break open shops; nothing can you steal, but thieves
Do lose it.   Steal not less, for this I give you;
And gold confound you howsoe'er!   Amen.

                              [Retires to his cave

   Third Thief.   He has almost charmed me from my
profession by persuading me to it.

   First Thief.   'T is in the malice of mankind that he
thus advises us; not to have us thrive in our mystery.

   Second Thief.   I'll believe him as an enemy, and give over
my trade.

   First Thief.   Let us first see peace in Athens; there is
no time so miserable but a man may be true.

                                   [Exeunt Thieves

Enter FLAVIUS

   Flav.   O you gods?
Is yond despised and ruinous man my lord?
Full of decay and failing; monument
And wonder of good deeds evilly bestowed!
O, what an alteration of honour
Has desperate want made!
What viler thing upon the earth than friends
Who can bring noblest minds to basest ends?
How rarely does it meet with this time's guise,
When man was wished to love his enemies!
Grant I may ever love, and rather woo
Those that would mischief me than those that do!
He has caught me in his eye: I will present
My honest grief unto him; and, as my lord,
Still serve him with my life.—My dearest master!

TIMON *comes forward from his cave*

   Tim.   Away! what art thou?
   Flav.   Have you forgot me, sir?
   Tim.   Why dost ask that?   I have forgot all men;
Then, if thou grant'st thou art a man, I have
Forgot thee.
   Flav.   An honest poor servant of yours.
   Tim.   Then I know thee not:

I ne'er had honest men about me; ay, all
I kept were knaves, to serve in meat to villains.
   Flav. The gods are witness,
Ne'er did poor steward wear a truer grief
For his undone lord, than mine eyes for you.
   Tim. What! dost thou weep?—Come nearer: then,
      I love thee,
Because thou art a woman, and disclaim'st
Flinty mankind, whose eyes do never give,
But thorough lust and laughter. Pity 's sleeping:
Strange times, that weep with laughing, not with weeping!
   Flav. I beg of you to know me, good my lord.
To accept my grief, and, whilst this poor wealth lasts,
To entertain me as your steward still.
   Tim.   Had I a steward
So true, so just, and now so comfortable?
It almost turns my dangerous nature wild.
Let me behold thy face. Surely this man
Was born of woman.—
Forgive my general and exceptless rashness,
Perpetual-sober gods! I do proclaim
One honest man,—mistake me not,—but one;
No more, I pray,—and he 's a steward.—
How fain would I have hated all mankind,
And thou redeem'st thyself: but all, save thee,
I fell with curses.
Methinks, thou art more honest now than wise;
For, by oppressing and betraying me,
Thou mightst have sooner got another service:
For many so arrive at second masters
Upon their first lord's neck. But tell me true.—
For I must ever doubt, though ne'er so sure,—
Is not thy kindness subtle covetous;
A usuring kindness, as rich men deal gifts,
Expecting in return twenty for one?
   Flav. No, my most worthy master, in whose breast
Doubt and suspect, alas, are placed too late.
You should have feared false times when you did feast:
Suspect still comes where an estate is least.
That which I show, heaven knows, is merely love:
Duty and zeal to your unmatchéd mind,
Care of your food and living, and, believe it,
My most honoured lord:
For any benefit that points to me,
Either in hope or present, I'd exchange
For this one wish,—that you had power and wealth
To requite me by making rich yourself.
   Tim. Look thee, 't is so.—Thou singly honest man,
Here, take:—the gods out of my misery.

Have sent thee treasure. Go, live rich, and happy;
But thus conditioned; thou shalt build from men;
Hate all, curse all: show charity to none.
But let the famished flesh slide from the bone,
Ere thou relieve the beggar; give to dogs
What thou deniest to men; let prisons swallow 'em,
Debts wither 'em to nothing; be men like blasted woods,
And may diseases lick up their false bloods!
And so, farewell, and thrive.
  Flav.   O, let me stay,
And comfort you, my master.
  Tim.   If thou hat'st
Curses, stay not; fly, whilst thou art blessed and free:
Ne'er see thou man, and let me ne'er see thee.

           [Exeunt severally

ACT FIVE

SCENE I.—The Woods. Before TIMON's Cave

Enter Poet and Painter

 Pain. As I took note of the place, it cannot be far
where he abides.
 Poet. What 's to be thought of him? Does the rumour
hold for true, that he 's so full of gold?
 Pain. Certain: Alcibiades reports it: Phrynia and
Timandra had gold of him: he likewise enriched poor,
straggling soldiers with great quantity. 'T is said he gave
unto his steward a mighty sum.
 Pet. Then this breaking of his has been but a try for
his friends.
 Pain. Nothing else; you shall see him a palm in Athens
again, and flourish with the highest. Therefore, 't is not
amiss, we tender our loves to him, in this supposed distress
of his: it will show honestly in us, and is very likely to
load our purposes with what they travail for, if it be a just
and true report that goes of his having.
 Poet. What have you now to present unto him?
 Pain. Nothing at this time but my visitation; only I
will promise him an excellent piece.
 Poet. I must serve him so too; tell him of an intent
that 's coming toward him.
 Pain. Good as the best. Promising is the very air
o' the time; it opens the eyes of expectation: performance
is ever the duller for his act; and, but in the plainer and
simpler kind of people, the deed of saying is quite out
of use. To promise is most courtly and fashionable:

performance is a kind of will, or testament, which argues
a great sickness in his judgment that makes it.

Enter TIMON *from his cave*

   Tim. [*Aside*] Excellent workman! Thou canst not
paint a man so bad as is thyself.
   Poet. I am thinking, what I shall say I have provided
for him. It must be a personating of himself: a satire
against the softness of prosperity, with a discovery of
the infinite flatteries that follow youth and opulency.
   Tim. [*Aside*] Must thou needs stand for a villain
in thine own work? Wilt thou whip thine own faults
in other men? Do so; I have gold for thee.
   Poet. Nay, let 's seek him:
Then do we sin against our own estate,
When we may profit meet and come too late.
   Pain. True:
When the day serves, before black-cornered night,
Find what thou want'st by free and offered light.
Come.
   Tim. [*Aside*] I'll meet you at the turn.
       What a god 's gold,
That he is worshipped in a baser temple
Than where swine feed!
'Tis thou that rigg'st the bark and plough'st the foam;
Settlest admiréd reverence in a slave:
To thee be worship! and thy saints for aye
Be crowned with plagues, that thee alone obey!
Fit I meet them.   [*Advancing*
   Poet. Hail, worthy Timon!
   Pain.   Our late noble master.
   Tim. Have I once lived to see two honest men?
   Poet. Sir,
Ha'ing often of your open bounty tasted,
Hearing you were retired, your friends fallen off,
Whose thankless natures—O abhorréd spirits!
Not all the whips of heaven are large enough—
What! to you,
Whose star-like nobleness gave life and influence
To their whole being! I'm rapt, and cannot cover
The monstrous bulk of this ingratitude
With any size of words.
   Tim. Let it go naked, men may see 't the better:
You, that are honest, by being what you are,
Make them best seen and known.
   Pain.   He and myself
Have travelled in the great shower of your gifts
And sweetly felt it.

Tim.   Ay, you are honest men.
Pain.   We are hither come to offer you our service.
Tim.   Most honest men! Why, how shall I requite
    you?
Can you eat roots, and drink cold water? no.
Both.   What we can do, we 'll do, to do you service.
Tim.   You are honest men. You have heard that I
    have gold;
I am sure you have; speak truth; you are honest men.
Pain.   So it is said, my noble lord; but therefore
Came not my friend, nor I.
Tim.   Good honest men!—Thou draw'st a counterfeit
Best in all Athens: thou art, indeed, the best;
Thou counterfeit'st most lively.
Pain.   So, so, my lord.
Tim.   Even so, sir, as I say.—And, for thy fiction,
Why, thy verse swells with stuff so fine and smooth,
That thou art even natural in thine art.—
But, for all this, my honest-natured friends,
I must needs say, you have a little fault:
Marry, it 's not monstrous in you; neither wish I
You take much pains to mend.
Both.   Beseech your honour
To make it known to us.
Tim.   You 'll take it ill.
Both.   Most thankfully, my lord.
Tim.   Will you, indeed?
Both.   Doubt it not, worthy lord.
Tim.   There 's never a one of you but trusts a knave
That mightily deceives you.
Both.   Do we, my lord?
Tim.   Ay, and you hear him cog, see him dissemble,
Know his gross patchery, love him, feed him,
Keep in your bosom; yet remain assured,
That he 's a made-up villain.
Pain.   I know none such, my lord.
Poet.   Nor I.
Tim.   Look you, I love you well; I 'll give you gold,
Rid me these villains from your companies:
Hang them or stab them, drown them in a draught,
Confound them by some course, and come to me,
I 'll give you gold enough.
Both.   Name them, my lord; let 's know them.
Tim.   You that way, and you this, but two in com-
    pany:—
Each man apart, all single and alone,
Yet an arch-villain keeps him company.
[*To the Painter*] If, where thou art, two villains shall
    not be,

256

Come not near him.—[*To the Poet*] If thou wouldst
    not reside
But where one villain is, then him abandon,—
Hence! pack! there 's gold; ye came for gold, ye slaves:
You have done work for me, there's payment: hence!
You are an alchymist, make gold of that.
Out rascal dogs!

                [*Exit, beating and driving them out*

Enter FLAVIUS *and two Senators*

  Flav. It is in vain that you would speak with Timon;
For he is set so only to himself,
That nothing but himself, which looks like man,
Is friendly with him.
  First Sen.   Bring us to his cave:
It is our pact and promise to the Athenians
To speak with Timon.
  Sec. Sen.   At all times alike
Men are not still the same. 'Twas time and griefs
That framed him thus: time, with his fairer hand,
Offering the fortunes of his former days,
The former man may make him. Bring us to him,
And chance it as it may.
  Flav.   Here is his cave.—
Peace and content be here! Lord Timon! Timon!
Look out, and speak to friends. The Athenians,
By two of their most reverend senate, greet thee:
Speak to them, noble Timon.

Enter TIMON

  Tim. Thou sun that comfort'st burn!—Speak, and
    be hanged:
For each true word a blister; and each false
Be as a cauterising to the root o' the tongue,
Consuming it with speaking!
  First Sen.   Worthy Timon,—
  Tim. Of none but such as you, and you of Timon.
  Sec. Sen. The senators of Athens greet thee, Timon.
  Tim. I thank them, and would send them back the
    plague,
Could I but catch it for them.
  First Sen.   O, forget
What we are sorry for ourselves in thee.
The senators with one consent of love
Entreat thee back to Athens; who have thought
On special dignities, which vacant lie
For thy best use and wearing.

Sec. Sen.   They confess
Toward thee forgetfulness too general, gross;
Which now the public body,—which doth seldom
Play the recanter,—feeling in itself
A lack of Timon's aid, hath sense withal
Of its own fail, restraining aid to Timon;
And send forth us, to make their sorrowed render,
Together with a recompense more fruitful
Than their offence can weigh down by the dram;
Ay, even such heaps and sums of love and wealth
As shall to thee blot out what wrongs were theirs,
And write in thee the figures of their love,
Ever to read them thine.
    Tim.   You witch me in it;
Surprise me to the very brink of tears:
Lend me a fool's heart, and a woman's eyes,
And I 'll beweep these comforts, worthy senators.
    First Sen.   Therefore, so please thee to return with us,
And of our Athens—thine and ours—to take
The captainship, thou shalt be met with thanks,
Allowed with absolute power, and thy good name
Live with authority:—soon we shall drive back
Of Alcibiades the approaches wild,
Who, like a boar too savage, doth root up
His country's peace,—
    Sec. Sen.   And shakes his threat'ning sword
Against the walls of Athens.
    First Sen.   Therefore, Timon,—
    Tim.   Well, sir, I will; therefore, I will, sir, thus:—
If Alcibiades kill my countrymen,
Let Alcibiades know this of Timon,
That Timon cares not.   But if he sack fair Athens,
And take our goodly agéd men by the beards,
Giving our holy virgins to the stain
Of contumelious, beastly, mad-brained war,
Then, let him know,—and tell him, Timon speaks it,—
In pity of our agéd, and our youth.
I cannot choose but tell him, that I care not,
And let him take 't at worst; for their knives care not.
While you have throats to answer; for myself,
There 's not a whittle in the unruly camp
But I do not prize it at my love before
The reverend'st throat in Athens.   So I leave you
To the protection of the prosperous gods,
As thieves to keepers.
    Flav.   Stay not: all 's in vain.
    Tim.   Why, I was writing of my epitaph;
It will be seen to-morrow.   My long sickness
Of health and living now begins to mend,

And nothing brings me all things.   Go; live still:
Be Alcibiades your plague, you his
And last so long enough!
   First Sen.   We speak in vain.
   Tim.   But yet I love my country, and am not
One that rejoices in the common wrack,
As common bruit doth put it.
   First Sen.   That 's well spoke.
   Tim.   Commend me to my loving countrymen,—
   First Sen.   These words become your lips as they pass
        through them.
   Sec. Sen.   And enter in our ears like great triumphers
In their applauding gates.
   Tim.   Commend me to them;
And tell them, that, to ease them of their griefs,
Their fears of hostile strokes, their achés, losses,
Their pangs of love, with other incident throes
That nature's fragile vessel doth sustain
In life's uncertain voyage, I will some kindness do them:
I'll teach them to prevent wild Alcibiades' wrath.
   Sec. Sen.   I like this well; he will return **again**.
   Tim.   I have a tree which grows here in my close,
That mine own use invites me to cut down,
And shortly must I fell it; tell my friends,
Tell Athens, in the sequence of degree,
From high to low throughout, that whoso please
To stop affliction, let him take his haste,
Come hither ere my tree hath felt the axe,
And hang himself.—I pray you, do my greeting.
   Flav.   Trouble him no further; thus you still shall
        find him.
   Tim.   Come not to me again; but say to Athens
Timon hath made his everlasting mansion
Upon the beachéd verge of the salt flood;
Whom once a day with his embosséd froth
The turbulent surge shall cover: thither come,
And let my grave-stone be your oracle.—
Lips, let sour words go by and language end
What is amiss, plague and infection mend!
Graves only be men's works, and death their gain!
Sun, hide thy beams!   Timon hath done his reign.
                      [Retires to his Cave
   First Sen.   His discontents are unremovably
Coupled to nature.
   Sec. Sen.   Our hope in him is dead.   Let us return,
And strain what other means is left unto us
In our dear peril.
   First Sen.   It requires swift foot.
                                [Exeunt

SCENE II.—The Walls of Athens
Enter two Senators and a Messenger

First Sen. Thou'st painfully discovered: are his files
As full as thy report?
Mess.   I've spoke the least;
Besides, his expedition promises
Present approach.
Sec. Sen. We stand much hazard, if they bring not Timon.
Mess. I met a courier, one mine ancient friend,
Whom, though in general part we were opposed,
Yet our old love made a particular force,
And made us speak like friends:—this man was riding
From Alcibiades to Timon's cave,
With letters of entreaty, which imported
His fellowship i' the cause against your city,
In part for his sake moved.

Enter the Senators from TIMON

First Sen.   Here come our brothers.
Third Sen. No talk of Timon; nothing of him expect,
The enemy's drum is heard, and fearful scouring
Doth choke the air with dust. In, and prepare:
Ours is the fall, I fear; our foe the snare.   [*Exeunt*

SCENE III.—The woods. TIMON'S Cave, and a rude
tomb seen
Enter a Soldier seeking TIMON

Sold. By all description, this should be the place.
Who's here? speak, ho!—No answer? What is this?
Timon is dead, who hath outstretched his span:
Some beast made this; there does not live a man.
Dead, sure; and this his grave.—
What 's on this tomb I cannot read; the character
I 'll take with wax:
Our captain hath in every figure skill;
An aged interpreter, though young in days.
Before proud Athens he 's set down by this,
Whose fall the mark of his ambition is.   [*Exit*

SCENE IV.—Before the Walls of Athens
Trumpets sound. Enter ALCIBIADES *and Forces*

Alcib. Sound to this coward and lascivious town
Our terrible approach.   [*A parley sounded*

Enter Senators on the walls

Till now you have gone on, and filled the time
With all licentious measure, making your wills

The scope of justice: till now, myself, and such
As slept within the shadow of your power,
Have wandered with our traversed arms, and breathed
Our sufferance vainly.   Now the time is flush,
When crouching marrow, in the bearer strong,
Cries, of itself, 'No more': now breathless wrong
Shall sit and pant in your great chairs of ease;
And pursy insolence shall break his wind
With fear and horrid flight.
  First Sen.   Noble and young,
When thy first griefs were but a mere conceit,
Ere thou hadst power or we had cause of fear,
We sent to thee; to give thy rages balm,
To wipe out our ingratitudes with loves
Above their quantity.
  Sec. Sen.   So did we woo
Transforméd Timon to our city's love,
By humble message and by promised means:
We were not all unkind, nor all deserve
The common stroke of war.
  First Sen.   These walls of ours
Were not erected by their hands from whom
You have received your grief; nor are they such,
That these great towers, trophies, schools, should fall
For private faults in them.
  Sec. Sen.   Nor are they living
Who were the motives that you first went out;
Shame, that they wanted cunning, in excess,
Hath broke their hearts.   March, noble lord,
Into our city with thy banners spread:
By decimation, and a tithéd death,
If thy revenges hunger for that food
Which nature loathes—take thou the destined tenth;
And by the hazard of the spotted die
Let die the spotted.
  First Sen.   All have not offended;
For those that were, it is not square to take
On those that are, revenges: crimes, like lands,
Are not inherited.   Then, dear countryman,
Bring in thy ranks, but leave without thy rage:
Spare thine Athenian cradle, and those kin
Which, in the bluster of thy wrath, must fall
With those that have offended.   Like a shepherd,
Approach the fold, and cull the infected forth,
But kill not altogether.
  Sec. Sen.   What thou wilt
Thou rather shalt enforce it with thy smile
Than hew to 't with thy sword.
  First Sen.   Set but thy foot

Against our rampired gates, and they shall ope,
So thou wilt send thy gentle heart before,
To say, thou 'lt enter friendly.
   Sec. Sen.   Throw thy glove,
Or any token of thine honour else,
That thou wilt use the wars as thy redress,
And not as our confusion, all thy powers
Shall make their harbour in our town, till we
Have sealed thy full desire.
   Alcib.   Then, there 's my glove:
Descend, and open your uncharged ports.
Those enemies of Timon's and mine own
Whom you yourselves shall set out for reproof,
Fall, and no more; and—to atone your fears
With my more noble meaning—not a man
Shall pass his quarter, or offend the stream
Of regular justice in your city's bounds,
But shall be rendered to your public laws
At heaviest answer.
   Both.   'Tis most nobly spoken.
   Alcib.   Descend, and keep your words.
                [The Senators descend, and open the gates

Enter a Soldier

   Sold.   My noble general, Timon is dead;
Entombed upon the very hem o' the sea:
And on his grave-stone this insculpture, which
With wax I brought away, whose soft impression
Interprets it for my poor ignorance.
   Alcib.   [*Reads*] '*Hear lies a wretched corse, of wretched
        soul bereft :*
Seek not my name; a plague consume you wicked caitiffs left!
Here lie I, Timon; who, alive, all living men did hate :
*Pass by, and curse thy fill; but pass, and stay not here
        thy gait.*'

These well express in thee thy latter spirits:
Though thou abhorr'dst in us our human griefs,
Scorn'dst our brain's flow, and those our droplets which
From niggard nature fall, yet rich conceit
Taught thee to make vast Neptune weep for aye
On thy low grave, on faults forgiven.   Dead
Is noble Timon; of whose memory
Hereafter more.—Bring me into your city,
And I will use the olive with my sword:
Make war breed peace; make peace stint war; make
        each
Prescribe to other, as each other's leech.—
Let our drums strike.   *[Exeunt*

TITUS ANDRONICUS

DRAMATIS PERSONÆ

SATURNINUS, *son to the late Emperor of Rome, and afterwards declared Emperor*

BASSIANUS, *brother to Saturninus ; in love with Lavinia*

TITUS ANDRONICUS, *a noble Roman, general against the Goths*

MARCUS ANDRONICUS, *Tribune of the People and brother to Titus*

LUCIUS
QUINTUS
MARTIUS
MUTIUS
} *sons to Titus Andronicus*

Young LUCIUS, *a boy, son to Lucius*

PUBLIUS, *son to Marcus the Tribune*

ÆMILIUS, *a noble Roman*

ALARBUS
DEMETRIUS
CHIRON
} *sons to Tamora*

AARON, *a Moor, beloved by Tamora*

A Captain, Tribune, Messenger, and Clown

Goths and Romans

TAMORA, *Queen of the Goths*

LAVINIA, *daughter to Titus Andronicus*

A Nurse, and a black child

Kinsmen of Titus, Senators, Tribunes, Officers, Soldiers, and Attendants

SCENE.—*Rome, and the country near it*

TITUS ANDRONICUS

ACT ONE

Scene I.—Rome. Before the Capitol

The Tomb of the Andronici *appearing ; the Tribunes and Senators aloft. Enter, below,* Saturninus *and his Followers at one side, and* Bassianus *and his Followers at the other, with drum and colours*

Sat. Noble patricians, patrons of my right,
Defend the justice of my cause with arms;
And, countrymen, my loving followers,
Plead my successive title with your swords.
I am his first-born son that was the last
That wore the imperial diadem of Rome:
Then let my father's honours live in me,
Nor wrong mine age with this indignity.
   Bass. Romans, friends, followers, favourers of my right,—
If ever Bassianus, Cæsar's son,
Were gracious in the eyes of royal Rome,
Keep then this passage to the Capitol;
And suffer not dishonour to approach
The imperial seat, to virtue consecrate,
To justice, continence, and nobility:
But let desert in pure election shine;
And, Romans, fight for freedom in your choice.

Enter Marcus Andronicus, *aloft, with the crown*

Marc. Princes, that strive by factions and by friends
Ambitiously for rule and empery,
Know that the people of Rome, for whom we stand
A special party, have by common voice,
In election for the Roman empery,
Chosen Andronicus, surnaméd Pius
For many good and great deserts to Rome:
A nobler man, a braver warrior,
Lives not this day within the city walls.
He by the senate is accited home
From weary wars against the barbarous Goths,
That, with his sons, a terror to our foes,
Hath yoked a nation strong, trained up in arms.

Ten years are spent since first he undertook
This cause of Rome, and chastiséd with arms
Our enemies' pride: five times he hath returned
Bleeding to Rome, bearing his valiant sons
In coffins from the field;
And now at last, laden with honour's spoils,
Returns the good Andronicus to Rome,
Renownéd Titus, flourishing in arms.
Let us entreat,—by honour of his name
Whom worthily you would have now succeed,
And in the Capitol and senate's right,
Whom you pretend to honour and adore,—
That you withdraw you, and abate your strength.
Dismiss your followers, and, as suitors should,
Plead your deserts in peace and humbleness.

   Sat. How fair the tribune speaks to calm my
       thoughts!
   Bass. Marcus Andronicus, so I do affy
In thy uprightness and integrity.
And so I love and honour thee and thine,
Thy noble brother Titus and his sons,
And her to whom my thoughts are humbled all,
Gracious Lavinia, Rome's rich ornament.
That I will here dismiss my loving friends,
And to my fortune's and the people's favour
Commit my cause in balance to be weighed.
           [Exeunt the Followers of Bassianus

   Sat. Friends, that have been thus forward in my
       right,
I thank you all, and here dismiss you all,
And to the love and favour of my country
Commit myself, my person, and the cause.
           [Exeunt the Followers of Saturninus

Rome, be as just and gracious unto me,
As I am confident and kind to thee.—
Open the gates, and let me in.
   Bass. Tribunes, and me, a poor competitor.
    [Flourish. Saturninus and Bassianus
               go up into the Capitol

Enter a Captain and others

   Cap. Romans, make way! The good Andronicus,
Patron of virtue, Rome's best champion,
Successful in the battles that he fights,
With honour and with fortune is returned
From where he circumscribéd with his sword,
And brought to yoke, the enemies of Rome.

Sound drums and trumpets, and then enter two of TITUS'S
*Sons. After them two Men bearing a coffin covered with
black ; then two other Sons. After them* TITUS ANDRON-
ICUS; *and then* TAMORA, *with* ALARBUS, CHIRON,
DEMETRIUS, AARON, *and other Goths, prisoners ; Soldiers
and People following. The Bearers set down the coffin, and*
TITUS *speaks*

Tit. Hail, Rome, victorious in thy mourning weeds!
Lo, as the bark that hath discharged her fraught
Returns with precious lading to the bay
From whence at first she weighed her anchorage,
Cometh Andronicus, bound with laurel boughs,
To re-salute his country with his tears,
Tears of true joy for his return to Rome.
Thou great defender of this Capitol,
Stand gracious to the rites that we intend!
Romans, of five-and-twenty valiant sons,
Half of the number that King Priam had,
Behold the poor remains, alive, and dead!
These that survive, let Rome reward with love;
These that I bring unto their latest home,
With burial amongst their ancestors.
Here Goths have given me leave to sheath my sword.
Titus, unkind and careless of thine own,
Why suffer'st thou thy sons, unburied yet,
To hover on the dreadful shore of Styx?—
Make way to lay them by their brethren,
                              [*The tomb is opened*
There greet in silence, as the dead are wont,
And sleep in peace, slain in your country's wars!
O sacred réceptacle of my joys,
Sweet cell of virtue and nobility,
How many sons of mine hast thou in store
That thou wilt never render to me more!
    Luc. Give us the proudest prisoner of the Goths,
That we may hew his limbs, and on a pile
Ad manes fratrum sacrifice his flesh,
Before this earthly prison of their bones;
That so the shadows be not unappeased,
Nor we disturbed with prodigies on earth.
    Tit. I give him you, the noblest that survives,
The eldest son of this distresséd queen.
    Tam. Stay, Roman brethren!—Gracious conqueror,
Victorious Titus, rue the tears I shed,
A mother's tears in passion for her son:
And if thy sons were ever dear to thee
O, think my son to be as dear to me.
Sufficeth not, that we are brought to Rome

To beautify thy triumphs and return,
Captive to thee and to thy Roman yoke;
But must my sons be slaughtered in the streets
For valiant doings in their country's cause?
O, if to fight for king and commonweal
Were piety in thine, it is in these.
Andronicus, stain not thy tomb with blood:
Wilt thou draw near the nature of the gods?
Draw near them then in being merciful:
Sweet mercy is nobility's true badge.
Thrice-noble Titus, spare my first-born son.
  Tit. Patient yourself, madam, and pardon me.
These are their brethren, whom you Goths beheld
Alive and dead; and for their brethren slain
Religiously they ask a sacrifice:
To this your son is marked, and die he must,
To appease their groaning shadows that are gone.
  Luc. Away with him! and make a fire straight;
And with our swords, upon a pile of wood,
Let's hew his limbs till they be clean consumed.
            [*Exeunt Lucius, Quintus, Martius, and Mutius,*
                                      with Alarbus
  Tam. O cruel, irreligious piety!
  Chi. Was ever Scythia half so barbarous?
  Dem. Oppose not Scythia to ambitious Rome.
Alarbus goes to rest, and we survive
To tremble under Titus' threatening look.
Then, madam, stand resolved; but hope withal,
The self-same gods that armed the Queen of Troy
With opportunity of sharp revenge
Upon the Thracian tyrant in his tent,
May favour Tamora, the Queen of Goths
(When Goths were Goths, and Tamora was queen),
To quit the bloody wrongs upon her foes.

Re-enter LUCIUS, QUINTUS, MARTIUS, *and* MUTIUS, *with*
                    their swords bloody

  Luc. See, lord and father, how we have performed
Our Roman rites.   Alarbus' limbs are lopped,
And entrails feed the sacrificing fire
Whose smoke like incense doth perfume the sky.
Remaineth nought, but to inter our brethren,
And with loud 'larums welcome them to Rome.
  Tit. Let it be so; and let Andronicus
Make this his latest farewell to their souls.
            [*Trumpets sounded, and the coffins laid in the tomb*
In peace and honour rest you here, my sons;
Rome's readiest champions, repose you here

Secure from worldly chances and mishaps!
Here lurks no treason, here no envy swells;
Here grows no damnéd drugs; here are no storms,
No noise, but silence and eternal sleep.
In peace and honour rest you here, my sons!

Enter LAVINIA

   Lav. In peace and honour live Lord Titus long;
My noble lord and father, live in fame.
Lo, at this tomb my tributary tears
I render for my brethren's obsequies:
And at thy feet I kneel, with tears of joy
Shed on the earth for thy return to Rome.
O, bless me here with thy victorious hand,
Whose fortune Rome's best citizens applaud.
   Tit. Kind Rome, that hast thus lovingly reserved
The cordial of mine age to glad my heart!—
Lavinia, live; outlive thy father's days,
And fame's eternal date, for virtue's praise!

Enter below MARCUS ANDRONICUS *and Tribunes ; re-enter*
      SATURNINUS, BASSIANUS, *and others*

   Marc. Long live Lord Titus, my belovéd brother,
Gracious triumpher in the eyes of Rome!
   Tit. Thanks, gentle tribune, noble brother Marcus.
   Marc. And welcome, nephews, from successful wars,
You that survive, and you that sleep in fame.
Fair lords, your fortunes are alike in all,
That in your country's service drew your swords;
But safer triumph is this funeral pomp,
That hath aspired to Solon's happiness,
And triumphs over chance in honour's bed.—
Titus Andronicus, the people of Rome,
Whose friend in justice thou has ever been,
Send thee by me, their tribune and their trust,
This palliament of white and spotless hue,
And name thee in election for the empire,
With these our late-deceaséd emperor's sons.
Be *candidatus*, then, and put it on,
And help to set a head on headless Rome.
   Tit. A better head her glorious body fits
Than his that shakes for age and feebleness.
What should I don this robe, and trouble you,—
Be chosen with proclamations to-day,
To-morrow yield up rule, resign my life,
And set abroad new business for you all?

Rome, I have been thy soldier forty years,
And led my country's strength successfully,
And buried one-and-twenty valiant sons,
Knighted in field, slain manfully in arms,
In right and service of their noble country.
Give me a staff of honour for mine age,
But not a sceptre to control the world:
Upright he held it, lords, that held it last.

    Marc.   Titus, thou shalt obtain and ask the empery.

    Sat.   Proud and ambitious tribune, canst thou tell?

    Tit.   Patience, Prince Saturninus.

    Sat.   Romans, do me right.—
Patricians, draw your swords, and sheathe them not
Till Saturninus be Rome's emperor.—
Andronicus, would thou wert shipped to hell,
Rather than rob me of the people's hearts.

    Luc.   Proud Saturnine, interrupter of the good
That noble-minded Titus means to thee!

    Tit.   Content thee, prince: I will restore to thee
The people's hearts, and wean them from themselves.

    Bass.   Andronicus, I do not flatter thee,
But honour thee, and will do till I die:
My faction if thou strengthen with thy friends,
I will most thankful be; and thanks to men
Of noble minds is honourable meed.

    Tit.   People of Rome, and noble tribunes here,
I ask your voices and your suffrages:
Will you bestow them friendly on Andronicus?

    Trib.   To gratify the good Andronicus,
And gratulate his safe return to Rome,
The people will accept whom he admits.

    Tit.   Tribunes, I thank you; and this suit I make,
That you create your emperor's eldest son,
Lord Saturnine, whose virtues will, I hope,
Reflect on Rome as Titan's rays on earth
And ripen justice in this commonweal:
Then, if you will elect by my advice,
Crown him, and say,—'Long live our emperor!'

    Marc.   With voices and applause of every sort,
Patricians, and plebeians, we create
Lord Saturninus Rome's great emperor
And say,—'Long live our Emperor Saturnine!'

                             [*A long flourish*

    Sat.   Titus Andronicus, for thy favours done
To us in our election this day,
I give thee thanks in part of thy deserts, .
And will with deeds requite thy gentleness:
And for an onset, Titus, to advance
Thy name and honourable family,

Lavinia will I make my empress,
Rome's royal mistress, mistress of my heart,
And in the sacred Pàntheon her espouse.
Tell me, Andronicus, doth this motion please thee?
    Tit. It doth, my worthy lord; and in this match
I hold me highly honoured of your grace:
And here, in sight of Rome, to Saturnine,
King and commander of our commonweal,
The wide world's emperor, do I consecrate
My sword, my chariot, and my prisoners;
Presents well worthy Rome's imperious lord;
Receive them then, the tribute that I owe,
Mine honour's ensigns humbled at thy feet.
    Sat. Thanks, noble Titus, father of my life!
How proud I am of thee and of thy gifts
Rome shall record; and when I do forget
The least of these unspeakable deserts,
Romans, forget your fealty to me.
    Tit. [*To Tamora*] Now, madam, are you prisoner to
                                an emperor;
To him that, for your honour and your state,
Will use you nobly and your followers.
    Sat. A goodly lady, trust me, of the hue
That I would choose, were I to choose anew.—
Clear up, fair queen, that cloudy countenance:
Though chance of war hath wrought this change of cheer,
Thou com'st not to be made a scorn in Rome:
Princely shall be thy usage every way.
Rest on my word, and let not discontent
Daunt all your hopes: madam, he comforts you,
Can make you greater than the Queen of Goths.—
Lavinia, you are not displeased with this?
    Lav. Not I, my lord; sith true nobility
Warrants these words in princely courtesy.
    Sat. Thanks, sweet Lavinia,—Romans, let us go,
Ransomless here we set our prisoners free:
Proclaim our honours, lords, with trump and drum.
    Bass. Lord Titus, by your leave, this maid is mine.
                                        [*Seizing Lavinia*
    Tit. How, sir? Are you in earnest, then, my lord?
    Bass. Ay, noble Titus; and resolved withal.
To do myself this reason and this right.
    Marc. *Suum cuique* is our Roman justice:
This prince in justice seizeth but his own.
    Luc. And that he will, and shall, if Lucius live.
    Tit. Traitors, avaunt! Where is the emperor's guard?
Treason, my lord! Lavinia is surprised.
    Sat. Surprised! by whom?
    Bass.   By him that justly may

271

Bear his betrothed from all the world away.
                    [*Exeunt Marcus and Bassianus, with Lavinia*
  Mut. Brothers, help to convey her hence away,
And with my sword I'll keep this door safe.
                    [*Exeunt Lucius, Quintus, and Martius*
  Tit. Follow, my lord, and I'll soon bring her back.
  Mut. My lord, you pass not here.
  Tit.   What, villain boy!
Barr'st me my way in Rome?   [*Kills Mutius*
  Mut.   Help, Lucius, help!

                    Re-enter LUCIUS

  Luc. My lord, you are unjust, and more than so;
In wrongful quarrel you have slain your son.
  Tit. Nor thou, nor he, are any sons of mine:
My sons would never so dishonour me.
Traitor, restore Lavinia to the emperor.
  Luc. Dead, if you will; but not to be his wife
That is another's lawful promised love.   [*Exit*
  Sat. No, Titus, no; the emperor needs her not,
Nor her, nor thee, nor any of thy stock:
I'll trust by leisure him that mocks me once;
Thee never, nor thy traitorous haughty sons,
Confederates all thus to dishonour me.
Was there none else in Rome to make a stale
But Saturnine? Full well, Andronicus,
Agree these deeds with that proud brag of thine,
That saidst, I begged the empire at thy hands.
  Tit. O monstrous! what reproachful words are these?
  Sat. But go thy ways; go, give that changing piece
To him that flourished for her with his sword.
A valiant son-in-law thou shalt enjoy;
One fit to bandy with thy lawless sons,
To ruffle in the commonwealth of Rome.
  Tit. These words are razors to my wounded heart.
  Sat. And therefore, lovely Tamora, Queen of Goths,
That, like the stately Phœbe 'mongst her nymphs
Dost overshine the gallant'st dames of Rome,
If thou be pleased with this my sudden choice,
Behold, I choose thee, Tamora, for my bride,
And will create thee Empress of Rome.
Speak, Queen of Goths, dost thou applaud my choice?
And here I swear by all the Roman gods,—
Sith priest and holy water are so near,
And tapers burn so bright, and every thing
In readiness for Hymenæus stand,—
I will not re-salute the streets of Rome,
                    272

Or climb my palace, till from forth this place
I lead espoused my bride along with me.
   Tam. And here, in sight of heaven, to Rome I swear,
If Saturnine advance the Queen of Goths
She will a handmaid be to his desires,
A loving nurse, a mother to his youth.
   Sat. Ascend, fair queen, Pantheon.—Lords, accompany
Your noble emperor, and his lovely bride
Sent by the heavens for Prince Saturnine,
Whose wisdom hath her fortune conqueréd.
There shall we consummate our spousal rites.
                       [Exeunt all but Titus
   Tit. I am not bid to wait upon this bride.
Titus, when wert thou wont to walk alone,
Dishonoured thus, and challengéd of wrongs?

Re-enter MARCUS, LUCIUS, QUINTUS, *and* MARTIUS

   Marc. O Titus, see! O, see what thou hast done!
In a bad quarrel slain a virtuous son.
   Tit. No, foolish tribune, no; no son of mine,
Nor thou, nor these, confederates in the deed
That hath dishonoured all our family:
Unworthy brother, and unworthy sons!
   Luc. But let us give him burial, as becomes:
Give Mutius burial with our brethren.
   Tit. Traitors, away! he rests not in this tomb.
This monument five hundred years hath stood,
Which I have sumptuously re-edified:
Here none but soldiers and Rome's servitors,
Repose in fame; none basely slain in brawls.
Bury him where you can; he comes not here.
   Marc. My lord, this is impiety in you.
My nephew Mutius' deeds do plead for him:
He must be buried with his brethren.
   Quint., Mart. And shall, or him we will accompany.
   Tit. And shall! What villain was it spake that word?
   Quint. He that would vouch it in any place but here.
   Tit. What! would you bury him in my despite?
   Marc. No, noble Titus; but entreat of thee
To pardon Mutius, and to bury him.
   Tit. Marcus, even thou hast struck upon my crest,
And with these boys mine honour thou hast wounded:
My foes I do repute you every one;
So, trouble me no more, but get you gone.
   Mart. He is not with himself: let us withdraw.
   Quint. Not I, till Mutius' bones be buriéd.
              [Marcus and the Sons of Titus kneel

Marc.   Brother, for in that name doth nature plead.—
Quint.   Father, and in that name doth nature speak.—
Tit.   Speak thou no more, if all the rest will speed.
Marc.   Renownéd Titus, more than half my soul!—
Luc.   Dear father, soul and substance of us all!—
Marc.   Suffer thy brother Marcus to inter
His noble nephew here in virtue's nest,
That died in honour and Lavinia's cause.
Thou art a Roman; be not barbarous:
The Greeks upon advice did bury Ajax
That slew himself; and wise Laertes' son
Did graciously plead for his funerals.
Let not young Mutius then, that was thy joy,
Be barred his entrance here.
Tit.   Rise, Marcus, rise.—
The dismall'st day is this that e'er I saw,
To be dishonoured by my sons in Rome!—
Well, bury him, and bury me the next.
                              [*Mutius is put into the tomb*
Luc.   There lie thy bones, sweet Mutius, with thy
          friends,
Till we with trophies do adorn thy tomb.
All.   No man shed tears for noble Mutius;
He lives in fame that died in virtue's cause.
Marc.   My lord,—to step out of these dreary dumps,—
How comes it that the subtle Queen of Goths
Is of a sudden thus advanced in Rome?
Tit.   I know not, Marcus, but I know it is;
Whether by device or no, the heavens can tell.
Is she not then beholding to the man
That brought her for this high good turn so far?
Yes, and will nobly him remunerate.

Flourish. Re-enter, at one door, SATURNINUS, *attended ;*
   TAMORA, DEMETRIUS, CHIRON, *and* AARON; *at the other
   door,* BASSIANUS, LAVINIA, *and others*

Sat.   So, Bassianus, you have played your prize:
God give you joy, sir, of your gallant bride!
Bass.   And you of yours, my lord!   I say no more,
Nor wish no less; and so I take my leave.
Sat.   Traitor, if Rome have law, or we have power,
Thou and thy faction shall repent this rape.
Bass.   Rape call you it, my lord, to seize my own,
My true-betrothéd love, and now my wife?
But let the laws of Rome determine all;
Meanwhile, I am possessed of that is mine.
Sat.   'T is good, sir: you are very short with us;
But, if we live, we 'll be as sharp with you.

Bass. My lord, what I have done, as best I may,
Answer I must, and shall do with my life.
Only thus much I give your grace to know:
By all the duties that I owe to Rome,
This noble gentleman, Lord Titus here,
Is in opinion and in honour wronged;
That, in the rescue of Lavinia,
With his own hand did slay his youngest son,
In zeal to you, and highly moved to wrath,
To be controlled in that he frankly gave.
Receive him then to favour, Saturnine,
That hath expressed himself, in all his deeds,
A father and a friend to thee and Rome.
    Tit. Prince Bassianus, leave to plead my deeds:
'T is thou, and those, that have dishonoured me.
Rome and the righteous heavens be my judge,
How I have loved and honoured Saturnine.
    Tam. My worthy lord, if ever Tamora
Were gracious in those princely eyes of thine,
Then hear me speak indifferently for all;
And at my suit, sweet, pardon what is past.
    Sat. What, madam! be dishonoured openly,
And basely put it up without revenge?
    Tam. Not so, my lord: the gods of Rome forfend,
I should be author to dishonour you!
But on mine honour dare I undertake
For good Lord Titus' innocence in all,
Whose fury not dissembled speaks his griefs.
Then, at my suit, look graciously on him;
Lose not so noble a friend on vain suppose,
Nor with sour looks afflict his gentle heart.—
[*Aside to Saturninus*] My lord, be ruled by me, be won
            at last;
Dissemble all your griefs and discontents:
You are but newly planted in your throne.
Lest then the people, and patricians too,
Upon a just survey, take Titus' part,
And so supplant you for ingratitude,
Which Rome reputes to be a heinous sin,
Yield at entreats, and then let me alone.
I 'll find a day to massacre them all,
And raze their faction and their family.
The cruel father, and his traitorous sons
To whom I suéd for my dear son's life;
And make them know what 't is to let a queen
Kneel in the streets, and beg for grace in vain.—
[*Aloud*] Come, come, sweet emperor;—come, Andro-
            nicus:—
Take up this good old man, and cheer the heart

That dies in tempest of thy angry frown.
   Sat. Rise, Titus, rise: my empress hath prevailed.
   Tit. I thank your majesty, and her, my lord.
These words, these looks, infuse new life in me.
   Tam. Titus, I am incorporate in Rome,
A Roman now adopted happily,
And must advise the emperor for his good.
This day all quarrels die, Andronicus;—
And let it be mine honour, good my lord,
That I have reconciled your friends and you.—
For you, Prince Bassianus, I have passed
My word and promise to the emperor,
That you will be more mild and tractable.—
And fear not, lords,—and you, Lavinia;—
By my advice, all humbled on your knees,
You shall ask pardon of his majesty.
   Luc. We do; and vow to heaven, and to his highness
That what we did was mildly, as we might,
Tendering our sister's honour, and our own.
   Marc. That on mine honour here I do protest.
   Sat. Away, and talk not: trouble us no more.—
   Tam. Nay, nay, sweet emperor, we must all be friends:
The tribune and his nephews kneel for grace;
I will not be denied: sweet heart, look back.
   Sat. Marcus, for thy sake, and thy brother's here,
And at my lovely Tamora's entreats,
I do remit these young men's heinous faults.
Stand up.
Lavinia, though you left me like a churl,
I found a friend; and sure as death I swore,
I would not part a bachelor from the priest.
Come; if the emperor's court can feast two brides,
You are my guest, Lavinia, and your friends.—
This day shall be a love-day, Tamora.
   Tit. To-morrow, an it please your majesty
To hunt the panther and the hart with me,
With horn and hound we 'll give your grace *bonjour.*
   Sat. Be it so, Titus, and gramercy too.
                         [*Trumpets.   Exeunt*

ACT TWO

Scene I.—Rome.   Before the Palace

Enter Aaron

   Aar. Now climbeth Tamora Olympus' top,
Safe out of fortune's shot; and sits aloft,

Secure of thunder's crack or lightning flash,
Advanced above pale envy's threat'ning reach.
As when the golden sun salutes the morn
And, having gilt the ocean with his beams,
Gallops the zodiac in his glistering coach
And overlooks the highest-peering hills;
So Tamora.
Upon her wit doth earthly honour wait,
And virtue stoops and trembles at her frown.
Then, Aaron, arm thy heart and fit thy thoughts
To mount aloft with thy imperial mistress.
And mount her pitch, whom thou in triumph long
Hast prisoner held fettered in amorous chains
And faster bound to Aaron's charming eyes
Than is Prometheus tied to Caucasus.
Away with slavish weeds and servile thoughts!
I will be bright, and shine in pearl and gold
To wait upon this new-made empress.
To wait, said I? to wanton with this queen,
This goddess, this Semiramis, this nymph,
This siren, that will charm Rome's Saturnine,
And see his shipwrack and his commonweal's.
Holla! what storm is this?

Enter DEMETRIUS *and* CHIRON, *braving*

Dem.   Chiron, thy years want wit, thy wit wants
          edge,
And manners, to intrude where I am graced,
And may, for aught thou know'st, affected be.
   Chi.   Demetrius, thou dost overween in all,
And so in this, to bear me down with braves.
'T is not the difference of a year or two
Makes me less gracious, thee more fortunate:
I am as able and as fit as thou
To serve, and to deserve my mistress' grace;
And that my sword upon thee shall approve,
And plead my passions for Lavinia's love.
   Aar.   Clubs, clubs! these lovers will not keep the
          peace.
   Dem.   Why, boy, although our mother, unadvised,
Gave you a dancing-rapier by your side,
Are you so desperate grown to threat your friends?
Go to; have your lath glued within your sheath
Till you know better how to handle it.
   Chi.   Meanwhile, sir, with the little skill I have,
Full well shalt thou perceive how much I dare.
   Dem.   Ay, boy, grow ye so brave?   [*They draw*
   Aar.   Why, how now, lords?

277

So near the emperor's palace dare you draw,
And maintain such a quarrel openly?
Full well I wot the ground of all this grudge:
I would not for a million of gold
The cause were known to them it most concerns;
Nor would your noble mother, for much more,
Be so dishonoured in the court of Rome.
For shame, put up.

  Dem.   Not I, till I have sheathed
My rapier in his bosom, and, withal,
Thrust those reproachful speeches down his throat
That he hath breathed in my dishonour here.

  Chi. For that I am prepared and full resolved,
Foul-spoken coward, that thunder'st with thy tongue
And with thy weapon nothing dar'st perform.

  Aar. Away, I say!
Now, by the gods that warlike Goths adore,
This petty brabble will undo us all.—
Why, lords,—and think you not how dangerous
It is to jet upon a prince's right?
What! is Lavinia then become so loose,
Or Bassianus so degenerate,
That for her love such quarrels may be broached
Without controlment, justice, or revenge?
Young lords, beware!—an should the empress know
This discord's ground, the music would not please.

  Chi. I care not, I, knew she and all the world:
I love Lavinia more than all the world.

  Dem. Youngling, learn thou to make some meaner
      choice:
Lavinia is thine elder brother's hope.

  Aar. Why, are ye mad? or know ye not, in Rome
How furious and impatient they be,
And cannot brook competitors in love?
I tell you, lords, you do but plot your deaths
By this device.

  Chi.   Aaron, a thousand deaths
Would I propose, to achieve her whom I love.

  Aar. To achieve her, how?

  Dem.   Why mak'st thou it so strange?
She is a woman, therefore may be wooed;
She is a woman, therefore may be won;
She is Lavinia, therefore must be loved.
What, man! more water glideth by the mill
Than wots the miller of; and easy it is
Of a cut loaf to steal a shive, we know:
Though Bassianus be the emperor's brother,
Better than he have yet worn Vulcan's badge.

  Aar. [*Aside*] Ay, and as good as Saturninus may.

Dem. Then, why should he despair that knows to court
  it
With words, fair looks, and liberality?
What! hast thou not full often struck a doe,
And borne her cleanly by the keeper's nose?
  Aar. Why, then, it seems, some certain snatch or so
Would serve your turns.
  Chi.   Ay, so the turn were served.
  Dem. Aaron, thou hast hit it.
  Aar.   Would you had hit it too;
Then should not we be tired with this ado.
Why, hark ye, hark ye,—and are you such fools,
To square for this? would it offend you then,
That both should speed?
  Chi.   Faith, not me.
  Dem. Nor me, so I were one.
  Aar. For shame, be friends, and join for that you jar.
'T is policy and stratagem must do
That you affect; and so must you resolve
That what you cannot as you would achieve
You must perforce accomplish as you may.
Take this of me: Lucrece was not more chaste
Than this Lavinia, Bassianus' love.
A speedier course than lingering languishment
Must we pursue, and I have found the path.
My lords, a solemn hunting is in hand,
There will the lovely Roman ladies troop:
The forest walks are wide and spacious,
And many unfrequented plots there are,
Fitted by kind for rape and villainy.
Single you thither then this dainty doe,
And strike her home by force, if not by words:
This way, or not at all, stand you in hope.
Come, come; our empress, with her sacred wit,
To villainy and vengeance consecrate,
Will we acquaint with all that we intend,
And she shall file our engines with advice
That will not suffer you to square yourselves,
But to your wishes' height advance you both.
The emperor's court is like the house of Fame,
The palace full of tongues, of eyes, of ears:
The woods are ruthless, dreadful, deaf, and dull;
There speak, and strike, brave boys, and take your turns;
There serve your lust, shadowed from heaven's eye,
And revel in Lavinia's treasury.
  Chi. Thy counsel, lad, smells of no cowardice.
  Dem. *Sit fas aut nefas*, till I find the stream
To cool this heat, a charm to calm these fits,
Per Styga, per manes vehor.   [*Exeunt*

SCENE II.—A Forest near Rome

Horns and cry of Hounds heard

Enter TITUS ANDRONICUS, *with Hunters, &c.,* MARCUS,
LUCIUS, QUINTUS, *and* MARTIUS

Tit.   The hunt is up, the morn is bright and grey,
The fields are fragrant, and the woods are green.
Uncouple here, and let us make a bay,
And wake the emperor and his lovely bride,
And rouse the prince, and ring a hunter's peal,
That all the court may echo with the noise.
Sons, let it be your charge, as it is ours,
To attend the emperor's person carefully:
I have been troubled in my sleep this night,
But dawning day new comfort hath inspired.

[Horns wind a peal

Enter SATURNINUS, TAMORA, BASSIANUS, LAVINIA,
DEMETRIUS, CHIRON, *and Attendants*

Tit.   Many good morrows to your majesty;—
Madam, to you as many and as good.—
I promiséd your grace a hunter's peal.
Sat.   And you have rung it lustily, my lords,
Somewhat too early for new-married ladies.
Bass.   Lavinia, how say you?
Lav.   I say, no;
I have been broad awake two hours and more.
Sat.   Come on then, horse and chariots let us have.
And to our sport. [*To Tamora*] Madam, now shall ye see
Our Roman hunting.
Marc.   I have dogs, my lord,
Will rouse the proudest panther in the chase,
And climb the highest promontory top.
Tit.   And I have horse will follow where the game
Makes way, and run like swallows o'er the plain.
Dem.   Chiron, we hunt not, we, with horse nor hound;
But hope to pluck a dainty doe to ground.

[Exeunt

SCENE III.—A Lonely Part of the Forest

Enter AARON, *with a bag of gold*

Aar.   He that had wit would think that I had none,
To bury so much gold under a tree,
And never after to inherit it.

Let him that thinks of me so abjectly
Know that this gold must coin a stratagem,
Which, cunningly effected, will beget
A very excellent piece of villainy:
And so repose, sweet gold, for their unrest.

[Hides the gold
That have their alms out of the empress' chest.

Enter TAMORA

Tam. My lovely Aaron, wherefore look'st thou sad,
When every thing doth make a gleeful boast?
The birds chaunt melody on every bush;
The snake lies rolléd in the cheerful sun;
The green leaves quiver with the cooling wind,
And make a chequered shadow on the ground.
Under their sweet shade, Aaron, let us sit,
And, whilst the babbling echo mocks the hounds,
Replying shrilly to the well-tuned horns,
As if a double hunt were heard at once,
Let us sit down and mark their yelping noise:
And—after conflict, such as was supposed
The wandering prince and Dido once enjoyed,
When with a happy storm they were surprised,
And curtained with a counsel-keeping cave—
We may, each wreathéd in the other's arms,
Our pastimes done, possess a golden slumber,
Whiles hounds, and horns, and sweet melodious birds,
Be unto us as in a nurse's song
Of lullaby, to bring her babe asleep.
Aar. Madam, though Venus govern your desires,
Saturn is dominator over mine.
What signifies my deadly-standing eye,
My silence, and my cloudy melancholy;
My fleece of woolly hair, that now uncurls
Even as an adder when she doth unroll
To do some fatal execution?
No, madam, these are no venereal signs:
Vengeance is in my heart, death in my hand.
Blood and revenge are hammering in my head.
Hark, Tamora, the empress of my soul,
Which never hopes more heaven than rests in thee,
This is the day of doom for Bassianus;
His Philomel must lose her tongue to-day:
Thy sons make pillage of her chastity,
And wash their hands in Bassianus' blood.
Seest thou this letter? take it up, I pray thee,
And give the king this fatal plotted scroll.—
Now question me no more; we are espied:

Here comes a parcel of our hopeful booty,
Which dreads not yet their lives' destruction.
    Tam.   Ah, my sweet Moor, sweeter to me than life!
    Aar.   No more, great empress. Bassianus comes;
Be cross with him; and I 'll go fetch thy sons
To back thy quarrels, whatsoe'er they be.   [*Exit*

Enter BASSIANUS and LAVINIA

    Bass.   Whom have we here? Rome's royal empress,
Unfurnished of her well beseeming troop?
Or is it Dian, habited like her,
Who hath abandonéd her holy groves,
To see the general hunting in this forest?
    Tam.   Saucy controller of my private steps!
Had I the power that some say Dian had
Thy temples should be planted presently
With horns as was Actæon's, and the hounds
Should drive upon thy new transforméd limbs,
Unmannerly intruder as thou art!
    Lav.   Under your patience, gentle empress,
'T is thought you have a goodly gift in horning;
And to be doubted that your Moor and you
Are singled forth to try experiments.
Jove shield your husband from his hounds to-day;
'T is pity they should take him for a stag.
    Bass.   Believe me, queen, your swarth Cimmerian
Doth make your honour of his body's hue,
Spotted, detested, and abominable.
Why are you séquestered from all your train,
Dismounted from your snow-white goodly steed,
And wandered hither to an obscure plot,
Accompanied but with a barbarous Moor,
If foul desire had not conducted you?
    Lav.   And being intercepted in your sport,
Great reason that my noble lord be rated
For sauciness!—I pray you, let us hence,
And let her joy her raven-coloured love;
This valley fits the purpose passing well.
    Bass.   The king, my brother, shall have note of this.
    Lav.   Ay, for these slips have made him noted long:
Good king, to be so mightily abused!
    Tam.   Why have I patience to endure all this?

Enter DEMETRIUS and CHIRON

    Dem.   How now, dear sovereign, and our gracious
       mother,
Why doth your highness look so pale and wan?
    Tam.   Have I not reason, think you, to look pale?

These two have ticed me hither to this place:
A barren detested vale you see it is;
The trees, though summer, yet forlorn and lean,
O'ercome with moss and baleful mistletoe:
Here never shines the sun; here nothing breeds,
Unless the nightly owl or fatal raven.
And when they showed me this abhorréd pit,
They told me, here, at dead time of the night,
A thousand fiends, a thousand hissing snakes,
Ten thousand swelling toads, as many urchins,
Would make such fearful and conduséd cries,
As any mortal body, hearing it,
Should straight fall mad, or else die suddenly.
No sooner had they told this hellish tale,
But straight they told me, they would bind me here
Unto the body of a dismal yew,
And leave me to this miserable death:
And then they called me foul adulteress,
Lascivious Goth, and all the bitterest terms
That ever ear did hear to such effect;
And, had you not by wondrous fortune come,
This vengeance on me had they executed.
Revenge it, as you love your mother's life
Or be not henceforth called my children.
    Dem.   This is a witness that I am thy son.
                             [Stabs Bassianus
    Chi.   And this for me, struck home to show my strength.
                             [Stabbing him likewise
    Lav.   Ay, come, Semiramis,—nay, barbarous Tamora;
For no name fits thy nature but thy own.
    Tam.   Give me thy poniard: you shall know, my boys,
Your mother's hand shall right your mother's wrong.
    Dem.   Stay, madam, here is more belongs to her:
First thrash the corn, then after burn the straw.
This minion stood upon her chastity
Upon her nuptial vow, her loyalty,
And, with that painted hope she braves your mightiness:
And shall she carry this unto her grave?
    Chi.   An if she do, I would I were an eunuch.
Drag hence her husband to some secret hole,
And make his dead trunk pillow to our lust.
    Tam.   But when ye have the honey ye desire,
Let not this wasp outlive, us both to sting.
    Chi.   I warrant you, madam, we will make that sure.—
Come, mistress, now perforce we will enjoy
That nice preservéd honesty of yours.
    Lav.   O Tamora! thou bear'st a woman's face,—
    Tam.   I will not hear her speak; away with her!
    Lav.   Sweet lords, entreat her hear me but a word.

Dem.   Listen, fair madam: let it be your glory
To see her tears; but be your heart to them
As unrelenting flint to drops of rain.
    Lav.   When did the tiger's young ones teach the dam?
O, do not learn her wrath; she taught it thee;
The milk thou suck'dst from her did turn to marble;
Even at thy teat thou hadst thy tyranny,
Yet every mother breeds not sons alike:
[*To Chiron*]   Do thou entreat her show a woman pity.
    Chi.   What, wouldst thou have me prove myself a
        bastard?
    Lav.   'T is true, the raven doth not hatch a lark:
Yet have I heard,—O, could I find it now!—
The lion moved with pity did endure
To have his princely paws pared all away.
Some say that ravens foster forlorn children,
The whilst their own birds famish in their nests:
O, be to me, though thy hard heart say no,
Nothing so kind, but something pitiful.
    Tam.   I know not what it means? away with her!
    Lav.   O! let me teach thee: for my father's sake,
That gave thee life, when well he might have slain thee,
Be not obdurate, open thy deaf ears.
    Tam.   Hadst thou in person ne'er offended me,
Even for his sake am I pitiless.—
Remember, boys, I poured forth tears in vain,
To save your brother from the sacrifice;
But fierce Andronicus would not relent.
Therefore, away with her, use her as you will:
The worse to her, the better loved of me.
    Lav.   O Tamora! be called a gentle queen,
And with thine own hands kill me in this place;
For 't is not life that I have begged so long:
Poor I was slain when Bassianus died.
    Tam.   What begg'st thou then? fond woman, let me
        go.
    Lav.   'T is present death I beg; and one thing more,
That womanhood denies my tongue to tell.
O, keep me from their worse than killing lust,
And tumble me into some loathsome pit
Where never man's eye may behold my body:
Do this, and be a charitable murderer.
    Tam.   So should I rob my sweet sons of their fee:
No, let them satisfy their lust on thee.
    Dem.   Away! for thou hast stayed us here too long.
    Lav.   No grace? no womanhood? Ah, beastly crea-
        ture!
The blot and enemy to our general name!
Confusion fall—

Chi. Nay, then I'll stop your mouth.—Bring thou
  her husband:
                              [*Dragging off Lavinia*
This is the hole where Aaron bid us hide him.
                              [*Exeunt Chiron and Demetrius*
  Tam. Farewell, my sons: see, that you make her sure.
Ne'er let my heart know merry cheer indeed,
Till all the Andronici be made away.
Now will I hence to seek my lovely Moor,
And let my spleenful sons this trull deflour.   [*Exit*

SCENE IV.—The Same

Enter AARON, *with* QUINTUS *and* MARTIUS

  Aar. Come on, my lords, the better foot before:
Straight will I bring you to the loathsome pit
Where I espied the panther fast asleep.
  Quint. My sight is very dull, whate'er it bodes.
  Mart. And mine, I promise you: were 't not for shame
Well could I leave our sport to sleep awhile.
                              [*Falls into the pit*
  Quint. What! art thou fallen?—What subtle hole is this
Whose mouth is covered with rude-growing briers,
Upon whose leaves are drops of new-shed blood,
As fresh as morning's dew distilled on flowers?
A very fatal place it seems to me.
Speak, brother, hast thou hurt thee with the fall?
  Mart. O brother! with the dismall'st object hurt,
That ever eye with sight made heart lament.
  Aar. [*Aside*] Now will I fetch the king to find them
  here,
That he thereby may give a likely guess,
How these were they that made away his brother.
                              [*Exit*
  Mart. Why dost not comfort me, and help me out
From this unhallowed and blood-stainéd hole?
  Quint. I am surprised with an uncouth fear;
A chilling sweat o'erruns my trembling joints:
My heart suspects more than mine eye can see.
  Mart. To prove thou has a true-divining heart,
Aaron and thou look down into this den,
And see a fearful sight of blood and death.
  Quint. Aaron is gone; and my compassionate heart
Will not permit mine eyes once to behold
The thing whereat it trembles by surmise.
O! tell me how it is; for ne'er till now
Was I a child, to fear I know not what.

Mart. Lord Bassianus lies embrewéd here,
All on a heap, like to a slaughtered lamb,
In this detested, dark, blood-drinking pit.
    Quint. If it be dark, how dost thou know 't is he?
    Mart. Upon his bloody finger he doth wear
A precious ring that lightens all the hole,
Which, like a taper in some monument,
Doth shine upon the dead man's earthly cheeks.
And shows the ragged entrails of this pit:
So pale did shine the moon on Pyramus
When he by night lay bathed in maiden blood.
O brother, help me with thy fainting hand—
If fear hath made thee faint, as me it hath—
Out of this fell devouring réceptacle,
As hateful as Cocytus' misty mouth.
    Quint. Reach me thy hand, that I may help thee out;
Or, wanting strength to do thee so much good,
I may be plucked into the swallowing womb
Of this deep pit, poor Bassianus' grave
I have no strength to pluck thee to the brink.
    Mart. Nor I no strength to climb without thy help.
    Quint. Thy hand once more; I will not loose again,
Till thou art here aloft, or I below.—
Thou canst not come to me; I come to thee.

                                            [*Falls in*

Enter SATURNINUS *and* AARON

Sat. Along with me:—I 'll see what hole is here,
And what he is that now is leaped into it.
Say, who art thou, that lately didst descend
Into this gaping hollow of the earth?
    Mart. The unhappy son of old Andronicus,
Brought hither in a most unlucky hour
To find thy brother Bassianus dead.
    Sat. My brother dead! I know, thou dost but jest:
He and his lady both are at the lodge
Upon the north side of this pleasant chase;
'T is not an hour since I left him there.
    Mart. We know not where you left him all alive,
But, out, alas! here have we found him dead.

Enter TAMORA, *with attendants;* TITUS ANDRONICUS, *and* LUCIUS

Tam. Where is my lord the king?
    Sat. Here, Tamora; though grieved with killing grief.
    Tam. Where is thy brother Bassianus?
    Sat. Now to the bottom dost thou search my wound:
Poor Bassianus here lies murderéd.

Tam. Then all too late I bring this fatal writ,
[Giving a letter
The complot of this timeless tragedy;
And wonder greatly that man's face can fold
In pleasing smiles such murderous tyranny.
    Sat. [*Reads*] "An if we miss to meet him hand-
        somely,—
Sweet huntsman, Bassianus 't is, we mean,—
Do thou much as dig the grave for him.
Thou know'st our meaning: look for thy reward
Among the nettles at the elder-tree,
Which overshades the mouth of that same pit
Where we decreed to bury Bassianus.
Do this, and purchase us thy lasting friends."
O Tamora! was ever heard the like?
This is the pit, and this the elder-tree.
Look, sirs, if you can find the huntsman out
That should have murdered Bassianus here.
    Aar. My gracious lord, here is the bag of gold.
[Showing it
    Sat. [*To Titus*] Two of thy whelps, fell curs of bloody
        kind,
Have here bereft my brother of his life.—
Sirs, drag them from the pit unto the prison:
There let them bide until we have devised
Some never-heard-of torturing pain for them.
    Tam. What! are they in this pit? O wondrous
        thing!
How easily murder is discoveréd!
    Tit. High emperor, upon my feeble knee
I beg this boon with tears not lightly shed;
That this fell fault of my acccurséd sons,
Accurséd, if the fault be proved in them,—
    Sat. If it be proved! you see, it is apparent—
Who found this letter? Tamora, was it you?
    Tam. Andronicus himself did take it up.
    Tit. I did, my lord: yet let me be their bail:
For, by my father's reverend tomb, I vow,
They shall be ready at your highness' will,
To answer their suspicion with their lives.
    Sat. Thou shalt not bail them: see, thou follow me.
Some bring the murdered body, some the murderers:
Let them not speak a word, the guilt is plain;
For, by my soul, were there worse end than death,
That end upon them should be executed.
    Tam. Andronicus, I will entreat the king:
Fear not thy sons, they shall do well enough.
    Tit. Come, Lucius, come; stay not to talk with them.
[Exeunt severally

287

SCENE V.—The Same

Enter DEMETRIUS *and* CHIRON, *with* LAVINIA *ravished ;
her hands cut off, and her tongue cut out*

Dem.   So, now go tell, an if thy tongue can speak,
Who 't was that cut thy tongue and ravished thee.
Chi.   Write down thy mind, bewray thy meaning so;
An if thy stumps will let thee, play the scribe.
Dem.   See, how with signs and tokens she can scrawl.
Chi.   Go home, call for sweet water, wash thy hands.
Dem.   She hath no tongue to call, nor hands to wash;
And so let 's leave her to her silent walks.
Chi.   An 't were my case, I should go hang myself.
Dem.   If thou hadst hands to help thee knit the cord.
                                    [*Exeunt Demetrius and Chiron*

Enter MARCUS, *from hunting*

Marc.   Who 's this?—my niece, that flies away so fast?
Cousin, a word: where is your husband?—
If I do dream, would all my wealth would wake me!
If I do wake, some planet strike me down,
That I may slumber in eternal sleep!—
Speak, gentle niece, what stern ungentle hands
Have lopped and hewed, and made thy body bare
Of her two branches, those sweet ornaments,
Whose circling shadows kings have sought to sleep in,
And might not gain so great a happiness
As have thy love?   Why dost not speak to me?—
Alas! a crimson river of warm blood
Like to a bubbling fountain stirred with wind,
Doth rise and fall between thy rosed lips,
Coming and going with thy honey breath.
But, sure, some Tereus hath deflouréd thee,
And, lest thou shouldst detect him, cut thy tongue.
Ah! now thou turn'st away thy face for shame;
And notwithstanding all this loss of blood,
As from a conduit with thee issuing spouts,
Yet do thy cheeks look red as Titan's face
Blushing to be encountered with a cloud.
Shall I speak for thee? shall I say, 't is so?
O, that I knew thy heart; and knew the beast,
That I might rail at him to ease my mind!
Sorrow concealéd, like an oven stopped,
Doth burn the heart to cinders where it is.
Fair Philomela, she but lost her tongue,
And in a tedious sampler sewed her mind:
But, lovely niece, that mean is cut from thee;

A craftier Tereus hast thou met withal,
And he hath cut those pretty fingers off,
That could have better sewed than Philomel.
O! had the monster seen those lily hands
Tremble like aspen-leaves upon a lute,
And make the silken strings delight to kiss them,
He would not then have touched them for his life;
Or had he heard the heavenly harmony,
Which that sweet tongue hath made,
He would have dropped his knife, and fell asleep,
As Cerberus at the Thracian poet's feet.
Come, let us go, and make thy father blind;
For such a sight will blind a father's eye:
One hour's storm will drown the fragrant meads;
What will whole months of tears thy father's eyes?
Do not draw back, for we will mourn with thee:
O, could our mourning ease thy misery!   [*Exeunt*

ACT THREE

Scene I.—Rome. A Street

Enter Senators, Tribunes, and Officers of Justice, with
Martius *and* Quintus, *bound, passing on to the place of*
execution; Titus *going before, pleading*

   Tit. Hear me, grave fathers! noble tribunes, stay!
For pity of mine age, whose youth was spent
In dangerous wars, whilst you securely slept;
For all my blood in Rome's great quarrel shed;
For all the frosty nights that I have watched;
And for these bitter tears, which now you see
Filling the aged wrinkles in my cheeks;
Be pitiful to my condemnéd sons,
Whose souls are not corrupted as 't is thought.
For two-and-twenty sons I never wept,
Because they died in honour's lofty bed:
For these, these, tribunes, in the dust I write
               [*Throwing himself on the ground*
My heart's deep languor, and my soul's sad tears.
Let my tears stanch the earth's dry appetite;
My son's sweet blood will make it shame and blush
     [*Exeunt Senators, Tribunes, &c., with the Prisoners*
O earth, I will befriend thee more with rain
That shall distil from these two ancient urns
Than youthful April shall with all his showers:
In summer's drought, I'll drop upon thee still;

In winter, with warm tears I'll melt the snow,
And keep eternal spring-time on thy face,
So thou refuse to drink my dear son's blood.

Enter LUCIUS, *with his sword drawn*

O reverend tribunes! gentle, aged men!
Unbind my sons, reverse the doom of death;
And let me say, that never wept before,
My tears are now prevailing orators.
   Luc. O noble father, you lament in vain:
The tribunes hear you not, no man is by,
And you recount your sorrows to a stone.
   Tit. Ah, Lucius, for thy brothers let me plead.—
Grave tribunes, once more I entreat of you.—
   Luc. My gracious lord, no tribune hears you speak.
   Tit. Why, 't is no matter, man: if they did hear,
They would not mark me, or if they did mark,
They would not pity me, yet plead I must,
And bootless unto them.
Therefore I tell my sorrows to the stones,
Who, though they cannot answer my distress,
Yet in some sort they are better than the tribunes,
For that they will not intercept my tale.
When I do weep, they, humbly at my feet,
Receive my tears, and seem to weep with me;
And were they but attiréd in grave weeds,
Rome could afford no tribune like to these.
A stone is soft as wax, tribunes more hard than stones;
A stone is silent, and offendeth not,
And tribunes with their tongues doom men to death.
                                  [Rises
But wherefore stand'st thou with thy weapon drawn?
   Luc. To rescue my two brothers from their death;
For which attempt the judges have pronounced
My everlasting doom of banishment.
   Tit. O happy man! they have befriended thee.
Why, foolish Lucius, dost thou not perceive,
That Rome is but a wilderness of tigers?
Tigers must prey; and Rome affords no prey
But me and mine: how happy art thou then,
From these devourers to be banishéd!
But who comes with our brother Marcus here?

Enter MARCUS *and* LAVINIA

   Marc. Titus, prepare thy aged eyes to weep;
Or, if not so, thy noble heart to break:
I bring consuming sorrow to thine age.
   Tit. Will it consume me? let me see it then.

Marc.   This was thy daughter.
Tit.   Why, Marcus, so she is.
Luc.   Ah me! this object kills me.
    Tit.   Faint-hearted boy, arise, and look upon her.—
Speak, my Lavinia, what accursèd hand
Hath made thee handless in thy father's sight?
What fool hath added water to the sea,
Or brought a faggot to bright-burning Troy?
My grief was at the height before thou cam'st,
And now, like Nilus, it disdaineth bounds.—
Give me a sword, I'll chop off my hands too,
For they have fought for Rome, and all in vain;
And they have nursed this woe, in feeding life;
In bootless prayer have they been held up,
And they have served me to effectless use:
Now all the service I require of them
Is that the one will help to cut the other.—
'T is well, Lavinia, that thou hast no hands,
For hands, to do Rome service, are but vain.
    Luc.   Speak, gentle sister, who hath martyred thee?
    Marc.   O, that delightful engine of her thoughts,
That blabbed them with such pleasing eloquence,
Is torn from forth that pretty hollow cage,
Where, like a sweet melodious bird, it sung
Sweet varied notes, enchanting every ear.
    Luc.   O, say thou for her, who hath done this deed?
    Marc.   O, thus I found her, straying in the park,
Seeking to hide herself, as doth the deer,
That hath received some unrecuring wound.
    Tit.   It was my deer; and he that wounded her
Hath hurt me more, than had he killed me dead:
For now I stand as one upon a rock,
Environed with a wilderness of sea,
Who marks the waxing tide grow wave by wave,
Expecting ever when some envious surge
Will in his brinish bowels swallow him.
This way to death my wretched sons are gone;
Here stands my other son, a banished man,
And here my brother, weeping at my woes;
But that which gives my soul the greatest spurn,
Is dear Lavinia, dearer than my soul.—
Had I but seen thy picture in this plight,
It would have madded me: what shall I do
Now I behold thy lively body so?
Thou hast no hands to wipe away thy tears
Nor tongue to tell me who hath martyred thee:
Thy husband he is dead, and for his death
Thy brothers are condemned and dead by this.
Look, Marcus; ah! son Lucius, look on her:

When I did name her brothers, then fresh tears
Stood on her cheeks, as doth the honey-dew
Upon a gathered lily almost withered.
  Marc. Perchance, she weeps because they killed her
    husband;
Perchance, because she knows them innocent.
  Tit. If they did kill thy husband, then be joyful,
Because the law hath ta'en revenge on them.——
No, no, they would not do so foul a deed;
Witness the sorrow that their sister makes.——
Gentle Lavinia, let me kiss thy lips,
Or make some sign how I may do thee ease.
Shall thy good uncle, and thy brother Lucius,
And thou, and I, sit round about some fountain,
Looking all downwards, to behold our cheeks
How they are stained, like meadows yet not dry,
With miry slime left on them by a flood?
And in the fountain shall we gaze so long,
Till the fresh taste be taken from that clearness,
And made a brine-pit with our bitter tears?
Or shall we cut away our hands, like thine?
Or shall we bite our tongues, and in dumb shows
Pass the remainder of our hateful days?
What shall we do? let us, that have our tongues,
Plot some device of further misery,
To make us wondered at in time to come.
  Luc. Sweet father, cease your tears; for at your grief,
See, how my wretched sister sobs and weeps.
  Marc. Patience, dear niece.——Good Titus, dry thine
    eyes.
  Tit. Ah, Marcus, Marcus! brother, well I wot,
Thy napkin cannot drink a tear of mine,
For thou, poor man, hast drowned it with thine own.
  Luc. Ah, my Lavinia! I will wipe thy cheeks.
  Tit. Mark, Marcus, mark! I understand her signs,
Had she a tongue to speak, now would she say
That to her brother which I said to thee:
His napkin, with his true tears all bewet,
Can do no service on her sorrowful cheeks.
O, what a sympathy of woe is this;
As far from help as limbo is from bliss!

     Enter AARON

  Aar. Titus Andronicus, my lord the emperor
Sends thee this word,——that, if thou love thy sons,
Let Marcus, Lucius, or thyself, old Titus,
Or any one of you, chop off your hand,
And send it to the king: he, for the same,

Will send thee hither both thy sons alive,
And that shall be the ransom for their fault.
　Tit.　O gracious emperor! O gentle Aaron!
Did ever raven sing so like a lark,
That gives sweet tidings of the sun's uprise?
With all my heart, I'll send the emperor
My hand.
Good Aaron, wilt thou help to chop it off?
　Luc.　Stay, father! for that noble hand of thine,
That hath thrown down so many enemies,
Shall not be sent: my hand will serve the turn.
My youth can better spare my blood than you,
And therefore mine shall save my brothers' lives.
　Marc.　Which of your hands hath not defended Rome,
And reared aloft the bloody battle-axe,
Writing destruction on the enemy's castle?
O, none of both but are of high desert.
My hand hath been but idle; let it serve
To ransom my two nephews from their death:
Then have I kept it to a worthy end.
　Aar.　Nay, come, agree, whose hand shall go along,
For fear they die before their pardon come.
　Marc.　My hand shall go.
　Luc.　　　　　　　　　By heaven, it shall not go!
　Tit.　Sirs, strive no more: such withered herbs as these
Are meet for plucking up, and therefore mine.
　Luc.　Sweet father, if I shall be thought thy son,
Let me redeem my brothers both from death.
　Marc.　And for our father's sake, and mother's care,
Now let me show a brother's love to thee.
　Tit.　Agree between you; I will spare my hand.
　Luc.　Then I'll go fetch an axe.
　Marc.　But I will use the axe.
　　　　　　　　　　　　[Exeunt Lucius and Marcus
　Tit.　Come hither, Aaron; I'll deceive them both:
Lend me thy hand, and I will give thee mine.
　Aar.　*[Aside]*　If that be called deceit, I will be honest,
And never, whilst I live, deceive men so:—
But I'll deceive you in another sort,
And that you 'll say, ere half an hour pass.
　　　　　　　　　　　　　　[Cuts off Titus's hand

Re-enter LUCIUS *and* MARCUS

　Tit.　Now, stay your strife; what shall be, is despatched.
Good Aaron, give his majesty my hand:
Tell him, it was a hand that warded him
From thousand dangers; bid him bury it:
More hath it merited; that let it have.

As for my sons, say, I account of them
As jewels purchased at an easy price;
And yet dear too, because I bought mine own.
   Aar.   I go, Andronicus; and, for thy hand,
Look by and by to have thy sons with thee
[*Aside*]   Their heads, I mean.—O, how this villainy
Doth fat me with the very thoughts of it!
Let fools do good, and fair men call for grace,
Aaron will have his soul black like his face.   [*Exit*
   Tit.   O, here I lift this one hand up to heaven,
And bow this feeble ruin to the earth:
If any power pities wretched tears,
To that I call.—[*To Lavinia*] What! wilt thou kneel with
      me?
Do then, dear heart; for heaven shall hear our prayers,
Or with our sighs we 'll breathe the welkin dim,
And stain the sun with fog, as sometime clouds
When they do hug him in their melting bosoms.
   Marc.   O, brother, speak with possibilities,
And do not break into these deep extremes.
   Tit.   Is not my sorrow deep, having no bottom?
Then be my passions bottomless with them.
   Marc.   But yet let reason govern thy lament.
   Tit.   If there were reason for these miseries,
Then into limits could I bind my woes.
When heaven doth weep, doth not the earth o'er-flow?
If the winds rage, doth not the sea wax mad,
Threat'ning the welkin with his big-swoln face?
And wilt thou have a reason for this coil?
I am the sea; hark, how her sighs do blow!
She is the weeping welkin, I the earth:
Then must my sea be movéd with her sighs;
Then must my earth with her continual tears
Become a deluge, overflowed and drowned:
For why, my bowels cannot hide her woes
But like a drunkard must I vomit them.
Then give me leave, for losers will have leave
To ease their stomachs with their bitter tongues.

Enter a Messenger, with two heads and a hand

   Mess.   Worthy Andronicus, ill art thou repaid
For that good hand thou sentst the emperor.
Here are the heads of thy two noble sons,
And here 's thy hand, in scorn to thee sent back:
Thy griefs their sports, thy resolution mocked;
That woe is me to think upon thy woes,
More than remembrance of my father's death.

                                  [*Exit*

Marc. Now let hot Ætna cool in Sicily,
And be my heart an ever-burning hell!
These miseries are more than may be borne.
To weep with them that weep doth ease some deal,
But sorrow flouted at is double death.
    Luc. Ah, that this sight should make so deep a wound,
And yet detested life not shrink thereat!
That ever death should let life bear his name,
Where life hath no more interest but to breathe!
                            [*Lavinia kisses Titus*
    Marc. Alas, poor heart! that kiss is comfortless,
As frozen water to a starvéd snake.
    Tit. When will this fearful slumber have an end?
    Marc. Now farewell, flattery: die, Andronicus.
Thou dost not slumber: see thy two sons' heads,
Thy warlike hand, thy mangled daughter here;
Thy other banished son with this dear sight
Struck pale and bloodless; and thy brother, I,
Even like a stony image, cold and numb.
Ah, now no more will I control thy griefs.
Rent off thy silver hair, thy other hand
Gnawing with thy teeth; and be this dismal sight
The closing up of our most wretched eyes!
Now is a time to storm; why art thou still?
    Tit. Ha, ha, ha!
    Marc. Why dost thou laugh? it fits not with this hour.
    Tit. Why, I have not another tear to shed:
Besides, this sorrow is an enemy,
And would usurp upon my watery eyes,
And make them blind with tributary tears;
Then, which way shall I find Revenge's cave?
For these two heads do seem to speak to me,
And threat me, I shall never come to bliss
Till all these mischiefs be returned again
Even in their throats that have committed them.
Come, let me see what task I have to do.—
You heavy people, circle me about,
That I may turn me to each one of you,
And swear unto my soul to right your wrongs.—
The vow is made.—Come, brother, take a head;
And in this hand the other will I bear.
Lavinia, thou shalt be employed in these things:
Bear thou my hand, sweet wench, between thy teeth.
As for thee, boy, go, get thee from my sight;
Thou art an exile, and thou must not stay:
Hie to the Goths, and raise an army there;
And if you love me, as I think you do,
Let 's kiss and part, for we have much to do.
                  [*Exeunt Titus, Marcus, and Lavinia*

Luc. Farewell, Andronicus, my noble father;
The wofull'st man that ever lived in Rome.
Farewell, proud Rome: till Lucius come again,
He leaves his pledges dearer than his life.
Farewell, Lavinia, my noble sister;
O, would thou wert as thou tofore hast been!
But now nor Lucius nor Lavinia lives
But in oblivion and hateful griefs.
If Lucius live, he will requite your wrongs,
And make proud Saturnine and his empress
Beg at the gates like Tarquin and his queen.
Now will I to the Goths, and raise a power,
To be revenged on Rome and Saturnine.   [*Exit*

SCENE II.—A Room in TITUS's House. A Banquet
set out

Enter TITUS, MARCUS, LAVINIA, *and young* LUCIUS, *a boy*

Tit. So, so; now sit; and look, you eat no more
Than will preserve just so much strength in us
As will revenge these bitter woes of ours.
Marcus, unknit that sorrow-wreathen knot:
Thy niece and I, poor creatures, want our hands,
And cannot passionate our tenfold grief
With folded arms. This poor right hand of mine
Is left to tyrannise upon my breast;
And when my heart, all mad with misery,
Beats in this hollow prison of my flesh,
Then thus I thump it down—
[*To Lavinia*] Thou map of woe, that thus dost talk in
        signs,
When thy poor heart beats with outrageous beating
Thou canst not strike it thus to make it still.
Wound it with sighing, girl, kill it with groans;
Or get some little knife between thy teeth,
And just against thy heart make thou a hole
That all the tears that thy poor eyes let fall
May run into that sink, and, soaking in,
Drown the lamenting fool in sea-salt tears.
    Marc. Fie, brother, fie! teach her not thus to lay
Such violent hands upon her tender life.
    Tit. How now! has sorrow made thee dote already?
Why, Marcus, no man should be mad but I.
What violent hands can she lay on her life?
Ah! wherefore dost thou urge the name of hands;
To bid Æneas tell the tale twice o'er
How Troy was burnt, and he made miserable?

O, handle not the theme, to talk of hands,
Lest we remember still that we have none,
Fie, fie! how franticly I square my talk,
As if we should forget we had no hands,
If Marcus did not name the word of hands!—
Come, let 's fall too; and, gentle girl, eat this.—
Here is no drink.   Hark, Marcus, what she says;
I can interpret all her martyred signs.
She says she drinks no other drink but tears,
Brewed with her sorrow, mashed upon her cheeks.
Speechless complainer, I will learn thy thought;
In thy dumb action will I be as perfect
As begging hermits in their holy prayers:
Thou shalt not sigh, nor hold thy stumps to heaven,
Nor wink, nor nod, nor kneel, nor make a sign,
But I, of these, will wrest an alphabet,
And, by still practice, learn to know thy meaning.
    Boy.   Good grandsire, leave these bitter deep laments:
Make my aunt merry with some pleasing tale.
    Marc.   Alas, the tender boy, in passion moved,
Doth weep to see his grandsire's heaviness.
    Tit.   Peace, tender sapling; thou art made of tears,
And tears will quickly melt thy life away.—
                 [*Marcus strikes the dish with a knife*
What dost thou strike at, Marcus, with thy knife?
    Marc.   At that that I have killed, my lord,—a fly.
    Tit.   Out on thee, murderer! thou kill'st my heart;
Mine eyes are cloyed with view of tyranny:
A deed of death, done on the innocent,
Becomes not Titus' brother.   Get thee gone;
I see, thou art not for my company.
    Marc.   Alas! my lord, I have but killed a fly.
    Tit.   But how, if that fly had a father and mother,
How would he hang his slender gilded wings
And buzz lamenting doings in the air?
Poor harmless fly,
That, with his pretty buzzing melody,
Came here to make us merry! and thou hast killed him.
    Marc.   Pardon me, sir: it was a black ill-favoured fly,
Like to the empress' Moor; therefore I killed him.
    Tit.   O, O, O!
Then pardon me for reprehending thee,
For thou hast done a charitable deed.
Give me thy knife, I will insult on him;
Flattering myself, as if it were the Moor,
Come hither purposely to poison me.—
There 's for thyself, and that 's for Tamora.
Ah, sirrah!—
Yet I think we are not brought so low

But that between us we can kill a fly
That comes in likeness of a coal-black Moor.
    Marc. Alas, poor man! grief has so wrought on him,
He takes false shadows for true substances.
    Tit. Come, take away.—Lavinia, go with me:
I 'll to thy closet; and go read with thee
Sad stories chancéd in the times of old.—
Come, boy, and go with me: thy sight is young,
And thou shalt read when mine begins to dazzle.

                                                [*Exeunt*

ACT FOUR

Scene I.—Rome. Before Titus's House

Enter Titus *and* Marcus. *Then enter young* Lucius,
Lavinia *running after him*

    Boy. Help, grandsire, help! my aunt Lavinia
Follows me everywhere, I know not why.—
Good uncle Marcus, see, how swift she comes!
Alas! sweet aunt, I know not what you mean.
    Marc. Stand by me, Lucius; do not fear thine aunt.
    Tit. She loves thee, boy, too well to do thee harm.
    Boy. Ay, when my father was in Rome, she did.
    Marc. What means my niece Lavinia by these signs?
    Tit. Fear her not, Lucius:—somewhat doth she
        mean.
See, Lucius, see, how much she makes of thee:
Somewhither would she have thee go with her.
Ah, boy! Cornelia never with more care
Read to her sons that she hath read to thee
Sweet poetry and Tully's Orator.
    Marc. Canst thou not guess wherefore she plies thee
        thus?
    Boy. My lord, I know not, I, nor can I guess,
Unless some fit or frenzy do possess her;
For I have heard my grandsire say full oft,
Extremity of griefs would make men mad;
And I have read that Hecuba of Troy
Ran mad through sorrow: that made me to fear;
Although, my lord, I know, my noble aunt
Loves me as dear as e'er my mother did,
And would not, but in fury, fright my youth;
Which made me down to throw my books, and fly,
Causeless, perhaps. But pardon me, sweet aunt;
And, madam, if my uncle Marcus go,

I will most willingly attend your ladyship.
    Marc. Lucius, I will.
              [*Lavinia turns over with her stumps the books*
                                which Lucius had let fall
    Tit. How now, Lavinia?—Marcus, what means this?
Some book there is that she desires to see.—
Which is it, girl, of these?—Open them, boy.
But thou art deeper read, and better skilled;
Come, and take choice of all my library,
And so beguile thy sorrow, till the heavens
Reveal the damned contriver of this deed.—
What book?
Why lifts she up her arms in sequence thus?
    Marc. I think, she means that there was more than one
Confederate in the fact:—ay, more there was;
Or else to heaven she heaves them for revenge.
    Tit. Lucius, what book is that she tosseth so?
    Boy. Grandsire, 't is Ovid's Metamorphoses:
My mother gave it me.
    Marc.   For love of her that 's gone,
Perhaps, she culled it from among the rest.
    Tit. Soft! so busily she turns the leaves!
Help her:
What would she find?—Lavinia, shall I read?
This is the tragic tale of Philomel,
And treats of Tereus' treason and his rape;
And rape, I fear, was root of thine annoy.
    Marc. See, brother, see! note, how she quotes the
          leaves.
    Tit. Lavinia, wert thou thus surprised, sweet girl,
Ravished and wronged, as Pilomela was,
Forced in the ruthless, vast, and gloomy woods?—
See, see!—
Ay, such a place there is, where we did hunt,—
O, had we never, never hunted there!
Patterned by that the poet here described,
By nature made for murders, and for rapes.
    Marc. O, why should nature build so foul a den,
Unless the gods delight in tragedies?
    Tit. Give signs, sweet girl, for here are none but friends,
What Roman lord it was durst do the deed:
Or slunk not Saturnine, as Tarquin erst,
That left the camp to sin in Lucrece's bed?
    Marc. Sit down, sweet niece:—brother, sit down by
          me.
Apollo, Pallas, Jove, or Mercury,
Inspire me, that I may this treason find!—
My lord, look here;—look here, Lavinia:
This sandy plot is plain; guide, if thou canst,

This after me.
    [*He writes his name with his staff, and guides it with
                               feet and mouth*
                  I have writ my name
Without the help of any hand at all.
Cursed be that heart that forced us to this shift!—
Write thou, good niece, and here display at last
What God will have discovered for revenge.
Heaven guide thy pen to print thy sorrows plain,
That we may know the traitors and the truth!
    [*She takes the staff in her mouth, and guides it with
                       her stumps, and writes*
  Tit. O, do you read, my lord, what she hath writ?
Stuprum—Chiron—Demetrius
  Marc. What, what!—the lustful sons of Tamora
Performers of this heinous, bloody deed?
  Tit. *Magni Dominator poli,*
Tam lentus audis selera? tam lentus vides?
  Marc. O, calm thee, gentle lord; although I know
There is enough written upon this earth
To stir a mutiny in the mildest thoughts,
And arm the minds of infants to exclaims.
My lord, kneel down with me; Lavinia, kneel;
And kneel, sweet boy, the Roman Hector's hope;
And swear with me,—as with the woful fere
And father of that chaste dishonoured dame,
Lord Junius Brutus sware for Lucrece' rape,—
That we will prosecute by good advice,
Mortal revenge upon these traitorous Goths,
And see their blood, or die with this reproach.
  Tit. 'T is sure enough, an you knew how;
But if you hunt these bear-whelps, then beware:
The dam will wake, an if she wind you once:
She 's with the lion deeply still in league,
And lulls him whilst she playeth on her back;
And when he sleeps will she do what she list.
You 're a young huntsman: Marcus, let alone;
And, come, I will go get a leaf of brass,
And with a gad of steel will write these words,
And lay it by. The angry northern wind
Will blow these sands like Sibyl's leaves abroad,
And where 's your lesson then?—Boy, what say you?
  Boy. I say, my lord, that if I were a man,
Their mother's bedchamber should not be safe
For these bad bondmen to the yoke of Rome.
  Marc. Ay, that 's my boy! thy father hath full oft
For his ungrateful country, done the like.
  Boy. And, uncle, so will I, an if I live.
  Tit. Come, go with me into mine armoury:

Lucius, I 'll fit thee; and withal my boy
Shall carry from me to the empress' sons
Presents, that I intend to send them both.
Come, come; thou 'lt do thy message, wilt thou not?
   Boy. Ay, with my dagger in their bosoms, grandsire.
   Tit. No, boy, not so; I'll teach thee another course.
Lavinia, come.—Marcus, look to my house:
Lucius and I 'll go brave it at the court;
Ay, marry, will we, sir; and we 'll be waited on.
                [*Exeunt Titus, Lavinia, and Boy*
   Marc. O heavens, can you hear a good man groan,
And not relent, or not compassion him?
Marcus, attend him in his ecstasy,
That hath more scars of sorrow in his heart
Than foemen's marks upon his battered shield;
But yet so just, that he will not revenge.—
Revenge the heavens for old Andronicus!   [*Exit*

SCENE II.—The Same.   A Room in the Palace

Enter AARON, DEMETRIUS, *and* CHIRON, *at one door;
at another door, young* LUCIUS, *and an Attendant, with
a bundle of weapons, and verses writ upon them*

   Chi. Demetrius, here 's the son of Lucius;
He hath some message to deliver us.
   Aar. Ay, some mad message from his mad grandfather.
   Boy. My lords, with all the humbleness I may,
I greet your honours from Andronicus;—
[*Aside*] And pray the Roman gods confound you both.
   Dem. Gramercy, lovely Lucius. What 's the news?
   Boy. [*Aside*] That you are both deciphered, that 's the news,
For villains marked with rape. [*To them*] May it please you,
My grandsire, well advised, hath sent by me
The goodliest weapons of his armoury,
To gratify your honourable youth,
The hope of Rome; for so he bade me say,
And so I do, and with his gifts present
Your lordships, that, whenever you have need,
You may be arméd and appointed well.
And so I leave you both [*aside*] like bloody villains.
                [*Exeunt Boy and Attendant*
   Dem. What 's here? A scroll; and written round about?

Let 's see:

> *Integer vitæ, scelerisque purus,*
> *Non eget Mauri jaculis nec arcu.*

   Chi. O, 't is a verse in Horace; I know it well:
I read it in the grammar long ago.
   Aar. Ay, just!—a verse in Horace;—right, you have
    it.
[*Aside*] Now, what a thing it is to be an ass!
Here 's no sound jest! the old man hath found their guilt,
And sends them weapons wrapped about with lines
That wound, beyond their feeling, to the quick;
But were our witty empress well afoot
She would applaud Andronicus' conceit:
But let her rest in her unrest awhile.—
[*To them*] And now, young lords, was 't not a happy star
Led us to Rome, strangers, and more than so,
Captives, to be advancéd to this height?
It did me good, before the palace gate
To brave the tribune in his brother's hearing.
   Dem. But me more good, to see so great a lord
Basely insinuate and send us gifts.
   Aar. Had he not reason, Lord Demetrius?
Did you not use his daughter very friendly?
   Dem. I would we had a thousand Roman dames
At such a bay, by turn to serve our lust.
   Chi. A charitable wish, and full of love.
   Aar. Here lacks but your mother for to say amen.
   Chi. And that would she for twenty thousand more.
   Dem. Come, let us go, and pray to all the gods
For our belovéd mother in her pains.
   Aar. [*Aside*] Pray to the devils; the gods have given us
    over.   [*Trumpets sound*
   Dem. Why do the emperor's trumpets flourish thus?
   Chi. Belike, for joy the emperor hath a son.
   Dem. Soft, who comes here?

Enter a Nurse, with a blackamoor Child

   Nur. Good morrow, lords. O, tell me, did you see
Aaron the Moor?
   Aar. Well, more or less, or ne'er a whit at all,
Here Aaron is; and what with Aaron now?
   Nur. O gentle Aaron, we are all undone.
Now help, or woe betide thee evermore!
   Aar. Why, what a caterwauling dost thou keep!
What dost thou wrap and fumble in thine arms?
   Nur. O, that which I would hide from heaven's eye,
Our empress' shame, and stately Rome's disgrace.—
She is delivered, lords, she is delivered.

Aar.   To whom?
Nur.   I mean she 's brought a-bed.
Aar.   Well, God give her good rest! What hath he
sent her?
Nur.   A devil.
Aar.   Why, then she is the devil's dam:
A joyful issue.
Nur.   A joyless, dismal, black, and sorrowful issue.
Here is the babe, as loathsome as a toad
Amongst the fairest breeders of our clime.
The empress sends it thee, thy stamp, thy seal,
And bids thee christen it with thy dagger's point.
Aar.   Out, you whore! Is black so base a hue?—
Sweet blowse, you are a beauteous blossom, sure.
Dem.   Villain, what hast thou done?
Aar.   That which thou canst not undo.
Chi.   Thou hast undone our mother.
Aar.   Villain, I have done thy mother.
Dem.   And therein, hellish dog, thou hast undone her
Woe to her chance, and damned her loathéd choice!
Accursed the offspring of so foul a fiend!
Chi.   It shall not live.
Aar.   It shall not die.
Nur.   Aaron, it must: the mother wills it so.
Aar.   What, must it, nurse? then let no man but I
Do execution on my flesh and blood.
Dem.   I 'll broach the tadpole on my rapier's point:
Nurse, give it me; my sword shall soon despatch it.
Aar.   Sooner this sword shall plough thy bowels up.
                    [*Takes the Child from the Nurse, and draws.*
Stay, murderous villains! will you kill your brother?
Now, by the burning tapers of the sky,
That shone so brightly when this boy was got,
He dies upon my scimitar's sharp point
That touches this my first-born son and heir.
I tell you, younglings, not Enceladus,
With all his threatening band of Typhon's brood,
Nor great Alcides, nor the god of war,
Shall seize this prey out of his father's hands.
What, what, ye sanguine, shallow-hearted boys!
Ye white limed walls? ye ale-house painted signs!·
Coal-black is better than another hue,
In that it scorns to bear another hue;
For all the water in the ocean
Can never turn the swan's black legs to white,
Although she lave them hourly in the flood.
Tell the empress from me, I am of age
To keep mine own; excuse it how she can.
Dem.   Wilt thou betray thy noble mistress thus?

Aar. My mistress is my mistress; this, myself;
The vigour, and the picture of my youth:
This before all the world do I prefer;
This, maugre all the world, will I keep safe,
Or some of you shall smoke for it in Rome.
    Dem. By this our mother is for ever shamed.
    Chi. Rome will despise her for this foul escape.
    Nur. The emperor in his rage will doom her death.
    Chi. I blush to think upon this ignomy.
    Aar. Why, there 's the privilege your beauty bears.
Fie, treacherous hue! that will betray with blushing
The close enacts and counsels of the heart:
Here 's a young lad framed of another leer.
Look, how the black slave smiles upon the father,
As who should say, 'Old lad, I am thine own.'
He is your brother, lords, sensibly fed
Of that self blood that first gave life to you;
And from that womb where you imprisoned were
He is enfranchiséd and come to light:
Nay, he is your brother by the surer side,
Although my seal be stampéd in his face.
    Nur. Aaron, what shall I say unto the empress?
    Dem. Advise thee, Aaron, what is to be done,
And we will all subscribe to thy advice:
Save thou the child, so we may all be safe.
    Aar. Then sit we down, and let us all consult.
My son and I will have the wind of you;
Keep there: now talk at pleasure of your safety.
                               [They sit
    Dem. How many women saw this child of his?
    Aar. Why, so brave lords: when we all join in league,
I am a lamb; but if you brave the Moor,
The chaféd boar, the mountain lioness,
The ocean swells not so as Aaron storms.—
But say again, how many saw the child?
    Nur. Cornelia the midwife, and myself,
And no one else but the delivered empress.
    Aar. The empress, the midwife, and yourself:
Two may keep counsel, when the third 's away.
Go to the empress; tell her this I said:
                               [Stabbing her
Weke, weke!—so cries a pig prepared to the spit.
    Dem. What mean'st thou, Aaron? wherefore didst
        thou this?
    Aar. O Lord, sir, 't is a deed of policy.
Shall she live to betray this guilt of ours,
A long-tongued babbling gossip? no, lords, no.
And now be it known to you my full intent.
Not far, one Muliteus, my countryman;

His wife but yesternight was brought to bed.
His child is like to her, fair as you are:
Go pack with him, and give the mother gold,
And tell them both the circumstance of all,
And how by this their child shall be advanced,
And be receivéd for the emperor's heir,
And substituted in the place of mine,
To calm this tempest whirling in the court;
And let the emperor dandle him for his own.
Hark ye, lords; you see, I have given her physic.
                                    [*Pointing to the Nurse*
And you must needs bestow her funeral;
The fields are near, and you are gallant grooms.
This done, see that you take no longer days,
But send the midwife presently to me.
The midwife and the nurse well made away,
Then let the ladies tattle what they please.
   Chi.   Aaron, I see thou wilt not trust the air
With secrets.
   Dem.   For this care of Tamora,
Herself and hers are highly bound to thee.
                        [*Exeunt Demetrius and Chiron, bearing off
                                    the dead Nurse*
   Aar.   Now to the Goths, as swift as swallows flies;
There to dispose this treasure in mine arms,
And secretly to greet the empress' friends.—
Come on, you thick-lipped slave, I'll bear you hence;
For it is you that puts us to our shifts:
I'll make you feed on berries and on roots,
And feed on curds and whey, and suck the goat,
And cabin in a cave; and bring you up
To be a warrior, and command a camp.
                                    [*Exit with the Child*

SCENE III.—Rome.   A Public Place

Enter TITUS, *bearing arrows, with letters on the end of them ;
with him* MARCUS, *young* LUCIUS, *and other Gentlemen,
with bows*

   Tit.   Come, Marcus, come;—kinsmen, this is the way.—
Sir boy, now let me see your archery;
Look ye draw home enough, and 't is there straight.
Terras Astræa reliquit :
Be you remembered, Marcus, she 's gone, she 's fled.
Sirs, take you to your tools.   You, cousins, shall
Go sound the ocean, and cast your nets,

Happily you may find her in the sea;
Yet there 's as little justice as at land.—
No; Publius and Sempronius, you must do it;
'T is you must dig with mattock, and with spade,
And pierce the inmost centre of the earth:
Then, when you come to Pluto's region,
I pray you, deliver him this petition;
Tell him, it is for justice and for aid,
And that it comes from old Andronicus,
Shaken with sorrows in ungrateful Rome.—
Ah, Rome!—Well, well; I made thee miserable.
That time I threw the people's suffrages
On him that thus doth tyrannise o'er me.—
Go, get you gone; and pray be careful all,
And leave you not a man-of-war unsearched:
This wicked emperor may have shipped her hence;
And, kinsmen, then we may go pipe for justice.
    Marc. O Publius! is not this a heavy case,
To see thy noble uncle thus distract?
    Pub. Therefore, my lord, it highly us concerns,
By day and night to attend him carefully;
And feed his humour kindly as we may,
Till time beget some careful remedy.
    Marc. Kinsmen, his sorrows are past remedy.
Join with the Goths, and with revengeful war
Take wreak on Rome for this ingratitude,
And vengeance on the traitor Saturnine.
    Tit. Publius, how now? how now, my masters?
What, have you met with her?
    Pub. No, my good lord; but Pluto sends you word,
If you will have revenge from hell, you shall:
Marry, for Justice, she is so employed,
He thinks, with Jove in heaven, or somewhere else,
So that perforce you must needs stay a time.
    Tit. He doth me wrong to feed me with delays.
I 'll dive into the burning lake below
And pull her out of Acheron by the heels.—
Marcus, we are but shrubs, no cedars we;
No big-boned men, framed of the Cyclops' size,
But metal, Marcus, steel to the very back;
Yet wrung with wrongs, more than our backs can bear:
And sith there is no justice in earth nor hell,
We will solicit heaven, and move the gods
To send down Justice for to wreak our wrongs.
Come, to this gear. You are a good archer, Marcus.
                                [*He gives them the arrow*
Ad Jovem, that 's for you:—here, *ad Apollinem :*—
Ad Martem, that 's for myself:—
Here, boy, to Pallas:—here, to Mercury:

To Saturn, Caius, not to Saturnine:
You were as good to shoot against the wind.—
To it, boy; Marcus, loose when I bid.
Of my word, I have written to effect;
There 's not a god left unsolicited.
    Marc. Kinsmen, shoot all your shafts into the court:
We will afflict the emperor in his pride.
    Tit. Now, masters, draw. [*They shoot*] O, well
    said, Lucius!
Good boy, in Virgo's lap: give it Pallas.
    Marc. My lord, I aim a mile beyond the moon:
Your letter is with Jupiter by this.
    Tit. Ha! Publius, Publius, what hast thou done?
See, see! thou hast shot off one of Taurus' horns.
    Marc. This was the sport, my lord: when Publius
    shot,
The Bull, being galled, gave Aries such a knock,
That down fell both the Ram's horns in the court;
And who should find them but the empress' villain?
She laughed, and told the Moor he should not choose
But give them to his master for a present.
    Tit. Why, there it goes: God give his lordship joy!

    Enter the Clown, with a basket and two pigeons in it

News! news from heaven! Marcus, the post is come.
Sirrah, what tidings? have you any letters?
Shall I have justice? what says Jupiter?
    Clo. Ho! the gibbet-maker? he says that he hath
taken them down again, for the man must not be hanged
till the next week.
    Tit. But what says Jupiter, I ask thee?
    Clo. Alas, sir! I know not Jupiter: I never drank
with him in all my life.
    Tit. Why, villain, art not thou the carrier?
    Clo. Ay, of my pigeons, sir; nothing else.
    Tit. Why, didst thou not come from heaven?
    Clo. From Heaven? alas, sir! I never came there.
God forbid, I should be so bold to press to heaven in my
young days. Why, I am going with my pigeons to the
tribunal plebs, to take up a matter of brawl betwixt my
uncle and one of the emperial's men.
    Marc. Why, sir, that is as fit as can be, to serve for
your oration; and let him deliver the pigeons to the emperor from you.
    Tit. Tell me, can you deliver an oration to the emperor
with a grace?
    Clo. Nay, truly, sir, I could never say grace in all my
life.

Tit. Sirrah, come hither. Make no more ado,
But give your pigeons to the emperor:
By me thou shalt have justice at his hands.
Hold, hold meanwhile, here's money for thy charges.
Give me pen and ink.—
Sirrah, can you with a grace deliver a supplication?
Clo. Ay, sir.
Tit. Then here is a supplication for you. And when
you come to him, at the first approach you must kneel;
then kiss his foot; then deliver up your pigeons; and then
look for your reward. I'll be at hand, sir; see you do it
bravely.
Clo. I warrant you, sir; let me alone.
Tit. Sirrah, hast thou a knife? Come, let me see it.—
Here, Marcus, fold it in the oration;
For thou hast made it like an humble suppliant:—
And when thou hast given it to the emperor,
Knock at my door, and tell me what he says.
Clo. God be with you, sir; I will.
Tit. Come, Marcus, let us go.—Publius, follow me.
[Exeunt

SCENE IV.—The Same. Before the Palace

Enter SATURNINUS, TAMORA, DEMETRIUS, CHIRON, *Lords,
and others:* SATURNINUS *with the arrows in his hand
that* TITUS *shot*

Sat. Why, lords, what wrongs are these? Was ever seen
An emperor in Rome thus overborne,
Troubled, confronted thus; and, for the extent
Of egal justice, used in such contempt?
My lords, you know, as do the mightful gods—
However these disturbers of our peace
Buz in the people's ears—there nought hath passed
But even with law against the wilful sons
Of old Andronicus. And what an if
His sorrows have so overwhelmed his wits,
Shall we be thus afflicted in his wreaks,
His fits, his frenzy, and his bitterness?
And now he writes to heaven for his redress:
See, here 's to Jove, and this to Mercury;
This to Apollo; this to the god of war;
Sweet scrolls to fly about the streets of Rome!
What 's this but libelling against the senate,
And blazoning our injustice every where?
A goodly humour, is it not, my lords?
As who would say, in Rome no justice were.

But if I live, his feigned ecstasies
Shall be no shelter to these outrages;
But he and his shall know, that justice lives
In Saturninus' health; whom, if he sleep,
He 'll so awake as he in fury shall
Cut off the proud'st conspirator that lives.
    Tam. My gracious lord, my lovely Saturnine,
Lord of my life, commander of my thoughts,
Calm thee, and bear the faults of Titus' age,
The effects of sorrow for his valiant sons,
Whose loss hath pierced him deep, and scarred his heart;
And rather comfort his distressed plight
Than prosecute the meanest, or the best,
For these contempts. [*Aside*] Why, thus it shall become
High-witted Tamora to gloze with all:
But, Titus, I have touched thee to the quick,
Thy life-blood out. If Aaron now be wise,
Then is all safe, the anchor 's in the port.—

Enter Clown

How now, good fellow! wouldst thou speak with us?
    Clo. Yes, forsooth, an your mistership be imperial.
    Tam. Empress I am, but yonder sits the emperor.
    Clo. 'T is he.—God and Saint Stephen give you good den. I have brought you a letter, and a couple of pigeons here.
                             [*Saturninus reads the letter*
    Sat. Go, take him away, and hang him presently.
    Clo. How much money must I have?
    Tam. Come, sirrah; you must be hanged.
    Clo. Hanged! By 'r lady, then I have brought up a neck to a fair end.   [*Exit, guarded*
    Sat. Despiteful and intolerable wrongs!
Shall I endure this monstrous villainy?
I know from whence this same device proceeds.
May this be borne?—As if his traitorous sons,
That died by law for murder of our brother,
Have by my means been butchered wrongfully!—
Go, drag the villain hither by the hair:
Nor age nor honour, shall shape privilege.—
For this proud mock I 'll be thy slaughterman;
Sly frantic wretch, that holpst to make me great,
In hope thyself should govern Rome and me.

Enter ÆMILIUS

What news with thee, Æmilius?
    Æmil. Arm, my lords! Rome never had more cause.
The Goths have gathered head, and with a power
Of high-resolvéd men, bent to the spoil,

They hither march amain, under conduct
Of Lucius, son to old Andronicus:
Who threats, in course of this revenge to do
As much as ever Coriolanus did.
   Sat. Is warlike Lucius general of the Goths?
These tidings nip me; and I hang the head
As flowers with frost, or grass beat down with storms.
Ay, now begin our sorrows to approach.
'T is he the common people love so much:
Myself hath often overheard them say,
When I have walkéd like a private man,
That Lucius' banishment was wrongfully,
And they have wished that Lucius were their emperor.
   Tam. Why should you fear? is not your city strong?
   Sat. Ay, but the citizens favour Lucius,
And will revolt from me to succour him.
   Tam. King, be thy thoughts imperious, like thy name.
Is the sun dimmed, that gnats do fly in it?
The eagle suffers little birds to sing,
And is not careful what they mean thereby,
Knowing that with the shadow of his wings
He can at pleasure stint their melody;
Even so may'st thou the giddy men of Rome.
Then cheer thy spirit, for know, thou emperor,
I will enchant the old Andronicus
With words more sweet and yet more dangerous
Than baits to fish or honey-stalks to sheep,
Whenas the one is wounded with the bait
The other rotted with delicious feed.
   Sat. But he will not entreat his son for us.
   Tam. If Tamora entreat him, then he will;
For I can smooth and fill his agéd ear
With golden promises, that, were his heart
Almost impregnable, his old ears deaf,
Yet should both ear and heart obey my tongue.—
[*To Æmilius*] Go thou before, be our ambassador:
Say that the emperor requests a parley
Of warlike Lucius, and appoint the meeting,
Even at his father's house, the old Andronicus.
   Sat. Æmilius, do this message honourably:
And if he stand on hostage for his safety,
Bid him demand what pledge will please him best.
   Æmil. Your bidding shall I do effectually.   [*Exit*
   Tam. Now will I to that old Andronicus,
And temper him with all the art I have
To pluck proud Lucius from the warlike Goths.
And now, sweet emperor, be blithe again,
And bury all thy fear in my devices.
   Sat. Then go successantly, and plead to him. [*Exeunt*

ACT FIVE

Scene I.—Plains near Rome

Enter Lucius, *and an army of Goths, with drum and colours*

    Luc. Approved warriors, and my faithful friends,
I have receivéd letters from great Rome,
Which signify what hate they bear their emperor,
And how desirous of our sight they are.
Therefore, great lords, be, as your titles witness,
Imperious, and impatient of your wrongs;
And wherein Rome hath done you any scath,
Let them make treble satisfaction.
    First Goth. Brave slip, sprung from the great Androni-
        cus,
Whose name was once our terror, now our comfort;
Whose high exploits and honourable deeds
Ingrateful Rome requites with foul contempt,
Be bold in us: we 'll follow where thou lead'st,
Like stinging bees in hottest summer's day,
Led by their master to the flowered fields,
And be avenged on curséd Tamora.
    Goths. And, as he saith, so say we all with him.
    Luc. I humbly thank him, and I thank you all.
But who comes here, led by a lusty Goth?

Enter a Goth, leading Aaron, *with his Child in his arms*

    Second Goth. Renownéd Lucius, from our troops I
        strayed,
To gaze upon a ruinous monastery;
And as I earnestly did fix mine eye
Upon the wasted building, suddenly
I heard a child cry underneath a wall.
I made unto the noise; when soon I heard
The crying babe controlled with this discourse:—
'Peace, tawny slave, half me, and half thy dam!
Did not thy hue bewray whose brat thou art,
Had nature lent thee but thy mother's look,
Villain, thou mightst have been an emperor:
But where the bull and cow are both milk-white,
They never do beget a coal-black calf.
Peace, villain, peace,'—even thus he rates the babe—
'For I must bear thee to a trusty Goth,
Who, when he knows thou art the empress' babe,
Will hold thee dearly for thy mother's sake.'

With this, my weapon drawn, I rushed upon him,
Surprised him suddenly, and brought him hither,
To use as you think needful of the man.
    Luc. O worthy Goth, this is the incarnate devil,
That robbed Andronicus of his good hand:
This is the pearl that pleased your empress' eye,
And here 's the base fruit of his burning lust.—
Say, wall-eyed slave, whither wouldst thou convey
This growing image of thy fiend-like face?
Why dost not speak? What! deaf? not a word?
A halter, soldiers! hang him on this tree,
And by his side his fruit of bastardy.
    Aar. Touch not the boy; he is of royal blood.
    Luc. Too like the sire for ever being good.—
First hang the child, that he may see it sprawl;
A sight to vex the father's soul withal.
Get me a ladder! [*A ladder brought, which Aaron is made*
                                        to ascend
    Aar.   Lucius, save the child;
And bear it from me to the empress.
If thou do this, I 'll show thee wondrous things
That highly may advantage thee to hear:
If thou wilt not, befall what may befall,
I 'll speak no more; but 'Vengeance rot you all!'
    Luc. Say on; an if it please me which thou speak'st,
Thy child shall live, and I will see it nourished.
    Aar. An if it please thee? why, assure thee Lucius,
'T will vex thy soul to hear what I shall speak;
For I must talk of murders, rapes, and massacres,
Acts of black night, abominable deeds,
Complots of mischief, treason, villainies
Ruthful to hear, yet piteously performed:
And this shall all be buried in my death,
Unless thou swear to me, my child shall live.
    Luc. Tell on thy mind: I say, thy child shall live.
    Aar. Swear that he shall, and then I will begin.
    Luc. Who should I swear by? thou believ'st no god:
That granted, how canst thou believe an oath?
    Aar. What if I do not? as, indeed, I do not;
Yet, for I know thou art religious,
And hast a thing within thee, calléd conscience,
With twenty popish tricks and ceremonies
Which I have seen thee careful to observe,
Therefore I urge thy oath:—for that I know
An idiot holds his bauble for a god,
And keeps the oath which by that god he swears,
To that I 'll urge him:—therefore, thou shalt vow
By that same god, what god soe'er it be,
That thou ador'st and hast in reverence,

To save my boy, to nourish, and bring him up;
Or else I will discover nought to thee.
    Luc. Even by my god I swear to thee I will.
    Aar. First know thou, I begot him on the empress.
    Luc. O most insatiate and luxurious woman!
    Aar. Tut! Lucius, this was but a deed of charity,
To that which thou shalt hear of me anon.
'T was her two sons that murdered Bassianus:
They cut thy sister's tongue, and ravished her,
And cut her hands, and trimmed her as thou saw'st.
    Luc. O détestable villain! call'st thou that trimming?
    Aar. Why, she was washed, and cut, and trimmed, and 't was
Trim sport for them that had the doing of it.
    Luc. O barbarous, beastly villains, like thyself!
    Aar. Indeed, I was their tutor to instruct them.
That codding spirit had they from their mother,
As sure a card as ever won the set;
Well, let my deeds be witness of my worth.
That bloody mind, I think, they learned of me,
As true a dog as ever fought at head.
I trained thy brethren to that guileful hole
Where the dead corse of Bassianus lay;
I wrote the letter that thy father found,
And hid the gold within the letter mentioned,
Confederate with the queen and her two sons;
And what not done, that thou hast cause to rue,
Wherein I had no stroke of mischief in it?
I played the cheater for thy father's hand,
And, when I had it, drew myself apart,
And almost broke my heart with extreme laughter.
I pryed me through the crevice of a wall,
When, for his hand, he had his two sons' heads;
Beheld his tears, and laughed so heartily,
That both mine eyes were rainy like to his:
And when I told the empress of this sport,
She swounded almost at my pleasing tale,
And for my tidings gave me twenty kisses.
    Goth. What, canst thou say all this, and never blush?
    Aar. Ay, like a black dog, as the saying is.
    Luc. Art thou not sorry for these heinous deeds?
    Aar. Ay, that I had not done a thousand more.
Even now I curse the day—and yet, I think
Few come within the compass of my curse—
Wherein I did not some notorious ill:
As kill a man, or else devise his death;
Ravish a maid, or plot the way to do it;
Accuse some innocent, and forswear myself;
Set deadly enmity between two friends;

Make poor men's cattle stray and break their necks;
Set fire on barns and hay-stacks in the night,
And bid the owners quench them with their tears.
Oft have I digged up dead men from their graves,
And set them upright at their dear friends' doors
Even when their sorrows almost were forgot;
And on their skins, as on the bark of trees,
Have with my knife carved in Roman letters,
'Let not your sorrow die, though I am dead.'
Tut! I have done a thousand dreadful things
As willingly as one would kill a fly;
And nothing grieves me heartily, indeed,
But that I cannot do ten thousand more.
    Luc. Bring down the devil, for he must not die
So sweet a death as hanging presently.
    Aar. If there be devils, 'would I were a devil,
To live and burn in everlasting fire:
So I might have your company in hell,
But to torment you with my bitter tongue!
    Luc. Sirs, stop his mouth, and let him speak no more.

Enter a Goth

    Goth. My lord, there is a messenger from Rome
Desires to be admitted to your presence.
    Luc. Let him come near.

Enter ÆMILIUS

Welcome, Æmilius! what 's the news from Rome?
    Æmil. Lord Lucius, and you princes of the Goths,
The Roman emperor greets you all by me:
And, for he understands you are in arms,
He craves a parley at your father's house,
Willing you to demand your hostages,
And they shall be immediately delivered.
    First Goth. What says our general?
    Luc. Æmilius, let the emperor give his pledges
Unto my father and my uncle Marcus,
And we will come.—March away.   *[Exeunt*

    SCENE II.—Rome. Before TITUS'S House

Enter TAMORA, DEMETRIUS, *and* CHIRON, disguised

    Tam. Thus in this strange and sad habiliment
I will encounter with Andronicus,
And say I am Revenge, sent from below,
To join with him and right his heinous wrongs.—

314

Knock at his study where they say he keeps
To ruminate strange plots of dire revenge:
Tell him, Revenge is come to join with him,
And work confusion on his enemies.   [*They knock*

           TITUS *opens his study door*
   Tit. Who doth molest my contemplation?
Is it your trick, to make me ope the door,
That so my sad decrees may fly away,
And all my study be to no effect?
You are deceived: for what I mean to do,
See here, in bloody lines I have set down;
And what is written shall be executed.
   Tam. Titus, I am come to talk with thee.
   Tit. No, not a word: how can I grace my talk,
Wanting a hand to give it action?
Thou hast the odds of me, therefore no more.
   Tam. If thou didst know me, thou wouldst talk with
     me.
   Tit. I am not mad; I know thee well enough:
Witness this wretched stump, witness these crimson
     lines;
Witness these trenches made by grief and care;
Witness the tiring day and heavy night;
Witness all sorrow, that I know thee well
For our proud empress, mighty Tamora.
Is not thy coming for my other hand?
   Tam. Know, thou sad man, I am not Tamora:
She is thy enemy, and I thy friend.
I am Revenge, sent from the infernal kingdom.
To ease the gnawing vulture of thy mind
By working wreakful vengeance on thy foes.
Come down, and welcome me to this world's light;
Confer with me of murder and of death.
There 's not a hollow cave or lurking-place,
No vast obscurity or misty vale,
Where bloody murder or detested rape
Can couch for fear, but I will find them out,
And in their ears tell them my dreadful name,
Revenge, which makes the foul offender quake.
   Tit. Art thou Revenge? and art thou sent to me,
To be a torment to mine enemies?
   Tam. I am; therefore come down, and welcome
     me.
   Tit. Do me some service, ere I come to thee.
Lo, by thy side where Rape and Murder stands;
Now give some 'surance that thou art Revenge:
Stab them, or tear them on thy chariot-wheels,
And then I'll come and be thy waggoner,
And whirl along with thee about the globe.

Provide two proper palfreys, black as jet,
To hale thy vengeful waggon swift away,
And find out murderers in their guilty caves:
And when thy car is loaden with their heads,
I will dismount, and by the waggon-wheel
Trot like a servile footman all day long,
Even from Hyperion's rising in the east
Until his very downfall in the sea:
And day by day I 'll do this heavy task,
So thou destroy Rapine and Murder there.

   Tam.   These are my ministers, and come with me.
   Tit.   Are these thy ministers? what are they called?
   Tam.   Rapine and Murder; therefore calléd so,
'Cause they take vengeance of such kind of men.
   Tit.   Good Lord, how like the empress' sons they are,
And you the empress! but we worldly men
Have miserable, mad-mistaking eyes.
O sweet Revenge! now do I come to thee;
And, if one arm's embracement will content thee,
I will embrace thee in it by and by.   [*Exit*
   Tam.   This closing with him fits his lunacy.
Whate'er I forge to feed his brain-sick fits
Do you uphold and maintain in your speeches.
For now he firmly takes me for Revenge;
And, being credulous in this mad thought,
I 'll make him send for Lucius, his son;
And, whilst I at a banquet hold him sure,
I 'll find some cunning practice out of hand
To scatter and disperse the giddy Goths,
Or, at the least, make them his enemies.
See, here he comes, and I must ply my theme.

Enter TITUS

   Tit.   Long have I been forlorn, and all for thee.
Welcome, dread Fury, to my woful house.—
Rapine and Murder, you are welcome too.—
How like the empress, and her sons you are!
Well are you fitted, had you but a Moor:—
Could not all hell afford you such a devil?
For, well I wot, the empress never wags,
But in her company there is a Moor;
And would you represent our queen aright,
It were convenient you had such a devil.
But welcome as you are.   What shall we do?
   Tam.   What wouldst thou have us do, Andronicus?
   Dem.   Show me a murderer, I 'll deal with him.
   Chi.   Show me a villain that hath done a rape,
And I am sent to be revenged on him.

Tam. Show me a thousand that have done thee wrong,
And I will be revengèd on them all.
Tit. Look round about the wicked streets of Rome,
And when thou find'st a man that 's like thyself,
Good Murder, stab him; he's a murderer.—
Go thou with him; and when it is thy hap
To find another that is like to thee,
Good Rapine, stab him: he 's a ravisher.—
Go thou with them; and in the emperor's court
There is a queen attended by a Moor:
Well may'st thou know her by thine own proportion,
For up and down she doth resemble thee.
I pray thee, do on them some violent death;
They have been violent to me and mine.
Tam. Well hast thou lessoned us: this shall we do.
But would it please thee, good Andronicus,
To send for Lucius, thy thrice-valiant son,
Who leads towards Rome a band of warlike Goths,
And bid him come and banquet at thy house:
When he is here, even at thy solemn feast,
I will bring in the empress and her sons,
The emperor himself, and all thy foes,
And at thy mercy shall they stoop and kneel,
And on them shalt thou ease thy angry heart.
What says Andronicus to this device?
Tit. Marcus, my brother!—'t is sad Titus calls.

Enter MARCUS

Go, gentle Marcus, to thy nephew Lucius;
Thou shalt inquire him out among the Goths:
Bid him repair to me, and bring with him
Some of the chiefest princes of the Goths;
Bid him encamp his soldiers where they are.
Tell him, the emperor, and the empress too,
Feast at my house, and he shall feast with them.
This do thou for my love, and so let him,
As he regards his aged father's life.
Marc. This will I do, and soon return again.

[*Exit*

Tam. Now will I hence about thy business,
And take my ministers along with me.
Tit. Nay, nay, let Rape and Murder stay with me,
Or else I 'll call my brother back again,
And cleave to no revenge but Lucius.
Tam. [*Aside to them*] What say you, boys? will you
    abide with him
Whiles I go tell my lord the emperor,
How I have governed our determined jest?

317

Yield to his humour, smooth and speak him fair,
And tarry with him till I turn again.
   Tit.   [*Aside*]   I know them all, though they suppose me
      mad.
And will o'erreach them in their own devices,
A pair of cursèd hell-hounds, and their dam.
   Dem.   Madam, depart at pleasure; leave us here.
   Tam.   Farewell, Andronicus: Revenge now goes
To lay a complot to betray thy foes.
   Tit.   I know thou dost; and, sweet Revenge, farewell.
                            [*Exit Tamora*
   Chi.   Tell us, old man, how shall we be employed?
   Tit.   Tut! I have work enough for you to do.—
Publius, come hither, Caius, and Valentine!

Enter PUBLIUS, *and others*

   Pub.   What is your will?
   Tit.   Know you these two?
   Pub.   The empress' sons
I take them, Chiron and Demetrius.
   Tit.   Fie, Publius, fie! thou art too much deceived;
The one is Murder, Rape is the other's name;
And therefore bind them, gentle Publius;
Caius, and Valentine, lay hands on them.
Oft have you heard me wish for such an hour,
And now I find it: therefore, bind them sure,
And stop their mouths if they begin to cry.
      [*Exit Titus—Publius, &c., seize Chiron and
                           Demetrius*
   Chi.   Villains, forbear! we are the empress' sons.
   Pub.   And therefore do we what we are commanded.—
Stop close their mouths, let them not speak a word.
Is he sure bound? look that you bind them fast.

Re-enter TITUS ANDRONICUS, *with* LAVINIA ; *she bearing
a basin, and he a knife.*

   Tit.   Come, come, Lavinia; look, thy foes are bound.—
Sir, stop their mouths; let them not speak to me,
But let them hear what fearful words I utter.—
O villains, Chiron and Demetrius!
Here stands the spring whom you have stained with mud;
This goodly summer with your winter mixed.
You killed her husband, and for that vile fault
Two of her brothers were condemned to death,
My hand cut off, and made a merry jest:
Both her sweet hands, her tongue, and that more dear
Than hands or tongue, her spotless chastity,

Inhuman traitors, you constrained and forced.
What would you say, if I should let you speak?
Villains, for shame you could not beg for grace.
Hark, wretches, how I mean to martyr you.
This one hand yet is left to cut your throats.
Whilst that Lavinia 'tween her stumps doth hold
The basin that receives your guilty blood.
You know, your mother means to feast with me,
And calls herself Revenge, and thinks me mad.—
Hark, villains; I will grind your bones to dust,
And with your blood and it I 'll make a paste;
And of the paste a coffin I will rear,
And make two pasties of your shameful heads;
And bid that strumpet, your unhallowed dam,
Like to the earth, swallow her own increase.
This is the feast that I have bid her to,
And this the banquet she shall surfeit on;
For worse than Philomel you used my daughter,
And worse than Progne I will be revenged.
And now prepare your throats.—Lavinia, come.
                              [*He cuts their throats*
Receive the blood: and when that they are dead,
Let me go grind their bones to powder small,
And with this hateful liquor temper it;
And in that paste let their vile heads be baked.—
Come, come, be every one officious
To make this banquet, which I wish may prove
More stern and bloody than the Centaurs' feast.
So, now bring them in, for I will play the cook,
And see them ready 'gainst their mother comes.
                    [*Exeunt, bearing the dead bodies*

SCENE III.—Court of TITUS's House.   Tables set out

Enter LUCIUS, MARCUS, *and Goths ; with* AARON *prisoner*

  Luc. Uncle Marcus, since 't is my father's mind,
That I repair to Rome, I am content.
  First Goth. And ours, with thine; befall what fortune
                will.
  Luc. Good uncle, take you in this barbarous Moor,
This ravenous tiger, this accursèd devil.
Let him receive no sustenance; fetter him
Till he be brought unto the empress' face,
For testimony of her foul proceedings.
And see the ambush of our friends be strong:
I fear the emperor means no good to us.
  Aar. Some devil whisper curses in mine ear

319

And prompt me, that my tongue may utter forth
The venomous malice of my swelling heart!
    Luc.   Away, inhuman dog! unhallowed slave!—
Sirs, help our uncle to convey him in.—
                        [*Exeunt Goths, with Aaron.   Trumpets sound*
The trumpets show the emperor is at hand.

        Enter SATURNINUS *and* TAMORA, *with Tribunes, and*
                        others

    Sat.   What! hath the firmament more suns than one?
    Luc.   What boots it thee to call thyself a sun?
    Marc.   Rome's emperor, and nephew, break the parle;
These quarrels must be quietly debated.
The feast is ready, which the careful Titus
Hath ordained to an honourable end,
For peace, for love, for league, and good to Rome:
Please you, therefore, draw nigh, and take your places.
    Sat.   Marcus, we will.   [*Hautboys sound*

Enter TITUS, *dressed like a cook,* LAVINIA, *veiled, young*
    LUCIUS, *and others.* TITUS *places the dishes on the table*

    Tit.   Welcome, my gracious lord; welcome, dread
            queen;
Welcome, ye warlike Goths; welcome, Lucius;
And welcome, all.   Although the cheer be poor,
'T will fill your stomachs: please you eat of it.
    Sat.   Why art thou thus attired, Andronicus?
    Tit.   Because I would be sure to have all well,
To entertain your highness and your empress.
    Tam.   We are beholding to you, good Andronicus.
    Tit.   An if your highness knew my heart, you were.
My lord, the emperor, resolve me this:
Was it well done of rash Virginius,
To slay his daughter with his own right hand,
Because she was enforced, stained, and deflower'd?
    Sat.   It was, Andronicus.
    Tit.   Your reason, mighty lord?
    Sat.   Because the girl should not survive her shame,
And by her presence still renew his sorrows.
    Tit.   A reason mighty, strong, and effectual;
A pattern, precedent, and lively warrant
For me, most wretched, to perform the like.—
Die, die, Lavinia, and thy shame with thee;
And with thy shame thy father's sorrow die!
                                    [*Kills* LAVINIA
    Sat.   What hast thou done, unnatural and unkind?
    Tit.   Killed her, for whom my tears have made me blind.

                            320

I am as woful as Virginius was,
And have a thousand times more cause than he
To do this outrage; and it is now done.
    Sat. What, was she ravished? tell, who did the deed?
    Tit. Will 't please you eat? will 't please your highness
        feed?
    Tam. Why hast thou slain thine only daughter thus?
    Tit. Not I; 't was Chiron, and Demetrius:
They ravished her and cut away her tongue,
And they, 't was they, that did her all this wrong.
    Sat. Go, fetch them hither to us presently.
    Tit. Why, there they are both, bakéd in that pie
Whereof their mother daintily hath fed.
Eating the flesh that she herself hath bred.
'T is true, 't is true; witness my knife's sharp point.
                         Killing Tamora
    Sat. Die, frantic wretch, for this accurséd deed!
                          [Killing Titus
    Luc. Can the son's eye behold his father bleed?
There 's meed for meed, death for a deadly deed.
[*Killing Saturninus. A great tumult. The people in
    confusion disperse. Marcus, Lucius, and their partisans,
    go up into the gallery*
    Marc. You sad-faced men, people and sons of Rome,
By uproar severed, like a flight of fowl
Scattered by winds and high tempestuous gusts,
O, let me teach you how to knit again
This scattered corn into one mutual sheaf,
These broken limbs again into one body,
Lest Rome herself be bane unto herself;
And she whom mighty kingdoms curtsy to,
Like a forlorn and desperate castaway,
Do shameful execution on herself.
But if my frosty signs and chaps of age,
Grave witnesses of true experience,
Cannot induce you to attend my words,—
[*To Lucius*] Speak, Rome's dear friend, as erst our ancestor
When with his solemn tongue he did discourse
To love-sick Dido's sad-attending ear
The story of that baleful burning night
When subtle Greeks surprised King Priam's Troy.
Tell us, what Simon hath bewitched our ears
Or who hath brought the fatal engine in
That gives our Troy, our Rome, the civil wound.—
My heart is not compact of flint nor steel,
Nor can I utter all our bitter grief;
But floods of tears will drown my oratory
And break my very utterance even in the time
When it should move you to attend me most,

Lending your kind commiseration.
Here is a captain, let him tell the tale;
Your hearts will throb and weep to hear him speak.
   Luc. Then, noble auditory, be it known to you,
That cursèd Chiron and Demetrius
Were they that murderèd our emperor's brother;
And they it was that ravishèd our sister.
For their fell faults our brothers were beheaded,
Our father's tears despised, and basely cozened
Of that true hand that fought Rome's quarrel out
And sent her enemies unto the grave:
Lastly, myself unkindly banishèd,
The gates shut on me, and turned weeping out,
To beg relief among Rome's enemies;
Who drowned their enmity in my true tears,
And oped their arms to embrace me as a friend.
I am the turned-forth, be it known to you,
That have preserved her welfare in my blood,
And from her bosom took the enemy's point,
Sheathing the steel in my adventurous body.
Alas, you know, I am no vaunter, I;
My scars can witness, dumb although they are,
That my report is just and full of truth.
But soft, methinks I do digress too much,
Citing my worthless praise. O, pardon me;
For, when no friends are by, men praise themselves.
   Marc. Now is my turn to speak. Behold this child;
Of this was Tamora deliverèd,
The issue of an irreligious Moor,
Chief architect and plotter of these woes.
The villain is alive in Titus' house,
Damned as he is, to witness this is true.
Now judge, what cause had Titus to revenge
These wrongs, unspeakable, past patience,
Or more than any living man could bear.
Now you have heard the truth, what say you, Romans?
Have we done aught amiss? Show us wherein,
And from the place where you behold us now,
The poor remainder of Andronici
Will hand in hand all headlong cast us down
And on the ragged stones beat forth our brains,
And make a mutual closure of our house.
Speak, Romans, speak! and if you say we shall,
Lo, hand in hand, Lucius and I will fall.
   Æmil Come, come, thou reverend man of Rome,
And bring our emperor gently in thy hand,
Lucius our emperor; for well I know,
The common voice do cry, it shall be so.
   Marc. Lucius, all hail! Rome's royal emperor!—

[*To Attendants*] Go, go into old Titus' sorrowful house,
And hither hale that misbelieving Moor,
To be adjudged some direful slaughtering death,
As punishment for his most wicked life.—

[*Lucius &c., descend*

Lucius, all hail! Rome's gracious governor!
   Luc.   Thanks gentle Romans: may I govern so,
To heal Rome's harms, and wipe away her woe!
But, gentle people, give me aim awhile,—
For nature puts me to a heavy task.—
Stand all aloof;—but, uncle, draw you near,
To shed obsequious tears upon this trunk.—
O, take this warm kiss on thy pale cold lips,

[*Kisses Titus*

These sorrowful drops upon thy blood-stained face,
The last true duties of thy noble son!
   Marc.   Tear for tear, and loving kiss for kiss,
Thy brother Marcus tenders on thy lips:
O, were the sum of these that I should pay
Countless and infinite, yet would I pay them.
   Luc.   Come, hither, boy: come, come, and learn of us
To melt in showers. Thy grandsire loved thee well;
Many a time he danced thee on his knee,
Sung thee asleep, his loving breast thy pillow;
Many a matter hath he told to thee
Meet and agreeing with thine infancy:
In that respect, then, like a loving child,
Shed yet some small drops from thy tender spring,
Because kind nature doth require it so:
Friends should associate friends in grief and woe.
Bid him farewell, commit him to the grave;
Do him that kindness, and take leave of him.
   Boy.   O grandsire, grandsire! even with all my heart
Would I were dead, so you did live again.—
O Lord! I cannot speak to him for weeping;
My tears will choke me, if I ope my mouth.

Enter Attendants, with AARON

   First Rom.   You sad Andronici, have done with woes!
Give sentence on this execrable wretch,
That hath been breeder of these dire events.
   Luc.   Set him breast-deep in earth, and famish him;
There let him stand, and rave, and cry for food:
If any one relieves or pities him,
For the offence he dies. This is our doom;
Some stay to see him fastened in the earth.
   Aar.   O, why should wrath be mute, and fury dumb?
I am no baby, I, that with base prayers

I should repent the evils I have done.
Ten thousand worse than ever yet I did
Would I perform, if I might have my will:
If one good deed in all my life I did,
I do repent it from my very soul.
    Luc.   Some loving friend convey the emperor hence,
And give him burial in his father's grave.
My father and Lavinia shall forthwith
Be closéd in our household's monument.
As for that heinous tiger, Tamora.
No funeral right, nor man in mournful weeds,
No mournful bell shall ring her burial;
But throw her forth to beasts and birds of prey.
Her life was beast-like and devoid of pity.
And, being so, shall have like want of pity,
See justice done on Aaron, that damned Moor,
By whom our heavy haps had their beginning:
Then, afterwards, to order well the state,
That like events may ne'er it ruinate.   [*Exeunt*

324